1312: AMONG THE ULTRAS

1312: AMONG THE ULTRAS

A journey with
the world's most
extreme fans

JAMES MONTAGUE

EBURY
PRESS

1 3 5 7 9 10 8 6 4 2

Ebury Press, an imprint of Ebury Publishing
20 Vauxhall Bridge Road
London SW1V 2SA

Ebury Press is part of the Penguin Random House group of companies
whose addresses can be found at global.penguinrandomhouse.com

Copyright © James Montague, 2020

James Montague has asserted his right to be identified as the author of this
Work in accordance with the Copyright, Designs and Patents Act 1988

First published by Ebury Press in 2020

www.penguin.co.uk

A CIP catalogue record for this book is available from the British Library

Hardback ISBN 9781529106282
Trade paperback ISBN 9781785039171

Typeset in 12/16 pt Fairfield LT Std
by Integra Software Services Pvt. Ltd, Pondicherry

Printed and bound in Great Britain by Clays Ltd, Elcograf S.p.A.

For Mila and Mitra, always

'In an expanding universe, time is on the side of the outcast. Those who once inhabited the suburbs of human contempt find that without changing their address they eventually live in the metropolis.'

Quentin Crisp, *The Naked Civil Servant*

CONTENTS

Author's Note

THE PART OF THE GAME I HAVE ALWAYS FOUND MOST INTERESTING has also been the most misunderstood: the supporters, and especially the ultras, the hooligans, the *barras bravas,* the *torcidas,* the maniacs, however the most passionate and extreme supporters have become known in their home countries. From a young age I was drawn to the danger and the mystery. It was a seductive culture of extremes. Watching that section behind the goal and being inexorably drawn to it was like holding up a magic eye painting. You either saw it or you didn't.

Yet, this was a world I could never be truly accepted by. Journalists are every bit the enemy as the police. Organised support groups are suspicious of those who want to write about them. This has dictated, to some degree, who and where I wrote about. Where access was impossible I decided against writing a full chapter. There were many aborted attempts, which is why there isn't more written in the book about Russia, Poland and Egypt. When the issue of access was worth writing about, like in Morocco, I have included it.

But, slowly, individuals and groups let me enter their worlds. This raised a number of ethical issues. Often I was adjacent to people whose views I disagreed with, and whose words many might find uncomfortable to read. I would hear stories of violence or racism. Often I would witness these too. By being there, was I giving a platform to the radical right or organised crime? Was I justifying their beliefs by relaying what they told me? But to understand the world, we need to know about it as it is, not what we wish it to be, no matter how uncomfortable that might make some people feel. This approach, I believe, is the only way to truly understand how this vast sub-culture came to be, and why it acts the way it does.

Another ethical consideration was identification. Most people I spoke to have asked for, and have been given, pseudonyms as talking to me would put them in danger. The exceptions are those who have such high profiles that they are virtual celebrities in their home countries. The ethics of writing this were always at the forefront of my mind. That voice in my head, I hope, allowed me to faithfully retell what I saw and heard whilst placing it in the social and political context that surrounded them. Ultimately, I always felt it was you, the reader, who should draw your own conclusions about what I have seen and written about.

Introduction

'I don't blame you for writing of me as you have. You had to believe other stories, but then I don't know if anyone would believe anything good of me anyway.'

Billy the Kid

Croatia

SPLIT

FIRST CAME THE FIRE AND THEN CAME THE FURY. A THICK, POISONOUS red smoke had enveloped all of us, stinging eyes and burning tongues with its distinctive metallic signature. For a short while you could see no more than the hand in front of your face as the songs deafened through the fog. Thousands had lit red flares and launched smoke bombs as they sang and jumped up and down, seemingly in unison. The north stand of the Poljud Stadium, home to the Torcida ultras of Hajduk Split, swayed. At our feet, across a narrow gap between two vast slabs of terrace, the concrete steps swung forwards and back, as if oscillating during an earthquake.

As the cloud moved down from the north stand and invaded the pitch, young men wearing balaclavas straddled the metal fence at the front, throwing red flares. They arced upwards, leaving a faint trace against the darkening sky, before landing on the edge of the grass where Hajduk were playing Dinamo Zagreb in the fiercest derby in Croatian football, the Eternal Derby. Others had been left to burn on the seats, starting a fire inside the north stand. There was no panic. The crowd simply shuffled a few metres away, ignoring the flames as they grew and the seats melted. A fire truck careered around the pitch and two firemen climbed in with a hosepipe to extinguish the danger.

The referee decided that the match had to be stopped. But the match was immaterial anyway and not just because Dinamo had already all but won the 2018/19 title. They had, after all, won 10 of the past 11 championships and Hajduk hadn't won the league in almost 15 years. No, what mattered was the show and the message. The Torcida was Europe's oldest organised supporters group, formed in 1950. What they said carried weight here. Even as the players waited for the man-made fog to clear, the Torcida in the north stand was busy coordinating alternating right-arm salutes, a call and response with the east stand as they sang to the tune of the 'Triumphal March' from Verdi's opera *Aida*. At the front the *capos* stood facing the north stand, their backs to the pitch, megaphones in hand, directing the thousands in song, most of them furious denunciations of their opponents from the capital.

'Kill, kill, kill the *purgera*,' the Torcida chanted, using the local Dalmatian slang word disparaging those from Zagreb.

Dinamo, and Zagreb, was the Torcida's main enemy for a number of complex, historical reasons. Before, back when Yugoslavia existed, the rivalry between the two had a familiar but largely benign root, based on the jealousies and feelings of neglect from those who lived far from the capital. But after the Croatian War of Independence, which ended in 1995, and following the dissolution of Yugoslavia, Dinamo and Hajduk were now the biggest teams in its fledgling independent league. The old enemies in Belgrade – Red Star and Partizan – were no longer on the fixture list. So the two turned on each other.

A small, black block of Dinamo Zagreb's ultras, the Bad Blue Boys, numbering perhaps a few hundred at most, were seated far away in a deserted upper part of the Poljud's west stand, quarantined from the rest of the stadium by vast blocks of empty seats. But this was the Torcida's show. Flags were passed down from the top of the stand to the bottom. Sheets of red and blue plastic had been left on each seat for the mosaic choreography that had long ago been mapped out. No one knew what it would say but your presence was a tacit acknowledgment of the message. A huge plastic banner was unfurled backwards, instantly creating a hot and humid atmosphere underneath. Each individual had their part to play in this collective piece of theatre. It was only later, after the match, that I would see a photograph of what the choreography looked like: a massive image of a supporter, arms outstretched, holding a scarf coloured the red and almost purple-blue of Torcida's badge. At the bottom, stretching across the entire north stand, was one word in huge white letters: 'ULTRAS'.

What do you see when you watch a football match? Do you see a team drama playing out in front of you? Do you see individual players exhibiting individual skills? Do you see a chess game of numbers, tactics and patterns? There is no right or wrong answer, but there are millions of people around the world who see the game in a completely different way. Just off the pitch, in the stands behind the goals, is a different way of understanding football, a subculture that has largely defined what the game of football has looked and felt like since the mid twentieth century: the ultras.

Yet we know virtually nothing about these groups of football fans who fill the stadiums with smoke. It is a culture that has developed its own rules and norms. It has lived outside of the law or at the very least in constant friction with it. It communicates through climactic public displays: huge banners, colourfully choreographed messages, political statements, smoke, tributes, denunciations, flares, violence and memorials. It is anti-authoritarian and has a virulent mistrust of both the police and the media. It is against the commercialisation of the game and the criminalisation of its brethren. It has developed an international network of friendships and enemies, its own code of honour and a deep sense of solidarity.

Football and the business of football is utterly ubiquitous. Billions watch and follow it, consuming every morsel even tangentially connected to it. The minutiae of every moment on the pitch is obsessively documented, as are the lives of the players who are meant to be the leading stars of this global entertainment product. The actions of owners, coaches, managers and administrators are under the microscope. But the fans? The *ultras*? In a sport where we know everything about everyone, they remain largely a mystery, castigated as the feared *other* on the one hand, whilst they aggressively protect their own hardwon anonymity and outsider status. The groups were spread across every continent with differing views and ideologies. Was it even possible to come to a single definition of what or who ultras are? The ultras had always been a mystery, hidden in plain sight.

Split is an ancient city found on Dalmatia's wild coastline, 400km and a five-hour drive from Zagreb. Over the centuries it has seen many empires pass over, through or around it: Romans, Greeks, Byzantines, Ottomans, Venetians, Italians, fascists and communists. Split had developed a Dalmatian and Croatian identity as well as a fierce opposition and resistance to any outsiders. There's even a word for it in the city: *dišpet*, a term of defiance that roughly means to oppose something no matter the consequences. '*Dišpet* means to be anti-everything,' as one member of the Torcida once told me. Split had *dišpet*. Dalmatia had *dišpet*. Torcida, and the ultras, had *dišpet* too. When Hajduk was formed in 1911 it was decided that their name would come from a type of Christian, Robin Hood-style guerilla fighter that emerged in Ottoman-controlled Europe in the eighteenth century.[1] During the Second World War, after Yugoslavia was invaded in 1941 and Split was annexed by the Italians, Hajduk refused lucrative offers to play in Italy's Serie A, which had been reconstituted as a national league by the government of fascist dictator Benito Mussolini in 1926. Later, when Germany retook Split, after the Italians briefly lost it to the partisans, Hajduk also turned down the chance to play in a new national competition set up by the pro-Nazi Ustaše who briefly ruled a short-lived independent Croatia under German patronage.

Instead, everyone at the club went to join the communist partisans fighting them, led by Josip Broz Tito. The team became a sort of Balkans propaganda version of the Harlem Globetrotters, playing exhibition games against Allied opposition in Croatia, Italy and the Middle East to raise awareness of their plight. Tito was so impressed he offered them the chance to move to Belgrade and become the official Yugoslav army team. They turned Tito down too.[2]

After the war Tito did eventually get his army team in Belgrade by founding Partizan. Hajduk meanwhile returned to Split and became an important symbol of Croatian identity, though the notion of national identity remained contentious. Tito had resurrected Yugoslavia as a federation of six socialist republics, attempting to subsume the regional differences into a communist whole. Yet when Hajduk supporters wanted to form a new type of supporter organisation, trying to replicate the songs and passions of Brazil's *torcida* fan groups at the 1950 World Cup finals, where Yugoslavia were competing, few in power thought that football supporters could reawaken dormant, and dangerous, nationalism. One apocryphal origins story claims that a group of sailors from the Croatian island of Korčula who had been at the tournament returned to Split with incredible tales of how Brazilian fans used instruments, flares and cunning to whip up an atmosphere that gave their team an advantage. The most likely explanation was the Yugoslav players themselves.

There were five Hajduk players in the Yugoslavia squad, a team that had already won the silver medal at the 1948 Olympics, including young goalkeeper Vladimir Beara. When Lev Yashin gave his acceptance speech for the 1963 Ballon D'Or, he told the crowd he wasn't the best player in the world. He wasn't even the best goalkeeper in the world. That honour was for Beara.[3] At the 1950 World Cup Yugoslavia were disappointingly knocked out by Brazil. But the crowd left its mark on the players. Just over 142,000 people were inside the Maracanã in Rio for that game. Up until then European football support had largely been sedate and disorganised. But Beara and fellow Hajduk player Bernard Vukas returned with fabulous tales of what they had seen, and heard, in the

Maracanã, which they told to a group of Hajduk fans studying in Zagreb. Beara recalled the alien sound of the *torcida* in the stadiums: 'They were like a machine that stomped for their homeland and their national team.'[4]

Those fans, in turn, decided they would try to replicate it. 'It's surely due to the stories we told them. There was no other way, because they didn't even know a thing like *torcida* could exist.'[5]

Hajduk Split's Torcida was to be founded just when a special atmosphere was needed for a very special game, four months after Yugoslavia lost to Brazil on the other side of the world. Hajduk was playing Red Star Belgrade in the penultimate match of the Yugoslav First League. Victory would all but secure Hajduk's first ever title. The leaders arranged for the Torcida members to be armed 'with school bells, trumpets, rattles and whistles and put them on the train to Split'.[6] On 28 October 1950 the Torcida was officially formed. With the help of local Communist Party apparatchiks, hundreds of Torcida members visited Red Star's team hotel, where they serenaded the players with 'a rousing concert, using instruments to discordant affect and upsetting their opponents' preparations'.[7] As many as 20,000 fans squeezed into the Stadion Stari plac, in the centre of Split, on 29 October to watch the game being played on a cinder pitch. The Torcida, and their instruments, had been denied entry until Hajduk's president (also a senior Communist Party official) intervened. One local communist newspaper described the stadium as 'like being in a cauldron. The battle on the pitch unfolded alongside the spectators' frenetic supporting ... everyone – both players on the pitch and spectators on the terraces – were struggling together.'[8]

The Torcida had successfully re-created Brazil's febrile atmosphere. But it got out of hand. Red Star's captain was punched in the face during the game by an opposition player, and when Hajduk scored late to secure a 2–1 victory – all but handing them the title in what would become Yugoslavia's only unbeaten title-winning season – the crowd invaded the pitch. That night the Torcida celebrated in the old city, with one member reading out Red Star Belgrade's obituary to the crowd. In Belgrade the spectacle was condemned, with one

newspaper bemoaning the Torcida's 'hellish racket' and its involvement in 'uncultured and obscene incidents'.[9] The Communist Party
was shaken by the Torcida's nakedly Croatian support, which they
feared would stir up nationalistic tendencies – especially as Croatia's
pro-fascist Ustaše had only been defeated five years before. The fallout was brutal. Three of Torcida's founders were stripped of their
party affiliations. Vjenceslav Žuvela, a shipping student from Korčula
who had been a driving force in its formation, was sentenced to three
years in prison, although that was later reduced to three months.
Croatia's red and white chessboard flag was banned from Hajduk's
club badge for 50 years. The Torcida lasted for just one match – it too
was banned. Even though it was short-lived, the Torcida would go on
to have a profound effect as Europe's first organised supporters group.
Hajduk Split had lived up to its reputation for *dišpet*. It was a rebel
club for a rebel city.

As Yugoslavia began to disintegrate into what would become a
ten-year descent towards a vicious ethno-nationalist war following the
death of Tito in 1980, the Torcida re-emerged as a nationalistic voice
in Split. It was mirrored in other Yugoslav republics by new supporters
groups, now heavily influenced by Italian ultra groups that had proliferated just over the Adriatic Sea. Each provided a forewarning of the
destructive nationalism that was to come. Matches between Dinamo
or Hajduk against Red Star Belgrade frequently ended in riots, with
their ultra groups leading the charge.

After the War of Independence Dinamo Zagreb replaced Red Star
as Hajduk's main rival. The country's new, nationalist president Franjo
Tuđman tried to make Dinamo Zagreb a team for the nation. He
hated the name 'Dinamo' for being too communist and the club was
briefly renamed Croatia Zagreb.[10] It was changed back to Dinamo in
February 2000, three months after Tuđman died. In the 2000s the
club would be run by Zdravko Mamić, the corrupt executive who had
controlled Croatian football and who was currently on the run somewhere in Bosnia having been convicted of fraud in his absence.[11]
Hajduk's ultras had led the protests against him and his enablers in
Croatian football. It was the Torcida who protested against the

Croatian Football Federation (HNS) at the 2016 European Championships when flares were thrown on to the pitch at St Etienne, even though Croatia were winning. Fighting broke out in the stands between Croatia fans afterwards.[12] In 2015 a huge swastika was painted on the Poljud pitch before a Euro 2016 qualifier against Italy, which was already being played behind closed doors due to racist chanting in an earlier game.[13] It was a presumed attempt to embarrass the federation in Zagreb even further. Mamić was even pushed into the Adriatic after coming out of a fancy restaurant on the nearby island of Brač. It was never confirmed that the perpetrator was a member of Torcida, but shortly after the incident Mamić shared a letter on social media which criticised them: 'The only thing you know is to hide behind the word "Torcida" and pretend you are heroes, and you did not say a word when Hajduk was being robbed.'[14]

That post was referring to the time in 2011 when Hajduk almost went out of business thanks to years of mismanagement and corruption. What it failed to mention was the fact that it was the Torcida that helped save the club with a model diametrically opposed to Mamić's profit-generating machine. A new organisation was set up called Naš Hajduk, or Our Hajduk, with the aim of running the club on strict, democratically accountable lines. They started to buy up shares and ultimately owned close to 25 per cent of the club, giving them a controlling stake.

'The only aim, the only focus, was to ensure a model that will assure democratic and transparent governing. Democratic elections for a supervisory board. The supervisory board then elects the CEO and [the] CEO runs the club,' explained Ivan Rilov, a Hajduk fan who runs Naš Hajduk. The Torcida had no interest in running the club themselves, but instead wanted to make sure all supporters had a final say over who did. He added that the fans were honourable. 'Last summer, we had a big fire here near Split. And who were the guys who were first in the line, you know, to help people? Torcida. A few years ago, you had big floods in northern Croatia, Torcida members were there immediately. When a hospital in Split needs blood donors, Torcida members are the first in line.'

The new model worked. There are now over 40,000 paid-up members. Rilov had received emails and letters from all around the world, not just football fans, but human-rights activists and lawyers who believed that Naš Hajduk promoted a rare, and successful, model in Croatia that others could follow – even if it hadn't led to a league title yet. It also showed the contradictory faces of the ultras movement. 'In Split, you know, we are always against something,' Rilov said. 'It's not very healthy but sometimes it can be really useful.'

On that particular derby day the Torcida gathered at a square near the old city to drink beer and sing. Earlier they had some important work to do, checking the IDs of anyone arriving at the bus or train station, to make sure no Bad Blue Boys from Zagreb were amongst the new arrivals. The route took you north, past the old Stari plac stadium, past the Torcida's headquarters, past the street stands grilling ćevapi, and into a small park that overlooked the magnificent Poljud Stadium on the banks of the Adriatic. The stadium, with its two-part shell-like roof, was designed by Boris Magaš and is considered one of Yugoslavia's last great architectural gems. It was featured in a recent exhibition at the New York Museum of Modern Art, a testament to Yugoslavia's utopian outlook before Tito's death.[15]

On the walk to the stadium the walls of passing houses, and apartment blocks, shops and malls, were covered in Hajduk graffiti, but also far-right symbols: swastikas, the Celtic cross, fascist number codes. One wall had the words *Nazi Razgazzi* (Italian for 'Nazi Boys') spray-painted on it. Hajduk may well have been founded as an anti-fascist club but in the twenty-first century things had become more complicated. A significant number of the Torcida, like elsewhere in Croatian society, had rehabilitated the Nazi-era Ustaše. It was not uncommon to hear the Ustaše chant '*Za dom spremni*' ('For the Homeland, ready'), the Croatian equivalent of *Sieg Heil*. It was especially prevalent around the commemoration of Operation Storm, the final decisive offensive of Croatia's 'Homeland War' of independence that killed hundreds of civilians and forced at least 200,000 Serbs to flee for their lives.[16] The event is celebrated by many in Croatia, but condemned as a largely unpunished war crime in Serbia. Ante Gotovina, who was the military commander of the campaign, was sentenced to 24 years in prison but later acquitted at the International Criminal Tribunal for the former Yugoslavia. Even the chant to the tune of Verdi's 'Triumphal March', with corresponding salutes between the north and west stand, one former Torcida member told me, clearly gave those who wanted it the chance to throw a fascist salute whilst claiming plausible deniability.

The police roughly checked everyone as we passed through the gates. On the stairway up to the main concourse members of the Torcida were collecting money in buckets. Usually the money was to pay for the choreography. But today it was money for a former club legend. He was sick and broke. So, as a gift, the Torcida wanted to raise €1,000 so that he too could own shares in the club. Despite the police searches, hundreds of flares had made it inside. After the choreography, after the smoke and the fire, a game of football had to be played. It was a drab 1–0 victory for Dinamo Zagreb. The most memorable moment, on the pitch at least, was when Hajduk's Mijo Caktaš was sent off for throwing out an elbow, sparking a 22-man brawl. As the full-time whistle was blown the songs continued: songs against Mamić, songs against Zagreb, songs against the HNS, songs against the Serbs. Songs against everything. Here, in the north stand, the Torcida existed in a free space where they made the rules. It was also an ephemeral experience. Everything, from the choreography, to the songs, to the banners, to the grievances against the capital and the calls for justice, was real. But they would also be replaced and renewed almost as soon as they touched the sky from season to season, one match to the next. Each act evaporated almost as soon as it had begun. But it still left a trace behind, the sketch of a permanent record in the collective memory. Like the petrified remains of an ancient animal; dissolved and forgotten, yet whose outline was forever seared on the rock.

PART ONE:
LOS PRIMEROS HINCHAS

'Have you ever entered an empty stadium? Try it. Stand in the middle of the field and listen. There is nothing less empty than an empty stadium. There is nothing less mute than stands bereft of spectators.'

Eduardo Galeano, *Soccer in Sun and Shadow*

1

Uruguay

MONTEVIDEO

There wasn't a soul outside the Estadio Centenario, but the Museo del Fútbol swung open its doors at precisely 10am anyway. The stadium had seen better days since it was completed in 1930 for the first ever World Cup finals but, up close, it remained an architectural miracle, with its 100m-tall, winged art deco tower – La Torre de los Homenajes – looming over the pitch and its sunken concrete bowl. The completion of the stadium was delayed as it had to be built during bouts of torrential rain, which meant that the tournament's opening games had to be played elsewhere. It was ready a few weeks later, for a handful of group games, both semi-finals and the inaugural World Cup final, Uruguay versus Argentina. Over 60,000 supporters – including as many as 20,000 away fans who had sailed over the

River Plate from Argentina – watched Uruguay win 4–2, after trailing 2–1 at half-time.

Usually, a country winning a World Cup with a population of just 1.75 million (as Uruguay had in 1930) would be a Black Swan event. But not here. For over 80 years Uruguay has overachieved when it came to football success, a story laid out inside the Museo del Fútbol, housed over two floors within the stadium. The museum was filled with cabinets of photos and objects; a tableau that told the story of how a tiny nation came to have such an outsized influence on the world game. On the ground floor, hanging near the entrance in a flat glass case, was a torn and threadbare blue-and-white-striped Uruguayan flag – with its distinctive Sun of May in the top left corner, adapted from the Inca god of the sun – that flew at the 1924 Olympics in Paris, where the Uruguayan team won gold. Upstairs were the boots that midfielder Roberto Figueroa wore when he scored in the replayed 1928 Olympic final in Amsterdam, a 2–1 victory over Argentina.

The centrepiece of the museum was a vast modern canvas that melded La Celeste's past and present. 'Los 23 Orientales' (The Eastern 23) was painted by a local artist, Santiago Vecino, before the 2018 World Cup finals in Russia. Two metres long and one metre high, it resembled a cartoonish version of *The Last Supper*, but set on a dusty battlefield. There was Egidio Arevalo Rios, lifting the 2011 Copa America, which Uruguay had won 15 times, more than any other South American nation. To the right was what looked like Edinson Cavani, kneeling and offering the Jules Rimet Trophy, which Uruguay won in 1930 and famously again in 1950 by beating Brazil in front of 200,000 supporters at the Maracanã. An unconscious Alvaro Pereira was held up by three team-mates, a nod to the moment during England versus Uruguay at the 2014 World Cup when he was knocked out by Raheem Sterling's knee. Uruguay would win that game 2–1, Luis Suarez scoring both goals. Suarez is the undoubted star of modern Uruguayan football and he was, of course, in the centre waving a blue flag. The team's captain Diego Godin was in the background, inexplicably riding a white stallion whilst holding a blue medieval-style banner with four gold stars, representing Uruguay's two World Cups and two Olympic gold medals. The Eiffel Tower, Christ the Redeemer, the Estadio Centenario and Moscow's St Basil's cathedral filled the skyline behind them.

Behind the portrait, and down the end of an adjacent side corridor, was a tribute to a man who had played a different but no less important role in the history of football. It was a framed photo, discoloured slightly green from age, of a heavy-set man approaching middle age, dressed in a three-piece suit and tie. He had a long moustache that curved downwards at the tips, and a salt-and-pepper goatee. It was an easy portrait to miss. The photo of Prudencio Miguel Reyes was taken in 1905. Reyes wasn't a footballer, nor did he hold any high-level position at any club or the Uruguayan FA. He was a saddler and leather worker who had been hired by Club Nacional de Football, then a recently formed *criollo* club in Montevideo, the first not to be run by the English but by Uruguayans. He had a functional but vitally important role on match day. He was the *hinchador*: the man in charge of manually inflating the heavy, leather balls before and during games. He became a regular fixture at Nacional's Estadio Gran Parque Central during the first decade of the twentieth century. But he wasn't like the other people in the stadium.

At the time, football in Uruguay was an art form to be savoured, like going to the opera or watching a play. Games of football, tennis, polo and even cricket looked much the same. Supporters would wear their best clothes and watch the game in what Nacional's Comision de Historia y Estadistica termed an 'classic Anglo-Saxon style'. In the wooden stands of the Parque Central, football was mostly a game of comportment and restraint where 'the public who attended matches maintained a certain seriousness.'[1] The exception was when a goal was scored but 'the display did not go beyond some applause or an exclamation of joy or disappointment'.[2]

Reyes was entirely different. Outside of the Parque Central he was, by all accounts, a quiet and unassuming man. But once he was inside the stadium, once he stepped on to the side of the pitch and the referee blew his whistle, he changed. During the match, in between blowing up balls, he would charge up and down the touchline, bellowing encouragement at the players. Then he would turn to the crowd and bellow at them, encouraging them to shout back, goading them into a response and coordinating chants of 'Nacional, Nacional, Nacional, let's go, Nacional!' to try and gain his team an advantage. During the first few games he received a puzzled response. Journalists wrote reports on how Nacional's *El Hincha Pelotas*, the ball inflator, was as much a part of the spectacle as the game itself. But he kept shouting and kept running until the crowd responded. Every passing home game saw more and more supporters follow the lead of 'fat Reyes' with his 'salami fingers', as the famed Uruguayan journalist Diego Lucero would later describe him. No one had ever seen anything like it. When visiting teams and supporters saw Reyes they started to chant and sing, taking this new form of encouragement back to their home stadiums. 'The word *"hincha"* was applied to the supporters of Nacional, because they shouted the most at the games,' the club wrote in their official history of Reyes. 'Later it spread to the other clubs, crossed the River Plate, and then projected out to the rest of the world.'

Today, in the entire Spanish-speaking world, the generic word used to describe crazy football fans is *hinchas*. Prudencio Miguel Reyes never won a World Cup or an Olympic medal. He died in obscurity in February 1948. No one is even sure where he was buried. But his alien way of supporting his team was revolutionary. It helped to break down the game's fourth wall and sparked a new type of relationship between those that watched football and those that played football. Football supporters were no longer passive. They had been cut loose to spread their infectious enthusiasm, and Prudencio Miguel Reyes was patient zero: the first *barra brava*, the first *torcedore*, the first ultra, the first fan, *El Primer Hincha*.

I had thought Mikael would be taller. For the past few weeks the two of us had been messaging on WhatsApp about our upcoming trip. We were due to meet 12,000km away in Montevideo to watch the Uruguayan *clasico* between Nacional and Peñarol. Mikael was one of the most connected figures in the European ultra scene. He was Swedish and had founded the first ever ultras group in Sweden, at his club Hammarby, back in the early 1990s. He lived and breathed Hammarby but Mikael had always known there was a wider world out there. He had told me how, when he was nine years old, he had watched the 1978 World Cup final between Argentina and the Netherlands transfixed, not by the game, but by the blue and white ticker-tape blitz that erupted from the terraces of the Estadio Monumental in Buenos Aires. Somehow he wanted to recreate that feeling at Hammarby. He travelled the world to spend time in other football cultures, bringing what he saw on foreign terraces back to Sweden. He had built deep relationships with Roma's ultras, in Austria with Rapid Wien and Panathinaikos in Greece, amongst others. But the reason we had been in contact was that he had lived for a year amongst the *barras bravas* in Argentina, especially the *barra* of Boca Juniors, and perhaps the most notorious supporters group in the world, La Doce, or 'The 12', a reference to them being Boca's twelfth man.

The global ultras movement was one built on trust and suspicion. Journalists weren't trusted, but there was an informal honour code between groups around the world. As long as someone could vouch for you, all the the doors were open. But if no one did, everything was closed. Like with ultras or hooligan groups in Europe, it was notoriously difficult for me to speak to anyone in the *barras bravas*. They were organised fan groups, often described as the South American version of ultras. They first emerged in Argentina, in their earliest incarnation, in the 1920s but soon spread throughout Spanish-speaking South America. The *barras* were the most passionate part of a club's *hinchas,* responsible for the atmosphere that made South American football unique and one of the most attractive fan experiences in the world. But they had also developed into something much darker and more violent, evolving past tribalistic football violence and into organised crime. The *barras* wielded a huge amount of power in Argentina and Uruguay, controlling every facet of trade around the stadium, from parking to tickets to drugs to food stalls and merchandise. Nacional versus Peñarol was one of the biggest *clasicos* in South America, and one of the most violent. But, unlike in Argentina where the violence had got so bad that away fans had been banned from the stadiums for six years now, the Nacional *barra*, La Banda del Parque, would be allowed to the game. Mikael was to be my guide, fixer and, I had assumed, my bodyguard.

Mikael was nearly 50 and a good foot shorter than me, with long hair in a ponytail and a long beard. He wore a light blue West Ham United T-shirt with 'Cockney Rejects' on the front, which barely covered his tattoos. There were several on his neck, including a large pink lipstick kiss, and more all over his body from the teams he had built friendships with over the years: Hammarby, naturally, but also the clubs he had visited that left the biggest impression on him. Roma, Rapid Wien and, of course, Boca Juniors too. On his leg there was a large tattoo of Andy Capp. The un-PC British cartoon had become a symbol of the global ultras movement. He had the world ULTRAS marked in large letters on his stomach.

'Hello, mate,' he said warmly, in slightly cockneyish English. A friend had vouched that he wasn't a maniac. In fact, he was a pacifist ultra who listened to death metal and had no time for the violent part of the scene. But he had also brought bad news. The Uruguayan *clasico* had been cancelled overnight. La Banda del Parque had more pressing issues to deal with. 'One of the *barra* leaders is in prison accused of murdering someone,' he said, matter-of-factly. He was sceptical about the veracity of the allegations. 'It's probably about power and money, as usual in South America.'

It was a horrific case. Six weeks earlier the bodies of two men – both members of La Banda del Parque – were found in a burned-out Volkswagen truck in the suburb of Tres Ombues. A month later three members of the same *barra* were arrested – one of them at Montevideo's airport after returning from watching Nacional play in the Copa Libertadores in Brazil against Atlético Mineiro. During the early court cases one of the accused's lawyers revealed that his client was allegedly being paid $U40,000 (about £800) a game by Nacional to help organise the displays and drums for the game, as well as keeping the rest of the *hinchas* in line.[3] Although the club denied it, this created a scandal and exposed what many Uruguayans had long suspected: that the clubs continued to keep the *barras* sweet with jobs and tickets. Uruguay was the richest and safest country in South America but there had been dozens of deaths in and around Uruguayan stadiums. The 2016 shooting of two Peñarol fans before a *clasico* was a watershed moment. One lost a kidney and the second died a month later. The league was suspended and a dozen members of La Banda del Parque were arrested. The next *clasico* at the Centenario was called off after Peñarol's Barra Amsterdam rioted, throwing gas canisters at the police; 150 people were arrested. The government announced they would crack down on the clubs if they continued to have a close relationship with the *barras*. The police meanwhile said they would refuse to go into the stadiums, ensuring that each club had to pay for their own security. But the fallout from the dead bodies found in a burned-out van showed that there was still a strong connection. In a 2017 testimony to the Uruguayan parliament the head of security for the country's football association, Rafael Peña, gave a dire warning that the *barras* 'had transformed themselves into true cartels that even fight for [control of] territory and the criminal activity they are involved in'. Any attempt to crack down on their activities, he said, 'always ends in extortion, without exception'.[4]

There was, as ever, a conspiracy theory from the Nacional fans. The official (and rather ludicrous) reason the football federation gave for postponing the game was a protest where four Nacional fans, including a ten-year-old girl, turned up at their headquarters to protest at the standard of refereeing in the previous game. The federation, the fans believed, wanted any pretext to avoid the *clasico* that weekend, especially as it came just before Peñarol was due to play a final and vitally important Copa Libertadores group match against Brazil's Flamengo. Instead, Peñarol would play River Plate from Montevideo in a half-empty Estadio Centenario. Later that evening Nacional played Progreso at the Parque Central. By the time Mikael and I had got to the stadium it was dark and raining hard. The first ever World Cup match took place here. USA versus Belgium kicked off at exactly the same time as France versus Mexico at the now defunct Estadio Pocitos, once the home of Peñarol. Mikael had brought with him a seemingly inexhaustible supply of Hammarby stickers, which he would leave on lampposts and road signs: 'Barra Brava Hammarby', 'Love Football, Hate Cops', and a sticker of Andy Capp, dressed in the green and white colours of Hammarby. A lone trombonist was warming up outside the west stand, home turf for La Banda del Parque. They entered their stand with percussions and drums. Only the lower, uncovered stand was filled up. There were dozens of blue, white and red banners and flags: 'Nacional We Will Die For You'; a large marijuana leaf and *Piedras Blanco,* the White Stones neighbourhood outside Montevideo; and in the middle, running the length of the entire stand was a banner that read '*La Primer Hinchada del Mundo*': 'The First Fans in the World'. Once they started singing and dancing they didn't stop, even at half-time when they were 3–0 up. The referee waited in the centre circle for two fully equipped riot police officers, complete with helmets and shields, to escort the players and officials off the field, even though there hadn't been a hint of violence. There had been tensions for months, said Pablo, a journalist for Nacional's TV station, so they were taking no chances.

The match ended 4–0 and the small group of La Banda del Parque kept singing, even after the final whistle.

> *Let's go tricolores*
> *Today we have to win*
> *El Primer Hincha*
> *He came to encourage you*
> *It doesn't matter to me*
> *Where you play*
> *Because wherever you are*
> *I will encourage you*
> *Nacional, I will always go with you*
> *Nacional, I want to see you as champions.*

Aside from being the etymological home to the *hincha*, the pitch at the Estadio Gran Parque Central appears to have played host to a series of important and sometimes macabre moments in Uruguayan history. 'The ghost of Miguel Reyes is still here,' said Ignacio Pou, the chief historian at Nacional, as we stood by the pitch of a now empty Parque Central. 'We have many ghosts here.' The stadium, Pou explained, was built on the spot where the revolutionary independence hero José Gervasio Artigas, who would spend his life fighting the colonial ambitions of the Spanish, Portuguese and British, was declared leader of the Uruguayan people in 1811. When Nacional was formed in 1899 they adopted the same blue, red and white colours that Artigas had popularised, and set the stage for their eternal rivalry with Peñarol.

'My father supported Nacional, who sported the red, white and blue of the country's great liberator José Artigas,' wrote the Uruguayan author Andreas Campomar in his book *Golazo*. 'I, on the other hand, became a fan of Peñarol, a working-class club that had originally been founded as the Central Uruguay Railway Cricket Club in the final decade of the nineteenth century.' Campomar wrote that it was the Nacional fans who wrapped what they saw as their unique Uruguayan-ness around themselves, whilst disparaging Peñarol for being a club for and of outsiders and immigrants. 'Hence,' he wrote of Peñarol's nickname, 'the Italianate soubriquet *mangare merda,* "shit eaters".' It was Peñarol's fans that did the dirty jobs no one else would do. They decided to own the classist barbs that were thrown their way.

In April 1920, the stadium was the site of a pistol duel between Uruguay's former president José Batlle y Ordóñez and Washington Beltrán, a journalist and politician. Batlle had been president twice and had been instrumental in helping to establish Uruguay's welfare state, especially when it came to workers' rights. But Beltrán wrote a scathing editorial calling Batlle a 'champion of fraud'. Batlle demanded the issue be settled by a duel, and Beltrán agreed to meet at Parque Central. 'The opponents met on a football field in the midst of pouring rain,' wrote the *New York Times*. 'Because of the rain the duelists decided to keep on their hats, but Beltrán changed his straw hat for a felt so that both might be on even terms.' The hat switch, however, didn't help. Both men missed but 'before Beltrán could fire a second shot he was struck by a bullet from Batlle's pistol and sank to the ground, mortally wounded'.[5]

Perhaps the most striking episode took place two years before and concerns one of Nacional's greatest players. Abdón Porte was a hard tackling but cultured centre half who was captain of Nacional for seven consecutive seasons between 1911 and 1918. His nickname was El Indio, because of his indigenous heritage, but in an era where complex racial hierarchies still dominated Brazilian and Argentinian football Porte rose to the top of the Uruguayan game, playing over 200 matches and winning four league titles. In 1918 he sustained a serious knee injury in the *clasico* against Peñarol. There were no substitutes at the time so Porte was sent up front. Nacional won 4–2 but Porte never fully recovered from the injury and Nacional had to replace him in the team. His last game was a 3–1 victory over Charley. He played well but later that evening, at a now silent and dark Parque Central, Abdón Porte walked on to the pitch one last time. He stood in the centre circle and, with a revolver in his hand, shot himself in the heart. He was found the next morning with two suicide notes in his hat. One read:

> *Nacional,*
> *Though in dust converted*
> *And in dust forever loved*
> *I shall never forget an instant*
> *How much I have loved you*
> *Farewell*[6]

Every professional footballer in Uruguay attended Porte's funeral. The procession was said to be 15km long. Over a hundred years later, his face now adorned a banner at the Parque Central's west stand, named in his honour, alongside the words *'Por la Sangre de Abdón'*: For Abdón's Blood. Porte had become a symbol of the sacrifices the crowd expected.

Football was crucial to developing Uruguay's identity; for example, the country became the first in South American to truly 'allow black players to play football', Pou explained. It was a tiny, multiracial country after waves of slavery and European immigration, buffeted by more powerful neighbours with colonialist ambitions. 'Football was the glue that united the country,' he added. 'We were a rather young nation between Brazil and Argentina. But football? It was the first thing in our history that we felt was something that was owned by us … It transformed Uruguayan society.'

Most of the stories that had been told about Uruguayan football had concentrated, rightly, on its outsized success on the pitch. On the stars that it had created. Less space had been given to explaining the phenomenon of the spectators and *why* Uruguay expressed such undoubted passion for the game. When Pou and the rest of Nacional's history commission started looking into the club's lost stories a few years ago they discovered press clippings, photos and minutes mentioning Miguel Reyes's pitch-side behaviour. In a famous photo of the Uruguay national team from 1914, which contained 11 Nacional players, there was only one other person in the shot. Miguel Reyes, literally the twelfth man. In his 1921 monograph *Group Psychology and the Analysis of the Ego* Sigmund Freud argued that crowds allowed groups with similar interests, held together by a shared love, to free their unconscious desires. Often a charismatic leader would replace a person's own ability to regulate their id, the base, instinctual element of our personalities. Reyes was Nacional's collective id. His behaviour, Pou discovered, was contagious. 'What makes us feel proud was that he was the first football fan to *feel* this way, to vibrate with fanaticism. To live the game,' said Pou. There was, he added, a 'huge difference between watching a movie and being in that movie'.

A half-hour's drive away, Ernesto Reyes laid out the few sepia-tinted photos he had of his great-grandfather on to a vintage card table covered in green felt. 'Here he is with my great-grandmother, they had five children,' he said. The photo had almost faded away. He laid another one down next to it, of Miguel Reyes with his wife on their wedding day. 'Miguel was a widower, which is why my great-grandmother is wearing black,' he explained. The small games room contained everything that was left and everything that was known about Prudencio Miguel Reyes. The same photo that hung in the Museo de Fútbol hung here too. There were receipts from his leather business. A few letters. Ticket stubs from Nacional games. A book that listed all the results from when Nacional played Peñarol. The first, on 15 July 1900, was a 2–0 victory to Peñarol. His mono-grammed *mate* gourd. And that was it. You could fit everything about Prudencio Miguel Reyes's life into a shoebox.

Miguel Reyes's story, Ernesto explained, was a disappearing leg-end. Reyes had died relatively young, leaving behind a widow and five young children. But no one knew how he died, or where he died. 'How much do you know about *your* great-grandfather?' Ernesto asked me. 'The story we knew was of our great-grandmother, and how she somehow survived with five children as a widow.' Ernesto and his two brothers had already grown up with a fanatic in the family. Their late father was obsessed with Nacional. 'He was an ultra fanatic,' Ernesto explained. So much so that his sons had to stop going with him to the games, as he argued with other fans. A colour picture of his father hung next to one of Miguel Reyes. Their father is smiling, his arms spread in Nacional's trophy room. Ernesto described one experience when his father took him to a Nacional game and he got into a furious row with some other *hinchas* nearby. It got so heated he took off his watch, a sign that a fight was brewing. 'It was a friendly match between Nacional A and Nacional B!' laughed Ernesto. 'And it ended up with a fight between my father and other Nacional fans.'

The family believed that whatever it was that had gripped Prudencio Miguel Reyes also afflicted their father, that it was 'in the blood'. 'It skips a generation,' Ernesto said. His grandfather, Miguel Reyes's son, was a quiet man who liked to play the clarinet and had little interest in football. But Ernesto's father was a full-blown, card-carrying *hin-cha*. Ernesto liked football, and he supported Nacional, but like his two brothers he could take it or leave it. Their children, however, were crazy for Nacional. 'He's part of the *barra,* standing below the flag,' he said of his son. 'He even goes to the basketball. He's a little bit crazy.' His eldest daughter had been afflicted too. 'She has the gene but we decided to stop her because she is a woman,' he said. It wasn't discrimination, he quickly added, but rather the knowledge of how dangerous the *barra* could be. 'I know that, yes, there's discrimination, but it was not very well perceived back then to have a women being a part of the *barra*. It's different now.'

The Reyes family had always wondered why an irrepressible passion for Nacional had afflicted their family every other generation. Prudencio Miguel Reyes gave them an answer. His life was still virtually unknown. He was now a folk tale, an apocryphal origins story. 'Every time we hear the word *hincha,* it is special for us,' said Ernesto as we left. He had heard that two clubs in Argentina – Huracán and Racing – were even arguing about which was the first to import the world *hincha* from Uruguay. 'It makes us proud.' His modern descendants had incorporated the legend of Prudencio Miguel Reyes into their family's story too, just as La Banda del Parque had.

The next day Mikael and I finally got to meet La Banda del Parque. Mikael received a message to expect Santino. He was, we were told, a big man with a skinhead who talked loud and fast. La Banda del Parque had been illusive so far. The arrest of their leader had spooked them, but Mikael made some calls. That evening Nacional was playing. It wasn't a football match but a basketball game, against Aguada, in the brand-new Antel Arena. Like in the European ultras scene, it didn't matter whether your team was playing football, basketball, water polo, even women's volleyball. The colours were the same and matches would be treated as such. An *entrada* was being planned, the procession that the *barra* would make to the stadium displaying their banners, often with fireworks, flares, smoke bombs and drums. Santino picked us up in his car, at dusk, dressed in a blue Nacional hoodie. He was a lawyer, he loudly explained, speaking at a thousand miles an hour as we screeched around corners a little too fast. He was also a long-time member of La Banda del Parque, although his role wasn't exactly clear. 'A lot of this, a lot of that,' he replied. He was free to move around the club and the stadium but was currently banned from attending any Nacional games, in any sport, on any match day. He had used his training to get out of most of his own legal troubles but there was little he could do when he was searched and arrested for possessing a gun. He drove us to a skate park near the Parque Central that had been covered in Nacional graffiti. There were about 50 people there, from the *barra*, preparing for the *entrada*. It was mostly young men. There was a blur of faces and names. Balls of marijuana were pressed into my hand, the only thing I had seen offered for free and in abundance. Since 2013 Uruguay had legalised weed and placed a maximum price per gram on it, virtually destroying the black market overnight.

'This is the *barra*, and there is nothing else,' explained Mateo, a heavy-set man wearing a baseball cap that had the word 'Winner' written on it. He was a famous member of the Banda del Parque, he told me. He'd just got out of prison.

What were you in prison for? I asked him.

'I shot two Peñarol fans,' he replied, making a pistol sign with each hand. He took out his phone and showed me the pictures of him in his prison cell, mostly smiling and giving the V-sign. His friend, Martin, had also just got out of prison. He walked with a stiff leg after nine years inside for robbery with a gun. Everyone was wired on crack or cocaine. One member of the *barra*, eyes wide and unblinking, offered me a plastic bag with a few scraps of paper in it. LSD. This was probably the worst place in the world to take LSD, so I politely declined. 'Shall we get the guns now?' he said. Santino swiped him around the head, as if admonishing a puppy.

Hundreds more joined us as Mikael told stories of the Swedish ultras scene in the broken Spanish he had picked up from his time in Argentina. Flares were passed around as the *barra* drank and smoked and sang songs about Nacional, about the *hinchas* and about their hatred of Peñarol. Without warning, everyone moved into the middle of the road. The traffic was stopped as the *entrada* formed, first with a few dozen people until there were hundreds of us marching down the road. The flags and the banners were unfolded as the procession moved noisily along the highway, traffic backed up behind us. Smoke bombs and flares made it impossible to see the road in front of us. Huge explosions came every few seconds. Next to us Santino was running along, checking how things were going. It became clear his role was to let La Banda del Parque get out of hand, but not *that* out of hand.

The procession reached its destination, the Antel Arena; a brand-new, modernist, glowing cube. The group broke in two. One walked down to the arena to take their places courtside, where they would make as much noise as they would at a home football game. The rest, around 50 people, stood in the park over the road. 'We call our group "The Blacklist",' said Mateo. Everyone here was banned from going in. The heirs to Prudencio Miguel Reyes had to make do with watching the Antel Arena glow from a distance.

2

Argentina

BUENOS AIRES

Mikael and I had extricated ourselves from Nacional's Banda la Parque in the early hours of the morning and were headed to Argentina. On a good day with a fair wind and calm waters the ferry across the River Plate, from Montevideo to Buenos Aires, takes just over two hours. The party had continued back at the skate park, but once the flares, the cocaine and the money had run out, the mood had turned darker, even if Mikael hadn't noticed. I dragged him out before the inevitable shake-down and, a few hours later, we were on the first boat. Along the way Mikael had told me about his life, which revolved around football. After forming Sweden's first ever ultras group in the early 1990s, he opened his own shop in Stockholm, selling the flags, scarves and shirts he had collected on his travels over the previous decade. 'A friend had an ice hockey sports shop,' he explained. 'I put a Fiorentina and Inter scarf in the window, because I like Roma, and it was gone the same day.' After that he began selling VHS and DVD copies of football fights from England, Germany, Holland, Greece, Brazil and Argentina. He took over the whole shop and business was good for a while, but after a few years the landlord raised the rent and that was that. He used his unexpected spare time to travel to Argentina, which he believed was the true heart and soul of global football fan culture, the best place on earth to watch a match. And there was only one team he wanted to see.

Boca Juniors, Argentina's most successful team, was founded in 1905 by Italian immigrants in the La Boca neighbourhood. Most had come from the north-western port city of Genoa. Today over 60 per cent of Argentinians can trace some kind of lineage to Italy. The club's Italian heritage was so strong that Boca Juniors' nickname is Los Xeneizes, derived from the word Genoese. Two different but remarkably similar football fan cultures developed on either side of the Atlantic: the ultras in Italy and, before that, the *barras bravas* in Argentina. *Barras bravas* roughly means 'brave gang' and they had loosely existed as rowdy, semi-organised groups of supporters since the 1920s. The name of Boca's *barra*, La Doce, originated in 1925 when Victoriano Caffarena – a wealthy man from the neighbourhood – bankrolled Boca's first ever tour to Europe. On the 22-day boat ride over the Atlantic ocean Caffarena became indispensable. He took training, massaged the players and ran errands. The tour was wildly successful and, by the end of a long trip, Caffarena was indistinguishable from the players. So, he was dubbed the "12th" man, a nickname that stuck until his death in 1972.[1] But by then La Doce's name had begun to mean something else. The *barra* became much more structured and hierarchical in the late 1960s and 70s, when the clubs recognised that the passionate support could be harnessed for an advantage on the pitch. The clubs began pitching in to help with transport, tickets and materials to make *trapos* (literally 'rags', but the word used in Argentina for the flags seen at football grounds). Gustavo Grabia, a journalist who has written extensively about Argentina's *barras*, points

towards Boca's former president Alberto J. Armando as the man who
started properly funding their *barra*, La Doce, in the 1960s to build
an atmosphere designed to intimidate their opponents both inside
the stadium and outside. For Boca legend Antonio Rattín, the former Argentina captain who was famously sent off against England
at the 1966 World Cup finals, it worked: 'In the Bombonera I remember seeing the faces of the rivals, pale when the whole stadium
began to sing.'[2]

The injection of money into the terraces would have unforeseen
consequences. The popularity of the *barra* exploded and turned particularly violent, increasing decade by decade. Mikael had seen the
modern incarnation first-hand. His first Boca game was in 2008, an
away match against Club Atlético Huracán in the Estadio Diego
Armando Maradona. The match had been moved to Argentinos
Juniors's home thanks to a stadium ban because of crowd violence. The
move hadn't calmed any potential tensions. An internal conflict between
two leaders of La Doce – known simply as 'The War' – had just begun.
It ended up in a riot and with Mikael in prison. Some infraction had
resulted in the police firing rubber bullets and filling the air with tear
gas. Mikael was one of 184 people arrested that night. He was taken to
a police station. No one spoke English and, back then, Mikael didn't
speak any Spanish either. But everyone was friendly, especially the
police officers. Pizzas and Cokes were ordered from outside regardless
of their incarceration. He was eventually released at 1am, after six hours
in the cells. But the next morning Mikael's distinctive face was all over
the newspapers. He'd kept the cuttings from that time. A full page of
the daily tabloid *Crónica* had a large picture of a smashed-up police bus
with a younger-looking Mikael – minus his beard and a few pounds –
walking sheepishly past it, his neck tattoo prominent. The headline
read: 'The "Internal" War Had Another Chapter'.

The incident had both advantages and disadvantages for Mikael.
On the one hand, for the general public at least, he was now the face
of the civil disobedience inherent in Argentina's *barras bravas*, especially Boca Juniors, the avatar of a violent, out-of-control football culture. On the other, everybody connected with La Doce now knew

him. 'People were coming to me in the street and saying: "You are the Swedish guy! We remember you!"' Mikael recalled. Since then he has worn a Boca Juniors tattoo on his chest.

Still, Mikael's unexpected infamy was ironic. He hated violence, but he always seemed to be close to the action. His next match in Buenos Aries, a third division game in the northern suburbs, ended in another riot with the police firing rubber bullets. He was only there to take a picture of the pyro show. Mikael tried to get away and hid behind an old man hobbling across the terrace.

Like a human shield? I asked him.

'No!' he replied, a little embarrassed at how that sounded spoken aloud. His logic was sound. The old man, he reasoned, would be the *last* person to get shot in that scenario. 'But they shot a young women in front of me. She just fell down onto the ground and someone carried her out. It was a little scary.' The furthest he went was stealing an opposing group's flag if the opportunity presented itself. 'And who doesn't enjoy that?' he said, as if it was common sense. 'I'm old school. I don't want to attack. I want a cold beer and a chat with my friends in the bar after.' He felt that the younger generation had it the wrong way round. The club was always, always the most important thing. He stayed in Argentina for a year, making connections and immersing himself in the supporter culture. The choreographies in Argentina's stadiums were the best in the world. The *barras* would arrange huge banners that would cover whole stands. These highly artistic *telon*, the Spanish for 'curtain', were unsurpassed, the best often making headlines around the world, like when the *barra* of second division side Godoy Cruz commissioned a vast *telon* 100m long with the faces of Maradona, Pope Francis (who's a big San Lorenzo fan) and Messi. The inscription read: *'Dios, el Papa y el Mesias'*. God, the Pope and the Messiah. The songs sung here were copied all across South America until they eventually reached Europe, bent and shaped into the local language, honouring local heroes, until no one could remember exactly where the original tune had come from. Ultras from all across Europe would, like Mikael, come and learn from the *barra*, before taking parts of it back home with them.

The passion also had a darker side, of course. The *barras bravas* had pretty much controlled Argentina's stadiums, and a lot more besides, since the 1980s. The game had become one of the most violent in the world. Dozens of fans died in football-related violence every year and away fans had been banned since 2013. A local campaign group, Salvemos al Fútbol, updates a list of every person killed at an Argentinian football match.[3] The first such fatality was in 1922. The Argentinian sociologist Amílcar Romero was the first to do pioneering studies into the nature of violence in Argentine football. He suggested that the death in 1958 of a River Plate fan killed by a policeman firing a tear-gas canister outside Vélez Sarsfield's Estadio Amalfitani was the tipping point that radicalised football supporters against the authorities, especially the police, and against each other.[4] He identified 1958 to 1983 as the period where the type of violence changed, reflecting both increased resources being pumped into the *barras* and a turbulent society beset by worker and student protests, coups, massacres and dictatorship, the so-called 'Dirty War' that saw thousands of left-wing activists, journalists and artists 'disappeared'. For Romero, the *barras* were the id of an unhappy and fractured society. Between 1922 and 1958, 16 football-related deaths had been recorded. As Romero pointed out, between 1958 and 1983 there were an average of five deaths a year (although that number includes the 71 supporters killed in the Gate 12 tragedy at the Estadio Monumental after a Boca versus River Plate match in 1968).

To this day, since 1922, 332 people have died in football-related violence in Argentina. Tens of thousands more have been injured. 'Organised violence here spread from football to the rest of society,' Romero would later say. 'In Europe it was the other way around.'[5]

The last fatality was on 9 December 2018 when a 21-year-old River Plate fan, Exequiel Neris, was stabbed to death by two Boca fans after the 2018 Copa Libertadores final, South America's equivalent of the Champions League final. The rivalry between River Plate and Boca was one of the fiercest in the world, the so-called *Superclasico*, but the two had never faced each other in the final of the Copa Libertadores before. As the 2018 tournament progressed, and the likelihood of a super *Superclasico* became reality, the authorities started to panic. 'Honestly, I prefer that a Brazilian [club] win instead of having that kind of final, because that would mean three weeks without sleep,' said Argentina's president Mauricio Macri when the two teams faced Brazilian opposition in the semi-finals. 'Do you know how much pressure that's going to be? The loser will need twenty years to recover.'[6] Macri knew what he was talking about. His first position in public life was a 12-year spell as president of Boca Juniors. He was narrowly elected by Boca's membership – its *socios* – in 1995 and used the success he enjoyed during that period (including four Copa Libertadores titles) as a springboard for elected office, first as mayor of Buenos Aires and then Argentina's presidency in 2015. A classified US intelligence cable from 2010, released by Wikileaks, described how then US ambassador Vilma Socorro Martínez invited Mayor Macri for lunch, where he openly discussed his presidential ambitions and Boca's role in his burgeoning political career. The cable read:

> He [Macri] described his presidency of the Boca Juniors Soccer Club as having been an outstanding political education (dealing with issues like access to press and locker rooms, distribution of seats, and business decisions in front of a membership of about 15,000) and said that the Club's national following was his greatest political asset. 'If I receive political support outside of Buenos Aires,' he said, 'in 90% of the cases it is for managing Boca and in 10% for being Mayor of Buenos Aires'.[7]

As he suspected, thanks to his 'political education', the 2018 super *Superclasico* was indeed a disaster for Argentina's image. The second game was called off after the Boca team bus was attacked by River Plate fans as it approached the Estadio Monumental. The police responded with tear gas, which some of the Boca players inhaled. The club tweeted videos from the locker room of them vomiting. The security situation was so dire it was decided that the game had to be played at a neutral venue.[8] Madrid was chosen, a huge humiliation given that the name of the tournament was chosen to honour the leaders who fought for independence from the Spanish and Portuguese. River Plate eventually won the title but CONMEBOL, South American football's governing body, decided that all future finals would now be a single game and played at a neutral venue.

Deaths between opposing fans had at least become rarer in recent years. Most deaths were now the settling of scores within different *barras*, largely due to the fact that they had now branched out into a variety of different businesses – ticket scalping, parking, protection rackets and drugs – that made them resemble mafia groups rather than supporter organisations. And La Doce, Boca Juniors' strongest *barra*, had seen many scores settled over the past decade. The group's leader Rafael di Zeo was both a showman and a feared leader. Since the mid-1990s he had built La Doce into a formidable and powerful money-making institution with deep political connections within Argentina's establishment. But money and power attracted rivals. When Rafa, as he is commonly known, was eventually jailed in 2007 for four years for his alleged role in a 1999 riot between the supporters of Boca and Chacarita Juniors, one of his underbosses, Mauro Martin, replaced him. Rafa was released in 2009 but Mauro had no intention of stepping down.

A bloody battle for supremacy followed – 'The War' – and dozens were killed. Mauro was even shot, but survived. Eventually a truce was agreed, with Rafa retaking the reins and Mauro closely involved as his number two. It was, Mikael explained, an uneasy truce that could break at any moment. Mikael had called an old friend from La Doce, who remembered him from his brief stint as the most recognisable hooligan in Buenos Aires. Mauro, he told us, had agreed to meet the following day in Bajo Flores, before Boca Juniors were due to play. It was their final Copa Libertadores group game against Brazil's Athletico Paranaense. Boca had already qualified for the knockout stages although, for Mikael, it was the chance to return to his beloved Estadio Alberto J. Armando, known affectionately as the 'Bombonera'. And there was at least one important thing to play for. A Boca Juniors victory would ensure that they remained in the same

side of the draw as River Plate, and raised the prospect of the two
meeting each other in the semi-finals. Mauricio Macri was wrong. It
wouldn't take 20 years for a club to recover from losing the Copa
Libertadores *Superclasico* final. Fate had conspired to offer Boca the
chance of redemption less than 12 months later.

Inside the tall, reconditioned space out in the western suburbs of
Buenos Aires, three artists were busily working on their cloth can-
vases. System of the Down was playing on the radio as jet-powered
spray cans hissed, the smell of solvent hanging heavily in the air. On
one wall, on a section of a huge white satin banner, one of the men
was painting a *telon* for San Lorenzo, filling in the colours of a pair of
drums whose outline had already been sketched out. Another worked
on an Argentina flag with the face of Eva Peron, for the *hinchas* of the
national team who were about to leave for the Copa America in Brazil.
Another was finishing off a smaller flag coloured blue and gold – for
the next Boca game – with its Twitter handle on it: '@Juvenil Xeneizes',
the young fans of Boca Juniors. 'This is not for La Doce, but for the
normal *hinchas*,' said Pepe Perretta, wearing a red trucker's hat with
'Buenos Aires Aerografia' emblazoned on the front. He took a moment
to check his team's handiwork, an unlit roll-up cigarette hanging from
his lip.

There was still some discussion about where exactly the vast flags
that covered whole stands at football matches – the *telon* – originated
from. But there was no doubt who, today, was the best *telon* artist in
the world. Pepe Perretta had made over a hundred of these vast can-
vases, each one telling a different story about the people who asked
for them to be made. Upstairs, in his office, Pepe's walls were covered
in pictures and signed shirts with Argentine legends. A section had
been cordoned off with an original piece of metal fence, complete
with barbed wire on the top, from the stadium of Pepe's beloved
Nueva Chicago. Behind the fence were hundreds of shirts and scarves,
and dozens of books and signed pictures of his hero Diego Maradona.
Messi had sent him a shirt too. Everything here had been sent by
hinchas, players and Popes alike, in appreciation for the huge pieces of

public art which Pepe had made honouring them. It was Pepe who had made the vast *telon* with the Pope, Messi and Maradona for the *barra* of Godoy Cruz.

Pepe's work had appeared on the curves and terraces of the biggest stadiums in the world: in Colombia and Chile; in Italy with Napoli, Inter, Lazio, Torino and Fiorentina; in Spain with Barcelona and Atlético Madrid. There were dozens of famous moments in Argentina too: a famous *telon* in honour of Sergio Agüero shortly before he left Independiente for Atlético Madrid. A 350m-long *telon* for Racing Club that filled the stadium. He'd just got off the phone from Saudi Arabia with an offer to make a flag that was 500m long, which would be a world record. But it all started in 2006 thanks in part to La Doce. Pepe was a biker and had used his art mainly to decorate helmets or petrol tanks. Occasionally he'd paint shopfronts too, although his father was dismissive of his artistic ambitions. Then, one day, he was approached by La Doce. They wanted him to paint a huge banner of a Boca shirt with the number '12' ringed, at the centre.

When it was unveiled to much fanfare, Pepe was inundated with calls from other *barras*. They too wanted their own unique flags and banners created. They would often come with a design and Pepe would adapt it, knowing what worked and what didn't. He would, he said, paint anything anyone wanted. Politics or religion didn't bother him. The famous Godoy Cruz *telon*, for example, included a map of Las Malvinas, the Falklands Islands. They took between five and fifteen days to make, often with some security, given that opposing *barras* would want to steal a flag as a sign of territorial supremacy. Sometimes dozens of people from the club concerned protected him whilst he painted. 'I put all my passion into them. Because that is what I am representing. The passion of the *barras*.' Pepe hadn't yet had a banner stolen, partly because he had managed something no one else could: moving between *barras* without rivalry or tribalism getting in the way, on account of his work.

The reason he had been accepted by rival *barras* was because of his one concrete rule: he never painted a flag *against* anyone.

Boca fans would ask for flags insulting River, but 'I always paint supporting the *barra*, but not against another club.' His stance of producing *telones* for anyone led, ultimately, to his one falling-out. Pepe was commissioned to make a large banner for River Plate. His father, who had always been dismissive of his art, was a River Plate fan. Pepe didn't tell his father about the banner until the two of them were in the Monumental and he saw his son's art being unfurled in front of an ecstatic audience first-hand. He died shortly afterwards, but had finally understood what his son had devoted his life to. Still the flag had consequences. La Doce ended contact with him.

On the face of it the *trapos,* the *telones*, the mosaic choreographies, made little sense. These were hugely ornate, technically difficult and expensive artistic projects to pull off. The message that was to be sent to the team or the outside world, whether that was a memorial or a warning or something more political, would last for a matter of seconds before it disappeared. Often they'd be burned afterwards, lest they ever fell into the hands of opposition fans. But to Pepe it made perfect sense. Technology meant that his creations would now exist on social media forever. But, above all else, they were an expression of pride and encouragement that was only ever meant to be fleeting and in close quarters. 'The origin of the flag in football was to show your passion for the neighbourhood at football matches,' he said. 'I've always understood it as some kind of heraldic or medieval thing. Your symbol representing you on the battlefield.'

Is there any club left that you would like to paint for? I asked him.

'For me, there is no club left!' he said, and he was right. It wasn't about clubs or teams. It was about stadiums. He didn't talk about Real Madrid, but rather the Bernabeu. He didn't talk about the *barra* of Club America or the *hinchas* of the Mexican national team. He talked about the Estadio Azteca. 'My art gallery is the fence and the field in the stadiums,' he said. 'The best way the world can show the art that I make is putting the flags in the best stadiums. You go to an art gallery to see paintings and the sculptures. And the stadiums are my art galleries.'

Mikael ordered himself a small flag for Hammarby before Pepe looked at his computer and realised he was running late. He had an important job to get to at Vélez Sarsfield's stadium. He jumped on to his black Harley-Davidson, cigarette in mouth, and roared towards the highway. Fifteen minutes later he was standing outside the Estadio José Amalfitani, where Pedro Paz was waiting for us. Pedro was a mountain of a man, over two metres tall, with long, dark shoulder-length hair.

'Jefe ultra,' Pepe said as we approached him. Pedro was the 'jefe', or chief, of the Vélez Sarsfield barra, La Pandilla. The security guard at the front barriers scrambled to his feet and whipped his pass out to let Pedro in as soon as he saw he was approaching. 'We want something special painted in our place,' Pedro said. He wanted a mural in the barra's headquarters. Pedro was friendly and charismatic as he showed us the club's history: the statue of a youngish Carlos Bianchi, a prolific goalscorer for the club who would go on to coach the team and win the Copa Libertadores and the Intercontinental Cup in 1994; the trophy cabinet that contained the spoils of Bianchi's prolific time as coach. Pedro was greeted as a returning hero every few steps. Old and young women left their desks and counters to hug him. Pedro knew everyone's name. As we walked past the swimming pool named after Marcos 'Marquitos' Lencina, the previous barracapo who had died in 2011, children ran out of their classes and mobbed him, jumping up to give him high-fives. He looked like Arnold Schwarzenegger on the second day undercover in Kindergarten Cop.

It was the first time I had seen just how much power the barras had within Argentinian football clubs. In fact Vélez's former president Raul Gamez had himself once been the head of Vélez's barra. He spent six months in prison for rioting against the police but had ingratiated himself into the club's internal politics and was eventually elected to run the club. But, like a rockabilly grandfather complaining about the K-pop the youngsters were listening to these days, he had been critical of the new generation of barras. 'We were "good lads" fifty years ago when society was different, there were others customs, drugs were not within our reach,'[9] he said. He was particularly critical of how political they had become. He was referencing the former president Cristina Fernandez de Kirchner, who had called the *barras* 'good lads' shortly before a government-funded trip for the leaders of the main groups to attend the 2010 World Cup in South Africa. But the political connections went even deeper than that. Unions, businesses, even political parties, often paid the *barras* to act in their interests against rivals. 'Politicians need [*barras*] and use them as violent manual labour,' said Gamez. 'Club directors want to get them off their backs, we make pacts with the *barras*, there's no option because there are no guarantees [for our safety].'[10]

Inside the dimly lit gym Pedro explained what he wanted: a mural to cover one large wall to honour his predecessor Marquitos. A freshly painted cartoon bulldog was drying on the adjacent wall. Pedro pulled out his phone by way of explanation and played a video from YouTube: his hero was Vélez's former goalkeeper José Luis Chilavert ('El Bulldog'), famed for his free kicks. Chilavert scored one from the half-way line against River Plate in 1996 and both scored *and* saved a penalty in the 1994 Copa Libertadores final.

It was time to go. We had to get to Bajo Flores for our meeting with Mauro, one of the most powerful figures within La Doce. But, just as we were about to leave, Mikael's phone rang. It was one of his contacts, who was closely aligned with Rafa. Juan, one of the oldest members of La Doce, had found out about the meeting and was immediately suspicious. 'He said we shouldn't go. He thinks it is a trap,' Mikael said, a little crestfallen. The meeting itself wasn't suspicious but *where* Mauro had agreed to meet us had set off alarm bells for Juan.

Mikael texted his man and told him his stomach was playing up.

Juan's office was a shrine to Boca Juniors. Behind his desk was a messy collage of his life. A framed signed shirt. Pictures of old matches, stadiums and long-departed friends from the *barra*. 'Yesterday when I told Rafa that you were going to meet Mauro in Bajo Flores, he said: "They are going to be robbed, watch out,"' said Juan, a powerfully built middle-aged man with thick grey hair who may have just saved mine and Mikael's lives. His handshake felt like he could crush my fingers to dust, if he chose to. A loaded shotgun was propped up in the corner. A bunch of shells held together by elastic bands stood on the shelf next to it. It was, he said, a gift from Aldo Rico, a former military man who led two failed coups in the 1980s.

What do you mean, 'robbed'? I asked.

'They can hit you, they can do whatever they want because it's like a mafia,' he replied. 'Maybe you [go] there and you go politely and maybe nothing happens. Maybe it does.'

Juan had known Rafa and Mauro for years because he was one of the grandees of La Doce. He had started going to the Bombonera with his father when he was eight years old. As soon as he walked into the stadium he was drawn to the action behind the goal, in the north end, where the *barra* sat, known as the *popular*. His father forbade him from going there, warning him it was dangerous. But Juan didn't listen. He began running away from home and sneaking to the games to join the *barra*, back when La Doce was run by a man called Tito Campo, known as The Butcher. Not because he was particularly skilled at carving people up. But because he was literally a butcher. His shop was outside the Bombonera. He'd receive tickets from the club and sell them on to fund the *trapos* for the group, and a little for himself on the side. It was here Juan met Rafael di Zeo, Rafa, who would go on to take control of La Doce himself.

For much of the 1970s The Butcher ran La Doce. The main focus was on support and, of course, stealing the opponents' flags. 'If La Doce [didn't] exist, I wouldn't be a fan of Boca,' said Juan. 'It's about the group of friends. The folkloric part was to go to their rivals and start taking out their flags or their T-shirts. That's the way it started. But then it started getting maybe more violent, chains, stones. It degenerated.' Juan didn't know why it degenerated. Maybe it was the drugs. Or the higher stakes that came with the amount of money in the game. Maybe it was the by-product of living in the dying embers of a dictatorship. The Butcher's reign came to an end after Boca Juniors played Rosario Central in 1981. Rosario won 1–0. Maradona, Juan remembered, missed a penalty. But The Butcher had told the rowdier members of La Doce that he'd sold out of tickets to the game. The group travelled to Rosario without tickets and were all arrested. There had already been a two-year power battle, and The Butcher's insult was the last straw.

'In La Boca, we set fire to his house,' Juan recalled. 'And he said: "I don't want to have anything to do with this."' The Butcher relinquished control and a new generation took power.

Juan took a photo down from the wall. It was a colour picture of him, a much younger version, with his arm around the shoulders of José Barrita. Barrita was better known as El Abuelo, The Grandfather, because of his grey hair. He was the next *barracapo*. The Grandfather was also something of a bohemian. 'José was some kind of hippie, you know? He didn't care about money,' said Juan. El Abuelo wasn't ostentatious and never appeared to have any cash. He drove a battered old Ford Falcon Ranchero but lived for the *barra*. He was attracted to the life of an outsider, and the adrenaline of conflict. It was during this period that the building blocks of what La Doce would become were laid. More money was demanded from the club. Players were expected to pay a percentage of their wages to keep the *barra* chanting their names. A foundation was set up so that La Doce could funnel its funds through it. For the club La Doce was also their eyes and ears, especially to keep their stars out of trouble. One famous example, Juan said, was the arrival in 1995 of Maradona and Claudio Caniggia. Both joined Boca looking to rebuild their careers after lengthy drug bans. Maradona's addiction to cocaine had already led to one 15-month ban whilst he was at Napoli. At the 1994 World Cup he failed another drugs test, this time for ephedrine.[11] Caniggia was a renowned party animal who served his own 13-month ban for taking cocaine when he played for Roma.[12] The pair had been the first signings under Macri, himself trying to rehabilitate his reputation as a diffident playboy, in an attempt to win over the Boca crowd and bring instant success. But the two players, according to Juan, were going out every night and then failing drugs tests back at the club. So Boca asked the *barra* to rein them in. 'Every time they saw Caniggia or Maradona partying, they had to stop them and warn them,' recalled Juan. 'Otherwise they would punch them!'

The 1980s and 90s were a time of violence. Juan was shot twice and stabbed four times. He pulled down an x-ray from his wall, from the time a bullet fired by a River Plate fan shattered his hip, which needed replacing. Behind the scenes Rafa and his brother Fernando were urging The Grandfather to take a more businesslike approach with the money they were generating. The two were becoming increasingly powerful just as The Grandfather's reign was coming to an end. The court cases were piling up when two River Plate fans were shot dead at a *Superclasico* in 1994. The courts never proved that The Grandfather was present but he was eventually jailed for nine years on a series of charges including extortion. Rafa visited The Grandfather in prison and a huge row erupted.

'Grandpa told Rafa the only thing that he wanted was to get to the top and be where he is now,' Juan said. José Barrita died in 2001, 20 days after coming out of prison, after contracting pneumonia. Rafa's La Doce was very different to Barrita's. 'Rafa wanted to make business. He started seeing the possibility of making business with the *barras* and the politics and everything,' said Juan. 'Macri, that is our president right now, used to be the president of Boca, so Rafa and I went and started advising him on how to take control and how to manage the club.'

This was dropped into conversation as if he was describing a meeting at a golf club. Yet it got to the nexus of power, money and influence that connected the *barras*, the football clubs and the political elite in Argentina. Mauricio Macri was elected Boca Juniors president in 1995 but, as Juan pointed out, he could not get elected unless he went through La Doce first. In fact, the payments from politicians, Juan said, were La Doce's biggest earners. The politicians expected a lot in return for hiring what Juan called 'human resources': attending rallies, breaking up protests, looting on demand, protection. It could all be bought at the right price. He explained how in 2003 some of the group were sent in to to break up a rally in support of the Brukman factory workers, a group of 50 women who had taken over their textiles factory and had become an internationally celebrated story.[13] That action cost just $20,000, 20 pizzas and a bus big enough to get everyone there and back. The timing of the action, Juan thought, might even have swayed the 2003 presidential election. La Doce knew to ask for much more next time.

And there was always a next time. Macri, Juan said, was no different to any other politician in Argentina. Macri had, of course, denied supporting La Doce. In *Hooligans*, a 2002 BBC series about football's troublemakers inside and outside of the UK, one episode, 'Foreign Fields', focused on La Doce and Argentina's *barras* ahead of a *Superclasico*. Rafa was interviewed, as was Mauricio Macri, who was younger, yet to go grey and in possession of a thin moustache. 'There's always been speculation about the relationship between football club presidents and hooligans,' Macri said. 'Club presidents as well as politicians used to use hooligans for their own purposes. But part of our new politics is to stop any contact with these sorts of people who base their power on violence.' He denied ever funding La Doce or giving them tickets knowing they would sell them on for a large profit. 'Perhaps I should say it in English. I've said it so many times. We do not give tickets to the hooligans.'

No one in Argentina believed that. Macri was the son of one of Argentina's richest businessmen. He lived in a gated community and was, Juan said, woefully unprepared to connect with Boca Junior's working-class fan base. 'The first meeting I had was with [this guy, he] was "living in a bubble", living in a private neighbourhood, in a different world,' said Juan. 'We taught him elementary things such as, leave your security guards outside. We suggested he should go to the *popular* and not to the *platea* [expensive seats]. We helped him with his campaign. He won ... and then he became hard.'

At the centre of all of it was Rafa. 'Rafa always had this thing of making money. He was very good at looking to the future and seeing how they can take money from everywhere.' The issue of just how much money La Doce made was complicated. According to a 2013 investigation in *La Nación*, the profit just from the one *trapitos*, the people hustling the parking spaces outside the Bombonera, was 300,000 pesos a match.[14] (In 2013, 300,000 pesos was worth nearly $60,000. But the collapse of Argentina's currency means that, at the time of writing, the same sum is worth around $5000. The journalist Gustavo Grabia suggested the organisation pulled in $400,000 a month.

But the true figure, according to Juan, was far higher. Tickets, parking, food and merchandising was the small part. 'The [rest] comes from the politicians, the unions when they ask for "human resources" for demonstrations or to fight against the police. And, on the other side, from the narcos.' On average, Juan said, La Doce pulled in at least $3 million a month, but it could easily increase depending on the business. 'And that's nothing. Normally it's more than three million per month. Only for the *barra*. Only Boca. Sometimes it's six [million], ten [million]. They can ask whatever money they want. And they pay.'

By the turn of the millennium La Doce was thriving. Rafa claimed a membership of 2,000 people. He was friends with Argentina's best players, including Maradona, who he was frequently pictured with. Everything was conducted in the open. La Doce was now operating 'adrenaline tours' for foreign tourists, who paid handsomely – 40 at a time – to watch a game in the *popular* at the Bombonera with the group.[15] The business model was so successful that La Doce even started a kind of 'university for ultras' around the world. For €5,000, groups could receive an education in how to set up a business like La Doce; from ticket scalping to writing terrace chants to making their own banners. At the end, each attendee was given a CD with songs from the Bombonera which would then be replicated and spread throughout Europe. 'La Doce is like Harvard,' Rafa said in a 2006 documentary aired on the Argentine TV channel Canal 9, 'a university to learn to be a *barra*.'[16] But eventually the law caught up with Rafa too. He was jailed in 2007 for his alleged role in a riot. Mauro took over parts of the business, and conflict began after the two had an argument when Mauro visited Rafa in prison.

Rafa was released in 2009 but conflict had already begun between their supporters. The two sides would turn up to matches, often taking opposite stands and hurling abuse at each other. A proxy war broke out, with supporters of both men fighting and dying. Mauro's mother,

Juan told me, had even been attacked. Nine months later Mauro's group was ambushed on its way to Rosario and he was shot in the stomach. He survived but, in the end, it was a Pekinese that handed La Doce back to Rafa. Maximiliano Mazzaro, Mauro's number two, was contacted by his brother-in-law, incensed that his neighbour, Ernesto Cirino, let his his pet dog urinate in his doorway. Cirino was beaten to death and Mazzaro and Mauro were jailed.[17] Although later acquitted and released, Rafa was back on top and the two men buried the hatchet.

The uneasy truce had held so far, even as the authorities had cracked down on the *barras*. Mauricio Macri was elected President of Argentina in 2015 and explicitly stood on a platform of reining in the power of the *barras* by building an elite, FBI-style unit to fight football violence. Rafa was pretty much banned from the Bombonera these days. Juan went to his filing cabinet and pulled out a thick file of cuttings and magazine front covers, covering the past few decades: stories about La Doce, The Grandfather, The War (between Mauro and Rafa). The most interesting aspect of his cuttings was the way Rafa was framed. He appeared on the front cover of glossy magazines. The inaugural issue of *Playboy* Argentina had an interview with Rafa: 'Man to Man with the Head of the Boca Barra'. Another magazine had Rafa on the cover in boxing gloves, sparring towards the camera, with the headline: 'The Ambassador of Fear'. He was treated like a rock star. 'Rafa, on the one side, he's very popular and famous,' Juan explained. 'But on the other side he's like a terrorist for some people. So it opens a lot of doors but it closes a lot of doors too.' I had hoped I could meet him after Boca's next game, but that seemed unlikely after what might have happened with Mauro.

It seemed like the power of the *barras* was an unsolvable issue. They were making too much money and had too much dirt on people in power. Maybe even on politicians at the highest level in Argentina. They were also revered as folk heroes, a constant and seductive presence in La Bombonera. Players came and went. Club presidents made and then broke promises before disappearing. But La Doce? They were always there with the same songs. It seemed that the only people who could possibly destroy the *barras*, were the *barras* themselves. 'We are all the time wondering what's going to happen because right now everything is OK, but tomorrow or the day after it can be total chaos and shooting,' Juan said. The War, he believed, would return. 'It's about to explode like a grenade.'

It was match day, the Copa Libertadores group match against Brazil's Athletico Paranaense, and the Bombonera shimmered gold and blue beneath the floodlights. It was a sell-out, as it was for every game, with 50,000 people expected. The police had tightly controlled every route to the stadium, closing roads and redirecting traffic. Still, there was a good chance I would miss the game. It was a tricky business getting a ticket to watch Boca play. La Doce controlled the trade, especially the most lucrative part of it: foreign tourists. A ticket, or at least 'borrowing' a Boca fan's membership card, could cost up to $400. Mikael was supposed to be using his contacts in La Doce to sort us both out but the scare with Mauro meant we had only managed to find one. As much as Mikael had wanted to help me out, he had come for this moment. Standing there, with the Bombonera illuminated and full of song, it was easy to see how he had been bewitched by this place. There was no way he was going to miss it, and I didn't want to stop him. He walked to the security gate and promised to meet me afterwards.

I did, however, have one last Hail Mary: my press card. I showed it at the ticket office. The man laughed, pulled down the shutter, locked up and left, tittering as he walked away. I went to another gate and made an impassioned plea at each line of security. Eventually one harassed guard opened the gate, just to get rid of me.

The Estadio Alberto J. Armando gets its nickname from its unusual architecture. When the Slovenian-born architect Viktor Sulčič was designing a prototype for the stadium in the mid-1930s he was inspired by a *Bombonera*, a box of chocolates. The ensuing design was compact and steep, giving each seat the feeling of being in the gods at the opera. With space at such a premium in the tightly packed La Boca neighbourhood, and no question that the stadium would ever be moved from its home – as River Plate had done by moving to the upmarket *barrio* of Núñez in 1926 – it was built, rebuilt and modified to make the best of what they had. They couldn't build out, so they built up instead, leading to its unique design; a sweeping three-tiered curve that bore down on the pitch from three sides, buttressed by a shallow block of corporate boxes along one side. From the air it looked less like a chocolate box and more like a cake of a football stadium that had been cut in half.

Walking into the Bombonera after a match had started was disorientating. The cumulative effect of constant song, driving Argentine drums and the steep drop to the pitch was vertiginous. You understood why the songs – quick, complicated and sung rather than shouted – and the *telon* from Argentina's stadiums were the most influential in the world: copied and adapted first by word of mouth and then thanks to the internet, and then replicated in stadiums from Madrid to Jakarta. But then something extraordinary happened. Athletico scored first. And the singing became louder. It was, Mikael told me later, always like that. In the seconds after the goal the Boca *hinchas* began to sing as if *they* had just gone in front. They sang the famous song 'Si, Señor', adapted from an early 1990s Argentinian rock song 'Y *Dale Aegria a mi Corazon*' by Fito Paez. River Plate and San Lorenzo both claim they adapted it first but no one can really be sure.

> And give joy, joy to my heart,
> The only thing I ask you [is] to win today
> The Copa Libertadores is my obsession,
> You have to leave your heart and soul,
> You'll see,
> We are not like the faggots of River Plate

Everyone was struggling with the sodden, cut-up pitch. Except for Carlos Tevez. Although the Argentina international striker had started on the bench, he was the undoubted star of this Boca team and the hero of the Bombonera. Tevez had grown up crushingly poor but fought his way out of the *barrio* and into Boca's first team. He won the

Copa Libertadores and the league and then started a journey that saw him play in Brazil for Corinthians before hopping across the Atlantic to make his name in Europe for West Ham, Manchester United, Manchester City and Juventus. This was his third spell at Boca after a brief, lucrative but embarrassing spell in Chinese football. But, as a child of the *barrio*, he was also seen as a player of the *barra*. A few weeks after re-signing, a picture was taken of Tevez enjoying an evening meal with Rafa and Mauro. No one succeeded at Boca without coming through La Doce first.

Tevez's introduction changed the game. He seemed to plough through the pitch even faster than his team-mates could run above it. Boca equalised shortly after going behind and then, in the 96th minute, deep in injury time, Tevez scored the winner. The noise was incredible, like a thousand musical instruments being thrown down a thousand staircases at the same time. Eventually, after the chaotic celebration, songs began to form again until the final whistle was blown. The songs didn't stop as the crowd moved like a wave, as one, outside and into La Boca's streets, filling them in all directions. It was so tightly packed I could barely reach for my vibrating phone. Mikael was waiting outside. We had to hurry. Rafa di Zeo had agreed to meet us. We had to leave straight away.

We half walked, half ran through the maze of dark, damp streets that surround the Bombonera, past lines of policemen and packs of celebrating fans. Past murals depicting Boca's undisputed hero, Diego Maradona. Past a mural with the Union Jack, a skull and crossbones at its centre, and the words: 'We Will Be Back in Malvinas with the Hand of Latin America'. Eventually, after several wrong turns, we arrived at the address. A petrol station. At first I thought we had arrived at the wrong place, until I saw an armed policeman standing guard at the corner of the shop. He left as soon as we arrived. A group of what looked like bodyguards approached us, one wearing a La Doce baseball cap, and invited us to walk down a dark, unlit side passage.

This was where La Doce did their business, in a car park behind a petrol station. Around 30 to 40 men were here, all in their thirties and forties: Rafa di Zeo's pretorian guard, the most trusted of his men. We stood in the middle of the car park as the men stared at us. Eventually, Juan came forward and explained the rules. There could be no pictures. No filming. No recording. Under no circumstances would I tell Rafa I was British. The Falklands War had not been forgotten. One of La Doce's older members, Mono (Monkey), was a veteran. I was to say, he insisted, that I was Swedish like Mikael, and writing about the club's connection to the Swedish flag. It is thought that Boca's blue and gold colours were inspired by a Swedish ship that was moored at the port just as they were deciding what colour the club's shirt should be. And I was, under no circumstances, to ask about The War between Rafa and Mauro. Mikael had warned me that I shouldn't mention the falling-out between the two. If I did, he would walk away before he heard an answer and leave me to my fate. He was convinced it could only end badly.

We stood in the middle of the car park for half an hour before Rafa unfolded himself out of the back of a car he was sitting in to finish some business. He walked forward and shook my hand. Rafa didn't look like one of Buenos Aires's most dangerous men. He was in his late fifties now, tall, with grey curtains parted in the middle. He wore a full, black Boca Juniors tracksuit. He looked more like a singer in a mid-90s nu-metal band, back for one last comeback show. A circle of his closest men formed tightly around us, but Rafa was immediately disarming, and was happy to be recorded.

What is La Doce? I asked him.

'It would be very complicated to say briefly,' he replied, before giving us an ultra-sanitised version of the past four decades. 'I've been in La Doce since I was sixteen years old, it's been forty years already. It's been a long time. There was another leader at that time [The Butcher]. When I arrived there, the leader stayed for two more years and after that another leader stayed in for some time; that one was my teacher [The Grandfather]. And then when the guys had a problem I assumed the role. Since the end of 1994 I've been taking care of the *barra*.'

What was your role in La Doce?

'A leader is the one who has more influence on everything,' he replied. 'Now it's different due to the advances of technology. Before, in order to be leader you had to fight against the other *hinchadas*. Everything was more violent. Today's more quiet. There's more control because of the government. When I started, to earn your place you had to fight. Always be there, at the front row ... Nowadays it's not the same.'

There's so much control, in fact, that he wasn't at today's game. He'd been banned from the stadium for two years but when the ban was due to be lifted a few weeks before today's game, the government issued a fresh four year ban against Rafa, Mauro and 126 other members of La Doce.[18] So he ended up watching it on TV instead. The *barra*, he said, '*is* against authority, against the police for sure. It is always against authorities. Therefore, nobody related to any authority is allowed to be part of the group. If they are, they're out and we punch him.' I asked him about the role of violence in the *barra,* and why the authorities feared La Doce. I could feel Mikael wincing behind me, but Rafa was comfortable talking about it.

'They are afraid of our power and of our violence,' he said. 'The times when we had a fight and they [the police] won, it was because they fired at us, you know? Without ammunition they wouldn't win. If this was like in Europe, where they only use sticks [instead of guns], everyone would be dead. In this country, to kill a cop is "valuable", I mean it is "well seen" in the jail environment when you are there due to killing a cop.'

He didn't shy away from the main issue. That the violence was enjoyable. 'I remember a match against Lanus, and I remember we fought against the police, here in the tribune,' he recalled of his favourite match. 'We kicked them out, all the way down the stairs to the streets. And we took [and kept] two guns from the police. I clearly remember it. And when we got inside the River [Plate] tribune in a stadium in Mar del Plata and we took away their flag. The most important one, most precious flag, the one that identifies them.'

Do you still love football? I asked him.

'Yes, I do,' he answered quickly. 'I would say that I love Boca more than football. I love Boca. Without Boca I don't know what I would have done.' He started laughing. 'I would have dedicated myself to the tennis!' Even when he was banned he wasn't far away. He was still friends with the players, especially Carlos Tevez. 'We have a really good relationship,' he said. 'He is also my friend. I had known him before he started playing.'

When the super-*Superclasico* between Boca and River was called off and moved to Madrid to be played, Rafa decided to stay in Buenos Aires. There was no guarantee he would be allowed into the stadium anyway. But when the Boca team bus left for the airport, tens of thousands of *hinchas* turned out to meet them, firing off rockets and banging drums. The coach inched through the sea of people. At the front, leading the coach through, were Rafa and Mauro.

Rafa didn't think he would be out of the stadium for long. He was a recognised public figure these days, which made things difficult. 'It has pros and cons,' he said. 'For example, the politicians, judges, the chief police officers. On one side they [publicly] reject me. But on the other side, they want to talk to you, to get closer, to arrange something with you.'

Politicians had always needed him. Macri had needed him. And in a way, at least how La Doce saw it, Macri wouldn't be president without their help. There would be presidential elections later in the year, which Macri could lose. There would, he believed, be a new president and a new security minister. 'It's not a legal problem, it's a political problem,' Rafa said. 'At the end of the year, when the politics change, I will be back.' Politicians came and went. But Rafa di Zeo and La Doce would always be there.

My time was up. We had been talking for half an hour, but it had felt like 30 seconds. It was also time to say goodbye to Mikael, who was staying in Argentina to see a few more matches whilst I headed for Brazil. 'I really thought you were going to mention The War,' he told me later, relieved. But we would see each other again, he said, in Stockholm, so that I could see for myself how Sweden had built one of the best ultra cultures in the world. Mikael, of course, would be my guide. Once our interview behind the petrol station was finished, Rafa di Zeo called over one of his men and told them to drive us back to our apartment. 'It's dangerous around here at this time,' he said in a rather fatherly manner. The driver joked that he had enough guns in the back of the car to retake Las Malvinas all by himself.

Before we left there was an awkward pause, as if Rafa expected something else to follow. For a moment I thought I'd offended him somehow. I looked to Mikael and the ring of burly *hinchas* around us, but he seemed happy enough. 'If you want to take some pictures, that is no problem!' Rafa said cheerily. I fumbled for my phone, unprepared for the sudden request. 'To commemorate this moment,' he said as we awkwardly posed, side by side. I snapped a selfie. Everyone had their picture taken with Rafa di Zeo: players, coaches, World Cup winners, pop singers, corrupt politicians, rock stars and soap actors. I was to be no exception.

3

Brazil

RIO DE JANEIRO

I WAS WAITING FOR CLÁUDIO CRUZ, THE FOUNDER OF RAÇA RUBRO-Negro, now Brazil's biggest *torcida organazada*. For the past few years, Cláudio wasn't really part of the scene. He owned a bar in Lapa. It had been open for an hour but Cláudio was nowhere to be seen. Every other shop and bar had its metal shutters down and locked. The only exception was Vaca Atolada, the Stuck Cow.[1] It was always like this on a sweltering Saturday afternoon. Lapa might be found in the centre of the north zone of Rio but Brazil's socio-economic geography didn't work like other places. The money and wealth hugged the sandy white coastline of Ipanema and Leblon. During the day at weekends the centre was abandoned, a product of urban flight and a fear of high crime. Lapa did, at least, come alive at night. It was famous as Rio's party district, but 5pm was a little early for most Cariocas. Except for the Stuck Cow. The barmen were busily preparing for that night's samba band whilst putting tables and chairs made from upturned beer crates out on to the pavement. I could wait, a barman said, as he placed a litre bottle of Brahma beer on my table and removed the top with one hand, in one movement. Cláudio was always late, he said.

The Stuck Cow was a fragment of Rio's dying bohemia. Inside the walls were plastered with old concert flyers. The toilets had vintage, slightly pornographic graffiti that someone had once tried to scrub away. The party tourists usually headed to the upmarket cocktail bars a couple of blocks down the road. But those that knew Lapa knew the Stuck Cow, and Cláudio too. He liked it that way; an awkward relic that doggedly hung on to its territory.

When Cláudio makes an entrance he doesn't so much say hello as launch himself on you. 'I had a dream, when I was a police officer, that I wanted a bar to be able to drink at cost price,' he said, after vigorously shaking my hand. He sat down and manoeuvred his crate across from mine. He didn't have long, he said. His musicians would be turning up soon for their soundcheck. But he stayed for two and a half hours, talking almost nonstop. He positioned himself so that he was exactly at his arm's length and, as he talked at a machine-gun pace, it was almost as if he shadow-boxed with me. As he made a point, he rapped his knuckles on the table to accentuate his words, sometimes doing the same by jabbing into my chest, explaining how he was *doente por Flamengo*: 'sick' for Clube de Regatas do Flamengo, one of Rio's biggest teams. He would use that word – *doente* – a lot when describing other fans. It was a badge of honour that noted their particular devotion or obsession with Flamengo.

The *torcida* began in Brazil as organised supporter groups, formed in the clubs of Rio and Sao Paulo around 1940. They had exploded in popularity and had developed a unique way of supporting their teams, usually led by a samba band alongside banners, fireworks and songs. But, like in Argentina with its *barras bravas*, the modern incarnation had become ultra-violent. Hundreds of supporters had been killed in fights and internecine conflicts since the 1980s. Thirty *torcedores* were killed in 2013 alone.[2] Brazil was already one of the most homicidal countries in the world, with around 50,000 people murdered in 2018.[3] It had legitimately become one of the most dangerous places in the world to watch a football match too. Cláudio's time was before then. He is in his sixties now, but seemed in good shape. He was short, with closely cropped dark hair. He wore a large round badge on his oversized shirt with the slogan 'Lula Livre!' – 'Free Lula', a message of support for Brazil's former president Lula da Silva, a leftist who came to power and reshaped modern Brazil at the turn of the millennium, dragging millions of people out of poverty. He was in jail now, on corruption charges, although his supporters – and there are still many of them, Cláudio included – thought his incarceration was a scandal, based on trumped-up charges designed to prevent him from standing in the presidential elections against Jair Bolsonaro. Bolsonaro was a far-right ex-military man who was a big fan of Brazil's vicious military junta that ruled from 1964 to 1985. Bolsonaro seemed to hate everybody: women, gay people, indigenous tribes, the Amazon itself. He called the dictatorship a 'glorious period'.[4] With Lula in jail, Bolsonaro won the 2018 presidential election and was now in power. Cláudio noticed that I had seen his badge. When he founded Raça in 1977, he said, it was 'a time of dictatorship'. *Raça* roughly translates as 'powerful desire' or a strong will; *rubro-negro* means 'red and black', the colours of Flamengo's shirt. When his *torcida* went to the stadium, they would all wear red shirts, but not because of the *rubro-negro*. 'Raça was the first *torcida* to wear a shirt that was different from the clubs,' he explained. 'It was red for the love of Flamengo and for the struggle to fight a left-wing fight.'

Football was famously brought to Brazil by Scotsman Charles Miller in 1894, but the sport started life as an upper-class pursuit that excluded its vast black and indigenous population. Slavery had only been abolished in 1888, Brazil being the last developed country to do so. It was thought that over a near 400-year period five million African slaves were shipped to Brazil. The US, in comparison, enslaved eight per cent of that number.[5] Flamengo started life as a rowing club and only started a football club when disgruntled members of their great rivals Fluminese defected. Their success in Rio when it was still the country's capital, combined with advances in radio technology and their matches being broadcast all across Brazil, meant they were the first team to have a truly nationwide following. Cláudio and pretty much every Flamengo fan you meet will tell you that they have anywhere between 30 and 40 million fans. More than the population of most countries, he told me proudly. It was through the radio that Cláudio was radicalised as a five-year-old, listening to Flamengo winning the championship in 1963. 'I started to cry, and I did not even know the meaning of the word champion. The announcer was shouting, "CHAMPIONS!" And it thrilled me.' He believed there was something deeper at work, perhaps with the red and black colours. 'These colours are the strongest colours in the world!' he said. 'The Sandinista flag was black and red. Hitler's swastika was black and red. Wherever there is red and black, there is fanaticism.'

He started Raça with his brother back when he was a teenager. His *torcida* started as a mixture of fanatical support and activism, painting graffiti and pasting up posters whilst, he said, 'fleeing from the army and their machine guns'. If a match was on the Sunday, they would arrive at the Maracanã on Friday night with thousands of rolls of toilet paper in the back of a truck. They would use the truck to jump over the fence and hide the rolls – which they would later throw on the pitch – and their fireworks and banners in the rafters. The problem was that the Maracanã was used by Rio's four big teams, so they couldn't take the risk of letting a rival *torcida* find their stash. 'If the guards saw us they'd shoot at us,' he said. They would bring water and bread and wait for two days. 'We would stay there without being able to shit,' he said, until the gate opened on Sunday and they could 'go outside with a bellyache'.

Violence wasn't then so ingrained with the *torcidas*. 'Rio de Janeiro was different then, understand?' he said. 'We had to run away from the cops who took care of the stadiums. Not from street violence, there was nothing like that. Even the *torcida* fights. They were fistfights. Maybe sometimes with drumsticks, from our bass drums.'

Later, when Raça were more established, Cláudio would arrange for a mimeograph to be brought into the stadium. 'We had a ... how do you say? A social network!' It was, Cláudio said, 'an old WhatsApp. It was our Instagram.' During the game a team of Raça members would essentially write an instant fanzine of the game. They would manually crank out the pages with their impressions of the match and other issues, like the high price of tickets, and distribute them in the stadium.

For Cláudio, supporting Flamengo was more than love. *Doente* was a good word to describe it. Something that overcame you, that you almost had no control over. But Raça had a bigger purpose. It was about resisting authority and showing people there was a way you could resist by doing things yourself. He was there for ten years, until he felt he was too old to connect with the young generation, as always happens on the terraces and in stadiums everywhere in the world. A new generation replacing the old.

The band had arrived and Cláudio had to go and do the sound-check. 'Raça was not just a *torcida organizada*,' he said. 'It changed people's behaviour,' making them more community focused, more aware politically of their surroundings.

If the founding of La Doce and the *barras bravas* reflected Argentina's unique passion for the game, Brazil's *torcida* had a more artistic beginning. The word *torcida* comes from the Portuguese word *torcer*, to twist or to wring. It came, I'd been told over and over, from the sight of the supporters, mainly women, who would nervously twist and wring their scarves or shirts as the game went on in the early days of Brazilian football. Others told me it came from the sight of twisted T-shirts being swung by fans over their heads. But recognised groups didn't start emerging until the end of the 1930s and beginning of the 1940s. And no one was more influential than Jayme de Carvalho. Carvalho arrived in Rio by ship from the north-eastern state of Bahia in 1927. He was 16 years old and looking for work. After selling sweets on a bus and then working in a clothes shop he found a job as a low-level civil servant in the Ministry of Justice. He adopted Flamengo and began leading something of a double life. He was a quiet government *funcionario* during the week, *doente* for Flamengo at the weekends. In 1942 he founded the Charanga, a carnival band that made a racket throughout the game, just like the street bands he remembered from his native Bahia when he was a child. The first time they were deployed, the goalkeeper of the opposing team complained to the referee, who took the players off the pitch.[6]

The name had come from the famed Brazilian composer Ary Barroso, a prolific writer and film-soundtrack composer who was nominated for an Oscar in 1945. He's most famous for writing 'Aquarela do Brasil', probably one of the most internationally famous songs ever written by a Brazilian. He too was *doente* for Flamengo and had a side career as a football commentator, sometimes incorporating pipes and a penny whistle as he spoke on Radio Tupi. At one Flamengo game he heard the ramshackle band play. 'My friends, this is not a group of musicians,' he said mockingly. 'This is a *charanga*.'[7] *Charanga* was a Brazilian word used to describe an amateurish band that played out of tune. But Jayme liked the name, the Charanga do Flamengo was born and Ary and Jayme would later become friends.

Both Jayme and his wife Laura would stitch and dye large banners to hang at the stadium. They would also wear the same red and black shirts that the players were wearing on the pitch, albeit home-made ones. For the Fla–Flu derby against Fluminese in October 1942, Jayme made a banner that said 'AVANTE FLAMENGO'.[8] When Flamengo equalised, Jayme and a friend jumped over the fence and ran on to the pitch, almost causing a riot amongst the 30,000 fans. The police dragged them off but decided against arresting them. Rio's famed sports journalist Mário Filho – whom the Maracanã was officially named after in 1966 – wrote a short article about the early days of Flamengo's fan culture. In 'Carnival in Springtime' he wrote how a police officer at the 1944 Rio State final flung himself to the floor when he heard a huge explosion. Jayme de Carvalho had thrown a 'dynamite bomb' on to the pitch. 'He lit a bomb. It went off covering the stadium with smoke and destroying the grass where it landed on the touchline. At the end of the match, which Flamengo won, Jayme led an impromptu procession of fans dancing and singing through the streets of Rio.'[9]

Fireworks and flags weren't uncommon in Brazilian stadiums, but the band was and the Charanga was soon copied across the country. The songs of the street and of carnival had been dragged into the stadiums and Jayme was Brazil's first super-fan. The club employed him, he was sent on foreign trips. He even had an endorsement deal with a clothing retailer. He was almost as famous as the players. So much so that he was appointed Comanada à Torcida Brasileira ahead of the 1950 World Cup finals. The Maracanã had just been finished, a stadium fit for a team that would inevitably be champions. Jayme was to bring the Charanga to an international stage but also help curb the crowd's rowdier instincts. 'Such was the concern in projecting an image of a sensible country, the authorities delegated a good part of the responsibility for controlling the fans' behaviour to Jaime de Carvalho,' wrote Bernardo Buarque de Hollanda in an essay in *Football and the Boundaries of History*. 'The organisers recognised the importance of a fan leader who would help the police chief to maintain good behaviour.' Which is what he did. Jayme and his Torcida Brasileira would be at every Brazil game. When Brazil were beating Spain 6–1, the crowd began to sing 'Bullfights in Brazil' written by Joao de Barros. Barros 'became emotional and cried when he heard his song being sung by a crowd estimated to be around 200,000 people'.[10]

When Brazil lost in the final game against Uruguay – the infamous Maracanazo ('Agony of Maracanã') that had a deep psychological impact not just on the players but on the country as a whole – the one silver lining was how the fans had taken the defeat with unexpected grace. But perhaps Jayme's most influential moment came earlier in the tournament, in the 2–0 victory against Yugoslavia. The film of that game isn't great – FIFA didn't start properly broadcasting the finals until 1954 – but in the footage that does exist you can see the fireworks, the banners and the band at the front. The noise of the 142,000-strong crowd led by the Charanga left an indelible mark on the visitors. Without Jayme de Carvalho and his Charanga, Hajduk Split's Torcida would never have been born.

Jayme de Carvalho was Cláudio's hero. Along with his wife Laura, Carvalho would lead the Charanga and the Torcida Brasileira at the World Cups in Switzerland, Sweden, Mexico and West Germany, taking the Charanga sound to an international audience until his death in 1976. Cláudio ran inside the bar and returned with a book. 'Jayme was the first fan in the world who took the club shirt and took to the bleachers,' he said as he handed it to me. It was a book Cláudio had written about Jayme, an album of history and photos from Jayme's life. 'You see the importance of Charanga do Flamengo?'

By the mid-1960s, Brazil was changing, with rapid urbanisation. A coup in 1964 saw the start of a decades-long military dictatorship. The new generation of fans were young, poor and eager for change. The *torcidas* were products of the club. Their leaders, even if they meant well as Jayme did, were seen as company men, and the younger fans wanted to break free of authority. New groups like Torcida Jovem do Flamengo were formed that actually booed their own team. Jayme de Carvalho, in his last years, dying of cancer, bemoaned the new attitude in letters to the Rio press. 'Flamengo teaches us to love Brazil above all else.'[11]

In 1968 Queen Elizabeth II made a state visit to Brazil. On the penultimate day she attended an all-star match between Rio and Sao Paolo, a team that featured Pelé. A crowd of 200,000 saw the *torcidas* of Botafogo, Vasco de Gama, Fluminese and Flamengo in their regular spots in the Maracanã.[12] Cláudio was there too. 'Out of nowhere, there was an advertisement for São Luiz Cookies, which was ...' he cleared his throat and started singing. 'Snack time, what a happy time, we want São Luiz cookies!' Almost immediately the crowd started chanting the jingle back, with one important change. 'Everyone started singing ...' he cleared his throat again. '"Snack time, what a happy time, we want the Queen's ass".' One story, later told by a left-wing newspaper, recounted how the Queen had told her hosts, shortly before handing Pelé the winning trophy, how beautiful the singing was. The mortified translator had to lie and say they were singing a tribute.

Raça became more than just a group of fans. It became a place where Rio's multiracial youth could gather. It was a haven of free expression, even if that was sometimes highly offensive. More and more *torcida* groups broke away to be independent of the clubs as the old-style *torcidas* from the previous generation, like the Charanga, withered. Cláudio told me he didn't like what had become nowadays of Brazil's *torcidas*. They had become connected to organised crime. The leaders, he said, made huge sums of money through merchandising and via bribes from the clubs, mainly through tickets that were then sold on. 'The values have changed,' he said, before saying something I didn't expect. 'I, for example, I do not like football.' It was Flamengo he loved, not the teams. All that mattered to Cláudio was the red and black.

Cláudio quit in 1987 and took a job with the police, where he was equally as difficult to control. 'In the police I was called a communist because I organised all the strikes,' he said proudly. 'I was arrested three times in the police for militancy.' When he retired ten years ago he bought the Stuck Cow, which had become a meeting point for the city's progressive activists: anti-facist *torcida* members from all of Rio's clubs met here, as did artists and politicos. Marielle Franco, the Rio politician who became famous for her work exposing police brutality but was assassinated in 2018, was a friend of Cláudio's and a regular at the Stuck Cow. Two former police officers were arrested and charged with her murder but there had been little progress in finding out who ordered the killing.[13] The new political environment had meant that Cláudio was taking drastic measures: he was coming out of retirement. The last leader of Raça had been arrested for allegedly murdering a rival fan. The group had been banned from going to the Maracanã for five years due to the violence. So the club's president had asked Cláudio to come back and clean up the mess, as a kind of consultant *capo*.

'After thirty years I've come back to rebuild Raça. But I said: "We're going to rebuild, we're going to debug the Raça. Take the shit people out. And if we keep only 20 per cent, we're reborn again,"' he said.

His plan was to restructure the group and introduce a parliament of sorts with elections at the start of the year, so the power wouldn't be in the hands of a single person. He wanted the *torcida* to return to the days of Jayme de Carvalho, when Brazilian music could be heard in the stadiums. 'Today, unfortunately, even the music of the Brazilian fans are Argentine songs,' he said caustically. 'And I think that shit is horrible ... We are going to bring back the samba again. Because the Raça was the first *torcida* that took the samba to the bleachers. Because it's joy.'

The band was now ready to play. In the time we had spent talking the Stuck Cow was now rammed full of people. The musicians all sat around a large table in the middle of his bar, as everyone crowded around them. Cláudio had work to do. 'If you control the song,' he said before going inside, 'you control the power.'

Rafael was waiting for me, with a red and black Flamengo shirt, outside my hotel at 9am on the dot. 'You should wear this,' he said, handing it to me. 'It would look strange if you were there without one.' Rafael was a young filmmaker who had taken me to the Stuck Cow and introduced me to Cláudio. He was also *doente* for Flamengo. It was Sunday and there was a game at the Maracanã against Chapecoense, the club who tragically lost almost their entire team in a plane crash the year before. They weren't a Rio club, so it wasn't a derby, but the match was expected to be a sell-out. This was rare in Brazilian football. There had been little violence inside the stadiums in the past few years but the journey to the games had become so dangerous that the average attendances in Brazil's Série A were now hovering around 15,000. Inverse to football's traditional logic, the big derbies were often the least well attended. The Maracanã was only half full when Fluminese played Botafogo the day before. But the league had come up with a novel solution: the 11am Sunday kick-off. 'I think it's better,' Rafael told me as we headed to Maracanã through oddly deserted streets. 'People try to blame the *torcidas* and say that they are violent. In Brazil they are afraid to go to the stadiums, that's why we have such low occupancy rates. But it's funny because we haven't had a big confrontation *inside* the stadium in a long time. They are rare.'

Raça had been banned from the Maracanã but Rafael hoped that Cláudio could turn things around, get the ban lifted and rekindle what the *torcida* was originally about. 'Now with Bolsonaro in power he [Cláudio] is trying to create the consciousness about the importance of the *torcidas,* and knowledge of what's happening in Brazil right now,' said Rafael. Cláudio truly believed that the *torcida* could be a bulwark against fascism, just as it was in his day. *Torcidas* at other football clubs were also organising. An anti-fascist *torcida* conference was being held at the end of the year.

'Lots of police support him,' said Rafael of Bolsonaro. 'Last month a guy went to a game at the Maracanã with a Flamengo anti-fascist T-shirt. They weren't allowed in. We are almost in a kind of dictatorship already, especially with the police.'

Meanwhile, the outside of the Maracanã was swamped as 60,000 diverse fans were swarming inside, filling the sold-out stadium. I had been to Rio before to witness the civil disturbances that had preceded the 2014 World Cup finals. On the street you would see the true Brazil; a highly diverse country. But the tickets for the World Cup, and the Confederations Cup before it, were so expensive that only the elite could afford them. The matches were a sea of white faces. The match today was a much closer representation of what Rio was. 'We have a lot of poor fans and the opposition would curse us: "Oh, the favelas, the favelas",' Rafael explained when the crowd started chanting after the national anthem was sung and the whistle was blown. 'We took that song and turned it around: "Favela, favela, there's a party in the favela".'

Flamengo quickly went 1–0 up and celebrated so loudly it felt like the stadium was vibrating. They later won a penalty but missed it and were booed off at half-time. 'It's never enough,' explained Rafael. 'If you score three, they want four.' But there was something missing. The bands, the Charanga sound, the fireworks and the flags. The violence and the subsequent police crackdown meant that it was impossible to recreate the look and feel of the old *torcida*. Rafael felt the authorities had been 'lazy', taking the same approach as the English authorities had towards hooliganism and punishing the whole fan base rather than violent individuals.

Flamengo won 2–1 and the booing at half-time was forgotten. As soon as the final whistle was blown, somewhere below us, a brass band struck up. We ran downstairs, pushing through the crowd until we found them. It was the Charanga do Flamengo: a trumpet, two horns, a bass drum and snare. They weren't allowed in the stands any more, but they had stayed alive and waited to play their songs, but only if Flamengo won. 'We are the first *torcida* in the world!' said Seu Gigi, the president of Charanga. Gigi was well into his seventies, with a bushy white moustache, and played the snare. He had been president for 40 years. There had only ever been three presidents: Jayme, his wife Laura who briefly took over after he died in 1976, and Gigi. 'We'll keep to [Jayme's] tradition and go on forever.'

And that was what the Charanga was these days: a band and a tradition, long overtaken by the *torcida* culture that now dominated Brazilian football. But the Charanga had not only changed how Brazilian football stadiums sounded. It had helped to sell Brazil's carnival look and sound to the world. They may be a historical relic these days, but as soon as they started playing, everyone instinctively knew what to do. A procession of thousands followed them out into the blazing midday sun. Drunk young *torcedores*, old women, children being thrown around on their parents' shoulders as they danced and sang Flamengo's anthem.

Once Flamengo,
Forever Flamengo,
I will always support Flamengo,
It is the greatest pleasure to see it shine,
Whether on the ground or at sea,
Once Flamengo,
Flamengo until I die.

PART TWO:
NO FACE, NO NAME

*'Man is least himself when he talks in his own person.
Give him a mask, and he will tell you the truth.'*

Oscar Wilde, 'The Critic as Artist'

4

Italy

WHAT, OR WHO, ARE THE ULTRAS? THE WORD IS OFTEN USED AS A synonym for hooliganism. But this is wrong. The word comes from the latin *ultra*, which means 'to go beyond', to be extreme. It was a term originally coined for the 'ultra-royaliste' faction in nineteenth-century France who supported the Bourbon monarchy. They were considered zealots even by Louis XVIII, who was restored to the throne after Napoleon Bonaparte was finally deposed.[1] The term was adopted by Italian football in the late 1960s, a time of great upheaval in the country. The Europe-wide student protest movement arrived just as the lines of the old social and religious order were being redrawn, with protests from the far left and the far right filling Italy's city and town squares. It was also a period of intense political violence, known as the '*Anni di piombo*', the 'Years of Lead'.

The first Italian ultra group, the Fossa dei Leoni at AC Milan, was founded in 1968. By 1969 Sampdoria fans had formed the Ultras Tito Cucchiaroni, named after their prolific Argentine striker. Torino formed the Ultras Granata in the same year (although they claim to have founded the first organised supporters group back in 1951). By the late 1970s the trend had spread throughout Italy. Many took names which reflected the tumultuous politics of the time. Roma's left-wing Fedayn, for example, was named after the Arabic word for guerilla fighters, which had been popularised by the Palestinian liberation struggle, itself a *cause célèbre* for the European left in the 1960s and beyond.[2]

These ultras stood in the cheapest section of the stadium, the *curva,* behind the goals, and brought the colour and political pageantry of the square to their part of the stadium. Huge banners with political messages, known as *choreographia,* were unfurled by the *tifosi,* the Italian word for fans. The word had its roots in typhus, a disease that exhibits symptoms of inaction and lethargy followed by bouts of mania. The groups were highly organised with flags, drums, songs and maritime distress flares, which started to be used by fans from port cities like Genoa.

Many groups adopted characters from popular films and comic books that they felt represented them, the outsiders and the anti-heroes: the Joker, the Droogs from *A Clockwork Orange* and, as I had discovered from Mikael's tattoo, the British cartoon character Andy Capp. The symbol of the Irriducibili, Lazio's avowedly fascist ultra group, is a bowler-hatted cartoon character called Mr Enrich. The ultras were also extremely hierarchical, run by a boss known as the *capo* who conducted his orchestra from the front, often with his back to the game. As the rivalries between teams inevitably bled into the ultra groups, each *tifosi* jealousy guarded their *curva* and their flags as each group tried to steal the others' standards. The ultras' flag had to be protected at all costs. This level of activity meant that it wasn't enough to just support a team on match day. You had to live it and breathe it seven days a week, as an evangelist, as a bodyguard, as a soldier. You had to go beyond.

*

Italy's ultra culture was a powerful and globally seductive force. Lorenzo Contucci could attest to that. His third-floor hospital room had a beautiful view of the Roman countryside, but he wasn't taking his confinement easy, nor particularly well. He was lying on his bed, in white hospital robes, in a private facility at AS Roma's Trigoria training ground on the outskirts of the city. He was taking phone calls from clients on his mobile phone despite his injuries. His left leg was in a cast, winched up, the result of crashing his scooter the day before. 'A car knocked me down,' he said, shifting awkwardly in his bed, just as his mobile phone rang again. As he spoke about a client's upcoming court case, the hospital phone by his bed also rang. Another client was in legal trouble and needed his assistance too. A broken leg wasn't going to stand in anyone's way; not Contucci's and certainly not his clients.

His popularity wasn't all that surprising given that he was a lawyer with a rare but lucrative specialism. He represented Italy's ultras when they invariably got into legal trouble. There was a long list of potential crimes and misdemeanours that could get you in hot water with the authorities: lighting pyro, setting off smoke bombs, firing rockets or, on occasion, brawling. But the ultras' main issue, and Contucci's specialism, was the hated *diffide* or banning orders, officially known as the Divieto di Accedere alle manifestazioni Sportive [DASPOs].

DASPOs were introduced in Italy in the mid-1990s but their use had exploded since 2007. They had become the single biggest bone of contention for ultras in Italy's supporter scene. Supporter groups accused the police of issuing them like confetti for petty and often ridiculous reasons. Contucci had become a master at overturning them, but the ultras didn't just come to him because of his high success rate. Although in his fifties, with a clean-shaven pate, Contucci understood the ultras better than almost everyone. He was one of them. Or, at least, he used to be. Back in the day he was an AS Roma ultra who cut his teeth in Rome's Stadio Olimpico, standing on the *curva sud* in the 1970s, 80s and 90s. And he had learned about the arbitrary nature of DASPOs in the same way every other ultra did: after getting arrested and banned himself.

During Roma's last Scudetto-winning season in 2000/01, Contucci was arrested at the stadium. He was already a qualified lawyer but was so incensed by the whole process that led to the banning order – which was issued by the police and not a judge, without any conviction of an actual crime – that he studied every facet of the law governing them. He challenged his case and won. It was, he said, one of the first cases where the police had been defeated. After that, he admitted, he became 'quite vindictive', and started to work on these cases across Italy. The law had been designed in haste and was ineffective. Contucci won almost all his cases.

Now he was the first person the ultras called on when they got into trouble, whether they were foot soldiers or *capos*. His renown was such that he got calls from ultras from Milan, Napoli and even Roma's hated rival Lazio. Now 50 per cent of his business dealt with ultra-related legal cases. Every lawyer he hired had once been an ultra too. 'We try to find lawyers from ultra groups, they can understand some things that the other lawyers don't understand,' he said.

What would that be? I asked.

'Basically the behaviour of police,' he replied. He explained that, in some cases, lawyers could be more on the side of the police than the client. 'Cases like Gabriele Sandri.'

The death of Gabriele Sandri, a Lazio supporter shot by police in 2007, was a pivotal moment for both ultras and the authorities. The case precipitated a crackdown on ultras whilst providing further proof to the supporter groups that the police could not be trusted.

Contucci's law firm was now trusted with even the most sensitive cases, and was currently working on one of his biggest. When Roma travelled to Liverpool for a 2018 Champions League semi-final, so did hundreds of ultras. A Liverpool fan, Sean Cox, was punched outside Anfield and was seriously injured. He was placed in an induced coma. When he emerged from this months later he could barely talk or walk. He had life-changing injuries.[3]

Three Roma ultras, from the group known as the Fedayn, had been arrested in the aftermath. One pleaded guilty to violent disorder, although the judge conceded that he hadn't been the Roma fan that threw the punch. A second was about to stand trial, hence Contucci's phone calls. A third had just been arrested in Rome and now faced extradition to the UK. Contucci had become momentarily infamous on Merseyside for directing some of the blame at Liverpool's police.

'There was terrible policing of public order outside the stadium,' he had said shortly after two Roma ultras were arrested. 'If Roma are to be punished, then I think UEFA also need to look at Liverpool for the senseless approach to public order.'[4] Contucci defended the rights of Italy's ultras, even – perhaps even especially – when it was unpopular. His livelihood depended on it, of course, but his understanding of the ultras, and his moral compass, had been forged on the *curva sud*.

Contucci first stepped on to the *curva sud* in 1980, when he was 13 years old. He'd been going to Rome's Stadio Olimpico for years with his father but had always been enraptured by the colour and song from the south stand. The stadium is home to the city's two biggest teams, and fiercest rivals. The *curva nord* is home to Lazio's ultras, including the infamous and openly fascist Irriducibili. The *curva sud* is home to the Roma ultras. Contucci joined the biggest group at that time, the Commandos Ultra Curva Sud, or CUCS, a kind of confederation of the most powerful ultra groups that existed on the *curva* at the time, renowned for their innovative, influential and gigantic choreography. They announced their new confederation on 9 January 1977, before a 3–0 victory against Sampdoria, by unfurling a 42m-long banner with the words 'Commando Ultra Curva Sud' on it. At the time it was the biggest banner ever seen in an Italian stadium.[5]

'I have to say it was one of the hardest mobs of the *curva sud*,' said Contucci. Violence was a constant factor in the *curva sud*, home and away, as was theft. 'Because people were so poor ... when you entered in the *curva*, you could feel very often the hand on your neck, looking for gold.' The ultras felt like they were, as Contucci put it, 'the defenders of the city of Rome'. Every other ultra group felt the same; that they too were defending their town and city squares from outsiders, from invaders.

Every town and city was infused with the politics of the time. Italy, and especially Rome, in the 1960s and 1970s was a politically violent place as far-left and far-right paramilitary groups engaged in tit-for-tat killings and reprisals. Hundreds of people were killed during the 'Years of Lead' through individual murders of activists, lawyers, politicians and businessmen, as well as scores of innocent people killed in terrorist acts. The Piazza Fontana bombing in Milan in 1969 is considered the opening salvo of the Years of Lead.[6] The most infamous incident was the brazen kidnapping in 1978, in Rome, of the former Italian prime minister Aldo Moro by the far-left Brigate Rosse, the Red Brigade. Five of his bodyguards were shot dead before Moro was bundled away. The authorities failed to find him and Moro was 'executed' 55 days later. His body was found stuffed into the back of a red Renault 4 abandoned near Rome's Mattei Palace.[7] The bombing of Bologna train station in 1980, killing 80, most likely carried out by a group of neo-fascists, was the deadliest single incident during those years of bloodshed. It also marked the beginning of the end of the Years of Lead. Many of the perpetrators of hundreds of acts of terrorism were never found. Those that were punished claimed they had been victims of a conspiracy. The truth around almost every incident was malleable and unknowable. Different political factions understood their own truth surrounding the causes of the Years of Lead.

It was during this period that Italy's *curve* became both a sanctuary from the bloodshed in the city squares and also a reflection of the times. 'The *curva sud* has always been the mirror of the city,' Contucci explained. As 1970s Rome was seen as being largely left wing, so was the *curva sud*. The city's football rivalry exposed both political and geographical differences. Rome is the capital of the Lazio region. SS Lazio largely represented those on the periphery of the city, and its supporters and ultra group, the Eagles, had always been broadly far right. Roma fans would dismissively call the Laziali *burini*; a newly pejorative term once used to describe the farmers who would come to Rome from the countryside to sell their butter.[8] Roma, on the other hand, represented the working-class community in Rome's inner-city heartlands, which was dominated by the Communist Party in the 1960s and 70s. Ultra groups often took their names from left-wing causes, like the Fedayn, the Fossa dei Leoni and Pantere (the Panthers), although there were also far-right ultra groups like Boys.

The English influence arrived at the same time CUCS was formed. In 1977 Liverpool played Borussia Mönchengladbach in the European Cup final at the Stadio Olimpico (Liverpool won 3–1). Scarves, two-pole flags and slower, more rhythmical chants started to be seen and heard on the *curva sud* in the months afterwards. One VHS tape brought from in England in 1984 was particularly influential: a match between Chelsea and Millwall. 'I brought it to *curva sud* and said to them that they should listen to this,' Contucci said. 'I still have that tape. Some of our chants from *today* are from that tape.'

The English influence can perhaps explain why the late 1970s and 1980s, as Contucci puts it, was 'pure hooliganism'. There was the gruesome death in 1979 of Lazio fan Vincenzo Paparelli, a 33-year-old father of two, before the *Derby della Capitale*. A flare fired from the *curva sud* struck Paparelli in his left eye and he died where he lay, in his wife's arms. To this day it is the only death recorded inside an Italian football stadium. Another infamous incident was the 1984 European Cup final again involving Liverpool, again at the Stadio Olimpico, but this time against Roma. Liverpool won but their fans left in a trail of blood. The *curva sud* attacked, and more than a dozen Liverpool fans were stabbed, mainly in the buttocks. But it was the week-by-week violence that was the most dangerous. Each away trip was seen by both the ultras and the authorities as an enemy army invading a city.

One of the worst away trips was to Bergamo, in the north of Italy, near Milan. It was a small, industrial, one-club city. Everyone supported Atalanta. There was chaos that day. 'We went into the *curva* and the Atalanta fans were worse than ultras. They were like Vikings.' Contucci described how the CUCS had to physically fight their way out of the stadium. 'From every street, every little way there was hundreds of these people with long hair trying to kill you,' he said. They reached their coach and escaped but revenge was already being planned. 'You start to think of the return game and that they must pay for what they've done in Bergamo,' he said. And so the cycle of violence continued. At no point did we discuss the match, or the actual score.

CUCS split in 1987 not because of Italian politics, and the world around it changing, but because of a transfer. Roma signed former Lazio midfielder Lionello Manfredonia from Juventus after selling their captain Carlo Ancelotti to Milan. This cross-city transfer, albeit an indirect one, provoked outrage on the *curva sud*. Manfredonia had, it was claimed, once made an offensive gesture towards them, an unforgivable sin. Boys had already left before CUCS split into pro- and anti-Manfredonia factions. CUCS never recovered and the *curva sud* began to change, becoming much more explicitly far-right. 'In the 1990s there started to be problems in Italy with immigration, so a part of the *curva* was more right wing, also exhibiting [far-right] symbols.'

By this point Contucci was in his thirties, virtually a grandfather in ultras terms. But he never lost the feeling of being an ultra, even if he couldn't be part of the scene in the same way any more. The question was, what were the ultras? Were they a gang? Hooligans? Activists? Were they a fraternity of football fans or an army of city-state soldiers? I asked Contucci whether he had ever defined it. He paused to think about it, turning off his phone. 'You know The Smiths? The singer Morrissey?' he finally answered. 'Morrissey said that hooligans are the patriots of their cities. It is a little different but, OK, I can say that ultras are the patriots of their cities.'

Defining what the ultras were had been harder than I thought. It was a question I had asked almost everyone I'd spoken to around the world. Each person gave me a different answer. Even *capos* of ultra groups would pause, exhale and struggle to define it when I asked them. Like Italy itself, any attempt to define and understand it was complicated, nuanced and multifaceted. It was, ultimately, almost impossible to arrive at an agreed truth about many things, ultras included.

'The ultras are people who go and live a passion seven days a week,' said Pierluigi Spagnolo, a journalist for the Milan-based *La Gazzetta dello Sport*. 'It's a seven-day-a-week routine where that group becomes your life, your structure, your social circle.' Spagnolo had just written a bestselling book about the history of Italian ultras: *I Ribelli Degli Stadi,* The Rebels of the Stadium. He'd grown up on the *curva* as a Bari fan. The supporters had always interested him more than the actual game of football and, as his career progressed, he wanted to tell the true story of the ultras as the 50th anniversary of the founding of Milan's Fossa dei Leoni approached. Yes, there was violence and, later, the links to organised crime, but there was also kinship, values and a certain egalitarianism. The *curva* was a space that saw no class, where a waiter could stand next to a lawyer, and which was anti-establishment to its bones. Telling the story of those 50 years also told a story about Italy too.

Part of the problem was accessing the scene itself. Ultras saw themselves as noble outlaws who lived outside a system of control. Journalists were, they believed, part of that system who painted them in a negative and unfair light, both to sensationalise violence (which helped sell newspapers or gain clicks) and to perpetuate a system they were ultimately beholden too. It often created a tension within those, like Spagnolo, who had cut their teeth on the *curva* but had later gone on to work at a newspaper. Once they stepped into the press area, in the fancy parts of the stadium, they ceased to be an ultra. Journalists were seen as much an enemy as the police. The result, Spagnolo believed, was a one-sided story that perpetuated the very worst aspects of Italian ultra culture, because journalists only came when someone had been killed, having no awareness of the scene.

Luckily I had some help. Like Spagnolo, Martino Simcik Arese had grown up more obsessed with what was happening on the *curva* than what was happening on the pitch. As a young Italian-American journalist for the Copa90 YouTube channel, with roots in Rome, it was inevitable that he would beat a path to the country's ultras scene, which he had documented and evangelised throughout his twenties. It wasn't always easy dealing with a complex network of values, rivalries and hatreds that were sometimes impossible to fathom, however. There is a word in Italian that ultras use, *gemellaggi*, which means 'twinning'. It began with groups in Italy agreeing a loose alliance based on shared political views. More broadly around the world today it is called a 'friendship': alliances between teams that share the same world view or even simply share the same colours. A friendship often meant taking on your friend's enemies – and your friend's friends – too. The Italian sociologist Antonio Roversi first applied an anthropological term – 'Bedouin Syndrome' – to explain this within ultra culture as early as 1991.[9]

A friendship could also develop between two groups because of a respected gesture or a tragedy. Hajduk Split's Torcida and Benfica's secretive No Name Boys forged probably the deepest friendship in the European ultras scene after three No Name Boys died in a car accident returning from a Champions League tie against Hajduk in 1994. When the Torcida returned they did so with flowers. It was a gesture that has never been forgotten. Twenty-five years later, when Dinamo Zagreb travelled to Benfica, so did the Torcida. Dinamo were met with a crowd every bit as hostile to them as if Benfica had been playing their great rival Sporting Lisbon. *The enemy of my friend is my enemy.*

The reason for the extreme rivalries between teams predated the Italian state, which was finally unified in 1871, a process referred to as the *risorgimento*, or rebirth (a word that Mussolini would adopt and repurpose during fascism half a century later). Football, at least the version codified by the British, would arrive in Italy 16 years later, first in Torino and then, in 1893, with the founding of the Genoa Cricket and Football Club, the oldest Italian club still in existence. But the Italian peninsular had been a patchwork of warring city-states and territories, often under partial occupation by various empires, for centuries. Unification made Italy but Italy didn't yet have a unified identity or even a commonly understood language. As Massimo d'Azeglio, a pioneer of Italian unification alongside Giuseppe Mazzini and Giuseppe Garibaldi, famously said: 'We have made Italy; now we must make Italians.'

This meant that most Italians felt a stronger connection to their towns, cities, and regions than to Rome, a concept known as *campanilismo*. The word is derived from the Italian for 'bell tower', as every town or city was built around a Catholic church. The differences between 'bell towers' is observable today in regional difference in food and wildly different dialects and language – 'almost as different as English is to Welsh', Martino said. Sicilian still contained many traces of Arabic from 400 years of Muslim rule. *Campanilismo* is now expressed most notably in the football stadium. So, obviously Italy has this extra aspect to its football tensions.'

Milan, where Spagnolo now lived and worked, was crucial to the development of ultra culture, and not just because the first recognised group was formed there in 1968. When the famed Argentine coach Helenio Herrera arrived in Serie A in 1960 as the coach of Inter Milan he revolutionised the game. He didn't invent the catenaccio style of play, with fixed defenders and a 'libero' sweeper operating behind them, but he adapted it with the most success, winning back-to-back European Cups for the Nerazzurri as well as three Scudettos. Herrera was known to be a brusque, pragmatic man as well as a visionary. He instilled dietary discipline, banned his players from smoking and drinking and introduced more psychological elements to his team's preparations. Such was his quest to eke out any kind of advantage, no matter how small, that he eventually turned to the *curva*. Herrera had grown up in Argentina but in the previous decade had enjoyed a successful spell coaching in Spain, experiencing La Liga's disorganised but raucous crowds. Herrera wanted to harness the '12th man' in the stadium. So, at Herrera's urging, Inter's president Angelo Moratti invested in forming an organised supporters group called il Moschettieri ('The Musketeers') who would now travel to away games and lay the foundations for the ultras that would come.[10] The end of the 1960s saw the formation of the Boys S.A.N. (Squadre d'Azione Nerazzurre), a far-right ultras group who have dominated the San Siro's *curva nord* ever since.

Elsewhere in Italy the *curva* took on the same colour of the city square or region. Bologna had always been a stronghold for the Italian Communist Party, the PCI. Livorno was the same, given that it was where the PCI was founded in 1921. The politics of the *curve* changed, just as society changed. As the left diminished as a political

force so too did leftist ultra groups. There was a high turnover of
ultra groups as generations changed, *capos* were removed or groups
simply disbanded. 'In the 1960s and 70s, the youth movement was
attracted to far-left culture,' said Spagnolo. 'Now it's the far right.'

The number of ultras boomed in the 1980s and 90s just as there
was a generational change. The new generation were young and disaf-
fected. Parochial city and cultural identity became even more important, as did the idea of protecting 'their' territory, all ideas that fitted
much better into a fascist world view than the idea of a socialist international fraternity. Racism became much more prevalent. Their inspiration was not 'the metropolitan street *guerrillero*, but Alex, the young
super-thug in *A Clockwork Orange*, whose effigy started to appear in
various *curvas*, replacing the "Che Guevara" portrait,' wrote Carlo
Balestri and Carlo Podaliri in their influential 1996 academic paper
'*Razzismo e cultura del calcio in Italia*'. 'The new groups were the result
of a period in which civil society was dominated by hedonism, exhibi-
tionism, and disaffection for political and social commitment. The
stylistic paradigm adopted by many new "ultra" members [was] often
chauvinist, violent and intolerant'.

The scene spread to every corner of Italy and then beyond its borders. The elaborate art of *choreographia* was copied, as was the *corteo*,
or procession, where the ultras would march together with their banners and flags to the stadium as a show of strength. Other ultras would
try and steal these symbols, often displaying them in their own end,
invariably upside down. It was the ultimate form of humiliation. The
banners sent messages to their opponents and the outside world: tributes to fallen ultras, poetry, solidarity or sometimes frustration and
unhappiness at the club's management and the wider world. At each
club the ultras were a powerful force, capable of changing the management's behaviour or protesting an unpopular signing. The ultras
opposed anything that resembled *moderno calcio*, modern football,
harking back to a semi-mythical bygone age where money hadn't cor-
rupted the beauty of the game. The clubs' management started to buy
them off, first with free tickets and then with a host of other induce-
ments like jobs (especially in security around match day) and access.

The ultras, and the management, knew they were indispensable to the product, to the show. Violence was simply an accepted by-product of the deal. 'It is a subculture that knows how to defend itself,' said Spagnolo. 'Otherwise it would get completely crushed.'

Until the late 1990s the enemy was clear. The opposite *curva*. The other bell tower. But that changed in Genoa in 2001. Genoa seems to have played a disproportionate role in the evolution of football culture in Italy – and beyond, as we've seen in Argentina. Turin may have been where the first Italian football clubs were established, but the British sailors that brought it there arrived in the port of Genoa.

In July 2001 huge protests rocked the city around the G8 summit. The summits had become a focal point for anti-globalisation protests, and 200,000 people had taken to the streets. Some of the protests turned ugly and the police began indiscriminately beating people. In one particularly brutal incident 150 police officers broke into the Diaz Pertini building; peaceful protestors, many of them sleeping, were savagely beaten – men and women, old and young – as the police shouted fascist and pro-Mussolini slogans.[12] The day before, a 23-year-old protester, Carlo Giuliani, was shot dead by the police. It was, Spagnolo said, a definitive moment in creating anti-police sentiment. 'You didn't [used to] go to the stadium to fight against the police,' he said. 'It largely begins at Genoa with the G8 and you see the police show this ugly side of itself.' When he returned home, he was more likely to see Lecce fans with 'All Cops Are Bastards' stickers than anything against their great rival Bari.

Three years later the 2004 Roma–Lazio derby was called off after a false rumour spread throughout the crowd that a child had been run over and killed by a police van outside the Stadio Olimpico. Three of Roma's *capotifosi* entered the pitch in the second half to tell their captain Francesco Totti that the match had to be abandoned. And it was.[13] Outside the Lazio and Roma ultras fought. Not against each other, but against the police; 150 officers were injured. In 2007 two deaths, and their very different responses, deepened that conflict. In February a Sicilian policeman, Filippo Raciti, was killed whilst ultras from Catania and Palermo rioted.[14] There was outrage over his death and all league and national-team football matches were cancelled. Raciti's death started a crackdown on the ultras. The Pisanu Laws, introduced as an anti-terrorist measure in 2005,[15] were used to curb their power but the death also brought in La Tessera del Tifoso, an ID-card system. Most of the ultras groups boycotted the Tessera card, meaning they could no longer travel to away games. In November the same year there was another death. Gabriele Sandri, a member of Lazio's Irriducibili, was shot and killed by a policeman. A scuffle had broken out between Juventus and Lazio ultras at a service station on their way to Milan. A police officer fired a warning shot in the air and another at the car (although he claimed the gun had gone off accidentally as he stumbled). That weekend's Serie A matches were not called off and ultras across Italy joined forces and rioted against a common enemy. Lazio's game against Inter was eventually called off. Atalanta's game against Milan was abandoned after seven minutes when the Curva Nord 1907 ultras tried to smash their way through the perspex glass barrier that separated them from the pitch.[16]

The three incidents – and the differing reactions to the deaths of Raciti and Sandri – led to what Spagnolo called the 'triangulation of conflict'. The main rival was now the state and its perceived repressive tools. And the police were the physical representation of that repression. 'Raciti dies and they stop the league. Sandri dies, as a football fan, and they keep the league going,' said Spagnolo. 'It becomes a symbol: "Yours are more valuable than ours. We're now at war."'

Gianvittorio de Gennaro's arms were covered in tattoos that honoured Roma. The first was a Subbuteo figure in Roma's famous *giallorossi* colours. The second was a picture of Agostino di Bartolomei, Roma's revered former captain. He was a Roman, a favourite of the *curva sud* and the beating heart of the team that reached the European Cup final against Liverpool in 1984 but lost on penalties. He never truly recovered from that loss at the Stadio Olimpico. The next season he was moved on to Milan. The ultras were so incensed with the transfer that they arranged for a huge banner that said: *'Ti Hanno Tolto La*

Roma Ma Non La Tua Curva' – 'They've Taken Roma Away From You But Not Your Curva'.[17] Ten years later, on 30 May 1994, on the anniversary of that final, Di Bartolomei committed suicide by shooting himself in the heart. Gianvittorio's third tattoo was a little less macabre: an image of Andy Capp. 'He's become a symbol for the ultras because he had a lot of trouble with the police,' said Gianvittorio, as we sat outside a cafe on a busy Rome street in the autumn sunshine.

For most of his adult life, Gianvittorio had stood on the *curva sud*. He was ultra to his bones. His father played rugby and didn't like football, so Gianvittorio went to his first match on his own, at 13, and jumped over the fence into the *curva sud*: Roma–Udinese, Halloween 1998. After that he was hooked. Now he was part of the Cor Core Acceso ('With the Heart Turned On') that sits under Gates 18 and 19 of the *curva sud*. 'You can recognise an ultra because he turns his back to the field. Roma at my back, Roma in front of me. This is the ultras way,' he explained when I asked what ultra meant to him. 'It's about turning around because the ultra has total faith in Roma. It's about making sure that the stand is contributing to Roma's victory. The focus is always giving an advantage. Analysing the game is not important. It's making sure that you're contributing to AS Roma being a superior team.'

Today he also writes for *il Romanista*, a daily newspaper that just covers Roma. 'It's a perspective from the stands so it becomes a sound box for a lot of the frustration that characterises the ultra culture in Italy today,' he explained when I asked how he walked the line between journalist and ultra. Earlier, the director of *il Romanista*, Tonino Cagnucci, had told me it was an almost impossible line to walk. 'I still have an ultra's heart, but you can't be that if you are a journalist,' he conceded. 'It's like being a Jewish Nazi.' But there were important issues to cover that other newspapers missed. Ticket prices, ID cards, the absurd length of prison sentences for seemingly minor infractions. And, of course, the *diffide*, the stadium bans. Which, Gianvittorio explained, didn't just mean a ban. It meant you had to go and sign in at the police station, once before the game and once at half-time. He had some first-hand experience. Back in 2011 he'd also been slapped with a *diffide*. He was banned from the *curva sud* for two years. 'Pyro,' he replied, when I asked why he had been banned. A friend had smuggled a heavily adapted flare, shortened and repurposed so it was the size of a packet of cigarettes, in his underwear. But he couldn't escape the 'thousands' of CCTV cameras inside the Stadio Olimpico, which later picked him out.

The *curva sud*, from Gianvittorio's perspective, is almost unrecognisable to what it was when CUCS held sway there. It was, he said, divided politically as much as anything else. The far right, especially the Boys ultra group, were dominant. Groups had become much more focused on their own identity rather than Rome's. They had also been smothered in new rules and regulations. Pyro and smoke were now outlawed. You needed special permission to bring a drum or a megaphone into the stadium. The Italian football authorities, and their cheerleaders in the mainstream newspapers, talked approvingly of the 'English model' as something to replicate. Whereas once the chants and fashion of English terrace culture had heavily influenced the *curva*, the authorities wanted to replicate what the British government did at the start of the 1990s: gentrifying football through all-seater stadiums and harsh laws against anyone who misbehaved around a football ground.

It had worked in making football safer and more accessible. But the old terrace culture which had proven to be so durable and influential, even today, around the world simply did not exist any more. The ultras feared they would be next unless they could stay one step ahead. There was certainly less conflict between ultra groups then there used to be. 'It is really hard to tell if the relationship has changed because of the politics,' he said, referring to Roma's rivalry with Lazio. Inter and Milan had long agreed a 'non-aggression' pact. Roma and Lazio's ultras had also moved much closer politically from where they used to be.

The problem was that when violence did occur it was often more extreme. Only recently one of his group was knocked out and was in a coma for a month. 'Because the repression is so heavy it's impossible for the two supporters to come into contact,' added Gianvittorio. 'So you can't really tell if it's the politics that made them closer or the fact that they can't even make it around the stadium.' Now, the police were more the enemy than the other team, except perhaps with Napoli. 'The last few years we were tough with the Napoli guys, when the kid from Naples was shot.'

'The kid from Naples' was Ciro Esposito. He was a 29-year-old ultra, in Rome for the 2014 Coppa Italia final between Napoli and Fiorentina. Esposito was shot in the chest as Roma ultras clashed with Napoli fans as they arrived at the Stadio Olimpico. He was taken to hospital but, inside the stadium, when news spread of the shooting, Napoli's ultras threatened to invade the pitch. Violence was only averted when Marek Hamšík, Napoli's captain, spoke to Napoli's *capo-tifosi*. Napoli won 3–1, the victorious fans invaded the pitch anyway and the club's owner Aurelio De Laurentiis dedicated the victory to the shot fan. Esposito died 50 days later. A former Roma ultra and 'extreme right wing militant' Daniele De Santis was sentenced to 16 years for the killing.[18] The shooting had a huge psychological effect in Naples too. 'Esposito', meaning 'exposed', is one of Italy's most common names. Its root is found in Italy's orphanages, especially in and around Naples, where babies were given the name (although the practice was later outlawed once Italy was unified). 'And Ciro is such a popular name you probably had a hundred guys in the stadium called Ciro Esposito,' Martino said. 'The entire city of Naples thought their son had died.'

Whilst the focus of most ultras was on the police, Napoli still endured a torrent of racist abuse, exposing the schism between the wealthy north of the country and the poorer south. Inter Milan were famously punished for banners that referred to a 1973 cholera out-break in the city, including 'Ciao cholera sufferers.'[19] Although, five years later, and encapsulating the complex and sometimes contradic-tory morality of the scene, Napoli's ultras would protest in solidarity with Milan's ultras after the latter were sanctioned for a similarly abu-sive banner. After Milan received a one-match stadium ban, Napoli's ultras flew a banner that said: '[We are] Naples cholera-sufferers. Now close our curva!', a defence of the right for Italian supporters to abuse each other. In December 2018 a *capo* of Varese, a lower-league team that had a friendship with Inter Milan's ultras based on their shared fascist values, was crushed to death by a van after attacking a Napoli supporters' bus outside the San Siro.[20]

Despite all this, Gianvittorio still believed in the ultras. Ultra groups were involved in a huge number of social projects, feeding the poor, helping the disabled, raising money for fallen ultras, even if they were your enemy. In fact, those values were most evident during death and memorial. 'In politics, if [Italy's far-right politician Matteo] Salvini was to die, get hit by a car, half of Italy would be having a party,' said Pierluigi Spagnola, the *Gazetta* journalist. 'When Gabriele Sandri, who was a known member of a far-right party, a member of the Irriducibili, died, you had [far-left] Livorno fans remembering him. The ultras movement can be more elevated and profound.' Gianvittorio also believed that ultras were vital for the game's commercial survival. 'The Italian product of football, you can't sell it if there's an empty stadium with no atmosphere. Sky even uses the pyro show in the commercials for Serie A. People around the world are looking for choreography and the pyro shows and not just the pitch. Not just twenty-two players.'

To save it, ultras had to join forces against *moderno calcio*, against the authorities and especially against the police. Even if that meant what had been previously unthinkable: being on the same side as Lazio. 'The enemy of my enemy is my friend, you know?'

I was in a tattoo parlour in an upmarket part of Rome. The waiting room was dominated by a huge painting of Augustus, the first Roman emperor, whose four-decade dictatorial rule crushed all dissent, brought order to the city and birthed a 200-year peace. A group of young, female American tourists sat underneath it, loudly discussing what they were going to get inked that morning. Andrea, the tattooist, nodded as Martino told him who we were and why we were there, wiping blood and excess ink away with tissue as his needle stained his customer's skin black. He couldn't be too careful. As one of the leaders of the Irriducibili, Lazio's pre-eminent ultra group, he was used to the attentions of outsiders, even if they were usually, and forcefully, rejected. They might be other ultra groups, journalists, the police, even Italy's secret service, who the group assumed were keeping tabs on them. Martino told him why we there: to meet probably the most infamous *capotifosi* in Italy.

Fabrizio Piscitelli was known more widely by his *nom de guerre*, Diabolik, taken from a famous Italian comic character of the same name. In the comics, Diabolik was an expert in pulling off complicated heists and was a master of disguise, always one step ahead of the police and the organised criminals he crossed along the way. Fabrizio was, like the members of the Irriducibili, an unrepentant fascist. Ever since the group emerged in the *curva nord* of the Stadio Olimpico and successfully took charge of it, the Irriducibili had earned a fearsome reputation for their organisation and strength in battle against other ultras. Their choreography was large, innovative and influential. They harnessed the symbols of Rome's fascist past, painting themselves as the natural continuation of it: Mussolini, the Celtic cross, the fasces (a bundle of rods with an axe that has become a global symbol of governance, and where the word 'fascism' originally comes from). Racism and anti-semitism were openly encouraged. They wielded a huge amount of power within the club and with the players. And Fabrizio had masterminded it all, branching out into merchandising earning millions of euros, as well as some more off the book interests. He had only recently been released from prison after being jailed in 2016 for drug trafficking. The Italian state had impounded more than €2 million in cash and other assets. He was back with the Irriducibili, for now, although not quite back at the stadium. Like almost everyone else involved in the ultras scene I had met in Italy, he too had been issued a *diffide*, a stadium banning order.

'OK, I'll ask Fabrizio,' Andrea said finally, wiping away the last of the blood and ink and admiring his handiwork. We would, he said, receive a call when a decision was made. We shouldn't miss it. A few hours later the phone rang. It was Andrea. We were to meet at the Irriducibili's headquarters in the district of Tuscolano at 10am sharp. 'Do not be late.'

*

The Irriducibili's headquarters can be found on Via Amulio, a quiet street in a residential area of Tuscolano. The white metal shutters on the building were pulled down but we were in the right place. The signposts nearby were covered in stickers from far-right ultra groups from around Europe: Spain, Bulgaria, Poland and beyond. Andrea arrived by scooter, along wth Gianni, another member of the Irriducibili, who unlocked the shutters and threw them up. They gave us a tour of their home, a high-ceilinged, industrial space where the Irriducibili would plan out and make their banners and choreographies. A half-built gym was in the middle of the main space, put together to help them train for fighting, I was told. Hanging from the wall of a mezzanine floor was a huge white banner, one of the Irriducibili's very first pieces of art: it featured Mr Enrich, the bowler-hat-wearing cartoon character that the Irriducibili would claim as their own. He was handcuffed, and in the middle of being taken away by two smug police officers. Unbeknownst to them, Mr Enrich was holding a bomb, its fuse lit, in his left hand. Another showed him aggressively swinging a boot.

Mr Enrich would prove to be quite profitable. Next door was one of the Irriducibili's merchandise shops. Since they formed in 1987 the group had built up its popular Original Fans brand. At one point they had 15 shops around Rome. Today you can buy stickers, bucket hats, T-shirts with far-right symbols like the Nazi-era Totenkopf skull or the Schwarze Sonne, the Black Sun symbol designed at the request of Himmler during the Second World War that has since been adopted by far-right movements across the world. You could buy 30-year anniversary T-shirts celebrating the Irriducibili's friendship with West Ham United's InterCity Firm. And, of course, a T-shirt with Mr Enrich swinging a boot. All around were stickers from like-minded ultras from around the world. White Power. Swastikas. A graphic of a policeman being shot in the head. A large wooden fasces was propped up against one wall. A red flag with a white circle containing a Celtic cross, reminiscent of the Nazi-era flag, had been placed high up in the room.

Fabrizio was going to be late, Gianni told us, as he showed us around the back of the building. He had an important meeting with his lawyer who was picking through the complex web of court judgments and appeals.

Behind the Irriducibili's headquarters is Via Acca Larentia, a short, seemingly nondescript road that nonetheless holds huge significance for the Irriducibili and Italian fascism in general. It was here that two teenage activists for the now-defunct neo-fascist Italian Social Movement (MSI) were gunned down in January 1978, presumably by left-wing extremists. A third was shot dead by the police following riots later that night. A brass plaque had been erected over the MSI party's former regional office to honour the three men. It read: 'Murdered by Communist Hatred and by Servants of the State'. The murders proved to be a tipping point for Francesca Mambro, an MSI militant who helped set up the neo-fascist Nuclei Armati Rivoluzionari militia along with her partner Valerio Fioravanti, a former child actor turned terrorist. After that, Mambro 'swore I would never go anywhere without a gun.'[21] Both Fioravanti and Mambro were later found guilty of plotting the Bologna train station massacre in 1980, the single biggest loss of the life in the Years of Lead. They have both always claimed their innocence, whilst admitting to a host of other political murders. But Mambro was sentenced to 84 years in prison (although she was paroled in 2013). Via Acca Larentia had now become a place of pilgrimage for Italy's far right. Every 7 January around 5,000 fascists, from Italy and around the world, march here to lay wreaths and give the straight-arm Roman salute. It was another example of the many wounds that still festered from the Years of Lead. Gianni pointed to a wreath, browned in the spring sunshine, still hanging from the wall, a reminder of the last anniversary a few months previously. Thousands of neo-fascists from CasaPound and Forza Nuova had been here for the memorial. Gianni pointed down. We were standing on a huge, black Celtic cross – perhaps six metres in diameter – which had been painted on the tiled floor.

Fabrizio didn't arrive until nightfall. After he had climbed out of his car with a bodyguard, two members of the Irriducibili stood to attention and gave a Roman salute. Diabolik was slightly built, with chiselled features. He was in his early fifties but looked much younger and was often photographed wearing glasses, giving him the disarming air of Louis Theroux. He wasn't wearing glasses today, and discounting any danger because of his boyish appearance would have been a mistake. He invited us inside and up to a mezzanine where he sat behind his desk. On the wall next to him was a portrait of Benito Mussolini. He sat down, rolled a joint, lit it and took a deep drag. He held it out to us with an unbroken stare, a test to see whether we would play by his rules or not. We complied. 'The people who run football assume the supporters are stupid and the truth is the supporter has been kind of stupid,' he said as he smoked. He was charismatic and relaxed. 'As much as we try to have this conflict between red and black, white and black, blue and light blue, whatever you want to call it. Who's that work in the interest of most? The owners of football, who get to cast us as these idiots.' He took another drag. 'Do you just want to know about the violence?'

No, I replied.

Although that wasn't true. I did want to know about the violence. But I also wanted to know about how the Irriducibili began. At least, I wanted to know Fabrizio's version of the story.

The Irriducibili began in 1987 when Fabrizio was 21, although he had been going to the stadium since he was 13. The Years of Lead had been the source of it all. 'I grew up in a red neighbourhood and directly across the street in front of me was the head of [Roma's ultra group] the Fedayn. He was a far-left activist and I grew up the opposite, far-right Lazio. That was a response to Roma being a leftist team in a leftist neighbourhood and Lazio having some of these fighters who were of the far right.' The government, Fabrizio believed, decided to kick political violence out of the square and into football, where it could be controlled.

The old hard-left loyalties were weakening and the first generation of ultras leaders were either too old or out of touch. The scene was stagnating. The death of Paparelli, when a Roma fan fired a flare into the *curva nord* in 1979, radicalised the younger generation of ultras. 'The old people wanted to calm down the tension and the young people said no, we're going to bring the Years of Lead to the stadium,' he said.

They were, Fabrizio recalled, 'like stray dogs'. They were all 14 or 15 years old, getting to the stadium first and causing trouble. 'We were the bad kids, we were the wild ones,' he said. 'Now, thirteen, fourteen, fifteen-year-olds, they don't grow up as fast. At the time, fifteen to sixteen, you became a man. I mean, look at it now. You can't be a bully. You can't call a faggot a faggot. You can't call a black guy a nigger. You're yellow, you're Chinese. It's political correctness. People aren't adults any more.'

They led a coup by example. They separated themselves from the other ultras and even the club itself. They refused to use the club-sanctioned coaches or trains. Instead they travelled on their own pillaging as they went and performing their own separate *corteo* when they arrived. Soon the biggest and most-established ultra group – the Eagles – was haemorrhaging members. 'We had a tradition of having a fight afterwards. Pretty soon you had this moment where there's a critical mass; twenty became two hundred, became three hundred, became four hundred. These young kids said: "No, fuck you, we're going to push the boundaries even harder".' The former West Ham and Lazio midfielder Paolo Di Canio used to be a member of the Irriducibili. In a 2002 BBC documentary, he describes standing on the *curva sud* during a Lazio home game and seeing their banner for the first time in 1987. Di Canio was famous for many things, one of them his unswerving fascination with Mussolini. He had a huge tattoo of Il Duce on his back and had frequently given the Roman salute after scoring for Lazio in the Stadio Olimpico. He recalled meeting Fabrizio too. 'Like in the team, you can see the people in the way they behave, the way they act. You recognise them as the leader,' he said.

By the early 90s Diabolik had elbowed his way to the top of the Irriducibili. Over the next decade the Irriducibili became notorious for their fighting, their choreography, which included witty retorts often adapted from classical literature (Dante's *Inferno* was a favourite), alongside viscerally racist and anti-Semitic banners and chants. They are too numerous to list in full: the constant booing and monkey chants directed at black players; the lionising of Serbian war criminal Željko Ražnatović after his murder in 2000 with a banner that said 'Honour to the Tiger, Arkan'; the constant mocking of Roma fans for being Jewish, owing to the fact that Rome's Jews were largely from the centre of the city ('Black Squad, Jewish Home End'; 'Auschwitz is your country, the gas chambers are your home'); stickers left all over the *curva sud* showing Anne-Frank and the words 'The Roma fan is a Jew'.

'We are a bunch of fucking bastards, basically,' Fabrizio freely admitted. He was utterly unrepentent of his racism and anti-Semitism.

In the 1990s the power of the Irriducibili grew as they took on more English influences, thanks to a surprising source. Off the back of a successful World Cup at Italia 90, Paul Gascoigne signed for Lazio. Before then, the Irriducibili would see English violence only fleetingly on the news, but the fans appreciated Gascoigne's anti-establishment tendencies. 'He influenced it so much because we would go to Gascoigne's house with his friend, a hooligan friend, and they'd like to have a couple of beers and discuss the culture and talk about all the different influences,' Fabrizio said. Gascoigne would, he added, burp into the microphones of journalists they told him the Irriducibili didn't like. After that an Irriducibili Union Jack was flown. They got rid of the drums and focused on a more English style of support, with scarves and songs only. The last player who the Irriducibili felt was 'one of ours' was Beppe Signore, the deadliest striker in Italy in the mid-90s. Signore almost signed for Parma in 1995 until thousands of Irriducibili came on to the street and protested violently. Incredibly, their actions led to the transfer being stopped, upsetting Lazio's owner Sergio Cragnotti so much that he threatened to sell his stake in the club.

It would not be the last time Cragnotti and the Irriducibili would fall out. Cragnotti was a millionaire who had built up Cirio, a vast food conglomerate. When he bought Lazio in the early 1990s he transformed the club, spending big money smashing transfer record after transfer record. Gascoigne was one of his first purchases. More big-money signings would follow until his investment finally saw some reward. In the 1999/2000 season, Lazio won their second Scudetto,

with Sven-Göran Eriksson in charge and a team including Roberto
Mancini, Marcelo Salas, Siniša Mihajlović and Alessandro Nesta.
They had a good claim at being considered the best team in the world
at the time. But soon after that Scudetto things would fall apart.
Cragnotti's business empire would collapse just as Diabolik's was
growing. The moment was captured in the brilliant BBC documentary *Hooligans* that followed Fabrizio in the weeks before the Rome
derby in March 2002 (in fact, it was the same 'Foreign Fields' episode
that also featured interviews with Rafa di Zeo and Mauricio Macri
ahead of the Superclasico between Boca Juniors and River Plate in
Argentina). It showed a man who seemed to have more control over
the club than Cragnotti. The Irriducibili now had their own headquarters, a radio station called 'The Voice of the North' as well as a
popular fanzine, plus the Original Fans brand and network of merchandise shops and warehouses around Rome. To keep the group
sweet they were being given as many as 800 tickets by Cragnotti's
management team for every home match, which would then be sold
on for a tidy profit. Fabrizio could waltz in and out of the stadium.

He was at the centre of it all: with a megaphone at the front of the
curva nord denouncing Roma; travelling with the Irriducibili to
Atalanta away and leading the Roman salutes; persuading the police
to allow a banner at the Rome derby that clearly had fascist connota-
tions. When there was a riot, Fabrizio was often there too, not throwing a punch, but regulating and controlling the behaviour from the
sidelines. The most striking moment came when hundreds of
Irriducibili members descended on Lazio's training ground, angry at
the team's recent form. At one point Alessandro Nesta, now the team's
captain, emerged to beckon Fabrizio inside. The players and the
Irriducibili held a meeting where a truce was agreed. Later, when the
French international Lilian Thuram refused to sign for Lazio because
of the Irriducibili's racist chants, Fabrizio somehow arranged a meeting with Thuram at his club Parma. 'It was very strange,' Thuram said
of that meeting. 'In Italy the fans are very powerful.'[22]

Fabrizio didn't see the rise of the Irriducibili as a story about greed
and power, but one about taking on a corrupt system at its own game.

He didn't really see the group as ultras at all, at least not in terms of supporting a team. He wasn't that crazy about football. 'I'm a little particular in that I don't even know a single player of Lazio that I like,' he told me. He loved Lazio but the Irriducibili were above Lazio. It was loyalty to the group and its internal values that he demanded. 'Family, tradition, honour,' he said. 'The state constantly wants to see you poor, empty, stupid. They want you to end up being an idiot. To us it's not about being apolitical football supporters. No, the value systems and being Lazio has to come first.'

How do you define ultra? I asked him.

'For me, we replaced the word "ultras" with the word "Irriducibili",' he said. 'The idea of being Irriducibili instead of an ultra means that you're an ultra with a bit of a purpose.' No one was making that much profit, he said. 'We always paid for the most lawyers, we've always reduced the away trips for people the most. The money was always spent to maintain the group. Massive amounts of people went to jail. There was every reason for the group to die.'

Everything changed after 2004 with the Rome derby, where the rumour of the dead child stopped the game, that sparked a crackdown by the police. 'You can read into all of the things that happened and the extent to which I was persecuted,' Fabrizio said. 'They tried to send me to jail. I was shot at.' Nevertheless, they kept rejuvenating the youth in the movement, meaning that the Irriducibili could continue.

At the same time, Sergio Cragnotti was forced to leave the club, later spending time in jail accused of financial mismanagement during the collapse of his company Cirio. He was replaced by Claudio Lotito, who tried to end the club's accommodation of the Irriducibili during the Cragnotti era. Lotito was put under immediate pressure with protests, critical banners on the *curva nord* and, later, death threats. Lotito was bad for business and bad for Diabolik and, in 2005, it appeared they had found a solution. A consortium headed by the former Lazio legend and president Giorgio Chinaglia – and aggressively championed by the Irriducibili – tried to buy the club. The problem was that the Italian authorities believed that the takeover was a front for the Camorra mafia to launder billions of euros.[23] Seven people were arrested and Chinaglia, who claimed no knowledge of the scheme, fled to the US. He died there in 2012, having never returned to Italy. The Irriducibili, meanwhile, were implicated in the intimidation. A police sting uncovered evidence that Fabrizio had also been involved in drug trafficking, moving vast amounts of hash from Spain to Italy, which led to millions of euros worth of his assets being frozen, including the trademark for Original Fans and Mr Enrich. Prosecutors had initially asked for as much as eight years in prison for Fabrizio's alleged role in the trafficking and the intimidation of Lotito.[24] It was suggested that the Albanian mafia might have been involved as well. There was now a complex web of court cases, summons, appeals and potential jail time all slowly inching their way through Italy's labyrinthine legal system, and slowly constricting Fabrizio.

As we spoke, business intervened. One member of the Irriducibili rushed up the stairs and, out of breath, whispered a message into Fabrizio's ear. He in turn wrote a message on a scrap of paper, folded it in half and passed it back to him. When a second man arrived, he walked over to him, cupped a hand over his ear and whispered another message, before he nodded, and jogged back down the stairs. 'Violence is something intrinsic with humans,' he said when he sat back down. He was brazenly unapologetic about his racism. 'Racism is something intrinsic in humans,' he said. 'All these things that are human nature that they try to repress today.'

Diabolik lamented what had become of the modern ultra movement. He was revered by groups, especially in eastern Europe, who saw his facist world view and method of management as something to aspire to, even if others felt that the crime and the politics poisoned the purity of the ultras movement. Technology, he said, was ruining everything. Everybody was posting pictures on Instagram. There was no anonymity any more. Even if it was possible to hide your identity – *no face, no name* – people were willingly giving away their movements on social media. When another ultras group wanted to communicate, through Facebook, he had no idea who he was conversing

with on the other side. 'Back in the day you had to go to a neighbourhood and find these people and you'd meet these people and so the
connections were more genuine,' he said. 'You and your ten thousand
friends on your Facebook group is nothing compared to my thousand
genuine friendships built over the years on the *curva*.' He also felt the
youth were less dedicated.

'The moment the kid is a little bit sceptical about writing something on a wall, about going into a fight: it's the moment we've lost.'
The hypocrisy, he said, was getting too much. 'For years the fans were
convenient to the clubs. We made you all your money, we were the
reason why you went to the stadium because we filled the stadium.
We made the choreography, we helped you kick out players when you
didn't want the player … And all of a sudden you guys went …' he
rubbed his hands together as if he was washing them, 'time for clean
football. As if we were the filthy ones in football when you are match-
fixing every game, half your presidents are corrupt.'

He gave the recent fall out about the Irriducibili's supposed ban
on women standing in the first ten rows of the *curva sud* – which, he
said, had been misinterpreted – as a prime example of the hypocrisy
of the footballing authorities. It was a story that went around the
world. Fabrizio claimed, not particularly convincingly, that it was misunderstood. 'The wording was also quite clever because it wasn't
"Don't bring women", it was "Don't bring non-ultras of Lazio into the
first ten rows".' Even if the explanation wasn't convincing, the hypocrisy was. 'What happens two weeks later? They choose to play the
Italian Super Cup final in Saudi Arabia and women have to sit in the
segregated section of the stadium because they want to profit off it!'

No one knew how long Fabrizio would be free, such was the
weight of legal cases against him. But he hoped, at least, to see Lazio
win the cup. In a few weeks they would play against Milan in the
semi-final of the Coppa Italia. Win that and there was a potential
final against Atalanta, a club whose ultras had shared a fierce and
violent ideological rivalry with Lazio for two decades. But, like many
Italian ultras, Fabrizio had shifted his hatred away from other groups
towards the state. Prison tended to have that effect, even if the world

seemed to have turned in his direction. Italy's most powerful man was Matteo Salvini, a far-right populist who enjoyed standing on Milan's *curva sud* with the ultras. But Fabrizio didn't trust 'this fake right. It's a world of hypocrisy. It's all bullshit. We don't trust any of them.' The only institution Fabrizio trusted or had any faith in was the Irriducibili. Any ultra that did support the system was not an ally. *The friend of my enemy is my enemy.* He dreamed one day that ultras, all ultras, could unite against who he and his Irriducibili viewed as the real enemy. 'To go against the globalists, against the fact the EU has taken away people's right to work, that it allows the Zionists to control all the economies of the world,' he said. 'We live under a dictator where the European Union controls us all. We don't live under a democracy. I want us all to gather and instead of meeting outside the stadium to have a fight we meet outside the European Union ready to fucking die.'

Fabrizio escorted us outside and shook our hands. His bodyguard unexpectedly hugged both me and Martino as we promised to call if Lazio reached the final. Martino and I found a cafe to talk about what had just happened. We felt relief and elation that we'd managed to speak to Diabolik. But then, as the adrenaline buzz subsided, we were left with the hangover from what we had seen and heard. How quickly the images of the far right had been normalised. How quickly we had been desensitised to the language. Were we complicit in telling Diabolik's story? For even sitting at the desk opposite him? I wondered whether, in one of the seemingly derelict buildings opposite the Irriducibili's headquarters on Via Amulio, there was a policeman crouched in the darkness, taking photos and wondering about Fabrizio Piscitelli's unfamiliar new guests.

BERGAMO

UNLESS YOU WERE A HARDCORE Atalantini, the Atleti Azzurri d'Italia was a difficult stadium to love. The roofless home ground of Atalanta was built during Mussolini's rule and was notorious for being both exposed to the elements and for providing lots of restricted sightlines. Aside from the blue and black ultras graffiti that covered its concrete exterior, it didn't look like it had much changed since it had been built. But Claudio Galimberti would give anything for one last chance to stand on the *curva nord*. Galimberti is the flamboyant *capotifosi* of Atalanta's main ultras group, the Curva Nord 1907. He was better known as il Bocia, or The Boy, a nickname he picked up when he started coming to the games because of his slight build and young age. His father had once played for Atalanta in the late 1940s but Bocia was orphaned young and instead found a new family on the *curva nord*. Bocia, of course, wasn't a boy any more. Martino and I waited for him in a bar next to the stadium, a small cafe with large windows on three sides. It was chosen – I was later told – so that any danger could be spotted in advance. One young ultra, dressed in English casual clothes and a bucket hat, entered first. He looked around to check no one else was inside before gesturing behind him. The ultras couldn't be too careful. Tomorrow was one of the biggest days in their history. Despite long periods of playing in Serie A, Atalanta had little silverware, just a solitary Coppa Italia in 1963. But tomorrow they would play their long-time rivals Lazio in the cup final, at the Stadio Olimpico in Rome.

With his grey stubble and sleeveless denim jacket, Bocia looked like a retired rock star. His longish hair was kept out of his face by a black bandana. Atalanta was an 'amazing thing', he said, that united people. 'We wouldn't know each other if it wasn't for Atalanta.' I felt like I knew Bocia already. During the 1980s and 90s Bergamo had a fearsome reputation. Anyone travelling there on an away day knew they would be met with fierce resistance. As the ultra lawyer Lorenzo Contucci had explained to me, getting into Bergamo was easy, but leaving was harder. You had to fight your way out. It was a one-club city with a strong left-wing culture that remained even as the *curve* around Italy moved towards neo-fascism. In spite of the poorly designed stadium, the Curva Nord 1907 was respected as one of the loudest in Italy, with exceptional choreography and a taste for pyro. There are thousands of videos of them in action on YouTube. Bocia was always at the front, standing on a fence and hanging forward by one arm from a beam, the other hand holding a megaphone which he was screaming into. He was exactly where he should be. 'It's something that's gone beyond the team,' he said when I asked him about Atalanta's ultras. There was friendship and camaraderie. 'There are people who have joined the ultras that, if it wasn't for the ultras group, they would have nothing else to live for. We can arrive with five hundred for a funeral. A thousand because someone overdoses on heroin, because that's the power of our group and people are blown away.'

The group that Bocia led was very different from Diabolik's Irriducibili. Both they and the Curva Nord 1907 didn't shy away from a fight. There was nothing he enjoyed more, Bocia said, than stealing the banners and flags of opposition fans. So many ultra groups came to Bergamo looking for a fight that they had to toughen up to survive. But the principles of the group were the polar opposite. Every lira, every euro that was taken off the *curva nord* was invested back into the group. There was no trademarked merchandise. No connections with organised crime. 'You make your materials and sell them but all the money goes back in the centre for the *curva* and for Atalanta because anybody seen making money off Atalanta will be disrobed, hung and crucified naked in front of the stand for the whole community to see,' he said, only half joking. 'Because Atalanta is something sacred. At times we publicly punished people for doing that.'

Bocia had seen other groups taken over by crime gangs. 'All the northern *curve* have been taken over by some sort of faction of organised crime,' he said. But not Atalanta. 'This place is still a space where even if we made bad decisions, our mothers would still be proud of us.'

It was this almost philosophical approach to ultras, the very definition of a *curva* replicating *campanilismo*, that made Bocia a cult hero, not just here, but in the rest of Europe. He was viewed as one of the last pure ultras, the last pure *capotifosi*. He would organise social work, projects for people with incurable diseases. Outreach projects for junkies and down-and-outs. The state may have washed their hands of them, but Atalanta could help. The *curva nord* could rehabilitate them. 'The ultras are the best friendships I've ever made. It's about helping the homeless person find a house. It's about building community and being part of Atalanta,' he explained. He spoke emotionally as if always on the verge of shedding a tear.

Outside, groups of men had started to mill around suspiciously. Bocia's young bodyguard sensed the danger and stormed out to find out who they were. It turned out they were fans of the Greek team Iraklis, who had travelled from Cyprus wearing 'Atalanta Salonicco' T-shirts. They had come just to have a picture taken with Bocia. Ultras had travelled from around Europe to be in Bergamo and show support not just for Atalanta, but for him too. Because, ultimately, he wasn't allowed into the Stadio Olimpico. Or the Atleti Azzurri d'Italia. Or, in fact, any stadium in Italy. 'I've basically been exiled from the city and from this space so long as they're playing a game here,' he said sadly. Bocia had been banned from the stadiums on and off for 23 years; and continuously since 2006 for a variety of offences. He threw a pig's head at a policeman, a neighbour of his, who had been under investigation for corruption. 'I got one and a half years for that,' he said. The ban was extended by two years after he travelled with 900 ultras to Dortmund, not to watch the Europa League game at the Westfalenstadion, but to 'breathe in' the atmosphere before watching the game in a city bar. Another time he got a ban after driving past the stadium at 11am on a Saturday morning. Atalanta wasn't playing, but AlbinoLeffe, Bergamo's second team in Serie C, were. Sitting here, next to the Atleti Azzurri d'Italia, was the closest he could get to the *curva nord*.

'I consider it quite an insidious thing because the police view me as the person who can bring people together. I can affect people in the stands by looking at them. I'm the glue that brings together the communities,' he said. 'Over the years I have never been involved in any issues with drugs, organised crime, politics. My only motivation was to go and see Atalanta and keep growing and building this thing. And I honestly don't think my time is done.'

He talked about Atalanta the way a spurned lover talks about the person who broke their heart. About the 'euphoria and madness' he felt during his favourite season, when Atalanta started the 2004/05

season in 'last place and finished in last place.' About the away trips
where thousands would follow him. About how, during Atalanta's rare
forays into Europe when he was a teenager, he would hide in the train
luggage compartments to get to away games as he had no passport or
ID. About the rush of standing in front of the *curva nord* and conduct-
ing his choir. It was one of the reasons why Bocia was considered a
folk hero in Bergamo. There was a fierce protective loyalty towards
him. A few weeks earlier, thousands marched in the centre of Bergamo
demanding that his *diffide* be rescinded so that he could attend the
last ever Atalanta home match in the *curva nord*, which was being
ripped down and rebuilt. All over Bergamo you saw graffiti: '*Libre
Bocia*' and '*Siamo Tutti Con Claudio*', 'We are all with Claudio'. The
same banner had been hanging in the *curva nord* all season. The
appeal was rejected. In response the ultras cancelled their annual
Festival of the Goddess, a raucous city-wide event that has become a
huge tourist boon for the city, in solidarity.

Yet, even after his constant friction with the police, he didn't buy
into the anti-police ethos seen in other *curve* in Italy and around the
world. 'Behind the suit I see a human. They might be the hero of
tomorrow,' he said. The enemy was the state, who made the laws, and
killed football. 'Everything in Belgium, everything in Germany, everything in England was all grey, it was all dead,' he said of what football
looked like to him then. 'And in Italy it was magic. Madness. Now it
has switched around; everything is grey in Italy because the state has
repressed too much.'

Bocia had considered going in disguise to Rome for the final. But
the risk wasn't worth it. Not for him, but for anyone around him who
would probably be punished just for standing next to him. 'Tomorrow
I'm going to be missing it like bread,' he said. He would, instead, take
the special 5am train that had been arranged for the Atalanta fans to
get to Rome. He'd travel as far as Pisa and hand his famous number-
eight jersey to a young fan who would wear it inside the stadium in his
stead. 'I'm getting emotional just thinking about it,' he said, staring
into his empty beer glass. He would be signing at the police station
instead. 'These are the best years of Atalanta. I'm still signing at a

police station. Twenty-five years of bans. Thirteen straight years. My parents died at a young age and I gave myself to Atalanta in place of them. These last hours, these times you give for your family? Since mine passed away I've given that time to Atalanta. And now I find myself sitting in a police station watching the game.' He had enjoyed Atalanta's rivalry with Lazio in the past. The *curva nord* had, like ultras groups across Italy, shown solidarity with them after the death of Gabriele Sandri. But their vastly different world views meant they had no contact with each other. 'Lazio is a *curva* that is always respected because of the good choreography, to follow the team they go everywhere, but I can't understand this vision of football where they've opened up businesses,' he said. 'Perhaps,' he added, 'I'm just a small-town person.'

Outside more supporters from around Europe turned up. Word had got around. Bocia was here. Later that night we would gather for a farewell dinner with the rest of the Curve Nord 1907. A group of ultras from Eintracht Frankfurt were there too as Bocia gave an emotional speech. He was probably the last true ultra *capotifosi* in Italian football. It wasn't about money, or power, or hatred. It was about the *curva* and the team and the city. The bell tower. 'At the end of the day the number one rule remains,' he had told me. 'If you don't know who my second keeper is and you don't know who's playing in the youth team, get the fuck out of here!'

Back in Rome, it started raining heavily just as the police started firing the tear gas. It was a few hours before the Coppa Italia final between Lazio and Atalanta was about to kick off. The Lazio ultras had been boisterous, letting off flares and smoke bombs, without too much aggression, although Diabolik had predicted that there might be some trouble. A week before, the Irriducibili's headquarters, where Martino and I had spoken to him, had been damaged in a bomb attack. 'If they want to go back to the terrorism of the 1970s, to that climate, we are ready. In fact, I can't wait and certainly won't hold back,' he said.[25] The Irriducibili were convinced that the bomb, which did minor damage to the front shutters but could have been much worse if someone had been passing by, had been placed by leftists. Before the semi-final against Milan the Irriducibili had unfurled a large banner praising Mussolini on the same square where his and his mistress's badly beaten bodies had been hung on meat hooks and displayed after being executed by the partisans. 'It is those who put the bomb that have shown fear. It is a cowardly act, done at night ... we are fascists, the last fascists of Rome.'[26]

Shortly before kick-off fighting broke out between the Lazio ultras and the police. The ultras hurled flares, smoke bombs and glass bottles that smashed on the floor. They commandeered a police car and set it on fire before the police rolled in, firing hundreds of tear-gas canisters, clearing the square we had stood in half an hour before. Fabrizio was, of course, not allowed to be there, just like Bocia. He was watching the game at the Irriducibili's HQ. Diabolik invited us to watch the game there but I had spent so much time with Italian ultras who had been banned from the stadiums that I hadn't actually been inside one yet. It was a decision I would later come to regret.

Over 20,000 Atalanta fans travelled to the capital. Bocia took the the 5am train and got off at Pisa, handing over his famous number-eight shirt as promised, before heading back to Bergamo to sign his name at the police station. There was virtually no pyro and no chore-ography in Stadio Olimpico. In the end it took two late goals for Lazio to win the cup. I remembered what Lorenzo Contucci, the Roma lawyer, had told me from his hospital bed. 'Ultras today are dead.' There was too much control and too much risk to be involved in the scene. He believed that the ultras that chose to still live that life, in the face of mass surveillance, were heroes. 'In the past we did what we wanted to do. But there was no CCTV or things like this. You can't ruin your life. But you don't just want to be a number on a seat.' The next battle would be against facial recognition.

Maybe the Italian ultra scene was dead, or at least hadn't yet realised it was dead, a zombie movement that would lurch on until it decayed into bone. But even as the *diffide* and CCTV and ID cards and facial-recognition technology had made it impossible for the ultras to organise like they did in the 1980s and 90s, the scene very much lived on, just in a different way. Like in the rest of Europe, supporters were taking control of their clubs in the lower divisions. Phoenix clubs were being set up and run by the fans for the fans. And ultras would turn up in numbers to watch their new/old teams. After all, their *diffide* was no longer applicable to their new team. And globally the influence of ultra culture had never been stronger. It might not have felt it to il Bocia and Diabolik, banned from watching the cup final. But the ultra movement that had begun in 1968 had taken root around the world, and flourished in the most unexpected places.

5

Serbia

BELGRADE

IN THAT SACRED HOUR BEFORE THE START OF A MATCH, THE atmosphere in the roads and pathways around the Rajko Mitić Stadium felt both invigoratingly fresh and like something frozen from a bygone age. The vast, slightly shabby sunken concrete bowl on the edge of the upmarket district of Dedinje was surrounded by the red and white of its host Crvena Zvezda, the Serbian name for Red Star Belgrade. In 2008 the stadium was named in Mitić's honour, shortly after his death. He had been arguably Zvezda's greatest player, captaining the team to five championships after the club was formed in the ashes of the post-Second World War period. But for most fans the stadium was still known by a nickname earned thanks to its vast size (at least 100,000 people watched Red Star play Bayern Munich in the semi-finals of the 1991 European Cup), the quality of the Brazilian-style football frequently on show and its intimidating atmosphere: the Marakana.

The days of six-figure attendances at the Marakana were long gone, but today it was likely to be a full house. It was a dark and muggy Sunday afternoon as thousands marched up the tree-lined Ljutice Bogdana. Groups of excited teenagers, fathers and mothers with sons and daughters, gangs of young men with skinheads smoking incessantly as they moved towards the north stand. We all moved past lines of riot police with militarised hardware, helmets and shields. Past hawkers sitting in front of sacks of *kikiriki* and *semenke* – salted nuts and pumpkin seeds – sold for a few dinars in a cone made from a scrap of that day's newspaper. Past the men and women selling knock-off flags and scarves. And past the walls of murals and graffiti: 'Kosovo je Srbija', a picture of a machine gun with the words 'UEFA Supports Terrorism' and, the most common graffiti of all, the word 'Delije', the name of Zvezda's famed ultras.

The sheer number of young people created a wide-eyed excitement that felt as fresh as dew, something anathema to English football where young people and the working class had largely been frozen out of the game at the highest level. But Zvezda was a club that, in a way, had been frozen in time. In 1991 the club won the European Cup by beating Marseille in the Italian city of Bari, where at least 30,000 Zvezda fans had travelled, most by boat from the Montenegrin port of Bar. For most of those around Europe who watched the game, the final was infamous for Zvezda's negative tactics that dragged its conclusion down to penalties. There should have been no need. This was a golden generation, a team of multi-ethnic players like the Serbian Siniša Mihajlović, Macedonian Darko Pančev, Croatian Robert Prosinečki and Romanian Miodrag Belodedici that played beautiful football. As Mihajlović would later admit, they shackled their attacking instincts to guarantee their place in history. They did what they needed to do for Zvezda to join European football's elite.[1]

A year later Zvezda beat Chile's Colo-Colo – the winners of the Copa Libertadores – in the Intercontinental Cup in Japan and became champions of the world just as Yugoslavia was entering one of the most harrowing conflicts of the twentieth century. The club, and the country, found itself isolated and sanctioned. The Yugoslav national team was kicked out of the 1992 European Championship – replaced by eventual winners Denmark – as a vicious inter-republic war killed thousands of innocent people. Just when the club should have been cementing its place at football's top table, as the European Cup made way for the Champions League and the modern, rebranded era of super-rich football was born, Zvezda – and the rest of Serbian football – withered. Over two decades were lost to war in Croatia, Bosnia and Kosovo, to hyper-inflation and economic sanctions and ruin, to NATO bombs over Belgrade. Zvezda had been on the periphery ever since, and the Marakana's murals told the story of Serbia's feelings of injustice.

This season, though, marked something of a comeback. Zvezda had reached the group stages of the Champions League for the first time since 1992, 26 years before. That was the last season Yugoslav teams were allowed to play in UEFA competition before a three-year ban. The club had returned to its rightful place, but in a vastly different, almost unrecognisable world. And although they didn't make it past the group stage, there were some memorable results along the way. I had stood pitch-side, freezing, next to the north stand where the Delije made the loudest noise I had ever heard in a stadium as Zvezda somehow beat Liverpool – who would go on to win the whole thing – 2–0. The two goals were scored by Milan Pavkov, an industrious everyman striker who was purchased for just €300,000 – a pittance in European terms – and had bounced between loan spells at his parent club and Radnički Niš. After the final whistle, the players did a lap of honour before settling in front of the north stand, where every player knew they had to pay tribute. Pavkov climbed in to be with the Delije as he was hailed as their new hero.

Today's game wasn't a high-profile European match or the latest instalment of the Eternal Derby against Partizan, whose stadium was just a few hundred metres away. No, today's game was against FK Napredak, a team from the southern city of Kruševac. The match would normally attract a few thousand supporters at best. But today was different. The championship, Zvezda's 30th, would officially be awarded to the team before kick-off, although that wasn't the most important 30th celebration. It was to be a celebration to mark the Delije's 30th birthday.

The Delije was formed on Orthodox Christmas Day, 7 January 1989. In the intervening years they had built a fearsome reputation. Not just for their choreography, pyro show, impenetrability, organisation and strength in numbers. But because of a war mythology from the time the warlord and career criminal Željko Ražnatović – known as Arkan – stood in the north stand and recruited from amongst the Delije. His Serb Volunteer Guard, known as Arkan's Tigers, became infamous as one of the cruellest and most bloodthirsty of the militias operating in Croatia and Bosnia during the Yugoslav Wars. Alongside the flags of assassinated *capos* and fallen friends were frequent images of ultra-nationalist heroes like the convicted war criminal Ratko Mladić, or the face of Draža Mihailović, the Second World War-era Četnik leader, a nationalist and royalist guerrilla force that eventually collaborated with the Nazis. Mihailović was executed after the war but in 2015 Serbia rehabilitated his reputation by quashing his 1946 conviction for high treason and war crimes.

The club was frequently handed stadium bans by UEFA, usually for racists chanting against Albanians. Before Zvezda returned to the Champions League group stages, two matches at the Marakana were played behind closed doors for the same reason. For the home play-off game against Red Bull Salzburg, the Delije arranged for the match to be shown on a big screen on a patch of scrubland behind the Marakana's south stand, the songs and flare smoke drifting over the otherwise empty stadium. Anger at the loss of Kosovo was a recurrent theme, especially UEFA's recognition of Kosovo in 2016. After that decision was made the Delije arranged a huge red and black mosaic choreography before the next home game at the Marakana, with 'UEFA' and a banner underneath it that read 'Supports Terrorism'. A common sight was a white flag with the outline of Kosovo coloured the red, white and blue of the

Serbian flag with a passport stamp on it, often with the words
'Kosovo is Serbia'.

But the real story of the Delije – and its association with Arkan
– was much more complicated than that. The Delije was today perhaps the most respected ultras group in Europe. Inside the stadium,
after the players had been handed their medals and the crowd had
displayed a huge red shirt with the number ten on it, in honour of
captain Nenad Milijaš who was retiring after the game, a mosaic choreography spread across three tribunes with the number '30' displayed
in white in the north stand. Red or white cards had been placed on
each seat alongside a letter with the Delije's insignia on it giving pre-
cise instructions as to when and how to display it. 'Let's make tonight
a memorable spectacle!' read the letter, signed 'Delije North'. And it
was. The game in front of us all was utterly immaterial as the real
show took place in the sweeping northern *curva*, which exploded in
smoke and bright red flares just as a vicious lightning storm ignited
over Belgrade, flooding the pitch and causing the game to be suspended twice. At one point the entire pitch was obscured not just by
smoke but by the thick curtain of warm rain and a strange fog it
helped to generate. On any other day the game would have been
abandoned. The centrepiece was a huge banner that looked like a
scene from Mario Brothers: a cartoon castle with oversized mush-
rooms. Underneath, on a red banner, were the words: *'U svetu postoji
jedno carstvo'*; 'There is one empire in the world'.

'It's from a children's song, like there is one place in the world
where everything is wonderful,' one member of the Delije later
explained to me. 'And for us it's the Marakana.' As the banner was
unfolded, and the children's song was played on the Marakana's loud-
speakers, the stadium sang as dozens of ultras – hoods up, faces covered by masks or scarves – fanned out around the stadium and lit
flashing flares and smoke bombs, creating a ring of light. A few more
had set up a firework display *inside* the tribune, firing rockets so close
to us – as the 40,000 crowd squeezed themselves under the covered
stands to escape the monsoon – that the concrete floor vibrated as the
rockets boomed.

Apparently, Zvezda won 3–0.

Josip Broz Tito died at 3.05pm, 4 May 1980, in a hospital in the Slovenian capital of Ljubljana. His death wasn't unexpected but still came as a shock. Yugoslavia's 'President for Life', the man who had led the partizans to victory against the Nazis in the Second World War before founding a socialist federation of six religiously and ethnically divergent Balkan nations, was 88 years old and in poor health. Tito had a taste for the high life, especially expensive Cuban cigars, and had long suffered from diabetes, but it was gangrene – after his left leg was amputated – that got him in the end. His death was announced throughout the federation almost simultaneously to a genuine out-pouring of grief. Just over four hours later, at the Poljud Stadium in Split, a match between Hajduk and Red Star Belgrade was abruptly halted and the players told to line up in the centre circle as Hajduk's president delivered the news over the stadium's loudspeaker. The announcement left many players in tears and the match was cancelled.[2]

Later that year, Hajduk Split's Torcida was revived. The name had been outlawed after the controversy that followed its founding in 1950. But as more space for expression opened in Yugoslav society, the terraces became louder and more organised until it was decided that the name 'Torcida' could safely be resurrected without the fear of reprisals. Dražen Lalić was there when Hajduk Split's Torcida was re-formed in 1980. Today, Lalić is a professor of sociology and political science at the University of Zagreb. He's in his sixties now but back in the early 1980s he was part of the new Torcida and wrote a book about his experiences in 1993 called *Torcida: A Look Inside*.

'There were a few hundreds of us, a hardcore of perhaps two hundred guys at the old stadium,' he said. The new Torcida was more than a connection to the club, but rather a chance to represent 'their city and their homeland'. Many of his fellow Torcida members, Lalić said, were Croat nationalists. The stadium provided a space for young dis-affected men like them – and it was mainly all men back then – to express ideas forbidden elsewhere in Yugoslav society. 'Some of the guys felt that to be part of the fan group is a proper way to express some political views,' he said, stressing that he wasn't a nationalist. 'During the eighties, in that time of the one-party socialist regime, to be a fan of football, punk or rock music, was actually the only way to express genuine beliefs and attitudes and values.'

Yugoslavia wasn't like the rest of communist Eastern Europe. Tito had been a dictator, that was true, but the leash wasn't as tight as in Czechoslovakia or Romania or East Germany. Ever since Tito fell out with Stalin in 1948, leaving Yugoslavia outside Moscow's control, the country walked a different, non-aligned path. There were limited free-market reforms that brought a higher standard of living in the 1960s and 70s. Although the level of dissent tolerated differed according to each of the six constituent socialist republics, Yugoslav society was relatively free when compared to, say, Poland or Hungary. The Yugoslav passport was famously heralded as one of the best in the world, with visa-free travel – east or west – to virtually everywhere bar the US. Wages were good. Young people could work in Germany and earn hard currency. 'It was a time when people were able to make a good living, and young people could find regular paid work ... and with their earnings they would go to the Italian border city of Trieste or to Vienna or even to London to witness the new subcultural trends and buy records,'[3] wrote Miljenko Jergović, in an essay on Yugoslavia's punk scene in the *New York Times*. The outside world didn't have to seep into Yugoslavia the same way it did with the rest of the Eastern Bloc, through smuggled books and contraband cassettes and LPs. It was welcomed in. Or, at the very least, tacitly accepted. Punk, hooliganism, ultras, heavy metal, had all percolated into the mainstream of youth culture. It was, as Lalić described it, 'Western-style communism'.

There was, however, a looming problem that was widely feared but never uttered in public: What would happen after Tito? The elderly communist elite coined the phrase 'After Tito, Tito',[4] which gave some indication as to the poor level of succession planning. Whilst he was alive Tito's answer to this, rather than grooming a successor who might threaten his power, was greater decentralisation.

There had been three constitutional rewrites in two decades that had given more and more autonomy and power not just to the republics but to two semi-autonomous regions in Serbia: Vojvodina in the north and Kosovo in the south. Many Serbs saw that 1974 change as an affront, and a tactic to dilute Belgrade's power within the state presidency.[5]

The issue of what came next was further obscured by Yugoslavia's economic miracle. But the 1970s boom, the sweet spot between Western capitalism and Eastern communism, revealed itself to be a mirage built on Western loans that needed to be repaid. In 1971, Yugoslavia's debt stood at $4 billion. By the early 1980s it was over five times that amount.[6] The correction was harsh, slashing living standards by up to half in just a few years. Yugoslavia went from being an upwardly mobile, rising industrial power to just another communist country with spiralling inflation, rapidly emptying shelves and a thriving black market. 'It's interesting that they pronounced the death of Tito during the match of Hajduk–Zvezda,' explained Lalić. 'Because Tito passed away, the economic and social crisis began, and a new generation of fans appeared.'

In the wake of Tito's death, organised supporters groups began to flourish with a markedly different philosophy. The Torcida took several thousand away fans to Stuttgart in the UEFA Cup in 1981. In fact, the home match against Stuttgart at the Poljud on 16 September 1981 was the first time the Torcida banner was raised at Hajduk since 29 October 1950. These twin Western cultural imports of punk and terrace culture from England and Italy had a huge influence on Yugoslav fan culture. The fashion, language and nihilism of punk had been fused with the attractive and dangerous violence of English hooliganism, whilst the proximity of Italy and its unique use of flares and choreography spread and then dominated the scene, influenced by Italian magazines like *Super Tifo*, which were widely available. But it was the proximity, as well as the freedom for travel and for cultural exchange, that saw the first wave of ultras outside of Italy reach Yugoslavia before spreading throughout the rest of the Balkans and southern Europe.

'Football fan groups became speakers, maybe one of the most important speakers of that change, that led to the decline, the crash, of Yugoslavia,' said Lalić,

In Belgrade, at the same time the Torcida was displaying its flag against Stuttgart, Dule Nedeljković was playing punk gigs with his band Radost Evrope, Joy of Europe, in a network of basements in the centre of the city. Today Nedeljković is one of Serbia's best-known novelists. In the early 1980s he was part of Yugoslavia's thriving punk scene, as well as a diehard Zvezda fan. The fashion and music of English and American punk had bled into the terraces. Dule pulled up his jumper and showed me the three tattoos on his right forearm: one for Crvena Zvezda, the words, in English, 'The Power and The Glory' (from the 1981 Cockney Rejects album of the same name) and a picture of the Droogs from *A Clockwork Orange*. 'The first city crews played rock and roll, punk rock, made art, made movies and then went to Red Star games,' he explained over coffee in his neighbourhood in the centre of Belgrade. In the beginning of the 1980s the north stand was as much a countercultural space as the basements that Dule would play in. Dule had travelled to London and New York, although he was in the rarefied position of working for JAT, Yugoslavia's national airline. He would return with records from American bands like MC5, the Ramones and the New York Dolls. Ted Nugent was a favourite. The music influenced the songs and fashion on the terraces because, he believed, the two came from the same place deep inside. 'When you play punk there has to be some rage,' he said. 'And this rage you have on the tribune. It's similar. When you are screaming, you are screaming against power.'

Red Star's fans had for years called themselves *cigani*, 'gypsy' in Serbian. It was originally a pejorative term from opposition fans remarking on the supposed low-class status of Red Star's followers. But the fact that the north stand was, as Dule described, home to 'delinquents and intellectuals' was one of its strengths. The first group to be formed was Ultras, in 1983, by Zoran Timić, known as Tima. Ultras brought the Italian taste for choreography and pyrotechnics to the Marakana. In 1985 the Red Devils were formed, named after the nickname for Manchester United, whom the founder supported. In 1987, as English hooliganism was becoming more widely known and respected, the Zulu Warriors were formed, named after Birmingham City's main hooligan group. They were also in contact with Italian ultra groups, and the terraces embraced the Italian singing: 'Tima was in touch with Italian ultras, spoke Italian and Italy was very, very near to go to a game or find pyrotechnics and make contacts there,' said Petar Ilić, a former member of Ultras who made a film about that time called *Zulu Warriors* for Vice Srbija.[7] There had been a few attempts to bring some order to the north stand before then, but Ultras was the first to succeed. 'Ultras used to fight but they were known for the choreographies,' said Ilić. 'And the Italian singing. It was like an opera on the terraces, man.'

If you look at old pictures from that time, especially in *Ćao Tifo*, a Belgrade magazine dedicated to terrace culture that would publish pictures of tifos and flags from Yugoslavia and around the world, it was striking how prominent the Union Jack and English language banners were.[8] 'We loved the English hooligans. It was the time of the fashionable English,' said Ilić. After the wars, and NATO's bombing of Belgrade in 1999, that all changed, and the groups became much more nationalistic. 'The younger supporters now, like Belgrade Boys [one of the current Delije sub-groups], when they see the pictures of Red Devils, American flag, English flag, they say: "What is that, man, they are the enemies." Now you have very nationalistic groups.'

The violence between supporter groups had been pretty widespread over the course of the 1980s. But it didn't begin to have an ethnic edge, at least not inside the Marakana, until the second half of the decade. Ilić began to notice it around 1987. 'Anxiety was there, you know? Everybody felt what was happening with the country.'

That year, 1987, was also when Slobodan Milošević rose to power within the Serbian Communist Party, largely by leveraging the emotive issue of Kosovo.[9] Kosovo is central to understanding modern Serbia. Wherever you are in Belgrade, you won't be more than ten metres away from graffiti that says: '1389'. It's the year of the Battle of

Kosovo, where a combined Balkan force of princes and knights were crushed by the Ottomans, ushering in five centuries of domination. Kosovo is seen as the site of Serbia's glorious defeat but also its spiritual home. Many Serbian Orthodox monasteries can be found throughout Kosovo today. But Kosovo had long been poor and neglected, with an economy dependent on mining. The Serbian population shrank to an overwhelming minority. The argument about why it shrank would form the ideological basis of the future conflict. On the one hand it appeared that ethnic Serbs were leaving for better economic opportunities elsewhere. But Milošević blamed the ethnic Albanian, largely Muslim, population for forcing Serbs out from their rightful place. In 1989 he became president of the Socialist Republic of Serbia. The rights of Kosovo Albanians were drastically reduced and in June that year he gave his famous Gazimestan speech at the site of the Battle of Kosovo, just outside Pristina, in front of up to a million people to mark its 600th anniversary, where he drove those themes home. His speech was seen as a harbinger for the wars to come.[11] The same month, in Croatia, a little-known former history professor and avowed Croatian ultra-nationalist, Franjo Tuđman, formed the Croatian Democratic Union, the HDZ.

In 1989 Zvezda's three main ultras groups – including dozens of smaller groups that had started because, in Ilić's telling, having your own group on the north was 'fashionable' – united to form one large umbrella organisation: the Delije. The name is hard to translate but it roughly means 'Heroes', or 'the brave ones'. It was at this time that Arkan appeared, but he didn't start the Delije, nor did he have absolute dominion over it. There was no doubt that Arkan was obsessed with Zvezda. The son of a Yugoslav air force captain, he discovered he had a taste for petty crime as a teenager. That morphed into robbery and extortion. He became a famous, almost romantic figure because of his criminal career in Europe as a brazen bank robber who would frequently break out of prison. But his criminal genius was helped somewhat by Yugoslavia's secret service. It was likely that he was a secret service asset, an assassin who would liquidate the Communist Party's dissident exiles.[12]

By the 1980s he was back in Yugoslavia, where he opened a cake shop whilst being given cover to make millions in the black market. But in 1989 his handlers thought the best use of his time was to take charge of the Delije and harness this young, organised, wellspring of Serbian nationalism. The north stand had something of an awakening. Songs were chanted and banners flown in support of Vuk Drašković and Vojislav Šešelj, two potential nationalist rivals to Milošević. 'Arkan didn't make Delije,' explained Ilić, but he filled the void that had been created by disputes and neighbourhood fights.

Ilić and the rest of the north stand had long known about Arkan thanks to his exploits in Europe in the 1970s. Goran Vuković, a famed Serbian gangster known as 'The Monkey', described his time robbing Western European banks with Arkan, shortly before Vuković was shot dead in Belgrade in 1994. 'Of all of us, Arkan robbed the most banks: he walked into them almost like they were self service stores,' he said. 'I don't know about politics, but as far as robbery was concerned, he was really unsurpassed. That is all he has done his entire life. Banks were his speciality, as well as escapes from prison. He managed to escape from the same prison two or three times. He even escaped from the Germans.'[13]

Arkan was ten years older than the other members of the Delije, and the younger men looked up to him. He was, Ilić said, 'very cold. Cold, cold. Like hell, man. But brave. And witty. His behaviour was like an old Belgrade gangster. You talk to him, and you feel like you are talking to an eagle, with the eagle eyes.' But not everyone was happy with his arrival.

'I didn't see him ever,' said Dule Nedeljković. There were even a few anti-Arkan songs. 'He did not make Delije. It's a lie. Delije was united by Tima, by Zulu Warriors.'

Ilić had seen him on the terraces more regularly. 'He was there, man. But not everyone was with him. He was there with his crew. He was very influential but not the main guy.'

Arkan's most famous match was perhaps one of the most written about, and misunderstood, games in the history of European football. On 13 May 1990, Dinamo Zagreb played Red Star Belgrade in

Zagreb's Maksimir Stadium. The game didn't finish thanks to rioting between Dinamo's ultras group the Bad Blue Boys, which was formed in 1986 and named after the Sean Penn film Bad Boys, and the Delije. As many as 5,000 Delije travelled from Belgrade for the game. As the fighting intensified under a hail of orange seats ripped from the concrete, Arkan can be seen in a brown suit next to the touchline, providing security for the bench.

'It was a tense atmosphere, a crazy atmosphere, it was intense,' said Miodrag Belodedici, who played in that match for Zvezda, when I asked him about it in 2017. 'At some point the fans, well, the railings were ripped off and people started going on to the pitch. The coaches said: "Go to the locker room. Now! Run!" Everyone ran.' The players were locked into their changing rooms as they heard the riot rage outside.

They didn't see perhaps the most iconic moment until after: Dinamo, and later Milan, striker Zvonimir Boban famously launching a flying kick into the face of a Yugoslav policeman. It was an image that would make him a hero amongst Croat nationalists who considered that match, and Boban's symbolic kick into the face of the Serbian-dominated Yugoslav police force, the 'first battle' of the war for Croatian independence. Later it turned out that the policeman wasn't a Serb at all but a man called Refik Ahmetović, a Bosnian muslim from Tuzla.[14]

'We were there for two hours,' Belodedici said of his time in the dressing room, remembering fans trying to get in through the small windows. Belodedici got to know Arkan, who was a regular presence around the team, flanked by two bodyguards, each carrying a bag whose contents was a secret. 'He was a dangerous guy,' he remembered.

The game had come at a delicate time. Just a few weeks before, Franjo Tuđman's HDZ party had won the first free elections held in Croatia. Conspiracy theories have emerged that either Serbian or Croatian intelligence had pre-planned the violence to spark conflict. Neither Nedeljković or Ilić were there. There was, Ilić said, a big memorial event for Draža Mihailović that most of the Delije's leaders attended instead. 'The main fist of fury of the Red Star was not there,' he offered as proof that it couldn't have been arranged from the Serbian side. But one person who said he was in Maksimir was the current Serbian president Aleksandar Vučić. Vučić was a former journalist and secretary general of the far-right Serbian Radical Party, founded by Vojislav Šešelj (Šešelj would later be found guilty of war crimes at the International Criminal Tribunal for the former Yugoslavia, the ICTY, in The Hague).[15] He came to prominence in the West during the last years of Milošević's rule, as a hardline Minister of Information during the Kosovo War and the subsequent NATO bombing of Belgrade. Since then he had rebranded himself as a pro-Western technocrat who wanted to take Serbia into the European Union. But in 1990 he was a 20-year-old student and rabid Zvezda fan. So much so, that in 2010 he gave an interview to the Serbian weekly news magazine *Vreme* where he described how he had been at the Maksimir with the 5,000 or so members of the Delije. He gave a detailed description of arriving by train in Zagreb under a hail of stones, hearing chants of 'beat the Četniks' by the Bad Blue Boys, of being close to the riot itself and then being questioned by the police afterwards. 'Whenever we went to Zagreb, we expected a fight,' Vučić said. 'I do not believe in the story that the war started at Maksimir. It only showed what the relations in society were.' Vučić may well be the world's first ultra president.[16]

The myth of the Maksimir has continued to be built. There is a monument outside the stadium that reads: 'To all the Dinamo fans for whom the war started on May 13, 1990, and ended with them laying down their lives on the altar of the Croatian homeland.' But the truth wasn't that clear-cut. The season continued after 'the war started'. Indeed, the Yugoslav First Division continued for another full season after that. Boban even continued playing for the Yugoslav national team. Neither was it a unique example of violence inside Yugoslav football, as Vučić hinted at in his interview, even if the nature of that violence changed.

Dražen Lalić's PhD looked at the issue of fan violence in Yugoslavia between 1988 and 1992. He concluded that as the federal state's power declined, inter-ethnic violence became much more prevalent. 'In that situation appeared great room, great space, great opportunity for football fan violence to become real,' he told me. Before then, the violence was almost a cartoonish ritual for territory or to steal scarves or a flag. But as the 1980s continued, each republic's supporter groups saw their rivals in ever more extremist terms. 'Not only as Croatian, but Ustaša,' said Lalić. 'Not only like Serbs, but like Četniks. Not only like Muslims, but like Balli Kombëtar [Second World War Albanian nationalists that also sided with the Nazis].'

What isn't disputed is what Arkan did next. Five months after Maksimir he formed his Serbian Volunteer Guard and recruited directly from the Delije. The terraces would prove to be a rich recruiting ground from across Yugoslavia as ultras from Torcida and Bad Blue Boys also headed for the front line. There are plaques and statues outside and inside their respective stadiums dedicated to the members of the Bad Blue Boys, Hajduk Spit's Torcida and the Delije who died in the wars that followed. As one member of the Torcida who had gone to war told Dražen Lalić in his 1993 book: 'Now it's like it was at the stadiums, only that they have given us weapons. This is above all a war of football supporters, because the supporters understood political developments when many of today's great politicians were still sycophants to the old government. In fact, we supporters have been fighting this war since 1980.'[17]

Arkan's Tigers would go on to commit horrific crimes. He was an effective commander who mixed military nous and cold-blooded ruthlessness with a rapacious thirst for looting the wealth of the areas he had helped to ethnically cleanse. The Tigers killed, raped and robbed thousands of Croats and Bosniak Muslims in eastern Croatia and north-eastern Bosnia.[18] It made him a very wealthy man. So wealthy, in fact, he would later try and take over Zvezda, not just the north stand. When he was rebuffed he purchased FK Obilić, an obscure team from Belgrade. Using a mixture of money and intimidation, Obilić won the title in 1998. There's a long list of anecdotes from former opposition players and referees who alleged that Arkan had threatened to shoot them if they didn't acquiesce in an Obilić victory.[19] Arkan's very visible presence within the club meant that UEFA threatened to bar Obilić from playing in the Champions League. A man accused of war crimes was not good for business. Arkan got around the proposed ban by transferring ownership of the club to his 25-year old wife Ceca. Ceca was one of Serbia's biggest turbo-folk singers. This gave the ICTY an opportunity. They would send spotters to games in Antwerp and Madrid in the hope of catching and arresting Arkan there, after they got a tip that he would turn up for Obilić away days abroad in disguise. Unsurprisingly, given his past record of escaping capture, they never caught him.[20]

But Arkan couldn't keep escaping forever. He was assassinated on 15 January 2000, shot dead in the lobby of Belgrade's Intercontinental hotel. No one was sure why he was killed but there were ample suspects. Perhaps he had outlived his usefulness. Perhaps an underworld dispute had got out of hand. Perhaps Slobodan Milošević feared he might tell the ICTY what he knew if he ever found himself in The Hague. After all, Arkan's lawyer had tried, and failed, to cut a deal with the court.[21] After his death the ICTY released Arkan's sealed indictment. He was wanted on charges of Crimes Against Humanity, Grave Breaches of the Geneva Convention and Violations of the Laws or Customs of War, relating to the Tiger's conduct when his forces seized the majority Bosnian Muslim town of Sanski Most. Seventy-eight people were murdered although it was likely that this indictment was just the tip of the iceberg.[22] Belgrade was a bleak place at the turn of the millennium. The economy had long been in free fall. According to Professor Steve Hanke, who was advising the Yugoslav government on economic policy in the mid-1990s, hyper-inflation was running at 313,000,000 per cent a month[23]. Belgrade had just been bombed by NATO because of Milošević's campaign in Kosovo and gangsters were shooting each other dead on the streets. The north stand had had enough. Now they sang: 'Slobodan, Kill Yourself', a reference to Milošević's dark family history. Both his father and mother had committed suicide.[23]

When hundreds of thousands of people, inspired by the student Otpor (resistance) movement, took to the streets on 5 October 2000, the Delije were at the front when the parliament was stormed. One of Arkan's lieutenants from the Tigers would play a pivotal role in the army and police *not* opening fire on them. Milorad Ulemek, known as 'Legija' ever since he spent a spell in the French Foreign Legion to escape the consequences of a failed robbery, was now in charge of the JSO, the unit that looked after Milošević's personal security. The night before the parliament was stormed one of the leading figures of the opposition, Zoran Djindjić, held a high-stakes meeting with Legija. 'He could kill me,' Djindjić said. 'It's worth the risk,' he reasoned. 'If there's anything I can do it's here and now. Later the price will be higher.' On a late-night drive around Belgrade the two men talked. Legija admitted that the next day would be a bloodbath. 'It's going to be a mess,' Legija told him. 'The orders are extreme.'[25]

In return for a promise that protestors would not shoot at his men, Legija assured Djindjić he would not give the orders to open fire. The two men shook on it.[26] When the final confrontation came, Legija and his JTO stood back as the Delije stormed the parliament and Milošević was removed from power. Legija had kept his word but the two men's paths would cross again, and Djindjić's words – that 'later the price will be higher' – would prove prophetic. Djindjić would rise to become prime minister in the new post-Milošević administration, and approved Milošević's extradition to The Hague. Milošević died in custody in 2006 while awaiting trial, but he lived longer than Djindjić. He was shot dead by a sniper in 2003 as he entered parliament. Legija was tried and convicted of his assassination.

'I want the whole world to know the truth that Arkan is not Red Star. Vučić is not Red Star,' said Dule Nedeljković. And they weren't. But it was clear that the ultras in Yugoslavia had been coveted and courted by those in power and that they had played their role in Yugoslav history. Back in 2000, just after Milošević had been removed from power, the radio station b92 held an award ceremony for those who had played the most important role in the October revolution. The Delije were awarded a plaque for their efforts. 'We would like to say thanks for the prize,' said Marko Vučković, the leader of a relatively new sub-group called the Ultra Boys. 'We hope that there will be no more occasions for such a prize.'[27]

Slobodan Georgiev, like all Red Star Belgrade fans his age, knows Zvezda's 1991 European Cup winning team like the back of his hand. Even so, a poster of the team was pinned to his office wall, more out of pride than necessity. Behind his desk was an aerial picture of the Marakana. 'I have a problem with going to the games now,' he said when I spotted the picture behind his shoulder. Georgiev is one of the Serbia's leading investigative journalists, for BIRN, the Balkans Investigative Reporting Network. There aren't many independent investigative journalists left in Serbia. Ever since Aleksandar Vučić came to power, first as prime minister in 2012 with his newly formed Serbian Progressive Party (SNS), and then switching to a newly empowered executive presidency in 2014, almost all independent media had been taken over by allies of Vučić, squeezed off the news-stands by local politicians loyal to Vučić, or forced out of business, after government advertisers refused to do any business with them. Georgiev has spent years looking into corruption and especially the relationships between politicians, the mafia and organised supporter groups, which was one of the reasons why he rarely visited the Marakana these days. This week, though, he had an even bigger problem to contend with. A recent story had resulted in him being trolled in a highly coordinated attack on social media. Georgiev's story focused on a picture of Vučić's brother Andrej – described as the president's 'éminence grise'[28] – and Zvonko Veselinović, a businessman from northern Kosovo who had long been suspected of involvement in organised crime.[29] It was the second picture linking Veselinović and Andrej Vučić. Shortly afterwards a professionally produced video was released anonymously online, complete with doom-laden music, call-ing Georgiev a traitor and a foreign-paid mercenary hell-bent on giv-ing Kosovo away to the Albanians.

BIRN wasn't dependent on Serbian money for survival. One of its funders was Open Society, George Soros's anti-corruption and pro-rule of law NGO. Soros had become a hate figure for illiberal regimes across Eastern Europe. Just in case the subtext was missed, the video was interspersed with pictures of Albanian prime minister Edi Rama and his then counterpart in Kosovo Ramush Haradinaj. Haradinaj had been the Kosovo Liberation Army commander for western Kosovo during the war and had twice been cleared of war crimes by the ICTY.[30] He was a despised figure in Serbia, living proof of the double standards at The Hague that punished Serbs but not Croats or Albanians for their war crimes. Oliver Ivanović, a Kosovo Serb politician who had openly criticised the ruling party, had received much the same treatment as Georgiev shortly before he was shot dead in the city of Mitrovica in northern Kosovo.[31]

'I was lucky,' Georgiev said. 'At least they didn't air it on TV.' Still, he was used to the threats by now, not least for his work detailing how Vučić and his political party had long courted and exploited Serbian ultra groups for his own political ends. 'Vučić is the political wing of hooligans,' he said, 'like Sinn Féin-IRA.'

The president's love of football was well documented. He had bolstered his man-of-the-people brand by highlighting his obsession with the game, and his involvement in, or at least proximity too, the Delije in the late 1980s. No one is really sure if he *was* at that famous Maksimir game in 1990, but it's now part of his personal mythology. He was in a prime seat to witness the Delije change from being countercultural, anti-authoritarian punks into, as Georgiev called it, 'the guardians of national interest'. He was also in the government when the Delije turned against it during the October 5 revolution in 2000, and was well aware of the power the north stand had. Serbian football clubs were, effectively, funded and run by the state. The labyrinthine ownership structures were a hangover from the communist era, which meant they were dependent on the largesse of those in power. When Vučić became deputy prime minister in 2012 Zvezda was in poor shape. Between 2008 and 2013 Partizan had won six titles in a row and had made the group stages of the Champions League. 'Vučić came to power and one of the first things he did was take the power in the club,' explained Georgiev. And he brought with him Slaviša Kokeza.

Kokeza had enjoyed a rapid rise. Today he is the president of the
Football Association of Serbia, the FSS. But back in 2008 he first
appeared in public with a heavily bandaged head and arm as a prop in
a press conference with Vučić. Vučić was still general-secretary of the
Serbian Radical Party and Kokeza was wheeled out as proof of police
brutality when an SRS rally in Belgrade turned violent.[32] By 2012
Vučić was deputy prime minister, Kokeza was a loyal functionary in
his new SNS political party and was appointed vice-president of
Zvezda. Up until then there had been frequent moments of public
violence involving organised supporter groups. The most high-profile
incident was a 2012 European Championship qualifier between Italy
and Serbia which was called off after Serbia fans rioted. Ivan Bogdanov,
one of the leaders of Zvezda's Ultra Boys, climbed the fence and
burned an Albanian flag with a flare. Earlier, Serbia's goalkeeper, former Zvezda player Vladimir Stojković, had been attacked for daring to
now play for Partizan.

The takeover in 2012 meant a clean slate. The Delije, according
to Georgiev, were given a long rope to operate on, allowing the leaders
to procure government contracts or pursue their interests in the black
economy whilst avoiding jail, even when convicted of serious crimes.
'It's organised like an army,' said Georgiev of how the Delije were set
up. 'In a very short period of time they can organise ten thousand men
here in Belgrade. I call you, then you call five men, then these five
men called fifty other men ...' Almost every rank and file member of
the Delije I have spoken to was anti-Vučić, but there are seldom any
anti-Vučić chants from the north stand today. The season after Vučić's
election Zvezda won the title and – even though Zvezda was prevented
from participating in the Champions League thanks to a UEFA ban
because of vast debts and unpaid players' wages – Partizan's domi-
nance was broken. Ever since Kokeza has stressed that Vučić had no
role in Zvezda's revival, and that the two teams receive the same funding, but few believe him, not least Partizan's ultras, the Grobari (the
grave diggers).

Like Zvezda proudly calling themselves *cigani*, Partizan had been
taunted as the grave diggers due to their sombre black and white

shirts before appropriating the term in the 1970s. The heart of Partizan's ultras stood in the *Jug*, the south stand of the Partizan Stadium. The Grobari was made up of smaller groups, the most famous of which had been Alcatraz, led by Miloš Radosavljević, known as Kimi. Slobodan Georgiev may well now be a target for the ruling party and its friendly media, but far worse was to happen to Brankica Stanković, who edited the Serbian anti-corruption TV show *Insajder*, when she crossed the Grobari. Her series of investigations back in 2009 blew the lid on the links between politicians, organised crime and some of the biggest ultra groups in Serbia. The programme was a bombshell, detailing how the leaders of the groups had been allowed virtual immunity in their black-market activities in return for agreeing to act as muscle for a string of nationalist protests. City rivalries were put to one side, she alleged, when a mob was raised to attack the US embassy in 2008 after Kosovo unilaterally announced independence. The police had to give her 24-hour protection for years after an incident at the Partizan Stadium when Partizan Belgrade beat Shakhtar Donetsk 1–0 in the Europa League. In the south stand, members of Alcatraz had brought along a blow-up sex doll and chanted: 'You're like a snake, you'll follow Ćuruvija, Brankica the whore.' Slavko Ćuruvija was an editor who was assassinated in Belgrade in 1999 after falling out with Slobodan Milošević's wife Mira over his reporting of Kosovo. The doll was passed around the stand and then stabbed. Kimi was sentenced to six months in prison.[33]

Just like in Argentina and the *barras bravas*, Serbia's ultras were both feared and respected. Club officials would ensure that the leaders would get tickets, a cut of transfer fees and even gate receipts in return for a quiet life. When a political opponent needed to be dealt with, there was a network of highly organised men ready to do what was needed. 'It's a business,' said Georgiev. But everything would change in 2009 after the murder of Brice Taton, a Toulouse fan beaten to death in a Belgrade bar. It was an incident serious enough that it warranted a US diplomatic cable from Belgrade to Washington detailing the alleged links between supporter groups and organised crime.[34] Several leading figures were arrested, including Ljubomir

Marković, known as Kića and one of the leaders of Alcatraz. Marković went on the run but was eventually caught and jailed for 30 years.[35] His arrest left a space to be filled. And that space was filled by a group called the Janičari. The Janičari was the name of an Ottoman regiment made up of Balkan fighters, usually the first-born son of any family who, by Ottoman law, had to be handed over. The new ultras weren't like the rest. Aleksandar Stanković, known as Sale the Mute, emerged as the new *capo*. But he had an unthinkable backstory. He had been a Zvezda fan, and was now switching to Partizan. In Serbia, this was as heretical as converting from Christianity to Islam. The new group, according to Georgiev, had the backing of the authorities and split the Grobari. Alcatraz and the other ultra factions were forced out and moved to the west stand. There was, at times, all-out war between the different groups. For Georgiev, the takeover was planned.

'What happened when Vučić came to power? He knew that he's going to have problems with Grobari, because they don't like him,' he said. 'So when he came to power, it was like, you know, "Vučiću *pederu*, Vučiću *pederu*" all the time. Vučić: You are gay, you're gay.' The chant, although clearly homophobic, had gained some traction in wider anti-government protests, just like the Delije's chant inviting Milošević to top himself. Vučić wouldn't allow the same thing to happen to him.

A ten-minute walk down the road, on the terrace of a smart Belgrade cafe next to a busy road, Bojana Pavlović was searching YouTube for the CCTV video footage she wanted to show me. 'Here it is,' she said, before playing it for me. 'That is Sale, there.' The colour footage from outside Partizan's stadium shows three well-built men approaching Partizan's general director before viciously beating his security guard. At one point one of the men stamps continuously on the security guard's head as he lies semi-conscious on the floor. One of the three was Sale the Mute. 'This was actually the first time when the public heard of these guys,' said Pavlović, an investigative journalist for KRIK, another of Serbia's dwindling number of independent news

websites. 'You can see,' she said, pointing to Sale, who is clearly directing the attack. 'You can obviously see that he's an important person.'
It wasn't obvious enough for Vučić. When the video was released to
uproar in the Serbian media the three men were arrested, but Sale
was released. When asked why, Vučić said that the man hadn't thrown
a punch and angrily denounced the media for daring to tell the police
who they can and can't arrest.[36] Sale's luck in avoiding arrest didn't
surprise Pavlović. He was already walking free after being convicted
and sentenced to five years in jail for drug offences. The courts kept
delaying his sentence after a series of unlikely excuses, including the
fact that he suffered from a bad knee.

There were other connections between Sale and Belgrade's police.
The effective quashing of his sentence, Pavlović believes, was the
quid pro quo to install Sale on the south stand. After Alcatraz was
displaced, the anti-Vučić chants stopped, at least from the south
stand. There were other examples that both Pavlović and Georgiev
gave of how politicians had used ultras for their own ends. One example was Belgrade's Gay Pride march. The event often turned violent
thanks to nationalist and religious counter-protesters that included
hundreds of ultras. The protests were highly embarrassing for the previous government. But, as Pavlović pointed out to me, from 2015 there
has been no violence during Gay Pride at all. Once in power, Pavlović
believes, the anti-Gay Pride protests were stopped. 'You can see from
that they're actually controlled,' she said.

Opposition politicians had begun to smell a rat. 'It is obvious that
the hooligan groups, which under similar circumstances only a few
years ago smashed Belgrade, are in a kind of coordination with the
authorities or people close to the current government,' said Bojan
Pajtić, who in 2016 was the leader of the centre-left Democratic Party
(DS). 'If someone from the DS had signed the Brussels agreement
[that started dialogue between Serbia and Kosovo], they would have
probably been crucified on Terazije [a main street and square in central Belgrade] as a traitor.'[37]

Pavlović wasn't a football fan, but she was curious as to why there
had been a surge in 'executions' on Belgrade's streets. The official

explanation was a turf war with the Montenegrin mafia, who had a large slice of Europe's drug trade imported through its ports. Belgrade was on the well-worn 'Balkan route' for both drug mules and people smugglers. Whilst many of the dead did have connections to organised crime, almost all were also members of various ultra groups. 'In 2015, we decided to follow things that are happening on the streets: killings, assassinations, fights, gang fights,' said Pavlović.

But it was the murder of Sale the Mute that pricked Pavlovic's attention. More than a dozen people involved in the organised supporters' scene have been murdered in recent years. KRIK has tried to document each death with an updatable infographic. Five months after the CCTV footage, Sale the Mute joined KRIK's data set. 'He was killed in front of the prison,' she said. 'His prison guard was sent on holiday. So we said: "OK, this is a big thing. We're going to look at what's happening here."' His reign in charge of Partizan's south stand ended in a hail of bullets when two men opened fire with automatic weapons as he sat in his Audi A6. He was hit by more than 50 bullets and died instantly.[38] Sale the Mute was a minor character in Serbia's underworld, but his death provoked a furious reaction from the government. Interior Minister Nebojša Stefanović gave an emotional statement as the news broke. 'He declared a war on mafia after his assassination,' said Pavlović. 'So we realised, OK, this is an important person.' Georgiev was equally as incredulous. 'When he was killed it was like a member of the government was killed,' he said. 'Who was he? Why was he so important?'

Serbia was almost impossible to understand. There was layer upon layer of intrigue and conspiracy, connections between the powerful, the underworld and the terraces. Vučić's son was even spotted at the 2018 World Cup in Russia with four members of the Janičari, all wearing the same white T-shirts with a map of Kosovo and the words 'No Surrender'. When asked about it Vučić lamented the fact that the press chose to criticise his family. 'My son has never done anything wrong,' he said.[39] It was a dangerous job, investigating organised crime whilst at the same time dealing with a state that was critical of your reporting. 'I went to a trial. And what they do is they come to support their friends,' said Pavlović. Inside the courtroom she met Veljko Belivuk, the man who took over the Janičari after Sale's killing. 'So they start talking to me.'

'Are you ever gonna write something nice about us?' And I was like, how do you know who I am?

'You're the only one who comes.' He sits next to me, gives me a pat on the knee and he says ...

'Oh, no, you're good. Do you want to talk to us? You know, because we're not as bad as you think. I'm going to tell you everything. I'm going to explain everything to you. The things that you were writing, you know, some of them are true, but you know, mostly you missed it. We hate cops and we're not good with them. We don't like that you're saying that we're good with the state.'

Belivuk never did call.

After a long, cold winter, the 159th Belgrade derby restarted the Serbian SuperLiga in bright sunshine. It was a Saturday afternoon and a friend, Aleksandar, had warned me not to wear anything red, and just stick to wearing all black like everybody else. This time we didn't walk up Ljutice Bogdana. Instead, as we approached the Marakana we veered left past the lines of militarised police and hoped that we'd reach the entrance to the south stand before anyone noticed us. Going to the Marakana as an away fan meant hiding Aleksandar's allegiance until the last minute, as if we were smuggling in a dirty secret.

Once we were around the back, we were presented with a choice. Hundreds of police officers and security guards had effectively divided the south stand into four sections, one for each of the warring Grobari factions. Aleksandar led us in with the Partizanovci, an anti-Janičari group which was effectively a pro-Kimi continuity Alcatraz. In every Eternal Derby I had been to, the police presence was there to keep the Grobari and Delije apart. But the security in the south was there to keep the Grobari away from *each other*. Abuse was shouted across the fences that divided the tribune. Flares and bottles followed. There was as much hatred for each other as there was for the *cigani* opposite. And then it stopped, in the 36th minute, when Nemanja Nikolić gave Partizan the lead. Zvezda were miles ahead in the league but Partizan hadn't beaten Zvezda at their place in a decade. Suddenly the divisions didn't matter. There was hope as the divided ultras sensed an upset. They weren't shouting at each other, they were shouting at the opposition.

Going down the rabbit hole of Serbia's ultras took you into every dark vice and conspiracy, one that made you doubt whether a derby considered the most heated in the world was even real. It was easy to forget that, at its core, this was about city tribalism and a game of football. Across the pitch, in the north stand, the Delije unleashed a fearsome pyro show.

'There is silence in the north against Vučić,' Dule Nedeljković had told me in a rather downbeat manner. 'But I don't know what's happened. The whole people are against him. People are ashamed when he says he is a big fan of Red Star. We haven't had protest in the stands like with Sloba [Slobodan Milošević].' There had been signs of resistance within the Grobari against what Aleksandar called 'the Gypsy entryists'. The previous season the simmering tension exploded during one Eternal Derby at the Partizan Stadium as the factions within the Grobari moved against the Janičari. In a bizarre moment a group were arrested who turned out to be Torcida ultras from Hajduk Split, invited to Belgrade to help defend the *Jug*.[40] But nothing united the Grobari, the true Grobari, more than the chance of a victory against Zvezda. The unity lasted as long as they were in the lead. With a few minutes left Milan Pavkov, who had scored twice against Liverpool earlier in the season, bundled home what turned out to be the equaliser. The abuse and the missiles restarted as hundreds of flares were lit. The Partizanovci chanted 'Vučiću *pederu*' as they ripped their chairs from the bolts and held them up like sacrificial offerings to the gods.

6

Greece and Macedonia

THESSALONIKI, GREECE

THE TENS OF THOUSANDS OF PAOK THESSALONIKI FANS DRESSED IN black and white would not be moved; not for the police horses trying to corral some order from the chaos, not for the armed officers on the ground with shields who were ignored, and certainly not for the arrival of the opposition's team bus which initially could not push through the throng shrouded in smoke from flares that were lit on its arrival. But when a convoy of expensive, blacked-out SUVs arrived, the monochrome sea parted instantaneously.

Ivan Ignatyevich Savvidis may have been banned from PAOK's Toumba Stadium, but this was his club. He'd bought it six years earlier. The king had arrived and no one was going to stop him. 'He comes to the stadium every game, he bids farewell to the players and then he goes back. That must be very difficult,' said Aris, a young season-ticket holder wearing a black and white Juventus top ('They are brothers,' he explained) standing outside and watching the scene unfold. In a few minutes' time PAOK was about to play the second leg of a Champions League play-off against Benfica. An unexpected 1–1 draw, with an away goal in Portugal, gave PAOK real hope of reaching the group stages of the Champions League for the first time. It was, Aris felt, the perfect riposte to the end of the previous Greek league season, where PAOK finished second to AEK Athens. Although that was only a tiny part of the real story. The Greek Superleague was shrouded in chaos as ultras groups fought pitched battles and the super-rich owners of each club fanned the flames of conspiracy.

PAOK's story began as the most compelling often do, with a gun and a sense of injustice. In March 2018, 30,000 people had crammed into Toumba to watch PAOK play AEK Athens. The two were neck and neck at the top of the league, a league dominated by Olympiacos – owned by the billionaire shipping magnate Evangelos Marinakis. Marinakis, a huge man with a bushy under-beard who inherited his fortune from his father, had bankrolled Olympiacos to 19 of the past 21 championships. But not this year. This year the league was between two teams who had been on the fringes for decades. The atmosphere was guaranteed to be fiery. The noise in Toumba, as one ultra described later, 'was like an earthquake'. An earthquake was an apt description of what followed when, with the scores at 0–0, the referee denied PAOK an 89th-minute winner. The pitch was invaded by incredulous PAOK staff. In the middle, striding briskly on to the pitch, was a short, bespectacled man with a grey beard and the air of a kindly uncle: Ivan Savvidis, a Russian oligarch and political ally of Vladimir Putin who has come to dominate Thessaloniki's fragile economy in recent years.

He was, of course, wearing a gun.[1]

Not many people outside of Greece knew about Savvidis, a tobacco tycoon who arrived in northern Greece over a decade ago and later embarked on an asset-buying spree as the Greek economy was on its knees. But here he was, with a gun on his hip, trying to remonstrate with the referee. 'I have never seen in my life, not even on YouTube or somewhere, that someone comes inside [of the pitch] with a gun and with their bodyguards,' Iranian midfielder Masoud Shojaei, who was on the pitch for AEK at the time, would later tell me. The game was abandoned and the pictures went viral. The league was suspended. Eventually AEK was awarded the match. PAOK had a further three points deducted. The incident, effectively, cost PAOK their first title in 33 years. AEK Athens gleefully celebrated their first in 24 years. Savvidis was banned from football stadiums in Greece for three years.[2]

As strange as it sounded, and as shocking as the images of Savvidis striding on the pitch to remonstrate wth the referee whilst displaying a pistol was, no one in Greece seemed *that* surprised that something like this had happened. Over the past ten years the game has been brought to its knees by violence, accusations of corruption and match-fixing. The individual acts are too numerous to list in full, but take the incident in March 2007 when the league was suspended for four weeks after a vicious mass brawl between hundreds of supporters of Olympiacos and Panathinaikos left one person dead. It later emerged that dozens of those implicated in the violence were leading ultras as well as Olympiacos club officials.[3] In 2008, there was six weeks of anti-police rioting after a Panathinaikos fan was killed by two Greek police officers.[4] Or the images of AEK Athens' Original 21 ultras, renowned for its left-wing and anti-fascist views, throwing Molotov cocktails at Ajax supporters during a Champions League game (UEFA only banned AEK from European competition for one season, suspended for two years).[5] It wasn't just football either. Football clubs in Greece, like many countries in Europe and north Africa, were one part of a wider association of sports. The ultras turned up in just as big numbers with just as many flares at a basketball game or a handball match. The stabbing in March 2007 when Olympiacos and Panathinaikos fans clashed happened before a women's volleyball match. For the ultras, their support transcended football.

Then there was the 2011 match-fixing scandal. Dozens of officials were accused and investigated for their involvement. Marinakis was named as a suspect in both that and a further 2015 match fixing scandal. There were even a few convictions with sentences of up to seven years.[6] PAOK, and its Gate 4 ultras, had always seen themselves to be on the receiving end of a vast conspiracy directed from Athens by the likes of Marinakis. Conspiracies rule in Greek football. The perception was that every referee is bought. Every incident that discredits your team is a false flag. The perception is that every politician and owner is corrupt and up to their knees in filth. Savvidis was seen as the antidote; a wealthy man, an outsider, not dependent on state patronage – at least not Greek state patronage – and clean of the corruption that seemed to blight Greek football. When violence marred a cup semi-final match against Olympiacos in 2012, and almost led FIFA to suspend the Greek FA, Savvidis withdrew PAOK from the second game. 'Greek football is undergoing an acute crisis – the healthy parties are fighting against a well-organised corrupt system,' he later explained in a statement. 'Every day we are welcoming more supporters of clean football in our ranks.' Marinakis was eventually cleared three years later of forming a match-fixing ring, but is still awaiting the outcome of an investigation into accusations of drug trafficking relating to a ship that was found to have two tonnes of heroin on it. He has denied any involvement. He later said that 'the prosecution against me is a product of a plot and it has nothing to do with the truth'.[8]

The national team wasn't immune either. As Greece's economy collapsed due to the 2008 global financial crisis, support for the neo-fascist Golden Dawn party spiked. For years they had been nurturing support on Greek football terraces. From 2000 onwards they set up the Galazia Stratia, or Blue Army, neo-Nazi supporters group of the national team, whose members have been implicated in the some horrific crimes, including the murder of asylum seekers.[9] The economic crisis saw support for the Golden Dawn go from 0.3 per cent to 7 per cent of the vote in the 2015 election, although it has been estimated that amongst police officers that figure could be as high as 50 per cent.[10] Nothing seemed to change the violence or the political polarisation bordering on extremism. Not stadium bans, not arrests, not league suspensions, not points deductions, not the threat of electronic ticketing. Electronic ticketing in particular had been fought off at all costs. One of the most important founding principles of all ultra movements is anonymity in the crowd. *No Face, No Name.* Electronic ticketing would change that. But it was impossible to implement. Greek ultras and hooligans were, it seemed, too powerful and impossible to tame.

The 2017/18 season began with the big four – Olympiacos, Panathinaikos, AEK and PAOK – sanctioned for their fans' behaviour the previous season; a total of 17 games were to be played behind closed doors for various acts of fan violence. In fact, the infamous PAOK–AEK game wasn't supposed to be played in front of any fans either. The previous game at Toumba, against Olympiacos, didn't even start. The Olympiacos coach Oscar Garcia was hit in the face with a till roll thrown by a PAOK fan. The referee called the game off, but PAOK – as every team in Greece does – sensed a conspiracy. 'This is a shadow play, a strategy that Olympiacos started implementing even ahead of the game, fantasising about [incidents] in its friendly media,' PAOK spokesperson Kyriakos Kyriakos said after the game, even though the incident could clearly be seen on TV. 'Just this morning, they warned us that they would leave the pitch at the slightest incident.'[11]

The fans were banned from the next game against AEK. But, incredibly, a Greek judge lifted the ban on the Sunday morning of the game. The fans poured in to Toumba, the goal was disallowed and Savvidis suddenly became the most famous man in Greece, if not the world. The problem had got so bad that FIFA appointed an official to monitor violence in the Greek league and threatened to exclude Greece from football's international body if it couldn't clean up the mess. That potential sanction had been dubbed 'Grexit' by the Greek press. 'The Grexit that looked distant is no longer impossible,' said FIFA's Herbert Hubel. 'Greek football [has] reached the edge of the cliff.'[12]

But it was a hard problem to solve. Ever since the the late 1960s, when organised supporter groups began to be formed, Greek terraces have had strong political identities forged in the times of dictatorship.

At first the rivalries were based more on traditional working-class versus middle-class antagonisms, but later they became much more
overtly political. There's still a heated argument as to who formed the
first fan group. Gate 13, from Athens' giants Panathinaikos, named
after the numbered section of the crumbling Leoforos Alexandras
Stadium they would sit in has a strong claim. Like the Original 21
ultras from AEK Athens, they traditionally have a hard-left, even
anarchist identity, whilst the Gate 7 ultras from Olympiacos have a
more nationalist outlook.

PAOK claims and even older lineage for its supporters group,
with SF Bellos Neapoli starting life in 1963. Today, the main groups
cluster around Gate 4, which was always known for its anti-fascist
outlook. That has changed over time as Golden Dawn has become
bigger in Thessaloniki. Like in the wider world, the centre ground
had crumbled, with people finding certainties in the far left, the far
right and in ultra-nationalism. There was now a Gate 4a, where anti-fa
PAOK fans sat, and Gate 4b for the rest. Fighting between the
two was not uncommon. After the end of Greece's military dictatorship in 1974, the number of supporter groups exploded, as did the
interest in them from some of the richest families in the country.
Choreography was less common than in Italy – except for at
Panathinaikos, the undisputed kings of Greek tifo – but pyro was
enthusiastically adopted. Almost all of those relationships turned
sour as the ultras' anti-establishment ethos rubbed up against the
greed of the Greek super-rich. But when Ivan Savvidis arrived in
northern Greece, and decided to buy PAOK in 2012, he was viewed
differently by PAOK fans. For one, he was an outsider, without the
baggage of Greek corruption. Although no one could answer why he
was there. 'He was not a guy that looked like he had bought a football team,' said Antonis Repanas, a former sports reporter in
Thessaloniki who covered Savvidis's arrival at PAOK. 'He looked
more like a guy who was going to create, in my opinion, a political
party.'

The city of Thessaloniki is by far the biggest in the region of
Greek Macedonia. It had long resented the capital, believing that

Athens got preferential treatment – economically, politically and cul-
turally – feelings that became especially acute after the 2008 financial crash. 'We usually say that PAOK is the only form of aggression
against the state which is Athenian-centred, so it [supporting PAOK]
does have some political weight,' explained Aris, the PAOK ultra.
Savvidis tapped into that and became a hero in Thessaloniki, and not
just because of the gun. He had invested millions of euros into a city.
He wasn't just getting a club. He was also acquiring an army of disaf-
fected Greek Macedonians desperate for a saviour. But still the question persisted. Why did Savvidis decide to come to Thessaloniki?
And why buy PAOK? One possible answer would emerge a few
months later. An investigation was released detailing how Russian
businessmen, with ties to the Kremlin, were allegedly funnelling
money into the hands of nationalist groups, especially football ultras,
in the neighbouring former Yugoslav Republic of Macedonia. The
money, allegedly, was a bid to thwart a referendum over whether
the country should change its name, end a long-standing dispute
with Greece and unlock membership to NATO and the EU. Far from
being PAOK's saviour, welcomed by the Gate 4 in spite of their long
history against the establishment, was Ivan Savvidis, in fact, working
for the Kremlin?

Ivan Savvidis was born into a poor Pontic Greek family in rural
Georgia in 1959, when it was part of the Soviet Union. The Pontic
Greeks had historically come from the southern shores of the Black
Sea, today in northern Turkey. They fled during the huge population
exchanges and massacres that Orthodox Christians faced during the
end of the Ottoman era and many found themselves in what would
become the Soviet Union, where Savvidis was born.[13]
    PAOK, the Greek club he would go on to buy, also has a refugee
history. It was formed in 1926 from recently arrived refugees from
Constantinople, now İstanbul. Savvidis left home at 15 and moved to
Rostov-on-Don, where he got a lowly job at the state-owned tobacco
company. The details are hazy about what he did next, but after the
Soviet Union disintegrated, he spent time in Greece before coming

back to become the general director when the tobacco factory was privatised. Donskoy Tabak became one of the biggest players in the Russian tobacco market. From there, Savvidis diversified, setting up Agrokom in 2004, which provided a home for his myriad assets, including Donskoy Tabak and 'the biggest cooked pork meat factory in South Russia'.[14] He also loved football and was president briefly of Russian team FC Rostov and then their smaller city rivals SKA Rostov.

Around the same time, Savvidis began his political career. In 2003 he entered Russia's Duma as a member of United Russia, the country's ruling party and long-time political home of Putin (although Putin chose to run as an independent in Russia's flawed 2018 presidential elections). He served until 2012. By then he had turned his attention to Greece, his ancestral homeland, and especially the northern region of Macedonia. Its biggest city, Thessaloniki, is also strategically important. The port is Greece's gateway to the Balkans, and the economic crisis presented an opportunity. Savvidis, after aligning himself with the left-wing government of Greek prime minister Alexis Tsipras and his SYRIZA party, went on a spending spree to purchase a whole range of assets at a knockdown price. He was part of a consortium that bought Thessaloniki's port, a key strategic asset for NATO (of which Greece is a member). Newspapers, a TV channel, tobacco companies, vast tracks of real estate and beach fronts, a water-bottling plant, not to mention hotels and other business have all been purchased by Savvidis.[15] In 2018 he sold Donskoy Tabak, as well as his Greek tobacco holdings, for $1.6 billion to Japan Tobacco, becoming Russia's latest billionaire.[16] He had come to dominate Thessaloniki's economy. But it was the 2012 acquisition of PAOK that transformed him into a local hero. He does not speak fluent Greek, but that hasn't stopped him building strong political links with the SYRIZA party, nor with Tsipras. 'He is creating power in northern Greece, amongst the Pontus and the fans of PAOK,' Repanas told me.

On the day of the Benfica match the city was covered in black and white. Many Greek Macedonians viewed Savvidis as a man who had done more for the city and region than their own government had over the past decade. 'In Thessaloniki he's very popular. He [created] a lot of jobs for the people,' said Todoros, a PAOK season-ticket holder who owned a restaurant in the centre of the city. The club held an important place in the region, as both the gatekeeper and the most visible sign of Greek Macedonian identity. Since 1991 Greece has been in a diplomatic dispute with its northern neighbour, the former Yugoslav Republic of Macedonia, over its name. The Greeks view the use of the name 'Macedonia' as an unconscionable appropriation of Greek history and, potentially, Greek territory. A fudge was agreed to allow the country to be called FYROM internationally, but a Greek veto at NATO and the EU had frozen the country's ambition to join either institution.

Under the previous Macedonian prime minster Nikola Gruevski, those antagonisms were deepened in part due to a beautification project of the capital – Skopje 2014 – that built huge monuments which Greece saw as appropriating their history.[17] The airport outside Skopje was even named after Alexander the Great, a beloved symbol of Greek, and Greek Macedonian, history. But Gruevski, and his VMRO-DPMNE party, was eventually removed from power following a wire-tapping scandal. Zoran Zaev, leader of the left-wing SDSM party, was elected prime minister in 2017, vowing to end the impasse and Macedonia's international isolation.[18] Earlier in 2018 Tsipras and Zaev met to thrash out the so-called Prespa Agreement, which would see Greek drop its objections in return for the country changing its name to the Republic of North Macedonia. The airport would also change its name. The move sparked violent protests in both Skopje and especially Thessaloniki.[19]

'All the people from northern Macedonia were involved and since PAOK is the greatest club in northern Macedonia the fans of PAOK were involved,' explained Aris the ultra. He too had protested. 'It is not a very political reaction. It is coming from inside us. We feel that it is unfair so we had to protest. Not as PAOK fans, but as Macedonians. As Greek Macedonians.' Like almost everyone else I spoke to in Thessaloniki, he didn't have a bad word to say about Savvidis. 'Of course he's loved, he deserves to be.'

Yet the protests caused a diplomatic stir in Greece and Macedonia. The Greek government expelled two Russian diplomats over alleged meddling in Greece's internal affairs, thought to be related to the name-change referendum.[20] Which is where Savvidis returns. Whilst his battles with the Greek footballing establishment were winning over fans in Thessaloniki, elsewhere questions were being asked about the reasons for his vast investments in the region, especially key NATO assets like the port, which seemed to correlate with the Kremlin's wider geo-political interests of thwarting NATO expansion. A few months after the gun incident, a report from the Organized Crime and Corruption Reporting Project (OCCRP), an international anti-corruption organisation, claimed that Savvidis had allegedly sent €300,000 in cash over the border and into the hands of nationalist groups in the former Yugoslav republic, especially the Komiti, a group of ultras connected to FK Vardar of Skopje, one of Macedonia's top teams. The aim, according to what OCCRP call 'interior ministry documents', was to spark protests and stir opposition to the name-change referendum.[21] FK Vardar is owned by another Russian tycoon, Sergei Solomenko, who also comes from Rostov, where Savvidis grew his power and wealth. The allegations brought a furious response from the Macedonian government. Zoran Zaev claimed that there was evidence that Greek businessmen 'sympathetic to the Russian cause' of preventing NATO expansion had paid money to Macedonians to 'commit acts of violence'.[22] Sure enough, the day after the Macedonia name-change agreement was made, the Komiti announced protests on its Facebook site.

Respected citizens of the republic of Macedonia, in these difficult moments for our homeland Macedonia, which is fiercely attacked by traitors and foreign aggressors, who by force and genocidal methods want to change us; identity, nation, language, history. We ask you to leave your party cards, each other's problems, forget the differences between you. We call for you to defend Macedonia. Gather your parents, brothers, sisters, relatives, friends. Come today in front of the assembly of the republic of Macedonia. Let's show that the ideals of freedom still live in our hearts.

Nearly 2,000 protestors turned up. A Molotov cocktail was thrown after they tried unsuccessfully to storm the parliament; 25 people were arrested.[23] Protests had also taken place in Thessaloniki. In June, thousands gathered at the International Fair where the SYRIZA party was holding a local meeting. PAOK ultras arrived in big numbers and several dozen managed to knock down the front door and protest inside. The police had to use batons and tear gas to retain control.

'The incidents which occurred in connection with the SYRIZA activities in Thessaloniki reflect the opinions of neither the Thessaloniki citizens, nor any other democratic citizen, nor any sensible fan club,' the party wrote in a statement after the incident. 'We expect the PAOK football club to condemn these actions, which are committed on behalf of the historical club PAOK association.' When Tsipras returned to Thessaloniki a few months later for an international expo, he announced that the government would donate state land for the building of PAOK's new stadium. More than 16,000 people, mainly PAOK fans, turned up to protest anyway.

Savvidis's Greek holding company released a statement denouncing the OCCRP investigation, and denied that he was in any way connected to the rash of anti-referendum protests involving ultra groups, calling the report 'totally false and highly slanderous'. The Macedonian government themselves seemed to back away from their early rhetoric too. When I called a Macedonian government spokesperson he declined to answer any direct questions on the affair and would only say that 'we have nothing to add on the matter'. A later statement said that Macedonia 'will continue to develop good bilateral relations with the Russian Federation' and it was 'aware of Russia's positions, it is well known that Russia has no problem with the integration of our entire region into the European Union, but we also know that they disagree with our NATO membership'. Cryptically, it also added: 'We know that some Russian actors have had some influence in other countries in the region before they become NATO members,' seemingly referring to the alleged Russian-backed coup plot in Montenegro shortly before it joined NATO. 'We are careful and we follow the developments.'

Back at Toumba, Savvidis pulled his slight frame out of his blacked-out SUV, stood at the entrance of the stadium and waved before climbing back in. The convoy sped away, past the police and into the distance.

Do you believe that Savvidis bought the club for the love of the team? I asked Aris.

'It depends on how you choose to see things,' he replied, suggesting I was being overly cynical. 'Maybe it is for the greater good. He is a businessman that wants to do well, and he employs people. I really believe he is a PAOK supporter.' In a country where the ultras had largely rejected and fought against the authorities, whether it was the police or the super-rich families that had bought and sold their clubs, Savvidis had managed to do something seemingly impossible: win over a group of ultras, indeed, an entire city, that was arguably the most suspicious when it came to outsiders, their money and their intentions towards them.

Once Savvidis had left Toumba, the stadium filled to bursting for the Champions League play-off. Before kick-off, a huge banner was displayed along one stand, in English. It read: 'Macedonia Is One and Only and It's Here'. Under a tremendous barrage of noise, PAOK took an early lead, giving the crowd hope. There was no 'ring of fire' this time – a now-infamous display by the ultras that saw them light pyro 360 degrees around Toumba – as the club had begged the ultras not to bring any flares. UEFA's strict rules against the use of pyro would lead to a stadium ban at the very least. But, soon enough, Benfica stormed back and ran away with the game, winning 4–1. There would be no earthquake in Thessaloniki that night, as the stadium emptied quietly and sullenly. Aris was sanguine in defeat. 'We go home,' he shrugged, 'and we continue to struggle.'

SKOPJE, FORMER YUGOSLAV REPUBLIC OF MACEDONIA

A FEW WEEKS AFTER THE game in Thessaloniki I headed north into
the former Yugoslav Republic of Macedonia and made contact with
the Komiti, the ultra group of FK Vardar that had been named in the
OCCRP investigation. The OCCRP claimed that Ivan Savvidis had
sent cash to them, and other nationalist groups, to incite protests. At
first the Komiti agreed to meet. Then something spooked them and
the meeting was off. But, out of the blue, a message arrived telling me
to be here in ten minutes, an abandoned shop, where Kiril hoped to
open a casino in a few weeks' time.

> We have some information that the questions will be political.
> We are ultras and Macedonian patriots. If you want you could
> send questions and I will respond.

'I agree to meet you because I said I would, and I am a man of my
word,' he said. Kiril was a short, powerfully built man and an intense
way of leaning his head in towards you as he spoke. But he was eager
to show that his word was his bond. 'In this business,' he said, referring to gambling, 'that is important. You might not be able to pay, I
will take your word. I don't, you take mine.' I didn't want to ever owe
Kiril money, but he was friendly. He explained that the state of his
casino was so bad – it did indeed look like a recently vacated squat –
that he probably wouldn't make it to that weekend's clash between FK
Vardar and Skopje rivals Rabotnički in the vast Philip II Stadium,
named after Alexander the Great's father. He had too much to do.
'Over here,' Kiril said, moving his short muscular frame over to a dais
that ran along one side of the room, 'this is where I will have a Texas
hold 'em table.' He strode to the other side, next to patch of stained,
ripped carpet. 'Slots.' Next to the door, that would be where the rou-
lette wheel would be. 'There is too much to do,' he said, rubbing his
hand over his shaved head. 'Too much.' Even though he was busy, he
did have one thing to say: 'I am a patriot.'

This wasn't a surprise. Ultras in Macedonia had long been intensely political, largely based on ethnic and religious lines. A quarter of the population is ethnically Albanian, although no one is sure given that the exact ethnic composition of the country is a politically explosive issue. There hasn't been a census since 2002. The last of the Yugoslav Wars was fought here, in 2001, between ethnic Albanians and Orthodox Christian Macedonians. Kiril's Komiti was unashamedly Macedonian, Christian and nationalist. It had also been connected to the government of the previous right-wing, nationalist government. Far from being an anti-establishment force in Macedonia – like ultras were in Greece and elsewhere around the world – the Komiti had been part of it. 'I don't agree with this, this 1312, this ACAB,' he said when I asked how the Komiti fits in with the ultras' popular anti-police ethos.

'Ultra is a special subculture, a special way of life in the stands and outside of it. Ultras implies belonging to a special psychology,' he would later say. 'But the police. They are my people. They are working people, like us. I am not against the police.'

Kiril was clear about opposing the name-change referendum; he saw the proposed name change as 'national treason' – an assault on Macedonian dignity. The group, which numbers between 2,000 and 4,000 depending on the game, had attended protests alongside other ultra groups, but only because they believed that the referendum was 'suicide' for Macedonia. He denied that the Komiti had taken any money from Savvidis or any foreign businessman for that matter.

Yet ultras being involved in political activity was nothing new in Macedonia, nor the rest of the Balkans. Nationalism had found a fertile home on Yugoslavia's football terraces. Red Star Belgrade had the Delije, Dinamo Zagreb the Bad Blue Boys, Partizan had the Grobari, Hajduk Split the Torcida. And Vardar had its Komiti.

Kiril explained how, in 1986, FK Vardar became the champions of the former Yugoslavia for the first time. With Darko Pančev up front – who would go on to score the goals that brought Red Star Belgrade the 1991 European Cup – FK Vardar became, briefly, the best team in Yugoslavia. But there was something deeper to that victory, 'an additional motivation', as Kiril put it, was 'the democratisation of the country', based on 'Macedonian patriotism, Christian ideology and the pronounced anti-communism among the founders of the group, who were guys from urban Skopje.' The name, he explained, came from a shortened version of the Turkish word *komitadji*, a term used during Ottoman rule for indigenous insurgent groups in the Balkans. After the Janičari, Hajduk and the Delije, it was the fourth word with Turkish roots I had heard used to name a nationalist ultra group in the Balkans.

Like Arkan with the Delije in Serbia, the Komiti also had its connections to the Yugoslav Wars. Its leader at the time was Johan Tarčulovski, who became the bodyguard for the Macedonian president and then joined a police tactical squad called the Special Operations Unit. Modelling himself on Arkan, the unit was nicknamed the Tigers. When fighting broke out between ethnic Albanian and Orthodox Christian Macedonians, Tarčulovski's unit gained a bloodthirsty reputation. On 12 August 2001, when a Macedonian army unit was attacked, killing several soldiers, Tarčulovski ordered that the nearby ethnically Albanian village of Ljuboten be attacked. Three people were murdered. Tarčulovski was charged with war crimes and brought to The Hague. On 10 July 2008 he was found guilty by the ICTY of 'ordering, planning and instigating the murder or three ethnic Albanian civilians in the village of Ljuboten' and 'of wanton destruction of twelve houses or other property and cruel treatment of thirteen ethnic Albanian civilians'. He was sentenced to 12 years in prison.[24] When he was released in 2013, he returned home to a hero's welcome. It was also revealed that his wife had been paid a €5,000 per month stipend for the entire time he had been in jail, a crazy sum compared to Macedonia's average wage.[25] He remains the only Macedonian found guilty of war crimes from the Yugoslav Wars, but that didn't hurt his political career and he was elected an MP for VRMO-DPMNE. When it was revealed that Macedonia's then prime minister Nikola Gruevski had ordered his political opponents to be wire-tapped, and the government eventually collapsed, a group of protestors attacked the parliament when Zoran Zaev was about to be sworn in. Zaev left with blood on his face and a cut to his forehead, but he assumed power. Tarčulovski was one of the MPs charged with helping the protesters to storm the building.[26]

Today, the biggest rivalries in Macedonia were based on ethnicity. 'FK Sloga,' answered Kiril when I asked which team Vardar shared its biggest rivalry with, using the old Yugoslav name for FK Shkupi. 'We basically do not consider [them] as ultras but rather a set of criminals and drug traffickers and fundamentalists under the protection of their political party DUI formed by former terrorists that protect them through their installed representatives in the police [and] judiciary.' It was a very clear answer.

The next day, at a smart cafe in a quiet, gentrified suburb of Skopje, Artan Grubi arrived dressed in an expensive shirt and jeans. 'It has been a while since anyone asked me about any of this,' he said as he sat down, looking a bit sheepish. Indeed, most people now saw a very different Artan Grubi. He was an MP in Macedonia's parliament who was also chief of staff for Ali Ahmeti, leader of the Democratic Union for Integration. The DUI is a party that represents the interests of Macedonia's ethic Albanian population and they were the current king makers in the parliament, as voters were evenly split between the right-wing, nationalist VMRO and the left-wing SDSM. In fact, it was the DUI switching sides that put Zoran Zaev into power, setting Macedonia on the path towards the name agreement with Greece.

But Grubi earned his political stripes elsewhere, on the football terraces. He was, in 1989, the founder of the Shvercerat, or 'the smugglers', an Albanian ultras group of FK Shkupi. 'The ultras make up a big interest group for political parties, they make up a constituency that every political party would like to have,' Grubi explained. 'They are well organised. They keep together. Function like a group, like an army. They are the engine of a political party in a protest movement.'

Ultra groups, Grubi believed, had become an important political constituency for everyone in Macedonia and across the former Yugoslavia. 'All of the political parties flirt with the groups,' he said. The *quid pro quo* would be, he added, help for transport to get to international matches, or to buy pyro. 'Also, when they cause trouble, they have protection from the police,' he added. That political connection became stronger under VMRO, with nationalist ultra groups being called into action against perceived opponents of the government,[27] whether to break up protests by Albanian groups, or to break up any LGBT events, as happened at the 2012 'March for Tolerance', which was attacked by masked ultras, injuring dozens.[28] The offices of the human rights group the Helsinki Committee was also attacked. 'It is a pre-nup agreement, a marriage agreement,' Grubi explained. 'They [ultras] get what they want. The politicians get what they want. And this is why they are in bed with one another.'

Grubi grew up in Čair, a district of Skopje with narrow cobbled streets that used to be the centre of the city under Ottoman rule. His father and brother played for the club. Grubi played too, as a goal-keeper, but he realised his skills were better suited for the terraces. 'It was the thing to do in the 1980s. Tito died, the groups started popping up. A wave was coming from England, primarily with the fashion,' he said when I asked why he set up the Shvercerat in the first place. 'It was a rebel voice against the establishment. We were seeing the conscription of soldiers who didn't really want to go. People started protesting. We started being a lot more aware of our ethnicity, much more aware we were different from one another, and in this sense we all found we could express our anger, our dissatisfaction.'

The terraces became an outlet for dissent. Incidents that took place the previous week, whether the arrest of a dissident or the racist beating of a prominent Albanian activist, would be the topic of that weekend's chants: short-lived political folk songs that would die soon after coming to life. 'You would express what you couldn't do at school. What you couldn't do in the family. What you couldn't do in public,' Grubi said.

Banners were made with anti-establishment slogans. As Čair was a poor district they were usually made, Grubi said, with stolen paint and cloth. 'It was always seen as the voice of anger. An incident would have happened that day, that week. And that would be the topic of the songs on the terraces.'

When Vardar and Shkupi played, the tension between the communities would play out on the terraces. And there was always violence. 'It was almost nationalistic, almost racist. Bad. On both sides,' he said, recalling one Komiti banner that said, 'Allah Is Gay'. 'That was 1994, '95. Imagine the reaction on the other side. "A Dead Albanian is a Good Albanian"; "Gas Chambers for the Albanians". Every song was related to the Albanians.'

By a quirk of fate, the leader of the Komiti, Johan Tarčulovski, also grew up in Čair. The two had known each other and became rivals, first as ultras leaders and then MPs. The two used to talk but the war in 2001 ended that. 'He was from the community and knew people. But then the hatred he had towards my community was shown in 2001 when he participated in the murder of innocent villagers and that is why he was sentenced by the war crimes tribunal,' said Grubi. 'How do you speak to someone like that?' Grubi's Shvercerat had often been the driving force of protests in favour of NATO involvement during the Kosovo War, or in solidarity with the Kosovo Liberation Army. In one famous incident from 2011, Grubi had helped arrange a protest against the building of an Orthodox church inside the city's fort, which they believed was an attempt by the then conservative government to rewrite the country's Albanian history. Grubi pulled up a YouTube video on his phone and played it. 'I'm pretty sure you'll find it anyway,' he sighed. The video starts off shaky. It's a cold, overcast day at the city's fort. The scaffolding of a half-built Orthodox church can be seen in the background and police lines on either side. Suddenly, one side breaks and groups of men charge at each other over an open field; on one side the Shvercerat, the other the Komiti. 'There, that's me!' he said, as a younger version of Grubi came into view. He threw a punch as someone attacked him but then appeared to get hit in the head with a rock. Grubi and 60 others were arrested and he was given a six-month suspended sentence. It was then that he decided that his time with the Shvercerat had come to an end. 'After 2011, I joined the party,' he said.

The reports that money had been funnelled from Ivan Savvidis to the Komiti did not surprise Grubi. Football, the terraces and political interests were intimately linked in the Balkans. He was in no doubt that VMRO and pro-Russian actors outside Macedonia were connected to other ultra groups. 'I am confident of that,' he said. 'I strongly believe that the Komiti is against the [Prespa] agreement, against the referendum, against the change of the name.' It was time for Grubi to go. As if to prove just how linked football and politics is in Macedonia, he had to get to FK Shkupi's next home game later that day. He was to give a speech in front of the fans, from the centre circle, before kick-off, to urge the Albanian community to vote in the referendum and agree the name change.

'Today at the match I'll be recalling to them that we are the first ones to organise tens of thousands of people to come out and protest in support of NATO,' he said. 'And now our time is to deliver on that.'

On the other side of the city, at a near empty Philip II Stadium, FK Vardar beat Rabotnički 2–0. The only noise came from the block of Komiti members, numbering a few hundred. Kiril was, of course, tied up with his new casino. But in his absence the Komiti, like PAOK's fans, had their own banner: 'The Name Is Our Identity'. The two groups, on either side of a nationalist divide, were unlikely allies against the referendum, but from diametrically opposed positions. *The enemy of my enemy is my friend.*

'We only want to be our on our own land,' Kiril later wrote to me. 'As the nineteenth-century British prime minister, William Ewart Gladstone, says, if Greece is of Greeks, Serbia is of the Serbs, Bulgaria of Bulgarians, why should it not be Macedonia to the Macedonians?'

A few weeks later the referendum vote passed peacefully, with 94 per cent of voters voting for the name change. But the opposition VMRO party instituted a boycott, meaning that the referendum only had a 36 per cent turnout, when 50 per cent was needed to approve it. It was something of a victory for those who opposed the name-change referendum, in Greece and in Macedonia. The question was whether Zaev's government would recognise the result, or carry on regardless.

Meanwhile, on the same day as the referendum vote, 700km southeast in Athens, PAOK beat Olympiacos 1–0 in a haze of flares and smoke to go top of the Greek Superleague. It had been a very good weekend for Ivan Savvidis.

7

Albania and Kosovo

DUBROVNIK, CROATIA

IT WAS AN EARLY SUNDAY MORNING IN DUBROVNIK AND THE CROATIAN port city hadn't yet filled its streets with the thousands upon thousands of tourists who now came here to pretend they were, in fact, in another city: King's Landing, the home of the Iron Throne in the HBO TV series *Game of Thrones*, which was filmed here. It seemed that Ana and I were the only people awake.

As we waited for Dubrovnik's only prison to open to visitors, Ana offered me some bread before she told me her story. Her 25-year-old son was here, on remand. 'He likes to drink and smoke grass,' she said, chewing awkwardly on her roll. One night, according to Ana, he got drunk. A house got burned down. She couldn't afford the lawyer's fees and she was expecting her son to be sentenced to three years in jail. So, every Sunday, Ana walked up the hill to hand over 50 euros she couldn't afford to her son so that he could buy food and cigarettes. 'He's young and gets crazy with his friends,' she said, holding back tears as a prison guard unlocked the large blue gate, slid it across, and invited us inside.

A few weeks previously I had received a message from a Croatian lawyer. His client, an Albanian citizen, had been jailed here for illegally crossing the Croatia–Montenegro border and was on the verge of being deported to Serbia where he faced a ten-year prison sentence. He feared for his life. His name was Ismail Morina and I had interviewed him before. Almost everyone in the Balkans had heard of him. Or, at the very least, if they didn't know his name, they knew what he did.

On 14 October 2014, Serbia hosted Albania in a Euro 2016 qualification match. The Partizan Stadium in the Serbian capital of Belgrade had been filled two hours before kick-off for what was a rare meeting between the two nations. They had not played each other since the 1960s. And for good reason. There was a long history of wars, massacres, counter-massacres and historic slights between them. But it was the 1999 Kosovo War that had defined their modern enmity. After Croatia and Slovenia had broken away, after the war that followed, after the evisceration of Bosnia, after Vukovar, Srebrenica and Operation Storm, and eventually after the 1995 Dayton Accords, an uneasy peace of new–old nations was agreed. But not for Kosovo. As I had seen with the Delije in Belgrade, Kosovo was a hugely emotive issue. For nationalists and the Serbian Orthodox Church, it was the cradle of their civilisation, but Slobodan Milošević had so successfully weaponised Kosovo and Serbian grievances over it in the mid-1980s that almost everyone, liberal or nationalist, had strong views that Kosovo was part of Serbia. Arms and men flowed from Albania into Kosovo via its porous border as the Kosovo Liberation Army fought the Serb-dominated Yugoslav Army. Thousands of lives were lost and the war brought NATO bombs to Belgrade before an uneasy peace was agreed. Kosovo unilaterally announced its independence in 2008 but it was neither truly independent nor, in reality, part of Serbia any more. It is difficult to describe the anger felt in Serbia to this day over NATO's bombing and Kosovo's independence, mirrored only by the equally unanimous gratitude felt by Kosovar Albanians for the West's intervention. There is little middle ground. At the Partizan Stadium, the humiliations forced on Serbia were being aired towards the Albanian team, the majority of whom were born in Kosovo. The match was deemed the highest risk by UEFA, meaning that away fans were banned. The only Albanians allowed into the stadium, officially, were the players, the coaching staff and a handful of VIPS, including the brother of Albanian prime minister Edi Rama and, I would later discover, Macedonian MP Artan Grubi.

'Ubi, ubi, ubi, Šiptar!'

'Kill, kill, kill [the] Albanians!' the crowd shouted.

As the first half progressed, it was Albania that had the best chances. The chants grew in volume. Objects were thrown on the pitch. Martin Atkinson, the English referee in charge of the match, had already halted the game twice because of the flares and missiles. Then, in the 42nd minute, and with the score at 0–0, an unfamiliar object appeared in the sky. Its humming could barely be heard above the noise. At first, no one knew what they were seeing. Then the chanting ceased.

Silence.

A quadcopter drone was gliding serenely down over the pitch.[1] Underneath, it was carrying a red and black flag. On it was the word 'Autochthonous' – derived from the ancient Greek word that means 'native' – and the faces of two Albanian nationalist heroes. On the left was Ismail Qemali, Albania's first prime minister, whose face also adorns the 500-lek note. On the right, Isa Boletini, a guerilla fighter and nationalist hero who led the Albanian revolt against Ottoman rule in 1912. The date at the top of the flag – 28/11/1912 – referred to the signing of the Albanian declaration of independence. The men were two very different figures who were crucial to the birth of the modern Albanian state. They died three years apart; Qemali in 1919 whilst in exile in Europe, Boletini in Podgorica in 1916 fighting Montenegrin and Serbia forces. But the truly controversial image was in the centre. A map of Greater Albania, one nation, uniting ethnic Albanians in the Balkans. It's a nationalist conceit that incorporates Kosovo and territory from eastern Montenegro, southern Serbia, half of Macedonia and a large chunk of north-western Greece. In the middle was the black double-headed eagle found on the Albanian flag.

The silence was temporary, like at the eye of a passing tornado. When Serbia defender Stefan Mitrović grabbed the flag and pulled the drone down, the Albanian players pounced, pre-empting what they thought would be an act of disrespect (Mitrović would later say he had no intention of doing anything other than handing the flag back to the Albanian players). A brawl erupted over the flag and the stadium exploded back into life.

'It was out of control, I was really scared for my players,' said Albania's captain Lorik Cana when I spoke to him a few months later. Cana had been born in Kosovo and fled the Yugoslav Wars for Switzerland as a child. As the Albanian players ran for the safety of the tunnel, several fans managed to get on to the pitch, throwing punches and plastic chairs. One was Ivan Bogdanov, one of the leading members of the Ultra Boys, one of the Delije's sub-groups.[2] It was only the quick thinking of the Serbian players that prevented serious injury. '[Aleksander] Kolarov and [Serbian captain Branislav] Ivanović really protected us,' said Cana. 'Without them we were in big trouble.' The match was abandoned. Eventually UEFA would award the three points to Albania and deduct a further three points off Serbia, effectively ending their chances of qualification.[3]

In the sanctuary of the dressing room the Albanian players treated their wounds – cuts and bruises, but nothing more serious – before the Serbian police burst in and searched the players' bags. They were looking for the drone's remote control. 'They thought one of us did this with the drone, which was ridiculous!' Cana said incredulously. When one wasn't found the blame centred on the Albanian delegation and the prime minister's brother. The Serbian authorities claimed the drone was the 'scenario of a terrorist action planned in advance'. But nothing was found on him either. There was no trace of the remote control or the pilot.

The drone's remote control was indeed nearby, but the police never found it. It lay on the stone floor of a Serb Orthodox church, dedicated to Archangel Gabriel, across Humska Street next to the stadium. As the police tore the dressing room apart looking for it, the real culprit lay in silence under a parked car near the church. When the coast was clear Ismail Morina climbed out and moved through the shadows of Belgrade's back streets, making his escape in a waiting car. It took a few months for the truth to come out, but far from being an Albanian or NATO conspiracy (as had been wildly speculated in Serbia's sclerotic tabloid press and on social media), the real pilot of the drone was in fact a slightly built crane operator with a an oversized mop of curly black hair who lived and worked in Milan. He was also a famed ultra from the Tifozat Kuq e Zi, or the Red and Black Fans– a confederation of ethnic-Albanian ultra and supporter groups from across the Balkans, as well as individual fans of Albanian ancestry from around the world – who supported the Albanian national team over land and sea. He went by the name of 'Ballist'; named after the Balli Kombëtar, an Albanian nationalist force that collaborated with the Nazis during the Second World War. Morina was hailed as a hero for his act of trolling, but it unleashed a furious response from Serbian politicians. That, in part, had led him to be imprisoned here after the Serbian government issued an Interpol Red Notice, requiring any government that came across Morina to arrest him immediately.

A bald prison officer barked at me to put everything from my pockets into a box, before taking me and Ana into a single room, divided by thick reinforced glass. There was a single long bench on either side and no dividers or individual phones. A few posters covered the walls on the visitors' side; a picture from Angry Birds and another cartoon that instructed how children of different ages should behave in the room. It took a few moments before I recognised that Morina, dressed in T-shirt and jeans, was sitting opposite me. It was over a year since I had seen him last. He was unrecognisable. His distinctive hair, a kind of unruly proto-afro, had been cut off, his beard shaved. He'd lost a lot of weight, despite already being

whippet-thin. He looked simultaneously ten years younger and terminally sick.

'The guards treat me well but I am not worried in here,' he said. I
couldn't hear him at first. I stood and pressed my right ear to the three
holes in the glass. 'I'm worried about what happens when I leave,' said
Ismail. 'They say I am a terrorist. I am not dangerous. You have met
me. You saw.' He looked terrified. 'If I go to Serbia, they will kill me.'

PREKAZ, KOSOVO, OCTOBER 2015: TWO YEARS EARLIER

ASIDE FROM THE PRESENCE OF armed soldiers in Kosovar uniforms, a
huge white marble graveyard that stretched out into the distance and
a semi-permanent scaffolding frame used to funnel hundreds of
selfie-taking tourists around its bullet-riddled facade, the house that
Adem Jashari built had remained as it was since the day he died. In
the late 1990s Jashari was one of the first commanders of the Kosovo
Liberation Army, a 'local tough' and family patriarch who was wanted
by the authorities for killing a Serbian policeman. He had thus far
avoided capture.[4] On 4 March 1998, Serbian special forces moved on
Jashari's house.[5] Whether they wanted to apprehend him or kill him
is still open to question. What isn't open to question is what happened
next. The house was shelled and a firefight followed during which 58
people, including Jashari, his brother, their wives and their children,
were killed. Two policeman also died. There was only one survivor in
the Jashari house, an 11-year-old girl. The massacre threw petrol on
the simmering embers of the conflict, which would soon lead to all
out war between the KLA and the Serb dominated Yugoslav army.
Today Jashari is considered a hero in Albania and Kosovo, but as a
terrorist by the Serbs.

The house was left as a memorial to the 'martyrs'. Huge holes
remained in the masonry, punched through by artillery shells.
Thousands of bullet holes seemed to cover almost every inch of the
brickwork. The house was now a site of pilgrimage, and a large crowd,
larger than normal, had gathered outside it. The several hundred men

and women were all members of the Tifozat Kuq e Zi, the Red and Black Fans. In a few days' time, Albania was to play a hugely important match. They were just one victory away from qualifying for Euro 2016. It would be Albania's first appearance at a major tournament. The team standing in their way was Serbia.

In the middle of the crowd stood a short man in his early thirties with wild, curly black hair and an American flag bandana around his neck. Teenage girls had surrounded Ismail Morina, taking it in turns to have a selfie with him, before the Red and Black moved as one towards the house. 'This,' Morina said grandly before going inside, 'is our Jerusalem.' He stopped to correct himself. 'This is our Mecca *and* our Jerusalem.' Morina was here as a guest of honour, invited by Adem Jashari's one surviving brother – who still lived next door – to be given an award for his role in flying the Belgrade drone the year before.

'You are a hero to the Albanians,' the frail old man said as he handed Morina a plaque fashioned from stone dug out of the Trepça mine in the north of Kosovo. In return, Morina handed him a flag. 'That was the original flag I was going to fly with the drone,' he explained after the ceremony. 'It was too heavy to fly. I couldn't lift it off the ground.'

The members of the Red and Black marched to the graves of the 58 men, women and children killed during the raid and chanted 'UCK' (pronounced 'Ou-Che-Ka'), the Albanian name for the KLA. This was just the first stop on a two-day patriotic tour of Kosovo's famous war graves and other nationalist sites, organised by the Red and Black, in preparation for the Serbia game.

'This is a spiritual place,' Morina said as we walked to the car and prepared for our next stop. 'You can see the past. And the the future.'

Ismail was the star attraction as we arrived at different towns, each with stories of massacres and bloodshed. Next was Deçan, to visit the village of another famous Kosovar clan: the Haradinaj family. The most famous member was Ramush Haradinaj, a former leader of the KLA who went by the name of Rambo. He was twice indicted, and twice acquitted by the ICTY, a scandal for many Serbs who believed he has blood on his hands. He resigned as prime minister of Kosovo in July 2019 after being summoned to give evidence at the new Kosovo Specialist Prosecution tribunal in The Hague. When he was acquitted by the ICTY for the second time, in 1998, Haradinaj had done much the same as Morina had seventeen years later: made a pilgrimage to KLA graves.

The Red and Black were welcomed to the war memorial and graveyard that Ramush Haradinaj built in the village of Gllogjan: a terrace of identical white stone graves stretching up the hill. A stone-built *kulas* (a traditional towered house) dominated the hill. Haradinaj's brother was buried here alongside dozens more killed during the war. Later, Haradinaj's father, Hilmi, would be buried here too. The Red and Black lined up in front of the large, white memorial stone. Morina was at the front, on his own, and gave a military salute. 'They have come here for a sacred place where heroes of our nation are,' said Deçan's mayor Rasim Selmanaj. 'It is an added motivation for winning the match.'

More stops followed. In each town mayors, former KLA commanders, former soldiers and well-wishers had turned up in large numbers to wish the Red and Black well for the upcoming match against Serbia. But, more importantly, to meet Ismail Morina. 'He's a hero. He showed that the Albanian flag cannot be thrown away or burned like in Genoa,' said Doni, a young member of the Red and Black who had travelled from Antwerp, where his family had fled when he was a child during the war. 'Genoa' had come up often in conversations with the Red and Black. Back in 2010 a European Championship qualification match between Italy and Serbia had to be abandoned because of rioting. But not before Ivan Bogdanov, the Red Star Belgrade ultra who also appeared on the pitch at the Partizan Stadium in 2014, climbed on top of the fence and burned an Albanian flag with a flare.[6] It was an act, I later discovered, that would have many unintended consequences.

As night fell the crowd arrived in the southern city of Prizren, seen as the spiritual home of modern Albanian nationalism, where the League of Prizren was formed in 1878. The Red and Black solemnly filed through the museum housed in the recently renovated building, after it was almost destroyed during the war in 1999. Morina stayed for photographs before leaving for Albania. I left with him.

After months of lurid speculation and conspiracy theories, the identity of the drone pilot was finally revealed when Morina gave an hour and twenty minute-long interview on Albanian TV. One million people viewed the interview on YouTube.[7] Far from being a suave provocation organised by the government, or a member of Albania's special forces, the culprit was Morina. He was both shy and at times maniacally extrovert, as if trying to live up to his new-found fame. But the truth was that the man who had executed possibly the most famous act of trolling in the history of football was a normal, flawed and unassuming character. The genesis of Morina's plan came five years previously. It was a plan that, 999 times out of 1,000, would have either (a) never left the bar in which had been devised or (b) failed at a dozen different places during its execution.

'I first had the idea after I had come back from work one day,' Morina said. He was now driving his Range Rover ('borrowed from my brother!') back from Kosovo to Tirana. A huge mountain of man, also a member of the Red and Black, sat in the back seat. 'My body-guard,' Morina said laughing.

That was back in the autumn of 2010, when he was working on a crane in Milan, travelling to Albania national team games with the Red and Black. He'd lived in Italy for four years with his Italian wife and two children. He returned to his apartment after one shift and, for the first and only time, didn't jump straight into the shower. 'Something told me I should turn on the television, so I did that first, which I never do,' he said. What he saw would change his life forever. Italy was play-ing Serbia in a Euro 2012 qualifier. Genoa. There had already been trouble in the run-up to the game, with Red Star ultras focusing their anger at goalkeeper Vladimir Stojković who had, via a spell at Sporting Lisbon, just moved on loan to rivals Partizan. This was considered a crime by the Delije. The game was abandoned after six minutes after flares and firecrackers were thrown on the pitch. And of course, Bogdanov was front and centre, burning the Albanian flag.

'I couldn't believe it, fuck you!' said Ismail. 'They weren't even playing Albania, why burn our flag?' Bogdanov, and 18 other Serbs, would be arrested. He was convicted and sentenced to three years and three months in prison but quickly deported to Serbia. Italy, meanwhile, were awarded the three points. For Morina, Bogdanov's actions had a longer gestation. And when the draw for Euro 2016 qualification was made, and Albania found themselves in the same group as Serbia, the outline of a plan first conceived nearly four years earlier came into view.

UEFA has rules preventing countries at war with each other, or with a recent past that would make hosting matches impossible, from being drawn in the same group. But as Albania and Serbia had not been at war against each other directly, no one thought to separate them. 'I saw the draw, and saw that the first game was in Belgrade,' said Ismail. 'Which was perfect. Perfect.'

Morina, or Ballist as he was widely known in the Albanian speaking world, was already well known amongst the Red and Black for his crazy antics at Albanian national team games. There was a famous video of him at a World Cup qualifier between Slovenia and Albania. Morina scaled the 10m-high mesh fence that separated the fans from the pitch just so he could hang an Albanian flag at the top.[8] The Red and Black were themselves an unusual group. Ultras were a manifestly local phenomenon. It was always club over country. In Italy, where the ultras embodied and eulogised the country's city-state roots – the 'bell towers' that took precedence over the relatively recent arrival of a unified Italian state – the national team was largely avoided by ultra groups. But the Red and Black weren't just a group that represented a national team as such. They represented an ethnicity, pulling together ethnic Albanians from home, from those spread across the Balkans and from the wider diaspora.

The Tifozat Kuq e Zi was formed on Christmas Day 2003. The aim, according to Fitim, one of the founding members, was to create a group 'to support all athletes representing the Red and Black colours' of the Albanian flag, 'with a special emphasis on the football national team'. They had a membership structure with different working groups for different types of activity. A €10 membership fee would cover the choreography and pyro. Their biggest achievement had been a 100m-long Albanian flag, weighing in at 360kg, which they displayed before a World Cup qualifier against Ukraine in 2005.

Fitim had been uneasy about calling the Red and Black an ultras group. 'If [being] ultras means using flares, displaying banners, messages ... then yes, we are,' he said. But, he added, the Red and Black left local identity behind. I'd met Fitim before. He was a softly spoken psephologist and family man who believed in a higher calling. 'Our philosophy is related to the national identity and the love for the country and every piece of land that breathes red and black.'

Still, being a confederation of ultras from across the Balkans, alongside individual members, was hard work; you had the Plisat of FC Prishtina in Kosovo, the Ballistët of KF Shkëndija and the Shvercerat of Shkupi in Macedonia, and also those in Albania itself, like the Guerrillas of Partizani Tirana. Most of the groups outside of Albania had a difficult relationship with their home countries, even in Kosovo itself. One of the most notorious ultras groups in Kosovo is FC Prishtina's Plisat. I went on the road with them and their leader, Spider, a former KLA fighter, to an away match in Prizren. They, like many young Kosovars, rejected the blue and yellow flag of Kosovo, which they saw as an imposition from the outside that denied hundreds of years of bloodshed and history.

'It is not our flag,' said Korab, a 23-year-old, softly spoken member of the Plisat as around 30 or so of us drove down in a fleet of minibuses for a league match against KF Liria.

'We believe in a united Albania,' said Atdhe, a 19-year-old student. 'There is no "greater Albania", only ethnic Albania. The KLA didn't fight for an independent Kosovo, but to unite all Albanians.'

On the small terrace of the ruined Përparim Thaçi Stadium in Prizren, named after a former Liria player who joined the KLA and was killed fighting in the war, the Plisat sang nationalist songs in the blinding sunshine. 'Most people in Kosovo believe their only national team is Albania, because nowhere in the world can you have two national teams,' said Arber, another member of the Plisat who spoke with a heavy English accent after living in London as a refugee. Kosovo, whilst officially unrecognised as a state, was recognised by FIFA and so had its own national team. But a younger generation rejected the 'new' flag and anthem. A new youth-inspired political movement, Vetëvendosje, followed a progressive but explicitly Albanian nationalist agenda. The party flag was the red and black Albanian flag. 'The KLA won the war with its emblem as the Albanian flag. It was an army for the Albanians,' said Arber. 'Kosovo is not a state. It is a temporary solution . . . until Kosovo can unite with Albania. Here the Plisat has the ideology that we will never support Kosovo. We already have one national team. That's Albania.'

Perhaps the best-known ethnic Albanian ultras group was the Ballistët of KF Shkëndija, from the Macedonian city of Tetovo, near the Kosovo border. Like Ismail Morina, the Ballistët named them-selves after the Second World War-era Balli Kombëtar. I met their spokesperson Bajram on the club's training pitch in Tetovo as the players worked out, balls occasionally missing us by centimetres and slamming into the metal fence next to us. 'Our national team is the Albanian national team. We do not support the Macedonia national team,' said Bajram. 'You can see pictures in the news. The Ballistët are coming,' he said, when I asked about their presence at Albania national team games.

KF Shkëndija's team colours were red and black, and they have, along with Vardar, been one of the most successful clubs in Macedonian football in recent years. The Ballistët rejected all Macedonian institu-tions apart from the football league. The ethnic problems were played out every weekend. The next game week, for instance, was to be played behind closed doors as tensions were high in the country. A military unit ended up killing ten people and destroying a whole neighbour-hood in Kumanovo looking for suspected ethnic Albanian terrorists.[9] 'We do not have any relationship with the the ultras of [non-Albanian] clubs,' said Bajram. 'We do not want to have any kind of relationship with the groups. They sing: "A good Albanian is a dead Albanian".'

Like Morina and the Red and Black, the Ballistët supported an ethnic Albania. He didn't use the term Greater Albania because, he said, 'that term promotes chauvinism. We do not want something that is foreign. We don't want something that belongs to someone else. We want our own.'

As the October 2014 match in Belgrade approached, Ismail Morina still had no idea exactly *what* he would do. Until he met up with a friend who had just bought a drone for his young son to play with. He saw the drone flying around the Milanese park and realised that, with a little bit of work, it could carry a banner or a flag. So he went out and bought a drone. He destroyed the first one. The second went the same way. By the time he had bought his third drone he had mastered it. 'I got used to it quickly because it was like when I drive my crane, I had a joystick. It's like playing on the PlayStation.' The next issue was how he would get the drone into the stadium. He used Google Earth to research the surrounding area. He flew to Belgrade and walked around the Marakana, checking potential sites from which he could fly the drone. With the plan set and the date approaching, it was only a few weeks before the match he realised he had been researching the wrong stadium. So he returned to Belgrade, scoped out the Partizan Stadium instead and settled on the Church of the Archangel Gabriel, a few hundred metres away. It provided the perfect cover. It had a large park, the church was unlocked and from the cupola Morina had a clear view of the stadium. Most importantly, it was within range of the drone that he had bought.

A few days before the match, Morina and a friend drove from Italy to Serbia. The car was searched at the Serbian border. Morina thought then that the game was up. 'They looked at everything and then found the drone in a box in the back,' he said. Morina explained to the Serb border guard that it was a gift for the son of a friend. The border guard handed the drone back and waved them through. 'It was unbelievable. After that there was nothing to stop me.' On YouTube there is a video of Morina in his hotel room in Belgrade, trying not to make any sound, as he uses a knife to cut away the lining from a case. Inside was the famous flag.

Morina positioned himself in the church grounds 17 hours before kick-off. He had already hidden the drone and the remote control in the church days before. The plan was for him to wait there until the game started. Security, he figured, would have been too tight if he had waited any longer. So he lay there, listening to the crowd arriving, singing, he said, anti-Albanian songs until, finally, he moved into position. There were a few teething problems. The first flag Morina tried (the flag he later presented to Adem Jashari's brother) was too heavy. But he had a back-up. As the match began, he could hear the crowd in the distance, although not what they were singing. Outside, the roads were deserted when Morina launched his drone into the air and into the Partizan Stadium.

'There was twenty seconds of silence,' Morina recalled of the moment the drone entered the stadium. 'I lowered the drone so that the players could see the flag, to give them courage.' But Morina had made an error. Serbia was playing in red and Albania in white. He flew the drone instinctively towards the red-shirted players believing them to be Albanian. When he realised his mistake he tried to power the drone into the sky. The original plan was for the drone to circle the stadium and then come back to the church, where Morina would collect the flag and jump into a car a kilometre away from the stadium. A friend would be waiting with the engine on. But Stefan Mitrović grabbed the drone, all hell broke loose, and Morina decided to abandon his post, leaving the remote control behind. Morina managed to escape before the police had flooded the area. But still he had to hide under a parked car when two policemen passed by. Once they were out of view he got up and walked as calmly as he could to the waiting car and drove south through the border and into Kosovo. 'I still thought I had failed at this point,' he said. 'Then I got a call from a friend in Italy. He told me: "Man, you're famous."'

And famous he was. His actions were discussed on Albanian national TV regularly, although not always favourably. In a region awash with conspiracy theories, he was accused of being a spy for numerous sides. 'One analyst on TV said I was both from ISIS, because the flag was black, and that I was paid by the Serbian secret service!' he said. Others were incredulous that it was an individual, and not a sophisticated foreign security service that had pulled it off. But once the truth was out he was greeted as a hero everywhere he went. His black flag was seemingly for sale on every street corner in Tirana. It wasn't just the 'victory' against the Serbs. It was also the fact that his action had somehow gained Albania the three points *and* saw their main rival effectively eliminated. Many believed that Morina was a big reason why Albania stood on the cusp of qualifying for their first ever major tournament. He would appear on stage at events where thousands would wave his famous black flag at him, his face projected six metres high on the screen behind him. There was adulation, yes, but he also received hundreds of death threats on Facebook and by SMS.

So, in the end Morina fled Italy and brought his family to Albania. According to the Serbian media, a businessman from Chicago even offered a €1 million reward for Morina's capture. 'I'm not worried about the Serbian state, but extremist groups,' he said. But the circus didn't stop. As the return game against Serbia approached, the interview requests and the appearances and the death threats kept coming. He was an active user of social media and announced on YouTube that he had been sent a special package from Bosnia. Aleksandar Vučić, then the Serbian prime minister, had recently attended the 20-year commemoration of the Srebrenica genocide. The Serbian government didn't recognise what happened as a genocide but Vučić attended anyway. There were scuffles and rocks were thrown. And apparently, he lost his glasses too.

'I have a little surprise …' Morina tells the camera that he'd received a package in the mail. He picks up a pair of glasses that look similar to the ones Vučić was wearing that day. He explained that he had been asked, if he got the opportunity, to give the glasses back to the prime minister of Serbia, Vučić, who would be in the stadium. There was, given his new hero status, no way Ismail wouldn't be there for the return game.

Once we had crossed the border into Albania, we drove through his home town of Kukës before pulling into a petrol station for a coffee. From the glove compartment he took out a gun and placed it in my hands, a Serbian-made Zastava pistol. It felt heavy, but I didn't immediately realise it was real. It was small and looked like a cigarette lighter. For a split second it crossed my mind that I should jokingly put the gun to my head and pull the trigger.

'It's real, man,' Ismail said, giving me a concerned look.

I gingerly handed the gun back to him.

Over the next few days, Ismail and I would travel around Tirana, meeting members of the Red and Black, whilst I asked about the drone incident, filling in the blanks where parts didn't make sense, or where parts of the story contradicted each other. There was no sense of danger or fear. Ismail Morina was a national hero and he could go wherever he wanted and speak to whomever he chose. The Red and Black had closed around him, offering him friendship and protection. He rarely gave interviews now and primarily interacted with the outside world using Facebook. Every day brought an avalanche of death threats: Serbian men, usually claiming they were ex-special forces, sending topless pictures of themselves wearing balaclavas. Or simply a collection of guns and knives spread out on a bed with a threat to slaughter everyone he knew. But it wasn't all bad, Ismail said. He also received hundreds of friend requests from beautiful Albanian women who sent him pictures in various states of undress.

The last time I saw Ismail Morina before he went to prison was in a cliff-top restaurant outside the costal city of Durrës, about 45 minutes' drive from the capital. We had agreed to meet there for dinner with a select group of the Red and Black. We knocked back blindingly strong rakia and talked about the moment he became the most famous man in Albania. He explained that he didn't hate Serbs, 'but the past has hurt us'. Of greater concern was how the Albanian authorities viewed him. Both the Albanian FA and UEFA had banned him from attending the game in Elbasan, about 50km from Tirana. The fear was that another drone would be flown into the stadium and there had been reports that Serbia's prime minister would be in attendance. There would be 2,000 police officers in Elbasan, and 500 Albanian special forces. Snipers would patrol the rooftops surrounding the stadium, ready to shoot down any drone that might appear. 'I am a danger man, they say!' Ismail laughed.[10] But, he said, his time as a drone provocateur was over.

With the bar closed, Ismail offered to drive back to Tirana. It was late and the restaurant was isolated, so we drove back down the winding, black, single lane towards the highway. Morina was excitable after checking his messages on Facebook. Suddenly, from the pocket of the car door, he pulled a second gun, a bigger one, and opened the window. He raised it outside and pulled the trigger.

Click.

He hadn't loaded it. Somehow he managed to drive the car at speed with his knees, send a message on Facebook, load the gun and cock the barrel all at the same time. He lifted the pistol out of the window again and blasted it three times in the air. The noise in the car was deafening. A spent shell flew out of the chamber and bounced off my forehead as Morina laughed until he had a coughing fit.

The rest of the journey was uneventful.

Morina pulled up outside my apartment in central Tirana. It was 2am but his night was not over. He was off to meet someone else, he said. We would meet tomorrow, and arrange our travel to the game together, he promised. I fell asleep that night dreaming of the sea.

I was awoken early the next morning by my phone. I'd received a message from my girlfriend telling me to check Twitter. Ismail Morina had been arrested, she said. I didn't believe it at first, as I'd only seen him a few hours earlier. But, sure enough, every news channel and radio station was leading with the story. I watched a local news channel in a cafe in Tirana. Morina had been arrested less than half an hour after I'd seen him last. The report had pictures of a dishevelled Morina standing in a dock wearing the same clothes I'd seen him in the night before. Next were pictures of his car. And then close-ups of the spent bullet shells in the footwell, not to mention a pile of 30 tickets for the Serbia game, one of them with Morina's name on it. It was then that I heard my name for the first time on Albanian TV news: the words 'Xhjems Montagu', 'American [sic] reporter' and 'New York Times'.

By coincidence, a story I had written about Morina for the *New York Times* had been published a few hours after his arrest.[11] In it I had mentioned the death threats, that he feared for his life, the fact that he carried a Zastava pistol purely for self-defence and, later on, his arrest too. But the police had briefed the media that they had arrested Morina *after* reading the article, which was impossible given that it was published after his arrest. But every TV channel and radio station ran with it anyway. My picture flashed up on the TV. 'Xhjems Montagu', read the caption. 'Amerikan reporter'. Almost immediately my phone buzzed again. It was a message from Ismail.

'Why you mention gun?!' read the message. 'Ismail now in jail. ALL YR FAULT!!' It was Morina's nephew, who now had control of Ismail's Facebook account whilst he was in jail.

Arresting Ismail for gun charges in Albania was like arresting a Dutch person in Amsterdam for carrying a bag of weed. Albania was a country awash with guns. Almost everyone had a gun thanks, in part, to the country's economy collapsing in 1997, which led to a full-blown uprising. Citizens stormed army bases and emptied weapons dumps. Kalashnikovs would change hands for $10 a pop.[12] But Ismail found himself in jail regardless, and the police were putting out a false story that I was the reason they arrested him. I spent the next few hours running from police station to police station looking for Ismail. Maybe I could explain to the police *why* he had a gun. That I'd seen the long list of death threats he'd received. That his life was in danger. But, when I found the right police station, no one wanted to speak to me. I was terrified, publicly fingered as the man who had put a national hero in jail. What if they came for me next?

It took all day, but I eventually got through to someone from the Red and Black. They too were trying to find Ismail and arrange a lawyer. 'He is in a lot of trouble,' one told me. He was denied bail and would spend the foreseeable future behind bars. He faced up to 15 years in jail. 'They have him on gun charges,' he added, leaving the statement of fact hanging in the air like an accusation.

*

On the morning of the Albania–Serbia match all the roads to Elbasan had been shut nine hours before kick-off. The highway was lined with checkpoints whilst the stadium itself was surrounded by a ring of armed officers. Residents of the tower blocks surrounding the stadium were told to stay inside and not let strangers into the building. There seemed to me more than the planned 2,000 police and 500 special forces officers on the streets. Snipers prepared themselves on the rooftops surrounding the Elbasan Arena, with little tents next to them just in case it rained. Huge, Russian-made helicopters flew overhead as the police practised crowd-control manoeuvres with water cannon and tear-gas canisters. 'It is for practice,' a police officer explained over the deafening sound of rotor blades overhead. Practice involved firing the water cannon into the crowd.

Still, the city had been full six hours before kick-off. There had been a carnival atmosphere gradually eroded by the constant rain and overbearing security. The stories of Ismail's arrest, and my supposed complicity in it, led the news for a second day. One claimed that Ismail had requested that he be given permission to watch the game in his cell, a request that was denied. I'd considered not going to the match, just in case an angry mob decided to take revenge. Outside the stadium a drunk member of the Red and Black recognised me, grabbed me by the lapels and shook me, trying to force me to make the eagle sign with both of my hands before he was prised off. He was angry and, like many of the Red and Black, blamed me for Ismail's arrest. A few minutes later I got a message from Fitim to meet him and a delegation of the Red and Black's leaders at the stadium. The group was sullen but not angry. Fitim apologised for his friend who had grabbed me in the street.

It turned out that the Albanian police had been following Ismail's movements for months. His high profile and hero status had been an acute embarrassment for the Albanian government ever since the diplomatic fallout from the drone. The prime minister Edi Rama had built something approaching a warm relationship with his Serbian counterpart, so much so that it looked like Vučić might even attend the game in Elbasan. But the drone incident was in danger of ruining all his work. The final straw, according to the Red and Black, was Vučić's glasses. Morina's deadpan offer on YouTube to hand his glasses back to him in Albania were interpreted as a threat. Ever since then he had been monitored, with the police waiting for the moment Morina put a foot wrong. They had followed his car from the cliff-top restaurant in Durrës and, after hearing the gunshots, took their opportunity once he had dropped me off to arrest him.

In the end, Vučić didn't come to the game. The Serbian national anthem was booed, and the fans chanted for the KLA, but the 12,000-strong crowd seemed nervous and subdued. Even one of the snipers on the roof of a building next to the stadium saw little danger, and moved into a tent erected nearby to keep out of the driving rain. Serbia ran out 2–0 winners. The victory party had been spoiled. Within an hour of the final whistle, Elbasan was silent and deserted. It was perhaps for the best that Ismail Morina was not allowed to watch the match in jail.

Albania qualified for their first European Championships with a surprisingly easy 3–0 victory over Armenia a few days later. The returning team were greeted as national heroes. Edi Rama held a reception for them as soon as they landed.[13] Tens of thousands celebrated on the streets of Tirana and across Albania. Ismail Morina, the man who had played an important part in Albania's qualification, would instead spend Christmas in jail, facing the prospect of a life-changing stretch in an Albanian prison. But then, after three months behind bars, there was a breakthrough. He would be released, but kept under house arrest. Eventually I was able to get in touch with him. I was worried he would blame me for his time inside, but he didn't. Morina's house arrest was due to end in January, then February, then April. Either way, he was done with the national team. Not the players and the fans, but the federation. He wouldn't be going to France for Euro 2016 even if he was allowed to leave the country, or even his house.

At least Morina's family house by the Albania–Kosovo border had a lot of room. It was spring and the land had bloomed. Fruit was ripening on the vine. 'Man, I am loving the nature,' he said. Earlier that day he was out planting trees before watching the news for the rest of the day. A terrorist attack had struck Belgium. 'Be careful, man.' He sent me a picture of his view, a beautiful blue sky, a wooden fence and green fields stretching out into the distance. Where I was sitting, it was grey and wet and cold and there was the suffocating feeling that ISIS could strike anywhere next. Perhaps it was safer where he was, planting trees in the Albanian sun, I offered.

'Yes!' he replied. 'I said the same thing to my brother just today.' And with that he logged off, to plant more trees in his little patch of earth. But he wasn't offline for long. As Euro 2016 approached, and interest in Albania's first ever competitive tournament grew, so did interest in Ismail, the man whose drone stunt had secured a priceless three qualification points. It was still a hugely controversial issue in Serbia, with some justification. Whilst there was no doubt about the anti-Albanian chanting, nor the violent reaction afterwards, the drone had sparked the whole thing off, endangered the players and, even worse from Belgrade's perspective, it was *Albania* that benefited from it. UEFA's reaction reinforced the wildly held perception in Serbia that it is unfairly treated in almost every international forum, be it in sport or politics. As the graffiti outside the Marakana says: 'UEFA Supports Terrorism'.

There were interviews and TV appearances. Babies were named after his flag. In fact, one famous song was written about a boy who had been named Autochthoni after the wording on Morina's flag. 'My Autochthonous Son', produced by Frrok Bardhi, was an Albanian folk-rock number, and Morina appears in the video wearing a *qeleshe*, a traditional Albanian white felt hat. At one point, looking a little embarrassed, he wraps a baby in his famous black flag.

Despite beating Romania in their final game, Albania went home from France early and that was the last I heard from Ismail for a while. I'd heard that he had gone missing from the family home. But that wasn't surprising. Morina's life wasn't in Albania. It was in Milan, with his Italian wife and two children. The authorities still had his passport, but that didn't mean much. Albania's eastern border with Kosovo is a border in name only – I've never had my passport checked crossing it – and the north-western border with Montenegro was almost as porous. You could cross with just an Albanian ID card. So, with the tournament over, he crossed to Montenegro with his ID, and managed to sneak into Croatia and then Slovenia. Once he was in Slovenia, and inside the Schengen area, the rest of the journey to Italy was straight-forward. And there he stayed, taking up his old job and getting back into family life. Until he got word that his father died. Ismail returned for the funeral but wasn't so lucky when he tried to cross back into Croatia on his way back home. He was spotted by a Croatian border guard. When they ran his name through the computer they discovered there was an Interpol Red Notice issued against him by Serbia over the drone incident. The nearest prison was Dubrovnik.

'They say I offended their flag. Their religion. I did not. I only showed history. Our flags,' he said quietly as we sat in the prison's visi-tors' room, separated by glass. Next to me Ana was crying as her son tried to console her. Morina knew that he wouldn't fare well in a Serbian jail. After everything I'd heard about the links between the terraces, organised crime, government and the courts, I wasn't sure he would last long in a Serbian jail either. Mind you, he wasn't 100 per cent safe out of jail. He felt sure that, one way or another, someone would come for him. He was, at least, being well looked after in prison. A Croatian prison was far nicer than an Albanian one and, as long as he had money, he could buy food. You could, he says, even order takeout. But that didn't matter. His wife was heavily pregnant with their third child. It was highly unlikely he would be able to hold his newborn baby as a free man any time soon. And if he was extra-dited to Serbia he feared he wouldn't last long. But he had found a lawyer and was trying to apply for political asylum on account of the threats against him.

The problem was that Ismail Morina's arrest had now become an issue of state. On the one hand, Albanians were wondering why the government wasn't using everything in its power to release a national hero. The Albanian football federation was against his incarceration. Albania's national team players had gone public, including the now retired former captain Lorik Cana, to 'Free Morina'. The Red and

Black had also mobilised, organising protests. Hundreds turned up in Tirana, led by Ismail's brother.

There was, however, a wider political game. There were long-standing diplomatic issues between Croatia and Serbia, for obvious reasons. Croatia refusing an extradition request for fears of Morina's safety would all but accuse Serbia's legal system of being incapable of holding a free trial. But if Croatia extradited him and he was killed, they would have blood on their hands. Initially the Dubrovnik court moved to have him extradited to Serbia as soon as possible. But the pressure from the Red and Black, amongst others, worked.

'The prime minister of Albania is against the extradition,' Fitim told me. 'The minister of defence and justice also.' The process was slowed. But he was no closer to being freed.

What do you want me to do? I asked Ismail.

'Tell them what you saw,' he replied as he was pulled away by the guards. 'Tell them about the threats.'

Our 15 minutes were up. Outside Ana dabbed her cheeks with a tissue. She would be back next week, she said, and every week after that. A few weeks later, Ismail Morina received good news by the prison phone: his wife had given birth to their third child, a boy.

Ismail Morina would spend the next year in prison. His Croatian lawyer, a garrulous Dubrovnik native who seemed to be the only person in the city who knew anything about extradition law, having, he told me half-drunk over dinner, 'saved the ass of a Russian oligarch' in a similar situation – kept dragging the case back from the brink. The Dubrovnik court would announce Morina was to be extradited. There would be howls of outrage in Tirana. A high-level politico in Zagreb would then assure the press that it would, ultimately, be a political decision. Angry statements would follow from the government in Belgrade. And the cycle would continue, involving the upper echelons of the Albanian, Croatian and Serbian government,[14] as well as the ultras from ethnic Albanian clubs.

'The way the Albanian government has treated Morina is a complete disaster, we are very angry about this,' Shkëndija's Ballistët said in a statement. Ismail's wife was terrified for his mental health, fearing that he would kill himself if his flight to Serbia was ever approved.

He did find some support from unexpected quarters in Serbia. Vojislav Šešelj, the ultra-nationalist founder of the Serbian Radical Party, a convicted war criminal who spent 11 years in The Hague and a former ally of Slobodan Milošević (although Milošević threw him in jail in 1994 for being too extreme), couldn't understand why Serbia was pursuing Ismail in the first place. 'Why do we need Morina?' he said, rather 'than dealing with Albanian criminals who are smuggling human organs' (a common accusation levelled at Albanians, especially during the Kosovo War).

Then there were the newspaper reports in Serbia that Milorad 'Legija' Ulemek, Arkan's loyal lieutenant who was serving a 40-year sentence for his role in the 2003 assassination of Serbian prime minister Zoran Djindjić, was planning a welcoming party for Ismail's arrival.[15] That couldn't have harmed Morina's argument that he wasn't safe in a Serbian jail.

In the end the political heat was too much and the Croatian justice minister decided to extradite him. To Italy. Morina had an Italian wife and Italian residency. They could deal with him. So, one night without warning, Morina was frogmarched out of his cell, taken to the port and put on a ferry to Bari with a one-way ticket. He was arrested as soon as he arrived. Undeterred, the Serbian authorities again applied for his extradition for the same charge of inciting racial and ethnic hatred, with a maximum term of eight years. But in July 2018, the Italian courts rejected it and Morina was finally free.[16] From the last time I had seen him as a free man, on the eve of Albania vs Serbia in October 2015, until July 2018, Ismail Morina had been in jail or under house arrest for almost three years.

MILAN, ITALY

THESE DAYS, ISMAIL MORINA PREFERRED life without a beard. He was sitting in an English pub, run by a Chinese owner, in a tiny Italian town outside Milan, surrounded by a group of Albanian ultras. They were in town to watch the Milan derby taking place later that day.

In jail he had learned Serbo-Croat and how to read Cyrillic, and kept up with the news, following the ongoing talks over Kosovo's future. A population exchange was openly being discussed in Belgrade and Pristina in a bid to break the deadlock. 'I think there will be a short war. A controlled war,' he said. 'I don't know who will get more from this. Vučić can't recognise Kosovo. It is a tough situation.' He believed only a 'blitzkrieg war' would create an outcome.

Ismail had been a free man for seven months. He'd returned to Milan to be with his wife and kids. He held his newborn son for the first time and took a new job, as a lorry driver. It was the first time we had spoken, face to face, since I'd sat opposite him in a Dubrovnik jail. The death threats had stopped, for now, although he still looked over his shoulder. He still received hundreds of requests to meet with him from fans around the world. Each was assessed as a potential security risk. The last group to visit was from Hajduk Split's Torcida. He showed me a picture of them all, dressed in the team's shirts, drinking beer at the same table we were sitting at now. *The enemy of my enemy is my friend.*

He had no interest in going to the Milan derby. He didn't want to stray too far from home. He hadn't seen the Albanian national team play since being arrested in Albania in 2015. He'd been invited to see Albania play Italy in Palermo, but the Red and Black were planning a *tifo* based on his famous flag, in criticism of the country's football federation, and he didn't want to be connected to it. He was happy here, in the bar, watching Liverpool play Fulham instead.

'The only thing is that I climbed in the church,' he said when I ask whether he regretted anything about that night on 14 October 2014. It had made him famous, and turned Ismail Morina into an Albanian folk hero. It had also ruined his life. But the only thing he regretted was flying the drone from a church. 'If any religious Serbs felt offended, I am sorry for this.'

As the memory of that night faded from the public's conscious-ness, so did the belief that Ismail Morina was in fact the real pilot of the drone. Everyone I spoke to in Belgrade couldn't believe that he was the culprit. There *had* to be a wider story. A bigger conspiracy. A nefarious hidden hand controlling the sequence of events. But the truth was even stranger. That a fanatical supporter, fuelled by the injustice of seeing his country's flag burned by a Serbian ultra four years previously, concocted a crazy plan that he somehow pulled off despite dozens of *Sliding Doors* moments where the plan could, and should, have failed.

Ismail still didn't know if he was on Interpol's database. He didn't fly, just in case. He admitted that the whole saga had ruined his life but now he was free to be with his family. We drove to a local McDonalds. 'I ask for ... how do you say in English ...?'

Forgiveness? I suggested as we approached the front door.

'Forgiveness. Yes. I ask for forgiveness. The rest? I feel only pride. It was all my idea. And all my abilities. All my stupidity. But all of it was mine.'

He walked into a brightly lit foyer where his wife and children were waiting, picked up his baby and kissed him on the forehead.

PART THREE:
AGAINST MODERN FOOTBALL

'He who fights with monsters should look to it that he himself does not become a monster.'

Friedrich Nietzsche, *Beyond Good and Evil*

8

Ukraine

KYIV, UKRAINE

SERHII FILIMONOV'S OFFICE CAN BE FOUND ON A CROSSROADS A FEW minutes' walk from Kyiv's Golden Gate, a replica of the city's original eleventh-century fortifications, now surrounded by European embassies and piles of grey snow slowly melting in the drizzle. The front door had recently been replaced, upgraded to a black, reinforced steel slab that could only be accessed by a high-tech electronic keypad.

The lift stopped on the fourth floor at a shabbily vintage network of rooms with high ceilings. Filimonov was sat in the largest room behind an oversized wooden desk wearing a 'Hard Rock Cafe: THAILAND' T-shirt, his left arm in a sling, fingers heavily bandaged. A tall metal cabinet, full of shotguns and ammunition, stood in the corner. Papers were piled up from Filimonov's new security business.

His Apple Mac was opened, the gleaming white 'Apple' symbol covered by a yellow and black sticker from his political party, the National Corps. He was young, in his mid-twenties; short but muscular, blondish hair cropped short with red wispish stubble on his chin. 'This,' he said, gingerly lifting up his injured arm, 'was a gift from the Greek police.'

Six days earlier, on Valentine's Day, Serhii was in Athens following his first true calling. His team, Dynamo Kyiv, was playing Olympiacos in the Europa League's Round of 32. As one of the leaders of the Rodychi, Dynamo's strongest hooligan firm, Serhii's presence was guaranteed. The Rodychi was famed for its strength in the European arranged-fight scene. Aside from a Molotov cocktail thrown at their bus on the way to the game, and a group of Olympiacos fans attacking their hotel the night before, it wasn't Olympiacos's Gate 7 ultras that had been the problem. It was the police who, Filimonov said, began beating them the moment they got inside the Karaiskakis Stadium in Piraeus. 'They were beating us so hard,' he said, examining his immobile left arm, 'I almost lost consciousness. I have never been beaten so hard before. My finger could even be amputated.' He missed the game, of course, a spirited 2–2 draw where Dynamo came from behind twice, with the Slovenian winger Benjamin Verbič scoring late in the game to give them the upper hand on away goals. Olympiacos would arrive for the return game tomorrow, although Filimonov was in no state to seek revenge even if he wanted to. Beside, as the head of the Kyiv chapter of the National Corps he had a full schedule of political actions in the coming days to plan and execute.

First, there was a protest, complete with banners and flares, outside a courthouse hearing the case surrounding the recent killing of a female activist. A few months previously Kateryna Handziuk, an advisor to the mayor in the city of Kherson, had been exposing local corruption in a variety of industries from logging to construction. Her regular Facebook posts didn't discriminate: police officers, government officials, well-known businessmen, they were all exposed for their alleged wrongdoing. But one morning, Handziuk was approached by a man who poured a litre of sulphuric acid all over her. She had burns covering a third of her body and underwent 11 operations. It took her five months to die. She was 33 years old. No one had yet been held to account for her death.[1]

Then there was a protest to mark the national day of the Ukrainian language and also the more bread-and-butter activism for which Filimonov and his National Corps had become known for in Kyiv in recent months: taking direct action against what they viewed as the corrupt and illegal purchase and development of prime Kyiv real estate by Ukrainian oligarchs. The group would often storm and occupy a recently acquired building, and 'neutralise' the onsite security, usually streaming it all on Facebook Live. They saw themselves as representatives of the people, fighting against the oligarchs.

This was how Filimonov filled his days; a carousel of training, football matches, arranged fights and direct action against the corrupt elite who – he believed – had for decades operated with impunity and were protected by a captured judiciary. But Filimonov wasn't a liberal activist, even though he found himself on the same side of the barricades alongside many left-wing protestors. The National Corps was a far-right, ultra-nationalist political party. Its roots came from the Azov battalion, a volunteer fighting force, largely populated by Ukrainian ultras and hooligans, the same ultras who had played an important role in the 2014 Maidan revolution that swept the Russian-backed president Viktor Yanukovych from power. When the war began in the east of the country, the ultras volunteered in huge numbers and left for the front line. Filimonov was one them. He was injured in the Battle of Ilovaisk, the lowest point of Ukraine's war, when the military was routed and as many as a thousand personnel were killed in a botched withdrawal operation. He returned home and was fast-tracked for a political career in the National Corps.

Ultra, hooligan, veteran, activist, politician; Filimonov was, in part, all of these things in a political landscape that had drastically changed since 2014. Groups like Azov and the National Corps now, allegedly, enjoyed the patronage and protection of some of the country's most powerful politicians, like Ukraine's minister of interior Arsen Avakov. They used new tactics that made groups like the

National Corps harder to pin down in post-revolution Ukraine, cutting across national barriers and ideological lines. Facebook and Instagram helped spread the message to a new audience.

Yet Filimonov's activism still managed to land him in jail regularly. Usually, he would be released after a large number of National Corps volunteers turned up with flares and banners. Filimonov certainly didn't feel like he was under the patronage of any great power. 'We fear we are being listened to,' he said, walking over to the window overlooking the street below. He thought they were under surveillance from a house across the street.

Are they watching us now? I asked.

'Yes,' he replied, staring at the building opposite.

Despite it being the fifth anniversary of the bloodiest day of the uprising, Maidan Nezalezhnosti, or Independence Square, was almost empty. This was the epicentre of the Euromaidan revolution that took place at the end of 2013 and the start of 2014, bringing hundreds of thousands of Ukrainians on to the street to depose President Yanukovych. The uprising was a long time in the making. Ever since independence from a Soviet Union only weeks away from its own demise, in 1991, Ukraine had been beset by economic and political failure. Political corruption was endemic. Real power lay, not in elected officials, but in a small network of oligarchs who enriched themselves in the post-communist fire sale of state assets, and used their wealth to manipulate politics and the economy for their own ends. Viktor Yanukovych was one such figure to benefit, a street thug from near Donetsk who, under the patronage of oligarchs from the Russian-speaking east of the country, rose to the highest political position. He almost came to power in 2004 when, as prime minister, he won the presidential election due to rampant ballot-box stuffing and after his opponent almost died from being mysteriously poisoned.[2] Yanukovych's first-round victory prompted mass street protests that became known as the Orange Revolution. A re-vote was ordered, Yanukovych was handily beaten and that, it was thought, was that. But, under the tutelage of Paul Manafort – President Donald Trump's

Ismail Morina, the pilot of the drone that flew over the Serbia versus Albania Euro 2016 qualification match in Belgrade, visiting Adem Jashari's house with the Tifozat Kuq e Zi. A few days later Morina would be arrested by Albanian police. October 2015, Prekaz, Kosovo.

A member of the Skifterat ultras of SC Gjilani with a smoke flare during the Gjilan Derby against Drita. The match is considered the biggest, and most passionate, in the Kosovar league. Gjilani scored a last minute winner. August 2016, Gjilan, Kosovo.

Members of the Ahlawy, the ultras of Al Ahly, march in the port city of Alexandria to mourn the deaths of several members during the Port Said massacre. A few weeks earlier 72 Al Ahly fans were killed at a match against Al Masry in Port Said. A court later found there had been collusion between the local authorities and rival ultras from Al Masry. March 2012, Alexandria, Egypt.

Thousands of members of the Ahlawy gather outside Al Ahly's training complex in Cairo to hear the verdict in the Port Said trial. Many came armed, some with home made guns, in case the verdict went against them. 21 people from Port Said were sentenced to death (although this was later reduced to ten). January 2013, Cairo, Egypt.

Riot police standing in front of graffiti made by the Delije, Red Star Belgrade's ultras, shortly before a Champions League match against Napoli at the Rajko Mitić Stadium, most commonly known as the Marakana. September 2018, Belgrade, Serbia.

Ultras from Partizan Belgrade, known as the Grobari – or 'Gravediggers' – rip out their seats and light flares during the Eternal Derby against Red Star Belgrade at the Marakana. March 2019, Belgrade, Serbia.

Ultras from Dynamo Kyiv light flares and unfurl a banner during a Europa League match at the Olympic Stadium against Olympiacos demanding justice for the anti-corruption activist Kateryna Handziuk. Handziuk was doused in acid and died three months later. The banner says: 'The Killers of Handziuk Must be Imprisoned.' February 2019, Kyiv, Ukraine.

Exiled ultras from Zorya Luhansk watch their team lose 5-0 to Dynamo Kyiv. Their home city of Luhansk, in the east of country, is under the control of pro-Russian forces. February 2019, Kyiv, Ukraine.

Riot police await the arrival of Ivan Savvidis, the Greek-Russian owner of PAOK, before a Champions League play off match at Toumba stadium against Benfica. Savvidis was serving a stadium ban for entering the pitch with a gun during a Greek league match six months previously. September 2018, Thessaloniki, Greece.

Anti-police graffiti next to Gate 4 at PAOK's Toumba stadium. September 2018, Thessaloniki, Greece.

Children playing football at a school in Kumanovo, North Macedonia. Twenty-five per cent of Kumanov's population is ethnically Albanian. Many schools are divided, one half is taught in Albanian, the other Macedonian. May 2015, Kumanovo, North Macedonia.

Graffiti honouring FK Vardar's ultras, the Komiti. September 2018, Skopje, North Macedonia.

Fans of Greek club Iraklis ask to have a picture taken with Il Bocia, the *capotifosi* of Italian club Atalanta (centre). Bocia has been banned from the stadium for most of the past 26 years, but he remains one of the most famous *capotifosi* in Italy. May 2019, Bergamo, Italy.

Graffiti outside the Stadio Olimpico honouring Gabriele Sandri before the Coppa Italia against Atalanta. Sandri was a member of Lazio's Irriducibili ultras. He was shot dead by a police officer in 2007. May 2019, Rome, Italy.

The inside of the Museo del Fútbol, at the Estadio Centenario in Montevideo. May 2019, Montevideo, Uruguay.

Mikael, the Swedish founder of the Hammarby Ultras, in Montevideo shortly after I met him. May 2019, Montevideo, Uruguay.

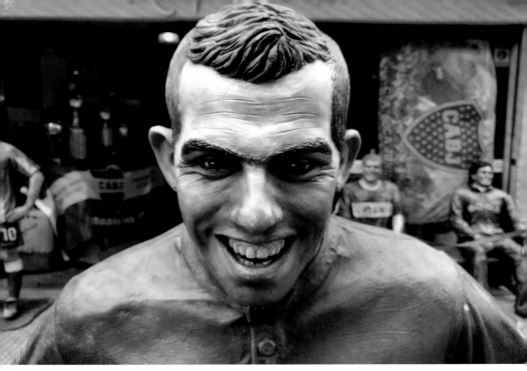

A statue of Carlos Tevez outside Boca Junior's Bombonera stadium. A statue of Maradona, sat down, can be seen over his left shoulder. May 2019, Buenos Aries, Argentina.

A mural in honour of Maradona, Boca Juniors' favourite son, outside the Bombonera. May 2019, Buenos Aries, Argentina.

Ultras of SC Freiburg in the north tribune of the Schwarzwald-stadion during a
1–1 draw with Hannover 96. December 2018, Freiburg im Breisgau, Germany.

1312 graffiti near Chemnitzer FC's Stadion an der Gellertstraße. December 2018,
Chemnitz, Germany.

A young fan of Beşiktaş leads the chants as the club's ultras, Çarşı, prepare for a home match against Başakşehir. April 2019, İstanbul, Turkey.

A fan of Başakşehir shows off his Beşiktaş tattoo. As Başakşehir is a new team, most fans grew up supporting other teams in the city. April 2019, İstanbul, Turkey.

Police armed with machine guns escort a convoy of Galatasaray ultras – known as UltrAslan – over the Bosphorus for their biggest match of the season: the Intercontinental Derby against Fenerbahçe. April 2019, İstanbul, Turkey.

Fans of Fenerbahçe put on a pyro show next to a statue of the Brazilian midfielder Alexsandro de Souza – a fan favourite who stayed at Fenerbahçe for eight years – shortly before the Intercontinental derby against Galatasaray at the Ülker Stadium, Kadıköy. April 2019, İstanbul, Turkey.

Fans of Raja Casablanca queueing up at the Stade Père Jégo in Casablanca.
The ground is usually home to Racing Athletic Club Casablanca but, with the
Stade Mohammed V being renovated Raja played their home game against Ittihad
Tanger here instead. April 2019, Casablanca, Morocco.

Ultras from Raja Casablanca watch their team play Ittihad Tanger at the Stade Père
Jégo. April 2019, Casablanca, Morocco.

Members of the 3252, the supporters' group of LA FC, show support for Gay Pride during a match against the Montreal Impact at the Banc of California Stadium. May 2019, Los Angeles, United States.

Breezy, one of the female *capos* of the 3252, is enveloped in smoke after LA FC score against Montreal Impact at the Banc of California Stadium. May 2019, Los Angeles, United States.

Ultras from Persija shortly before boarding a coach for the 24 hour journey east to watch their team play PSS Sleman in a pre-season tournament. A few hours later we were being chased by a group of machete-wielding ultras from Persija's arch rivals, Persib Bandung. March 2019, Bogor, Indonesia.

A Persija fan wearing an anti-Persib Bandung T-shirt after making the long trip east to watch his team play PSS Sleman in a pre-season tournament. March 2019, Sleman Regency, Indonesia.

A Persija *capo* with a megaphone straddles the fence at the Maguwoharjo International Stadium and urges the 12,000 away fans who have made the long trip east to sing. March 2019, Sleman Regency, Indonesia.

former campaign chairman who is now in a US jail for tax and bank fraud – and the money of Ukraine's richest man, Rinat Akhmetov, Yanukovych made an incredible political comeback and won the 2010 presidential election. He jailed his most prominent opponents – like Yulia Tymoshenko – once in power.[3]

Ukraine is a vast, complex country rich in mineral wealth. The east, where most of this mineral wealth is found, largely speaks Russian, with many looking to Moscow rather than Kyiv; the west speaks Ukrainian (although most Ukrainians speak some Russian) and is a stronghold for Ukrainian nationalism and those who look towards Western Europe. At the end of 2013 Yanukovych was faced with a choice: to look east or to look west. The president had promised to sign an Association Agreement with the EU, a signal to the country's young population that Ukraine was seeking a closer future with Western Europe. But Russia, who had a strong influence over its neighbour, opposed it. Russian President Vladimir Putin feared that another key trading partner and strategic asset would be lost to his rivals in the West. Yanukovych pulled out of signing the documents under pressure from Moscow. Huge numbers of protesters descended on city squares across the country, centred on Kyiv, in the following weeks.

The conflict escalated in mid-January when Yanukovych signed a so-called 'dictatorship law' that gave him almost unlimited power to suppress any dissent. On the evening of 18 February the police stormed the protest camp on Maidan. Twenty-seven people were killed, including seven police officers. Snipers began killing protesters, the vast majority killed five years ago today, on 20 February; 48 protestors died, four police officers. Over 100 protesters were killed across a three-day period. They have since been named the 'heavenly hundred'. A makeshift memorial snakes up the road next to the square, towards Instytutska Street, where most were shot: a long line of shrines, each with a photo of the protestor who had been killed. Shortly after, Yanukovych fled the capital and crossed the border into Russia, where he sought refuge. The protesters had won, even if it came at a high price. But it was a victory that, in part, had an unusual key actor. Large numbers of ultras from Ukraine's football teams had joined the activists and protestors in the square.

Under communism, when Ukraine was part of the Soviet Union, football hooliganism had gained a surprising foothold. The 1972 UEFA Cup Winners' Cup final between Glasgow Rangers and Dynamo Moscow was disrupted by a violent pitch invasion that swung the game in Rangers' favour. Dynamo, wrote Avram Liebenau for Pushkin House, 'never got over the injustice of nearly completing one of the greatest comebacks in European footballing history'. And that was just one legacy from that game. 'As the underbelly of European football beamed into Soviet living rooms,' Liebenau wrote, 'Russian youths saw rebellion, escapism and camaraderie in creating their own.'[4]

The violence and the fashion were based on British hooliganism, and especially punk. One particularly notable fight took place on 19 September 1987, when Spartak Moscow arrived in Ukraine for their game against Dynamo Kyiv. The day before, Spartak players out shopping in Kyiv had been attacked by a group of Dynamo fans, and after the game a riot broke out that shocked Moscow's political establishment. 'There was an explosion in a telephone booth and the clothes of one Spartak fan were set alight. Passengers's suitcases were thrown on the rails. I turned my back and was stupefied. An avalanche of people rolled over the platform. A real bloody battle began. Even girls were fighting,' an eyewitness told the *Moscovsky Komsomolets* newspaper.[5] There were several other riots across the Soviet Union that season, most notably in Georgia and Lithuania. The authorities feared that football tribalism and connected violence were becoming outlets for expressions of dangerous nationalistic impulses. They responded by banning alcohol in the stadiums, strictly segregating fans and, in some cases, banning away support altogether. It was even suggested that, at one point, the authorities were considering hosting arranged fighting tournaments between fan groups 'to blow off steam in the stadium rather than in the streets outside'.[6]

The fall of communism and the disintegration of the Soviet Union ended the regular confrontations between Dynamo and Spartak, but each newly independent state, including Ukraine, now had its own hooliganism problem to deal with. The new era of openness and the possibility for travel meant that new influences entered Eastern European football, melding the colour and pageantry of the Italian ultra scene with heavily British-styled hooligan violence and fashion. It was the second wave of ultra groups spreading throughout Europe, not just in Eastern Europe but northern Europe too, especially Germany, the Netherlands and Scandinavia. By the end of the 1990s almost all Ukrainian, Russian and Polish teams had both ultra groups – that dealt with the pyro and match atmosphere – and firms that dealt with the organised violence. In Russia and Ukraine the organised fight scene became known as *okolofutbola*, Russian for 'around football'. In Poland it was known as *ustawka*. At most clubs the two groups – ultras and firms – had become indistinguishable from each other.

The arranged fight scene was now incredibly popular across all of Eastern and northern Europe. Gone were the days of lagered-up British hooligans swarming a city centre in a disorganised brawl. Now highly trained MMA fighters compete in organised mass fights with rules and norms. The changing of the guard, from a now defunct English hooligan culture to the now dominant arranged fight scene from Eastern Europe and Germany, came in Marseille at Euro 2016. On 10 June, before England played Russia, a group of about 150 Russian men attacked England fans drinking in the Old Port. The level of violence and organisation was shocking. 'It was like nothing I've ever seen before,' said Steve Neill of Northumbria Police. 'The Russians came with serious intent to carry out barbaric violence. They were highly organised, very effective. We saw football hooliganism on a different level.'[7]

The violence at first appeared to be a PR victory for Russia.

Russia's president Vladimir Putin could afford a smirk and a few derogatory remarks about the England fans' poor performance. English football hooliganism, after all, had been all but eradicated in the Premier League era. But the violence also exposed the close links that the Kremlin and various far-right and ultra-nationalist politicians had with ultra groups in Russia. Alexander Shprygin, a former Dynamo Moscow fighter who had set up the Union of Russian Fans (at the behest, he said, of the FSB, the successor to the KGB), explained how for ten years politicians would provide transport for their firms to games, in return for 'security', a ruse so that they could be called upon whenever far-right street violence was deemed politically expedient. Shprygin had been pictured with Putin on several occasions. But Shprygin had chartered the flights to Marseille for the hooligans. With two years to go before Russia's own World Cup, they were effectively excommunicated.

'For ten years we were supported by the government,' said Shprygin. 'After France, the government stopped supporting us.'[8]

Serhii Filimonov thrived in the *okolofutbola* scene. Ukraine's ultra groups and associated firms, like almost every single firm and the majority of ultra groups in Eastern Europe, were firmly far right, ultra-nationalist and steeped in a culture of violence. Before the revolution they were regarded as something of a nuisance, with regular reports of clashes between fans inside and outside Ukraine's stadiums. The most trained and dedicated, however, kept a lower profile, arranging fights with other firms in faraway locations, sometimes involving 10, 20, even 100 people at a time. Secluded forests, far from the police, were a favourite spot. They trained with almost military dedication.

The ultras converged on Maidan, not to try and force Ukraine to take a pro-EU direction as most of the activists demanded. They were as anti-EU as many in the east of the country. As Sergiy, a Metalist Kharkiv ultra told a Ukrainian TV documentary about football supporters and Maidan called *Ultras*, he hoped 'for an independent Ukraine. Independent from Europe and Russia.'[9] Former hated rivals found themselves on the same side for once and, most importantly, had an important skill that few in Maidan had – regular experience of fighting with the police.

'I was coming back home from my girlfriend's just prior to Maidan and I was jumped by twenty anti-fa [anti-fascist] fans from Arsenal Kyiv. I was more than angry,' Filimonov recalled of those days before the protests began. Arsenal Kyiv was the only leading club in Ukraine with left-wing ultras. 'When Maidan started, I saw the same guys there! But I said this was not the time. So, I shook their hands. We have these ideological and club differences, but we shook hands. Maidan is not left wing or right wing, Nazi or Commie, or whatever. This was the war against Yanukovych.'

By early January 2014 Dynamo's ultras had formed a defence battalion, designed to protect the protestors against the *titushky*, pro-government thugs that many believed were paid to attack them. 'We appeal to all those who have yet to join the defence of Kyiv from these bastard sellouts,' one Dynamo ultras group, the White Boys Club, announced on their VK page, the Russian equivalent of Facebook: 'We're not going out in favour of joining Europe ... Not against Russia and Russians!!! We're going out ... FOR THE PEOPLE OF KYIV, FOR OUR CITY, FOR OUR COUNTRY, FOR OUR HONOR!' The next day, Yanukovych announced his so-called 'Dictatorship Laws'.

Volunteer 'defence forces' began springing up everywhere, to support the protestors in their town and city squares. As well as the ultras from teams that would most obviously support Maidan – Dnipro and especially Karpaty Lviv, from the far west of Ukraine and known for their ultra-nationalist views – support also came from ultras in the east and south, whose constituency was traditionally pro-Russian: Zorya Luhansk, Metalist Kharkiv, Chornomorets Odessa and Metalurg Zaporizhya. There were also the ultras of Tavriya Simferopol and Sevastopol in the soon to be annexed Crimea, many of whom also supported Maidan. 'They were visibly the most organised,' said Pavel Klymenko, who was working as an activist focusing on far-right groups in football in Ukraine at the time of Maidan. 'Whereas the other people were like office managers, and went on instinct, they [the ultras] were organised, they knew how to defend themselves.'

The days leading up to the bloodiest hours of the Maidan uprising were chaotic. The ultras, Filimonov said, took to the front lines 'to give the people who were at Maidan a feeling of security and understanding that they are being guarded. They won't fight physically, right? But it gives them the feeling that they have some backup and people who are willing to give up their health and lives for this noble cause.' The authorities quickly caught up with him. He discovered that he was a wanted man. His mother had been taken into custody and told that he was on, in effect, a government kill list. 'They told her: "Your boy is a criminal, he will be killed, and it will end up really badly." But on this paper was all sorts of data. Pictures, the way I dressed, where I hung out.'

The protestors were not outnumbered but they were out-armed, something Filimonov felt he needed to urgently redress. 'We knew they [the police] were taking over Maidan and we knew that we needed arms,' he said. 'And the crime guys didn't want to sell guns because they knew they would be used against them. So we made homemade guns.' After car-jacking a Porsche that belonged to the security of one local oligarch, they took their pistols, hijacked a trolley bus and rammed it to the front of the protest to form a barrier before setting it on fire. Filimonov also had, he told me, a grenade, a gift from a friend that he smuggled back from Russia after attending his father's funeral. Twice he considered using it. One time, he said, he stood over a group of 50 police officers at the October Palace, grenade in hand, and considered the consequences of dropping it in. He decided against it. In the fighting that followed Filimonov and about 40 of his colleagues ended up being pushed back and cornered. They decided to flee to the recently evacuated Canadian embassy, as one of their group had a Canadian passport. After easily pushing past the security, they sheltered there for two days. They even considered applying for asylum in Canada, where they would train, regroup and return to fight another day.

The incident went unreported for a year, until the Canadian Press, a Canadian news agency, pieced together what was a serious breach of security protocol. 'I understand there was a Canadian passport holder associated in some way with the group,' said Roman Waschuk, the Canadian ambassador. The opening of the doors was 'a gesture designed to react and to reach out to the people suffering in the turmoil'.[10]

Protestors seriously injured when the police stormed the Maidan protest camp on 18 February were treated on the lobby floor before being ferried to hospital in the embassy's mini van, which was later found burned out and abandoned. 'From what I was told, it was several days and they left flowers on departure,' Waschuk said.

After Yanukovych fled east Filimonov left the embassy and began planning for what he believed was the inevitable war to come. Russia's annexation of Crimea, first by force and later through a flawed referendum, was the catalyst. He travelled to Dnipropetrovsk with a group of like-minded Dynamo fans. There he met with the ultras from Dnipro, a team that had a friendship with Dynamo. Around 50 of his group signed up for a new volunteer fighting force, the Azov battalion, led by Andriy Biletsky, a long-time political leader of the far right who had founded the National Socialist Assembly, a coalition of extreme nationalist, radical right and neo-Nazi groups. His aim, back then at least, was to 'lead the white races of the world in a final crusade ... against Semite-led *Untermenschen*'.[11] (He has since denied that he ever espoused anti-semitic views.) When Maidan began, Biletsky was in jail in his native Kharkiv on what he and his supporters believed were politically motivated charges following an armed scuffle in the Patriot of Ukraine headquarters. Four days after Yanukovych fled for Russia, Ukraine's parliament, the Rada, passed a law to free all political prisoners. The interior minister Arsen Avakov signed a law that allowed for the creation of volunteer fighting forces up to 12,000 strong. Biletsky was released, headed east, and became the first commander of Azov, the roots of which can be found in a volunteer fighting force set up by ultras from Kharkiv, where Avakov was governor.[12]

I'd first heard of Azov back in the summer of 2014. I was in Kyiv to watch Shakhtar Donetsk play. The war meant that the Ukrainian champions were now exiled in Kyiv, and later Lviv in the far west of the country. At a league game I'd met the Shakhtar ultras who had travelled hundreds of miles for the game. I'd assumed they would be pro-Russian, but instead I discovered that they supported Maidan and several were planning on signing up for a newly created volunteer regiment to fight in the east. Some wanted to be 'part of Russia', said Vladyslav, a 21-year-old finance student who I'd met outside the ground. 'Normal people want to stay. I am a patriot. I love my country. I love Ukraine. We all speak Russian. Since a kid, Russian is my mother tongue. Our problem is corruption, not Russian speakers.' Throughout the game the ultras let off black smoke bombs and pyro as Shakhtar cruised to an easy 5–0 victory. 'Some boys who were at the match today took the military oath and will go to Donbass,' Vladyslav told me later. Sure enough, the next day, the Shakhtar Ultras Twitter account announced that a group of ultras had been sworn in (as many as 75 according to Vladyslav), joined Azov and were now headed for Donbass.[13]

Azov's first real action was in Mariupol, a vitally important Black Sea port city in the Donbass region and close to the Russian border. Ukraine's second largest metals plant, the Illich Steel and Iron Works, owned by Metinvest, employed 60,000 people, processing steel for anything from shipbuilding to oil pipelines. In 2018 it made $1.2 billion profit[14] for the company's owner, Rinat Akhmetov, who also owns Shakhtar Donetsk (and is a former financial backer of Yanukovych). Filimonov arrived in Mariupol with virtually no equipment and nothing to fight with. 'During the training I only had five bullets. We looked like bums. I had a supermarket security uniform,' Filimonov said.

What was your job in Azov? I asked him.

'The storming group,' he replied.

What did that involve?

'I must go first into the building and kill everyone,' he answered matter-of-factly.

The liberation of Mariupol in June 2014 made Azov's name. The Ukrainian film *Ultras* laid out how the various ultras groups who had previously been enemies came together. The importance of the ultras was clear: 65 per cent of Azov's fighters came from the scene. 'They [the ultras] came to Azov in groups and ready-to-go teams because of *okolofutbola*,' Biletsky said in the film.[15]

They first had to deal with long-seated resentments and hatreds. In the Ukrainian ultras scene there had been a loose alliance of friendships between Dnipro, Dynamo and Lviv against an alliance of Kharkiv, Odessa and Shakhtar Donetsk. The war had united the enemies. The head of Dnipro's ultras, Rodion Kudryashov, or Radik, played a key role in the battle as commander of reconnaissance, spending two weeks behind enemy lines plotting a path to the city's recapture. 'A lot of people got to know the name Azov after we put our hearts into Mariupol's defence,' he said. 'We were already ideologically ready to defend our country.'[16]

It wasn't just troops that were needed. Hundreds more joined volunteer organisations to procure weapons and equipment for Ukraine's poorly armed soldiers. Roman Sinitcyn co-founded Narodny Tyl, the People's Home Front. 'We bought a hundred tonnes of equipment for soldiers,' he said when we met in a cafe near Filimonov's office. They even helped other ultra groups buy theirs, whether thermals or Chinese-made drones or even rifles. Sinitcyn was a member of the Crusaders, the ultras group of Volyn Lutsk. Half of the group, around 100 men, joined the fighting on the front line whilst the rest, once the league restarted, raised money and promoted recruitment. Sinitcyn's skill, though, was getting weapons and other equipment to the front line, something that was illegal. 'But not if they are bought for hunting!' he said. 'By law you can buy everything as a hunter.' Many of Azov's vehicles came from the People's Front too, like second hand, British made Land Rovers they would equip with hand-made armour.

After a string of humiliating defeats for the Ukrainian army, Mariupol proved that the Russian-backed forces (and the Russian military itself) could be stopped. Azov made the city their base. Filimonov's military career would end two months later at Ukraine's military nadir: the Battle of Ilovaisk. As many as a thousand servicemen were killed in a botched raid on the city of Ilovaisk, designed to cut the rebels' supply lines. Regular Russian forces moved in, and when the Ukrainian military realised they had been encircled they arranged a ceasefire to retreat. But the Russians didn't abide by it and Filimonov was caught in an ambush.[17] 'Our commander said that we should try to escape but not everyone will survive,' he recalled. 'We should run and not stop when someone falls, because it will be our death too.' He threw a smoke grenade and began running as the 'enemy began shooting from all the barrels they had'. A grenade exploded above him and knocked Filimonov to the floor. 'I hallucinated that my legs were torn off, I felt like I was inside a black-and-white film about World War Two in the fight with Nazis,' he said. He'd been hit by shrapnel on his back, legs and arms. Filimonov's front-line war was over.

Filimonov examined his damaged hand as he recounted his war story, as if it was as fresh to him as wet paint. He was young, articulate and charismatic. It was difficult to square the activist-veteran-ultra with the far-right views of his political party. He certainly didn't think of himself as a fascist and he didn't use overtly racist language. Instead he talked about corruption and bringing oligarchs to justice. His Instagram account was a carefully curated mix of football casual fashion, family-man snaps with his wife and young son, and topless shots of him working out or training other recruits on how to handle a machine gun. He had, amongst others, the Tryzub (trident), Ukraine's coat of arms, tattooed on his chest, below the words 'VICTORY OR VALHALLA'. Other photos showed him in jail or standing trial, something that happened regularly after he undertook what he called 'civic action'.

Maidan and the war didn't just make Azov's name. It also rehabilitated the reputation of Ukraine's ultras. Before the uprising they were seen as irrelevant, violent and racist. A 2012 BBC documentary that aired before Ukraine was due to co-host the European Championship with Poland showed thousands of fans of Karpaty Lviv giving Nazi salutes and abusing black players. In Kharkiv they interviewed a Metalist ultra who was also a leader of the Patriots of Ukraine, another far-right organisation that was led by Andriy Biletsky. Although they denied being neo-Nazis, you could see hundreds of ultras giving Nazi salutes before they attacked a group of Indian students. Their party flag included a symbol similar to the neo-Nazi *wolfsangel* insignia.

Biletsky would use that symbol again after he disbanded the Patriots of Ukraine, incorporating it into Azov's flag.[18]

The war, and Maidan, changed everything, offering legitimacy to both ultras and the far right. 'Let us applaud the heroic soccer fans of Dnipro Cherkasy, Karpaty Lviv, and Vorskla Poltava!' said Oleh Tyahnybok, the leader of the nationalist, far-right Svoboda party. 'This is where solidarity starts. This is where patriotism starts.'[19]

Maidan had formed an unlikely coalition; ultras and the far right making common cause with liberal activists. 'For many Ukrainians this issue of what exact ideology the people have in this conflict with Russia is secondary,' said Andreas Umland, a political scientist at the Institute for Euro-Atlantic Cooperation, and an expert on Ukrainian and Russian politics. 'The far right is strongly anti-Russian, anti-Putin. And that's more important than the reason *why* they are against Russia.'

Pavel Klymenko, the activist who now works for FARE which monitors racism in Europe's stadiums (and publishes a country-by-country guide to far-right symbols that can be seen in stadiums[20]), believed that the role of the ultras has been romanticised and their connections to the far right glossed over. 'Even someone from a village in deepest western Ukraine would know that the ultras are the good guys,' he said, arguing that the prevailing narrative is that they joined the protest, joined the war, and that 'everything said against them is Russian propaganda'. Klymenko had long been in conflict with Ukraine's ultras for regularly pointing out the connections between fans involved in violence and figures in and around Azov and other far-right groups. When he published an investigation into the beating of four black supporters at a 2015 Champions League match between Dynamo and Chelsea, which implicated the Rodychi and led to sanctions by UEFA, he began to receive death threats. His previous work had seen the leader of the neo-Nazi C14 movement post an investigation that 'proved' Klymenko had received one million dollars from the Kremlin to smear 'Ukraine's heroes'.

'I quit using public transport for half a year. I didn't go out on the street further than two blocks from my apartment,' he said. 'It was difficult for a few months. Your face is on prime time saying you've got a million dollars for organising Ukrainian provocations.' Although Klymenko was present at the start of Maidan, he stopped going when the ultras turned up. 'It was exactly around the time local far-right hooligans were hunting me after [the] Ukraine sanction, so meeting them on Maidan was not the best plan,' he said. He no longer lives in Kyiv.

The National Corps burst on to the scene as a new political force in October 2016 when thousands marched through Kyiv in balaclavas and military fatigues carrying flaming torches. They chanted 'Death to enemies!' and 'Glory to the nation!' as Andriy Biletsky was voted in as party leader for a four-year term. At the same time a new force, the National Militia, emerged as the militant street wing of the party. 'When the authorities are impotent and cannot solve issues of vital importance for society, then simple, ordinary people are forced to take responsibility upon themselves,' Biletsky said.[21]

It had been a decision by Ukraine's interior minister Arsen Avakov to incorporate Azov into the regular army's National Guard in 2014. 'Although presented as a means to defuse the ultra-nationalist battalion, [this move] led to its explosive growth and branching out into the National Corps political party and increasingly assertive National Militia street movement,' wrote journalist Oleksiy Kuzmenko in an investigation for Bellingcat.[22] An interior ministry spokesman would later deny that Avakov had anything to do with the National Corps, who seemed to be well equipped and well funded. 'I'd like to hear on what such assumptions are grounded,' Arsen Shevchenko told the Ukrainian news agency UNIAN when asked about Avakov's alleged links to the far right.[23]

Since Maidan there has been a roll call of violent events involving emboldened far-right groups, including one nasty incident when the National Militia invaded a Roma camp near Kyiv before later destroying it, mocking women and children as they fled. They even streamed it all on Facebook Live.[24] There have since been other attacks on Roma camps, as well as on LGBT events and marches celebrating women's rights. These involved a host of organisations from the same far-right eco-systems: groups like C14, Right Sector, and Tradition and Order. In all cases the police did little to intervene. The inaction prompted four prominent human rights groups – Amnesty International, Front Line Defenders, Freedom House and Human Rights Watch – to release a joint open letter to Avakov. 'Hiding under a veneer of patriotism and what they describe as "traditional values", members of these groups have been vocal about their contempt for and intent to harm women's rights activists, ethnic minorities, lesbian, gay, bisexual, transgender, and intersex (LGBTI) people, and others who hold views that differ from their own,' they wrote. 'The near-total impunity enjoyed by members of groups that promote hatred and discrimination through violent means creates the impression that these attacks are tolerated by the Ukrainian authorities.'[25]

Despite a weight of evidence and, even though the US State Department declared the National Corps 'a nationalist hate group', they have denied they are a neo-Nazi organisation. 'I can assure you we are not neo-Nazis; we are simply people who want to change our country for the better,' said Ihor Vdovin, a spokesman for the National Militia.[26] Groups like the National Corps have often been highlighted in Russia's tightly controlled media, which frame Maidan not as a people's uprising, but an illegitimate fascist takeover abetted by a CIA obsessed with fomenting 'colour revolutions' in Russia's back yard. This has led to Ukraine's authorities defensively playing down accusations that the far right is gaining a foothold in the country, pointing out that, electorally speaking, far-right parties rarely meet the 5 per cent threshold needed to gain MPs in the parliament. Biletsky, who won a seat in the Rada in the 2014 parliamentary elections, was thought to be considering running in the presidential elections taking place in March and April 2019, but he never announced his candidacy (one poll had him at 0.0 per cent).

For Andreas Umland, the lack of electoral support for the far right was a reflection of Ukraine's complex and varied electorate. 'The ultras that have ended up now in Azov and partly with the far-right parties, I still wonder what exactly their ideology is,' he said. 'Some of them are clearly neo-Nazi, but others may not be and that may be a sort of general patriotism. It is sometimes very difficult to distinguish this sort of liberationist nationalism and the ultra-nationalism.'

Filimonov also denied that he was a neo-Nazi. To prove that his concern was 'corruption, about the need to stop stealing' rather than the issues that agitate neo-Nazis the most, he took me to a nearby building with a small park that, he said, his group was trying to save from development by a corrupt local oligarch he believed was working for Russian interests. We passed one wall on Striletska Street showing a huge, kitsch Zodiac mural depicting Maidan. A snake, with Putin's head, was being controlled with a rope. 'Behind this building is Sophia Tszigar, the most important building in Ukraine. It was built about a thousand years ago,' he said. 'In Ukraine you had buildings. In Russia, only frogs. Oligarchs want to destroy this building and build a hotel.' He gets out his phone and shows me a video from a TV news report a year before. In it, they report how a building site was invaded by a group of protestors from the National Corps. It shows the men, all dressed in black, vaulting over the fences and attacking the security as they trash the site. Filimonov comes on the screen, ripped from his Facebook Live stream. He's laughing as he helps smash down a fence, neck veins bulging. He enjoyed his work.

When we returned to his office, it was full of Azov veterans, including Maliar, who sat quietly by the window. He was covered in tattoos, his longish black hair swept to one side. He had a pronounced scar on his neck, partially covered by a 'VICTORY OR VALHALLA' tattoo. In one of Bellingcat's open-source investigations it found a trove of pictures of Maliar (which means 'painter' in Ukrainian; according to Filimonov he designed and made the *tifos* and protest banners). One photo from Instagram showed him with four swastika tattoos on his head. A video from one protest during Maidan showed him in front of several hundred policemen, swinging a long chain into the front row. Another photo captured him on the pitch shortly after his team, Dnipro, beat Napoli in the semi-finals of the Europa League in 2015. He had removed his top, revealing a distinctive skull tattoo covering most of his body, and invaded the pitch whilst carrying a black flag showing the white supremacist Celtic cross. UEFA forced Dnipro to play the next game behind closed doors and fined them €50,000. But, in the office, Maliar sat quietly and didn't talk. In another life he could have passed as a singer in an emo band. 'It's not right to say we are ultra right or ultra left,' said Filimonov when I asked again about his and the National Corps politics.

Over the coming months I'd keep tabs on the National Corps. I'd watch their protests, often posted on various Facebook sites, or their ephemeral Instagram stories. Filimonov was often there, arm still in a brace, trying to organise an angry crowd, dressed in black, their faces covered, as the election approached. There was the video of Filimonov 'arresting' Rafael Lusvarghi, a Brazilian who had become famous in Russia after he volunteered to fight with the separatists in Luhansk. Filimonov had caught him in Kyiv and marched him to the offices of the SBU, Ukraine's secret service, roughing him up a little along the way. Lusvarghi would later be handed a 13-year jail sentence.

Social media would also have a slew of posts and photos, stretching back years. I'd come across photos of people I'd shaken hands with who, in topless photos, had the numbers 14, 18 and 88 tattooed on their body. The number 88 refers to an alphabet number code that spells 'HH': Heil Hitler. 18 is the alphabet code for 'AH': Adolf Hitler. The number 14 referred to the '14 Words', a invocation coined by the American white supremacist and ideologue David Lane: 'We must secure the existence of our people and a future for white children.' Lane died in 2007 in a US prison after being convicted of being involved in the murder of a Jewish radio host. His writing makes him probably the most influential white supremacist in the world. Lane's final published book of essays was entitled *Victory or Valhalla*.

Everywhere I looked there were connections to far-right words, codes and tattoos steeped in Nazi lore. Filimonov and Rodion, the Dnipro ultra who had also made a name for himself in the war and was now also rising quickly within the National Corps, were considered clean cut and upwardly mobile. They'd shown bravery and guile on the front line and proved themselves to be capable organisers, both in *okolofutbola* and the ultra scenes. Now they were being rewarded with, or groomed for, upwardly mobile political positions in civilian life. Perhaps more importantly, both could wear a suit and tie without a swastika or Hitler number code poking out from their cuffs or collars. But not if Filimonov wore shorts, as he has a Totenkopf skull – a symbol used by the SS – tattooed on his right knee. Maliar would have had a harder time explaining away his tattoos if he ever sought office. The presidential elections were a few weeks away, and although Biletsky decided against standing, the National Corps had been appointed as one of the election's official observers. There were parliamentary elections coming up too, and it was touch and go whether they would reach the 5 per cent threshold. On Independence Square I had seen a National Corps gazebo, where volunteers handed out election leaflets, even though they didn't have a candidate. It listed the party's achievements so far, which read more like a Green Party manifesto: a drive to donate blood for wounded veterans, donations for animal shelters, the replanting of hundreds of trees and direct action against crooked real-estate developers. Certainly there was nothing there about protecting the purity and sanctity of the white race. At the top of the leaflet it read:

> We, the party of the people, are responsible before the Ukrainian people. As long as our state is in a catastrophic position, only the National Corps will be the saviour of our country. Our ideology originates from the people

Below were the pictures of two men. Biletsky, the party leader, and Filimonov. Filimonov was sure he would be on the party's list. True change, he believed, could only come from being on the inside. But Filimonov seemed happiest on the street, whether it was in football or politics. When he was young, he said, his options were either a life of crime or being a sportsman. He was a good wrestler, so it was only a matter of time before he was propositioned to try his hand at fighting in the *okolofutbola* scene. He enjoyed it, and so began his association with the ultras. There are fewer fights at home, of course, as the war truce between the different ultras groups had more or less held since 2014. 'Except Chornomorets [Odessa],' explained Filimonov as he found a video on his phone, 'because they have stayed friends with [the ultras of Russian team] Spartak Moscow. But we fight in the forest.'

He showed me a video of the last fight, a brutal 60 vs 60 affair against Eintracht Frankfurt which Dynamo won convincingly. The next video was in an open field, taken a few days before, involving Dynamo's 'Youth' team and their friends Metalist Kharkiv in an open field. A group of around a dozen men run forward and smash into their opponents. Most of the Kharkiv firm are wearing red T-shirts with a swastika in the middle.

Metalist went out of business in 2016 after the oligarch that funded the team, Serhiy Kurchenko, fled the country following Maidan. All that was left of the club today was its firm.

Do you like football?

'I think no,' Filimonov replied. 'I don't know the names of our players at Dynamo.' It was all about the fighting. Another video came up, this time of a fight with GKS Katowice in Poland. 'When we came to Poland, to Katowice, we found the Polish ultras, and we said, "Let's fight",' he recalled. But there was a hitch. 'They said: "We can't, we have a fight with our enemy." Warsaw or Kraków, I can't remember. "Today you are our friend. What do you need? Cocaine? Girls?"'

But that wasn't for him or the rest of the Rodychi. 'Fanatics,' Filimonov said, 'don't like cocaine or alcohol.' The scene involves hard training. 'Our guys like marijuana,' he said. And with that Maliar took out a knife and silently constructed a homemade bong out of two plastic Sprite bottles, then lit the pipe.

The Rodychi sit in Sector 21 of Kyiv's Olympic Stadium at every game. It was the return leg of the Europa League Round of 32 against Olympiacos, on a bitingly cold February night. The night before, Filimonov's crew went out looking for Olympiacos fans to exact revenge for the events of a week earlier, but to no avail. This was probably for the best. Filimonov would later show me a police intelligence report that, he said, had been leaked to him, outlining how he would likely try and get revenge on Olympiacos's ultras because of his finger, and be ready to bring him in. It had already dropped below minus-five as kick-off approached, but almost 50,000 people were already here. On the other side of the vast stadium, rebuilt for Euro 2012, some Dynamo ultras – the White Boys Club – had constructed an elaborate choreography of a skull wearing a blue ice hockey helmet in Sector 41. It was to bring attention to the plight of Sokil Kyiv, the city's famed ice hockey team and academy, which was about to go out of business. Around 2,000 ultras, most with their faces covered, sang elaborate, choreographed chants. In the middle of the flags (One read: 'Hasta La Vista, Separatista'), scarves and endless streams of blue, white and red pyro and smoke bombs, was a Croatian flag. A delegation of the Bad Blue Boys from Dinamo Zagreb were in town. The two ultra groups had forged a deep friendship due to the war in the East. It wasn't just Ukrainians who were drawn to the front. Nationalists from all around the world rallied to Ukraine's cause, whilst Russia saw hundreds of fighters arrive from its allies. Croatia allied with Ukraine. Serbian fighters, with its close relationship with its Orthodox brother Russia, often fought for the other side. To honour their guests, the Dynamo Kyiv ultras started a chant. Within seconds, thousands were joining in.

'Ubi, ubi, ubi, Serbina!'

'Death, death, death, [to the] Serbs.'

Filimonov arrived late, with his wife, carrying his young son. 'This is his first game!' he said, beaming. He was accompanied by his usual crew, including Maliar and Rodion Kudryashov, the head of Dnipro's ultras, now one of the highest-ranked members of the National Corps. Filimonov was a little disappointed by the lack of Olympiacos fans, pointing up to the small block of supporters protected by hundreds of riot police with his one good arm. 'I wanted revenge for my finger!' One member of the Rodychi in a hood, face covered with a scarf, ran towards their sector, lit a flare and hurled it towards them. But it fell well short.

I asked why he sat in a separate section to the rest of the ultras, and he explained that there had been a disagreement, that some of the ultras had had contact with the police that he didn't approve of. 'They are ultras. We are hooligans.'

Filimonov walked through the crowd and seemed to shake everyone's hand. On the pitch, Dynamo took the lead thanks to a wonderful goal from their new Spanish signing Fran Sol. Filimonov, though, didn't stay long. It had been a busy few hours. There was another civil action for Kateryna Handziuk, the murdered activist: this time a banner at the courthouse with the names of the people they accused of ordering her murder. And then a banner and a Facebook Live video to honour International Mother Language Day. Above us in the upper tier of the stadium a new protest began. Red flares were lit and a banner was hung at the front calling for justice for Handziuk. It read: 'The Killers Of Handziuk Must Be Imprisoned'. Dynamo held on to win 1–0 and reached the quarter-finals of the tournament, but Filimonov didn't stay to see the celebrations. He was gone by half-time as the ultras sang for Kateryna Handziuk and for the death of the Serbs.

MARIUPOL, UKRAINE

THE UKRAINIAN NATIONAL ANTHEM WAS being played, out of old, crackly speakers, for the small crowd who had gathered at the Volodymyr Boiko Stadium, home of Mariupol FC. Only a few hundred people had turned up for the Saturday afternoon kick-off, in the freezing cold, to watch the home team play Olimpik Donetsk, another team from the Donbass region. They stood, with their hands on their hearts, and sang along.

'We are here for one of the most boring football matches you could have, Mariupol against Olimpik Donetsk,' said Anton Trebukhov wearily as he shelled sunflower seeds. I had almost missed the start of the game, and the restart of the Ukrainian Premier League after its winter break, arriving at the stadium just as the anthems began. Mariupol was 750km away from Kyiv, a bone-shaking 24-hour drive east over broken, potholed, unlit roads. The closer you got to the city, the more evidence of the war presented itself: abandoned trenches, machine-gun nests, huge anti-tank spikes and concrete road blocks set up by the Ukrainian military.

After the initial flash-bang of Crimea's annexation, the battle over Donetsk, and the taking (and retaking) of Mariupol, the war had settled into a rhythm. More than 10,000 people, civilians and troops, had died since 2014 but the front line was still 'hot'. People were still dying every day, but it rarely made the international news any more. Whilst every other team from the Donbass region had headed west to find a temporary home and safety in Kyiv, Kharkiv and Lviv, FC Mariupol had decided to stay. So did Trebukhov who, like Filimonov, took a similar route from the terraces into organised politics. He was one of the Mariupol FC's ultra leaders who now ran the Mariupol office of the National Corps. But right now, in this empty freezing stadium, he lamented what had become of his club. If Azov was formed and powered by the fanaticism and organisation of Ukraine's ultras, in the city where Azov is the official protector, the war had destroyed its fan culture.

'We formed back in the 1990s but the main peak in our developments was 2012 to 2014, we had several good victories in *okolofutbola*,' Trebukhov said sadly. 'But then the war erupted.' He pointed into the distance. 'The war is there, twenty kilometres away.'

A scattering of families and old men in the stands were all that remained of Mariupol's once vibrant fan culture. The club's two firms, Project 32 and Youth, were barely functioning. 'It really hurts me how the tribune is empty, how we have lost spectators,' he said. Fifty of his group joined Azov, and were still with them a few miles from here.

Suddenly a penalty was awarded to Mariupol, scored by the Ukrainian youth international Oleksandr Pikhalyonok, one of half a dozen players on loan from Shakhtar Donetsk. On the halfway line a new banner had been hung up: 'We Are Stronger Together'.

'But now I'm getting a little bit more cheerful,' said Trebukhov, rubbing his hands and finally cracking a smile. 'Even though this looks dull, and no fans are here.'

Like Filimonov, Trebukhov volunteered and joined the front line with Azov in 2014. But he soon worked out he wasn't a frontline military man, and instead turned his attention to the National Corps when it was founded in 2016. The association with Azov, who were widely seen as liberators and protectors of the city, meant that they immediately found some popularity. They now had as many as 20,000 active supporters, Trebukhov said. He too was preparing for the parliamentary elections as well as the local municipality elections, hoping to transform street power into real power. Until then it was a similar treadmill of civil action and football matches. On one occasion the two came together. 'When Dynamo Kyiv came to town,' he said, 'it heated up.'

Mariupol had become more than just a calling card for Azov and the National Corps. The city's name was often used as shorthand by mainstream politicians in Kyiv, especially the president Petro Poroshenko, for a symbol of resistance to Russia. So when Dynamo Kyiv announced that it would not be travelling to the port city to fulfil a league fixture in August 2017 due to the proximity of the front line, they upset all the wrong people. 'Matches in Mariupol are a great opportunity to demonstrate that we have a single country, we have strong special services and an army,' said Andriy Pavelko, the president of Ukraine's football federation.[27] But this didn't mollify Dynamo's board, who claimed that three of Ukraine's security agencies had told the club their safety could not be guaranteed.

'Will the main squad leave for the match against Mariupol? Under the current conditions and in these circumstances, of course it won't,' said Dynamo's vice-president Andriy Madzianovsky.[28]

This created a problem for the government. Mariupol was the country's second biggest port, and home to the vast Illich Steel Works in the centre of Mariupol. Even if you couldn't see it, you could feel it. It emitted a constant low hum, day and night. For Ukrainian politicians like Poroshenko, an essential part of projecting normality involved portraying Mariupol as safe and secure under the Ukrainian military. Dynamo's refusal to travel to the match ran counter to that. The match was awarded to Mariupol FC but when the fixture came up again, Dynamo was effectively shamed into turning up. This time, Poroshenko declared that he would in fact attend the game, leaving Dynamo's management with a tough choice: fulfil the fixture, or be

embarrassed by the country's president and be made to look unpatri-
otic. Dynamo's president Ihor Surkis took the news, and a Court for
Arbitration in Sport decision to uphold Dynamo's punishment of a
3–0 forfeit to Mariupol, pretty badly. 'You all know full well that our
supporters were some of the initiators of the Revolution of Dignity,' he
told the TV show *ProFutbol* – using the Ukrainian term for Maidan
– before wrongly accusing some of the ultras of Shakhtar of fighting
for the separatists.[29]

So Dynamo turned up in April 2018, along with a thousand ultras.
One anti-federation flag in the away sector depicted the Ukrainian
coat of arms as a guillotine. Poroshenko flew in by helicopter as promised, but the match – a 3–2 victory for Dynamo – did not go smoothly,
and for once it had nothing to do with the war. Trebukhov, what was
left of Mariupol's ultras and their counterparts from Dynamo used
the match to send a message to Poroshenko. One banner read:
'Suitcase, Train, Maldives', a reference to Poroshenko's recent holiday
to the Maldives that cost half a million euros.

'It was, in a way, fun,' recalled Trebukhov as Mariupol took a 2–1
lead against Olimpik from another penalty. 'It provoked this whole
thing to get a little bit heated up. There were a lot of fans. There were
pyrotechnics. Lots of things going on. And then behind there,' he
said, pointing to the left, where a group of policemen were standing
next to piles of snow, trying to keep warm, 'we had a good fight.'

Once the game was finished, ultras from both sides met behind
the main stand. Not to fight each other, but to fight the common
enemy: the police. Trebukhov, he would later show me, had bought a
vehicle registration plate for his car that had the numbers 1312 on it.
'We were fighting against the police with the Dynamo ultras,' he said
whilst showing me the video. As Poroshenko was whisked away to his
waiting helicopter, several hundred young men, their faces covered,
threw smoke bombs and rocks at the banks of police in riot gear who
had moved in to clear the stadium. Nine police officers were injured.

The next day Trebukhov took me to an Azov event at a local gym
in the city. The walls surrounding the boxing ring and wrestling mats
were covered in Azov and National Corps flags, as well as more

explicit far-right imagery. One black flag displayed a large Tyr rune, a Nordic symbol that was used by the Third Reich on the badge of the Nazis' first paramilitary training school. Today, though, was a show of unity, a Sunday morning Cross Fit competition that had brought together members of Azov from the police, the navy and, now, the National Guard, which it had been incorporated into. Heavy metal blared out as the groups of hyper-muscled men raced against the clock to lift and pull and run.

'This is one of the most important cities for the war and its liberation broke the "Russian spring" ideology,' said 'Kir', a military commander at Azov's officer school with a huge beard, still panting from winning his heat. 'They captured Donetsk and Crimea, and wanted to build a [land] bridge [between the two] but their ideas were crushed in Mariupol. Crushed by Azov. We protected this city three times.' Azov and the National Corps appeared to have been completely integrated into Ukraine's political sphere. They had made themselves invaluable to the revolution and, now, invaluable to the protection of Mariupol. The ultras' past misdeeds – the violence, the racism – were all but forgotten. After all, the city hadn't been hit by any Russian-made Grad rockets since 2017, when a market was hit in an eastern suburb, killing ten people. But the skirmishes still took place every day a few miles from here.

The road east, towards the frontline, passed rows and rows of large anti-tank spikes. Every 200m a Ukrainian army road block stopped us and questioned who we were. A sign warned not to step off the road. The snow-covered fields were heavily mined. It was now, perhaps, the most heavily mined area in the world. According to the Ukrainian government, nearly a thousand civilians had been killed by mines since the war began. The army eventually stopped us at Lebedynske, one kilometre from the front line and within range of Russian snipers. Buildings all around had huge chunks missing after being hit by artillery fire. A handful of people still lived here, moving through the wreckage of their town. Muffled booms could be felt more than they could be heard. They began slowly at first, before the gap between them got shorter and shorter. The rebels had begun their daily artillery fire. It was time, the soldier told me, to leave.

KYIV, UKRAINE

TWENTY-FOUR HOURS LATER, AFTER ANOTHER bone-shaking drive back to Kyiv, the Olympic Stadium was filled with the sound of Ukraine's national anthem, if not many home supporters. It was the last fixture of the first round of the Ukrainian Premier League's restart and, although the stadium was virtually empty, the section reserved for the away fans was almost full of exiles in their new home. Dynamo Kyiv was playing Zorya Luhansk, a team from the city found the furthest east in Ukraine and currently under the control of the Luhansk People's Republic. Everyone here was a refugee, relocated to Kyiv. The team, too, played its home games away from Luhansk, in the city of Zaporizhia about 300km west of the Russian border. The move hadn't done them much harm on the pitch. Over the past three seasons since the war began Zorya had finished fourth twice and third once. In 2016 they qualified for the Europe League, playing eventual winners Manchester United in the group stage (United travelled to the safety of Odessa, over 800km away from Luhansk, and won 2–0).

In the centre, a small group of around a hundred were the only people chanting. They were holding up a white flag with a tiger painted on it and the words 'Black and White', the name of their ultras group. I took a picture and someone grabbed my arm: Vladislav, the Zorya Luhansk ultra I had agreed to meet here. 'Let's talk after the game,' he said. Dynamo ran out easy 5–0 winners.

In a cafe next door Vladislav Ovcharenko began to tell me his story. He looked younger than his 21 years and almost unrecognisable from the video I had seen earlier seen of him. Today, sitting at the table, Vladislav had put on a little weight and grown his hair, shaving it on one side and styling it a little like Cristiano Ronaldo. But just over a year before, he had been part of a prisoner swap arranged between the Ukrainian government and the Luhansk People's Republic (LPR). Ukrainian TV captured the moment he got off the coach after crossing the front line. He was gaunt after 15 months in prison, hair shaved. A phone was thrust into his hand. It was President Poroshenko, who had been involved in brokering his freedom. 'Mr President, on behalf of all the guys, thank you, thank you to all of Ukraine,' he said. He had been held in a separatist jail, alongside his friend Artem Akhmerov, since his arrest and conviction for treason 18 months before.

Both were members of Zorya's Black and White ultras who had been caught undertaking subtle acts of resistance and uploading the videos on YouTube. One video saw them taking a Ukrainian flag to the centre of the city and flying it in the square, wearing hoods and covering their faces with scarves. They became famous for their small, incognito acts of rebellion whilst infuriating the pro-Russian authorities, who called them a 'pro-fascist cell' that was 'spying for Ukrainian intelligence'. But when they were eventually arrested in 2016 after filming themselves burning an LPR flag, the book was thrown at them. Artem got 13 years; Vladislav was sentenced to 17 years. 'I was thrown in a basement,' Vladislav said of his imprisonment. 'It was just a pit without any water or a toilet.'

As the situation in the east deteriorated in February 2014, after the former president Yanukovych had fled to Russia, the Ukrainian league was suspended. But when it returned it was clear that the fixtures in the east of the country were a potential powder keg. There were, Vladislav said, around 500 ultras at every home game. He wasn't part of its hooligan firm. He wasn't a fighter. He'd come through the Zorya youth academy and had once hoped to make it as a player. So, instead, he took care of the choreo, pyro and chants, which were resolutely pro-Ukrainian even as the city was being taken over by the pro-Russian LPR. 'For me, the ultras, they are people who always support their team, no matter what, during defeats or victories, who never betray their native colours, which they treasure in their hearts since birth,' he said. 'The people who will root for their team and prove it in the terrace, in the hooligan scene, everywhere. These are people who will be totally faithful to their colours, their ideals, their club and their country.'

Gradually, all pro-Ukrainian voices were snuffed out. At a home game against Mariupol in April the riot police surrounded their tribune as they were attacked by pro-Russian supporters. The next day rebel forces stormed and occupied the offices of the SBU in Donetsk and Luhansk. That was the last game Zorya played in their city.

The situation in Luhansk was like a horror movie. Dead bodies littered the streets. For long periods Luhansk had no power and no water. The remains of over 500 civilians killed in the city were quickly decomposing due to the lack of electricity in the morgue.[30] 'Luhansk turned into a kind of Chernobyl,' Vladislav said of that time. 'You leave the house and you're not sure that you will ever return. You can be accused of spying for Ukraine. You can be shot dead, because you have a pro-Ukrainian position. They perceive you as an enemy. They are looking for you, they want to kill and destroy you, you shouldn't exist. If you're an ultra of Zorya Luhansk, you're a threat.'

The war had left dozens of football clubs on the other side of the front line. Moving to the safer cities in the west was of course no problem for teams with huge resources like Shakhtar Donetsk. It was impossible for three teams in the Crimea who now found themselves annexed and entered into the Russian pyramid, until UEFA intervened after protests from the Ukrainian federation. One, Tavriya Simferopol, had won Ukraine's first post-independence championship. Today there are two 'Tavriya' clubs; one that plays in a new Crimean league, and a phoenix club set up by a group of Tavriya ultras that is based in Ukraine, near Kherson, playing in the lower leagues.[31]

When the LPR overran Luhansk, 80 per cent of the Black and White left to fight in the Azov battalion. But Vladislav stayed. He was only 18 and his parents needed him. Rather than fight, Vladislav went about making videos showing his little acts of rebellion. He was spurred into action by a speech Poroshenko gave claiming there weren't any patriots left in Luhansk and Donetsk. 'We wanted to show that the people of Luhansk are worth fighting for,' he said. So Vladislav went about trying to prove to the outside world Poroshenko was wrong, posting a video of him holding a Ukrainian flag next to an 'I love Luhansk' sign in the centre of the city. When one of his best friends was killed they made a banner that read: 'Avenge the death of the Great Knights', one of the ten commandments of the Organisation of Ukrainian Nationalists, a confederation of nationalist and far-right groups formed in the late 1920s. The OUN was once lead by Stepan Bandera, a Ukrainian nationalist and Nazi collaborator whose organisation many believe was responsible for the massacre of Jews and Poles during World War Two. Yet Bandera is considered an independence hero by the Ukrainian far-right today. It was a phrase often used by Azov. But the final straw was when Vladislav was filmed in the middle of the forest burning the LPR's flag.

When the LPR took over all the state institutions they also had access to the police database. There was a file on the ultras and their political proclivities. They simply went through the list until they found their man and called him in for questioning. They said: "We want to talk with you, we know that you are Zorya ultras, we need to talk for two to three hours." But finally, as everyone knows, the "conversation" lasted for one and a half years.' Vladislav was accused of leaking reconnaissance data to the SBU. When they found communications between himself and members of the Black and White who were now in Azov, it was all the proof they needed. He was thrown into his pit, a windowless basement cell. He was tortured, beaten, and then found guilty of treason in a kangaroo court. After a few months he was taken to a regular detention centre. 'On the first day of detention there were beatings without interrogations, without questions, we were just beaten,' he recalled. At least he had a toilet and regular meals, even if they were usually handed 'lukewarm Ukrainian borscht or pearl-barley porridge with worms'.

His cellmates were all criminals convicted before the troubles who now found themselves under the control of a new sheriff. 'They were just regular people – sort of ordinary killers, thieves, and so on.' Rather than releasing them, the LPR began their sentences from scratch. Vladislav was in a bad way physically and psychologically. He felt abandoned and lost. 'The murderers and thieves, they helped me to recover mentally,' he said. 'When I came back after being sentenced to seventeen years, they hugged me and said: "Bro, hold on!"'

But back in Kyiv the two had not be forgotten. Filimonov and the Dynamo Kyiv ultras were holding regular protest marches demanding their release, and giving their cases prominence on the news. So much so that, after 18 months in jail, on 27 December 2017, at 8am, the two ultras were suddenly taken from the detention centre and driven to the front line. A prisoner exchange had been agreed and the two were on the list. They were walked over the line, taken to a waiting coach and handed a phone with Poroshenko on the line.

'My personal opinion is [it was] because a lot of people, those from Dynamo Kyiv, Chornomorets Odessa and Mariupol football club, participated in marches to support Artem Akhmerov and me,' he believed. 'The response was huge in the country. It was the ultras. It was the reason I was released.' It was an intense two hours talking to Vladislav. He was clearly still feeling the psychological effects of his detention. Guilt, mainly, for being included in the prison swap. He felt that he didn't deserve it, when there were fighters being kept in the same detention centre he was in. He was reunited with his family and his girlfriend. There was a job waiting for him at the Ukrainian football federation, organising tournaments for veterans and children internally displaced by the war. The ultras in exile were his connection not just to his club, but to the home he couldn't return to.

It was late now, gone 1am. The bar was closing and Vladislav's girlfriend, who had waited patiently as he recounted what happened to him, wanted to go home. He believed he would return to Luhansk one day. 'All those people at the match today, they were from Luhansk. Many of them have seen the war,' he explained. They weren't just ultras, but also journalists and engineers and doctors. 'These people will be able to rebuild Luhansk from scratch in the future. They can restore Luhansk out of the ruins. I still believe in our movement and in the ultras.'

Can your team, and the ultras, survive in exile? I asked him.

'I believe that Zorya was, is and will be the club of Luhansk. There's nothing that will change that,' he said before the two left, arm in arm, down into the Olimpiiska metro station.

Outside the main municipal building in Kyiv, just a few minutes' walk from Independence Square, Filimonov and his crew were trying to unroll a banner against another corrupt real-estate developer. It was drizzling, the rain falling harder with each passing minute, sometimes turning into snow. As more police arrived, and the conditions started to deteriorate, Filimonov started thinking about taking shelter and finding some food. 'It is about corruption,' he replied when I asked what his vision for Ukraine was. 'But for real changes you'll need real power. We'll be representatives of real people, we'll be MPs of real civil activity, we'll thoroughly analyse laws which we will vote for. That will be our role in the Rada.' He stopped and pointed to a police-man nearby, filming us as we talked. 'We're being watched.'

When the presidential elections arrived, the National Corps wasn't on the ticket. But they played their role as election observers whilst often disrupting rallies by President Poroshenko. I could always spot Filimonov at the front thanks to his arm brace. A corruption scandal broke that alleged that a key presidential ally on Poroshenko's national security council had profited by smuggling military parts from Russia and selling them at hugely inflated prices to the Ukrainian army. Poroshenko was crushed in the election, losing out to Volodymyr Zelensky, an actor with zero political experience and an unclear politi-cal agenda. He had played the role of president in a famous Ukrainian Netflix series, *Servant of the People*. Zelensky plays Vasyl, a teacher who accidentally becomes president of Ukraine after a secretly recorded video of him railing against corruption goes viral. For Ukrainians jaded by years of corruption and war, a fake president seemed as good a bet as anyone.

Meanwhile, Zelensky moved the elections for Ukrainian's parlia-ment forward from October to July. The question was whether the National Corps could make an electoral breakthrough so that, as Filimonov told me, he could wield power on the inside of the system, whether at these elections, or at the Kyiv municipality election in 2020. 'I'll be on our party's list of candidacies,' he told me confidently.

There was little doubt that Ukraine's ultras, and their organisation and experience when it came to violence, helped at Maidan, helped to force Yanukovych out of office, and helped to retake Mariupol. The issue was what they did after returning to civilian life. Far-right groups had used their popularity to mainstream extremist ideas by presenting them, not as fascist, but as nationalistic, or simple patriotism. As a skeptical Pavel Klymenko had told me, 'They try to present themselves as Robin Hood.' The truth was often markedly different. It was true that, as Klymenko pointed out, the issue of fascism in Ukraine had become 'basically an instrument of propaganda.' It was also true that the war with Russia had 'given many in Ukraine an immunity to accusations of fascism.' The reputation of Stepan Bandera, for example, had been revived. Ukraine's parliament had passed a law declaring 1 January – Bandera's birthday – to be a national holiday. Revolution and war had created an unusual coalition that meant 'Ukrainian liberals were a bit blind' to the overt fascism many displayed. 'They see these people as just civic activists,' said Klymenko. 'These guys when they attack people or burn a Roma camp, they are always called "an activist", very neutral. Very positive. They are never highlighted as neo-Nazis or asked why they burn the Roma camp.' I was in no doubt Filimonov saw himself as an agent of change. The question was: what change did he want to bring?

With the protest coming to an end, I said goodbye to Filimonov and Maliar. Later that day they had another protest for Kateryna Handziuk. Five men, all veterans of the war, would later be convicted for the attack. But no one faced justice for ordering it. There was also a street campaign to grant citizenship to the foreign fighters from Russia, Belarus, Croatia and beyond who had joined Ukraine's volunteer battalions. In some cases, they were now effectively stateless. 'It is vital for some of them to get Ukrainian citizenship,' he said, 'because they, who came from Russia or Belarus, can't go home, because they'll be imprisoned there.' There was also some upcoming arranged football fights with other firms across Europe to train for, once his finger had fully healed, of course. And then there was the next round of the Europa League, against Chelsea. He was looking forward to that. 'It's true, I don't like football,' he said, before leaving to plan his next civil action. 'But I like it when we win a tough game.'

9

Germany

DORTMUND, GERMANY

EVEN ITS GREATEST EVANGELIST WOULD STRUGGLE TO CALL Dortmund a beautiful city, but when the Westfalenstadion is surrounded by a halo of blazing light, and filled with 80,000 people, the city – or at least this small part of it – is truly a thing of wonder. Borussia Dortmund were about to play Werder Bremen and were top of the Bundesliga. As it did for every home evening kick-off, the Signal Iduna Park, as it was now contractually known, glowed like a recently landed UFO as the city streamed towards it dressed in *schwarzgelb*, the yellow and black. Dortmund is an industrial city in the far west of Germany – the economic centre of the Ruhr – that got rich from its abundant coal mines and steel factories, not to mention its copious number of breweries. The club's ultras regularly fly banners that claim

Dortmund is the country's *Bierhaupstadt,* Germany's beer capital. Its importance to the Nazi war effort meant it was targeted and largely destroyed by Allied bombers during the Second World War. Bombing campaigns in 1943 and 1944 reduced what had been a beautiful, gothic city that had once been a key member in the Hanseatic League (a kind of fourteenth-century mercantile proto-EU) to rubble. Over 6,000 civilians perished.

Today there is virtually nothing left of Dortmund's historic centre, replaced by functional, post-war concrete shopping blocks and modern glass malls. Its fortunes have waxed and waned since; rebuilt to thrive after the war before a long and painful industrial decline in the 1980s. But through the good times and the bad, the black and yellow can be seen in virtually every shop, in every cafe. Borussia Dortmund has become a symbol of pride and something of a mirror. The fortunes of the city, the club and its supporters have always been tightly intertwined; the club thrived during the 1960s, becoming the first German team to win a European title when they beat Liverpool in the Cup Winners' Cup in 1966.

'Dortmund was a working city, many working in mining. It was not a very clean place,' recalled Theo Bücker, an intense but friendly German coach I had met whilst he was in charge of the Lebanon national team a few years ago. He had also played for Dortmund between 1969 and 1973, something which he was asked about in Beirut, he told me, every single day. 'The people, beside work, only had football, everyone was addicted to Borussia Dortmund . . . Football was their religion.'

The club sank during the 1970s and 80s and almost went out of business. The 1990s saw a resurrection and, under coach Ottmar Hitzfeld, an unlikely 1997 Champions League title before a foolish floatation on the stock market in 2000 intended to take advantage of financial deregulation and cheap credit.[1] They very nearly lost their shirts in the process.[2] The club is now enjoying a renaissance, kick-started in part when Jürgen Klopp was hired as coach and Dortmund matched Bayern Munich at a time when they seemed unimpeachable. Against the corporate excess of Bayern, Dortmund felt like a rock and roll underdog that provided the best fan experience of any club in Europe. Cheap tickets. Cheap beer. Standing. Pyro. Choreography. Incessant chanting no matter the score. The experience was so focused on the supporters that thousands of foreign fans flew to Dortmund every weekend to marvel at what football might have been for them had their own clubs not sold their soul. The club estimates that, at every home game, a thousand fans come from England alone.

And the soul of Dortmund was the *Südtribüne*, the south stand, and its famous 'Yellow Wall'. It is the largest free-standing terrace in Europe. Up to 25,000 stand here at every home game, slightly less when there's a European tie, producing a wall of sound enveloped by and entwined with yellow flags and banners. The aesthetic – the flags, the banners, the huge choreographies – was a relatively new arrival, created by German ultras who have proliferated since the late 1990s. The Yellow Wall was created by Dortmund's three ultra groups: Desperados, JuBos and, the biggest, The Unity.

At the end of the 1990s German fan culture rapidly changed. Before then German terraces had largely copied the English model of support. There were more indigenous flourishes, like the *kutten*, groups of largely male supporters, synonymous with wearing cut-off jean jackets covered in pin badges (*Kutte* is the German word for a denim vest). But there was also a long tradition of hooliganism, even if it wasn't always called that. 'If you look at the history of violence in German football, there has never been a German football without any violence,' said Robert Claus, an academic and writer who has exhaustively studied hooliganism, fan culture and the far right in Germany. There were, he told me, records of outbreaks of organised violence at football matches in Mannheim going back to the 1920s. It was only in the early 1970s, when British hooliganism had popularised the term, that the first hooligan groups, with names and some form of organisational structure, came into being. 'The first groups which actually named themselves hooligans are in the Gelhsenszene with Shalke 04, around the winter of '78/79,' Claus explained.

There had always been a strong connection to the far right too. Dortmund had its own problematic group, the Borussenfront, founded in 1982 by the notorious neo-Nazi Siegfried Borchardt, a key figure in Dortmund's far-right scene known as 'SS-Sigi'.

But in 1984 a player transfer started a process of change.[3] German international Hans-Peter Briegel had spent almost his entire playing career at Kaiserslautern before signing for Hellas Verona in Italy. He arrived in the aftermath of a huge match-fixing scandal which had led to the Italian FA randomising which referees would handle each game (before then, a commission had appointed the referees, leaving the system open to corruption). The 1984/85 season saw Italy's big teams fall away as Hellas Verona won their first (and so far only) Scudetto. There was always room in Verona's vast, half-empty Stadio Marcantonio Bentegodi, and that season they had some new guests: Kaiserslautern fans coming to see Briegel, their club legend. Whilst Briegel left Verona with a Scudetto, the German supporters left with a new outlook heavily influenced by the Italian ultra scene, pyro and choreography chief amongst them. A few years later, more than a hundred flares were lit when Kaiserslautern played Barcelona in the 1991 European Cup. 'It was visible proof,' Uli Hesse wrote in *Building the Yellow Wall*, 'that German football supporters were beginning to move away from the classic English fan culture they had sought to emulate for three decades.'[4]

The early 1990s was a time of huge upheaval in Germany and German football. The fall of the Berlin Wall in 1989 eventually led to the country's reunification in 1990 and the merging of East Germany's football clubs into West Germany's football association, the Deutscher Fußball Bund [DFB]. Two East German teams played in the first united Bundesliga, expanded to 20 teams for the 1991/92 season: Hansa Rostock and Dynamo Dresden. Dresden survived, but Rostock was relegated. Another important development in 1992 was the introduction by the DFB of what would turn out to be a hugely successful network of Supporter Liaison Officers. Each club would have a bridge between the supporter groups and the clubs, ostensibly to try and deal with the violence and far-right politics that had afflicted the terraces.

The following year saw the introduction of the *Koordinationsstelle Fanprojekte,* a government-funded scheme that gave money to clubs and supporter groups to work on eliminating violence and racism.

The more inclusive attitude to German fan culture had deep roots that went back as far as the nineteenth century. German football clubs began life as membership organisations rather than limited companies as had been the case from the very early days of English football. Birmingham City, then Small Heath FC, became the first English club to become a Limited Liability Company all the way back in 1888. According to the DFB, in 2017 there were 25,000 football clubs in Germany, across 21 regional federations. More importantly, there were some seven million members, all having a say on how their club, and football in general, was being run. German fans were part of the club and part of the solution. English fans were treated as if they were part of the problem and then, later on in the 1990s, more like customers.

When it became clear that the increasing financial success of German football made the old amateur model of ownership hard to maintain whilst competing in Europe, a new system was introduced in 1998: '50+1'. This allowed some outside investment in football clubs but it left the power in the hands of the membership, who would always own 50 per cent plus one share. The members would vote for the president and the composition of the board. The advent of the internet and the arrival on German terrestrial TV of Italy's Serie A, by far the most colourful and successful league in the world during the 1990s, created a perfect storm: a game where supporters were valued, their opinions were listened to, where standing had been fiercely protected by the supporters even as stadiums were modernised in the run-up to the 2006 World Cup (and which meant fans hadn't been priced out of the game) and, in the ultras, a method of not only supporting your team but also influencing the club and wider society.

'By the beginning of 2000 they [ultra groups] really became ubiquitous in Germany,' says Jonas Gabler, one of Germany's leading academics who studies the ultra movement. It was, in its own way, a form of gentrification from Germany's hooligan past, which was rooted in the country's working class.

There were many theories as to why the second wave of the ultras movement spread to eastern and northern Europe: the fall of communism, the beginnings of the internet, the arrival of Italian football on free-to-air TV, even influential player transfers. But Jan-Henrik Gruszecki can point to another reason: boredom. Gruszecki agreed to meet me in an organic Italian cafe in the centre of Dortmund. It had been, given most ultras disdain for the media, surprisingly easy to meet a man who played a pivotal role in building Germany's ultra culture, and building the Yellow Wall. As a teenager Janni, as he is more commonly known, had started watching Italian football on television. He founded one of Dortmund's first ultra groups, the Desperados, back in 1999 when he was 14. Janni could still be found most Saturdays in the Yellow Wall, even though he was now a father, a filmmaker and far from the youth that defines ultra culture. 'We were just so bored by the bad atmosphere in Dortmund and inspired by Italian ultra,' he said.

The arrival of Italian football on free-to-air television brought the colour and the fire of the *curva* into every front room. The internet sped up communications, helping to spread ideas and techniques and songs. The goings-on at influential clubs or on influential *curva* no longer needed to be exchanged by letter or by photograph in the mail. 'We were a little bit inspired by Empoli,' said Janni, 'because there was a group called the Empoli Desperados.' This chimed with Janni and his Dortmund-supporting friends. Dortmund was in the far west of Germany and had accrued a reputation of being in managed decline following the collapse of its heavy industry in the 1980s. For Janni, his part of Germany was as much the 'wild west' as anywhere else.

The Desperados started with 20 people but soon had ballooned to 150. Membership of the group was three euros, money that would go on pyro and other materials. The issues that would excite or agitate them would go on their banners at home games. Against modern football. Against commercialisation. Even 50+1 was too far for Janni. Instead he wanted '100 minus zero'; total fan control. It was an era where the ultras were slowly replacing the hooligans, which caused some friction. The Desperados would often get, as Janni said, 'our asses kicked' and their banners stolen, the ultimate disrespect in the ultra scene. Such disrespect would often lead a group, like a shamed Japanese general, to liquidate itself. And there was some tension within the *Südtribüne* too, especially on away trips, due to the mix of left- and right-wing 'Oi!' skins that shared the bus. Oi! was a late-stage iteration of skinhead punk from the England that proudly wore its working-class roots against the so-called intellectualisation of the original punk movement. The Cockney Rejects was the best example, a band almost synonymous with West Ham United and its InterCity Firm after recording a punk version of 'I'm Forever Blowing Bubbles'.

'Everybody was united by Borussia Dortmund ... but there were more disagreements.' Janni helped form The Unity a few years later, which still runs the core of the *Südtribüne's* choreo and other activity today. 'The Unity was united by a kind of apolitical, anti-racist common sense,' he told me. 'For us, politics means being anti-racist, which for me isn't a novel way of thinking.' But in Dortmund, he said, it needed many years to develop.

It wasn't just in Dortmund. Whilst right-wing and apolitical ultras groups were common in Germany, there were just as many left-wing and anti-fascist ultras groups too. In Italy and almost everywhere else in southern and eastern Europe I had visited, ultras had moved rightward, towards ultra-nationalism and sometimes outright neo-fascism. But a large number of ultra groups in Germany bucked the trend. And even if the politics of various groups differed, they found that there was common ground on the key issues. They were against tough policing. In favour of the 50+1 rule. Against high ticket prices and Monday night football. One of Janni's most famous actions was the '12:12' campaign, which saw the *Südtribüne*, and other tribunes across Germany, go silent for the first 12 minutes and 12 seconds of a match because of new safety measures brought in that reduced the number of available away tickets.

The structure of ultra groups has led to a proliferation of sup-porter-led activism in Germany's stadiums. Banners and choreo would send whatever message was important to them that week, not just to the stadium but around the world, meaning that any choreography produced by The Unity, according to Jonas Gabler, was on 'TV in the best time. The choreography made by Dortmund fans in the semi-final of the Champions League [in 2015] was seen by billions of peo-ple.[5] I think this is also one of the things that is so fascinating for young people that you have such a big visibility.' Today Germany prob-ably has the most politically active, and politically influential, ultra culture in the world. 'When the German ultras copied the Italian model they always said, "We don't want to be politicised like them"', added Gabler. 'There was this idea that we are neither brown, for fas-cist, nor red [for communist]. We are only black and yellow for Borussia Dortmund. But there was a critique from anti-discrimination initia-tives that said, OK, not saying anything when someone uses a racist term, this is political if you don't intervene.'

After being *capo* of the Desperados for seven years, Janni left for Argentina. Like Mikael, he had gone to immerse himself in the anar-chic, undiluted fan culture of South America. He came back six years later and although he wasn't part of the Desperados any more, he remained part of The Unity. Janni was 34 now and had seen the scene change over the past 20 years. Social media, especially Instagram and Facebook, had helped to glorify the more violent parts of the scene, which Janni had always rejected. 'Violence is more important than before,' he said of The current youth movement. 'It's more important to rob a flag or scarf or to raid another ultra group.' And the old battle with the far-right wasn't over either. A few weeks before today's game, when Dortmund beat Bayern Munich 3–2, some old faces returned to the Yellow Wall. During the game two well-known neo-Nazi hooli-gans turned up at Block 13, the area in the *Südtribüne* behind the goal where the hardcore of The Unity's ultras stand.

Sven Kahlin had been an active Dortmund hooligan until he was jailed for seven years for manslaughter, and Timo Kersting was a pro MMA fighter with deep links in the local neo-Nazi scene.[6] He had been banned from football for five years for holding up a banner supporting a local far-right political party. The men arrived with members of the Northside hooligan crew and then demanded that the ultras shake their hand as a sign of fealty. A few men were later seen giving the Nazi salute and shouting 'Sieg Heil'.[7] This was after an incident a few months before when members of the Northside had barricaded 50 members of The Unity in their club house. 'The ultras were forbidden from leaving the base and were made to listen while the hooligans announced new "rules" to bring about a "de-politicisation" of the *Südtribüne*,' wrote Matt Ford for Deutsche Welle. 'In other words: no more anti-racist, anti-fascist or anti-homophobic messages. No more left-leaning politics.'[8]

Janni wasn't too worried about their return. The Yellow Wall was too big. It was heterogeneous, meaning that a single message or political action wouldn't be agreed by everyone. But this was the strength of the ultra movement and of the Yellow Wall. Janni believed the far right didn't have the critical mass any more to impose its will on the *Südtribüne*. 'They are not many people. But they are strong, powerful people and they tried to re-win the terraces they have lost,' he said. 'They don't have a chance because we have changed the mindset of the stands ... But we have to fight daily to keep this mindset.'

As it got darker, and kick-off between Dortmund and Werder Bremen approached, the police began to stir. Hundreds of officers in riot gear and a few dozen on horseback moved towards the thick line of supporters approaching the stadium with rolled-up banners. They surrounded them and brought them to a halt. 'A lot of people on the security side of the government already don't like us,' said Ben, standing away from the commotion. Ben was the nominal leader of Caillera, one of Werder Bremen's seven ultra groups. A small, multicultural group of young ultras had come with him to talk about Caillera, which had become one of the best known in Germany largely because of its anti-facist activism: Haggi, a tall blondish man who looked like he could be a surfer, and Hakeem, who was quieter. Werder Bremen's fan scene, today, was considered almost as left wing as St Pauli, the famously progressive club from nearby Hamburg. Caillera had been at the forefront with banners and choreo attacking the far-right. At an Action Against Fascism day earlier in the season they covered the lower stand of the east tribune in their Weserstadion in banners:

> *'Racism kills'*
> *'Against Fascism'*
> *'Nazis Out of the Stadiums'*
> *'Refugees Welcome'*[9]

The largest banner, in the centre of the lower east stand behind the goal, read: 'Football Fans Are Watched, And The Eyes Are Shut With The Far-Right', a dig at the police, who they believed harboured sympathies for the far-right.[10] Their action led, in part, to the club's president Dr Hubertus Hess-Grunewald announcing that supporters of the far-right AfD party (which won 13 per cent of the vote in Germany's 2017 federal parliamentary elections) were not welcome at the club. 'It's a shame that sports clubs like Werder have become a part of [German Chancellor Angela] Merkel's refugee industry,' an AfD spokesperson responded.[11] When a far-right march, connected in part to the local hooligan scene, turned violent in the eastern city of Chemnitz, Caillera raised a series of banners naming other cities where attacks had taken place. 'The Nazi Mob Is Raging, And The State Cooperates. Germany, You're Shit,' read the largest.[12]

'Because we have brains and we're not assholes,' was how Ben explained Caillera's stance. 'We have seven ultra groups. I think four of us have almost exactly the same political view. Maybe some worry more about sexism than others, but [the] bottom line is we are all anti-fascist.'

It didn't always look like that at Werder Bremen's Weserstadion. For years it was far-right hooligans that dominated the scene. One of the key figures was Hannes Ostendorf, the founder and lead singer of far-right punk band Kategorie C. Ostendorf had a long trail of connections to Bremen's neo-Nazi punk and hooligan scene. His brother Henrik was a political organiser who was convicted of trying to burn down a refugee centre in 1991.[13] Hannes had been connected to Standart Bremen (sometimes known as Standart 88, with the number code that corresponded to 'HH' in the alphabet, for Heil Hitler). It was Werder's oldest hooligan firm.

As the 1998 World Cup in France approached, the band released an album of songs glorifying the far right as well as hooligan terrace culture. The band was named after the designation given to football fans by the local police. 'Category A' were deemed harmless, ultras who flew banners and flags. 'Category B' was for those who let pyro and fireworks off in the stadium. 'Category C' was reserved for those involved in the worst of the violence. France 98 was a wake-up call for the German authorities about the strength and reach of German hooligans. A French gendarme called Daniel Nivel was badly beaten in Lens. The beating left him paralysed and led to a long period of soul-searching in German football.[14]

By the mid-2000s, a small number of Werder fans, Ben and Haggi included, had had enough. They set up some small ultra groups and tried to co-exist. But that ended in 2007 at the birthday party of their group Racaille Vert, being hosted in the club's east stand. (They took their name, Ben told me, from the 2005 Paris riots, when then interior minister Nicolas Sarkozy referred to those rioting in the banlieue as *racaille*, more or less 'scumbags' in French. 'Caillera' is the verlan reverse-slang for 'racaille'. *Vert*, French for green, is the colour of Werder.) The night ended when 25 skinheads dressed in black, members of Werder's neo-Nazi hooligan group Nordsturm Hansestadt Bremen, stormed the party. The attackers subdued the crowd, calling out names and demanding that their anti-racist songs and banners stopped. It very nearly destroyed their movement. After that, they were confronted with three options. Disband; accede to the people who had assaulted them and become apolitical; or carry on and risk serious harm. They doubled down, changed their name to Caillera (adapted from Racaille) and, alongside other groups like Infamous Youth, decided to carry on.

Their numbers swelled until they were the dominant force in the east stand. The turning point was an away game in Bochum in 2008, when 11 members of Nordsturm tried to unroll their black banner with a burning skull and the away section revolted. Their flag was torn down as Werder ultras chanted 'Nazis out!' over and over until the Bochum fans joined in too. Eleven men had to be escorted away 'for their own protection', according to the Bochum police.[15] In one respect the writing was on the wall for German hooligans, at least when it came to their presence at football matches. The 2006 World Cup was a chance to regenerate old and tired stadiums, but it also allowed the police to rethink how they controlled German fan culture, introducing police stations into football stadiums and driving the hooligans underground, even if it couldn't eliminate them entirely.

It had succeeded in removing the right-wing element at Werder Bremen, though. 'Everyone is against the Nazis, basically,' said Ben when I asked what the stadium looked like today. They hadn't been able to change anyone's mind, but they now outnumbered them.

It took four years for the case against the Nordsturm hooligans who had attacked the Racaille Vert party in 2007 to go to court. They pleaded guilty and only received fines. The same group was implicated in another attack on a party in 2012, before Kategorie C gained wider notoriety in 2014 by playing at a Hooligans Against Salafists [HoGeSa] rally in Cologne. More than 5,000 hooligans and neo-Nazis attended, ostensibly to protest against the rise of radical Islam. Ostendorf had written a song especially for the event:

> Today they butchered sheep and cows
> Tomorrow may be Christian children
> Hooligans Against Salafists
> We don't want a religious state[16]

The demonstration ended in riots. Standart Bremen was officially disbanded in 2015 following a German court case against a Dynamo Dresden hooligan group, when the court ruled that membership of it, or groups like it, could be considered membership of a 'criminal organisation'.

For Ben and Haggi, Werder Bremen was a political education, and an opportunity to harness a platform, as much as anything else. 'It's crazy to think that politics have nothing to do with soccer because it has everything to do with it. There are eighty thousand people here right now.' Who was, and who wasn't, allowed into their section was tightly controlled. Any banners or songs they didn't agree with would mean immediate banishment. 'We will not tolerate racist behaviour, right-wing behaviour,' said Ben. 'Our main goal was that everyone, no matter what race you're from, which sex you're from, which sexual orientation whatsoever, that you should feel welcome and safe to support our team.' When I asked about how many ultras wanted to be apolitical, the Caillera thought it was impossible. Tolerance, Ben said, was seen as a political act. *Not* doing anything was a political act too. For Ben, Haggi and the rest of Caillera, it was impossible to be an apolitical ultra.

And yet there was more that bound ultras groups together than divided them. The fight against the commercialisation of football cut across ideological barriers. Every time I asked for a group to define what ultra was or is they came down to roughly the same answer: a collective, a brotherhood, where the group is the biggest single thing in your life. And, of course, fighting control by the police united everyone, even though Caillera and other left-wing groups believed that they, and groups like them, were treated more harshly than the far-right hooligans. 'It's pretty easy to see which side they [the police] are on because they like to use racist insults. They like to use sexist insults,' said Ben. 'That tells us that politically, they're not our friends.' The way they were treated pointed, Ben said, to something deeper. A number of Werder ultras had their houses raided by police looking for pyro and banners. When a group of Werder ultras clashed recently with a hooligan firm in Bremen, the police, Ben said, tried charging bystanders who were there for 'psychologically supporting' the violence. Haggi explained how they had been denied entrance to the past three derbies with Hamburg because the police objected to *how* they had travelled to the game. And they were always on the lookout for unfamiliar faces.

The German ultras scene had been relatively open to journalists and academic researchers compared to Eastern Europe, the Balkans and even Italy. But that had changed in recent years. In 2014 a well-known academic named Martin Thein was outed as an alleged agent for the *Verfassungsschutz*, German domestic intelligence. He'd spent years studying the scene, especially in Nuremberg, and had even published a well-regarded book, *Ultras Offside: Portrait of a Daring Fan Culture.* 'It was a big scandal,' said Jonas Gabler, who had worked with Thein but didn't suspect anything. Thein disappeared into thin air.

'I tried to follow Martin Thein for several months after my revelation but this guy [has been] completely invisible since then,' said Rafael Buschmann, who broke the story for *Der Spiegel.* 'His family, his flat, his former job in the university. Everything was invisible from one day to the other.'

Ben and Haggi couldn't really understand why the state used so many resources to control them. No one had died in German football since the 1980s. Pyro hadn't caused any injures. A new form of 'cold pyro' invented in Denmark which burned at a much lower temperature was being tested by the club. 'I think it's crazy how much money and how much manpower they throw at us,' said Ben, insisting that the scene is all about pushing boundaries and testing limits. 'Ultras has been, and probably will always be, that. You have certain rules given by society and you will break certain rules. That's it with a youth culture. Young people trying to test what they can do and what they can't do.'

There wouldn't be any political banners today – all their efforts were being focused on the restart of the season, after the winter break, in a few months' time. Werder were about to celebrate their 120th birthday. They were planning something special.

But today was all about Dortmund. The Yellow Wall was vast and intimidating, a loud constant weight that pressed you from the front. When it roared the players responded, but the most important moment didn't come during the game, nor at the final whistle as Dortmund ran out 2–1 winners. Before kick-off Nuri Şahin approached the Yellow Wall. He was born in Germany to Turkish immigrant parents and had been at Dortmund, on and off, since he was 12 years old; he was a key player during their modern-day success. A few months before he had signed for Werder Bremen but the Yellow Wall never had the chance to say goodbye. In his white and green training jacket, Şahin approached the Yellow Wall. He stood there, with tears in his eyes, as 80,000 people, home and away, chanted his name.

FREIBURG IM BREISGAU

YOU WOULD BE HARD PRESSED to find any stadium in Europe where you could stand closer to the pitch than at SC Freiburg's Schwarzwald-stadion. At the front of the *Nordtribüne*, where the ultras stood, you could just about touch the goal net if you leaned forward over the advertising hoarding. It was cold, a freezing Wednesday night game, and the small, compact stadium – the smallest in the Bundesliga – was full, as it was for every home match. A sea of red and white flags stretched out behind me; flags for individual ultra groups, others eulogising the city. There was a ubiquitous banner against the heavy-handedness of the authorities ('Freiburg City: Police State'), solidarity banners with the names of ultras who had recently been handed stadium bans and another that was always here for every game, in Italian: '*Diffidanti con noi*': Banned Fans With Us. Two had been specially made for today's match, and for today's opponent. One was in support of 50+1. The other read: '*Kind Verschwindet*'. 'Kind Disappear'. The game was against bottom-of-the-table Hannover 96 and the banner was directed at one of German ultras' biggest hate figures, Martin Kind, the president of Hannover.

Kind had been the most vocal opponent of the 50+1 model of ownership in German football. And Freiburg's ultras had been one of the most vocal, and successful, in opposing him. Kind had made his fortune in hearing aids and, over the past decade, had argued in the press and in the courts that 50+1 was a restraint on his investment. It prevented, he believed, German clubs from competing in Europe against countries that allowed almost unlimited investment. He believed that it entrenched the advantage of the big clubs like Bayern Munich to the detriment of smaller teams like Hannover. 'It stops clubs from being on the same level,' Kind told me back in 2010 when I asked him about his unpopular and seemingly quixotic campaign. 'In England, France, Italy, Spain and Russia, there is no "50+1" … Look at us. We have a $70 million turnover per season and we don't make any profit. With that amount of money, we don't have any business or sporting future.'

Over the following decade he had persisted, doggedly trying to overturn a system that had been held up as a model for supporters around the world to aspire too. Or at the very least he wanted to gain an exemption, something which had controversially been allowed in the past. When the rule was brought in in 1998 Wolfsburg and Bayer Leverkusen were treated as special cases. Both had been formed long ago as, essentially, workers' teams, the former funded by Volkswagen, the latter by the pharmaceutical giant Bayer. The rules had prevented the kind of takeovers by billionaire owners that have changed the shape of football, and the relationship between the supporters and their clubs, in England especially, but France, Italy and other European countries too. Two clubs in particular had managed to upset Germany's ultras by successfully applying for an exception to 50+1. Hoffenheim, a fifth-division team from a village of just 3,000 people, was transformed by the software tycoon Dietmar Hopp into a regular Bundesliga team with a Bundesliga-standard stadium. In 2015 the DFB and DFL (the German football league) approved Hopp's full takeover of the club as it met their criteria for making an exemption, given that Hopp had invested €300 million over a 20-year period. Much more controversial was the existence of RB Leipzig. In 2009 the Austrian energy-drink manufacturer Red Bull bought the playing licence from a fifth-division club in Saxony, SSV Markranstadt. They changed its name to RB Leipzig (claiming that the RB stood for *Rasenballsport*, 'Lawn Ball Sports' in German, rather than Red Bull, as league rules prevent the use of sponsors in club names), spent hundreds of millions of euros on transfers and flew up the divisions. They managed to satisfy the 50+1 rule by having a tiny membership board that cost thousands of euros a year to join. The club was run by a 'membership' organisation in spirit only. In reality it was run by Red Bull employees. With every new promotion protests followed: 15 minutes of silence at the start of a match; away game boycotts; stands filled with ultras wearing all-black ponchos as if at a funeral. Dynamo Dresden ultras even threw a severed bull's head on to the pitch during a 2016 cup match. RB Leipzig subsequently threw away a two-goal lead and were knocked out on penalties. Dresden were later fined €60,000 and were handed a one-match partial stadium closure.[17]

Hoffenheim and RB Leipzig remain pariahs for gaining an exemption to 50+1, which is supported with an almost religious fervour by German ultras. Borussia Dortmund's ultras, plus the ultras at Bayern Munich and 1.FC Koln, have boycotted every away game since RB Leipzig reached the Bundesliga, and arranged for protests and a hostile reception for every home game. Some of the banners in the Yellow Wall were so explicit that the *Südtribüne* was shut down for one game by the DFB.[18] Hoffenheim's owner had not escaped either. When Dortmund travelled to Hoffenheim in May 2018 the ultras unfolded a white banner with owner Dietmar Hopp's face, a red crosshair and the words 'Hasta la Vista, Hopp'. Others chanted 'Son of a Whore'. The incident led to five Dortmund fans being charged with defamation and fined. The culprits were found 'with the help of high-resolution video cameras and directional microphones built into the roof of the away section at the PreZero Arena on Hopp's instruction in January 2018'.[19] The decision was appealed.

None of this had put Kind off trying to smash the system. Not even Hannover 96's own ultras, who began boycotting matches, or staging silent sit-ins, with banners urging *Kind Muss Weg* (Kind Must Go) when Hannover were promoted back to the Bundesliga. At one game the ultras marched to the stadium with a coffin, to declare the 'death of the people's game'. Inside the ground they hung a banner that said: 'Here lies the people's game and the participation of the membership, killed by the burden of money and corruption, murdered by the DFL fat cats.' Still, the system had held, but a few months later, in the spring of 2018, it looked like Kind might finally get his way and, in the process, terminally undermine a system that had, uniquely, placed the fans and the ultras at the centre of the game. And he would have likely got away with it if it hadn't been for the ultras of Hannover and Freiburg.

I met Manu and Helen two and a half hours before kick-off at a coffee shop at the end of the tram line near the stadium. Manu was a leading member of Freiburg's ultras group Corrillo. Helen was an academic who was part of the Supporters Crew Freiburg, one of the *Fanprojekte* that mediated between the club and the ultras on various issues. At the beginning of 2018 it appeared like 50+1 was in real jeopardy. 'It was a very bad season,' explained Helen. Bayern Munich was running away with the title, all but winning it by the winter break. German clubs had been underwhelming in European competition and the familiar hand-wringing resurfaced from various club presidents. 'They were saying: "OK, we need more money to be competitive," because that's their solution for everything,' said Helen. 'If you get more money, everything's getting better.'

Manu agreed. 'Look at Football Leaks,' he said, referencing the reporting by *Der Spiegel* based on a huge trove of material from the Portuguese whistle-blower Rui Pinto. 'There are people in football who are criminals. There are people in football who use football for geopolitics, like Man City, like PSG, so it's not then about the sports any more.'

Manu and Helen wanted to give a unified voice to the fans who supported 50+1. They knew that the ultras at Hannover had been fighting what looked like a losing battle against Martin Kind. So they came up with a plan, a plan that seemed fairly vanilla at the time. The DFL would be holding its annual general meeting in March 2018 and the issue of 50+1 would be discussed and more than likely put to a vote. So Manu, the Corrillo and Helen devised a campaign called '50+1 Stays!' It was, essentially, a glorified petition but it turned out to be the right move at the right time. The petition went viral. Within four days a thousand different supporter organisations and ultra groups had signed it. After eight days 3,000 had signed it, representing hundreds of thousands of ultras, members and individual supporters, a big chunk of whom had voting rights within their clubs' membership associations.

Just before the vote was due to take place in Frankfurt, Manu, Helen and representatives from Pro Verein 1896, a Hannover 96 fan group that had been the most prominent in campaigning against Kind, travelled to the meeting. They printed out all the names of the people that had signed it, and unrolled the metres-long petition next to the hall where the vote would take place. Each club chairman had to walk past it. 'It was about thirty metres long!' said Manu.

The vote was put to the 36 teams in Germany's top two divisions and a majority decided to keep it. The CEO of Borussia Dortmund conceded that he had no choice but to vote to keep 50+1 because the majority of his 150,000 members were hugely in favour it. So 50+1 survived, for the time being.[20] 'We also managed to increase transparency at the general meetings of the DFL,' Manu said. 'In the end, everyone knew [who voted for or against]. Freiburg and Dortmund voted and wanted to retain 50+1. Bayern Munich voted against.'

At times in German football it seemed like more effort was going into fan activism than watching the games. Take the issue of Monday night football. Germany is a vast country and travel to away games can take a long time. Monday night football made it almost impossible for away fans to travel to see their team without taking days off from work. So when it was widened to include the second tier in the 2017/18 season, the fans revolted. There was, of course, choreography that aired the ultras displeasure, like the famous Garfield 'We Hate Mondays' banner used by Werder Bremen. But there were also more innovative protests. Borussia Dortmund emptied the Yellow Wall for one game, against Ausburg, silencing the stadium. Eintracht Frankfurt supporters perhaps engaged in the most famous protest, throwing thousands of tennis balls on to the pitch. Later they covered one of the goals in toilet paper too. Eventually it was decided that Monday night football was more trouble than it was worth. 'The DFL can confirm that a decision was made as early as September to abandon Monday games in the Bundesliga when the next media rights deal is negotiated,'[21] the DFL announced.

Any given month saw hundreds of protests in German football stadiums. Take December 2018. The Ultras Tifo forum listed over a hundred separate posts with nearly 300 pictures detailing choreography at games across five divisions, almost all of them dealing with some form of activism. There were anti-police banners at Stuttgart ('1312 → 80 Stadium Bans. Against All City And Stadium Bans' and 'All Cops are Bastards'); SV Wehen Wiesbaden protested against television, in English ('Football Is For You And Me, Not For Fucking Pay TV'). Borussia Monchengladbach ultras were angry at VAR ('*Scheiss Videobeweis*') and e-sports ('*e-Sports Stoppen!*'). A Bayern Munich ultras group, Schickeria, had shown their unhappiness with the club's sponsorship deal with Qatar Airways. Nuremberg showed solidarity with Rapid Wien ultras (with whom they share a friendship), who had been prevented from attending the Vienna derby after they had arranged a *tifo* at a previous game that turned one whole stand green and white with the numbers '1312'. Their Europa League game against Rangers had taken place a few weeks before, on 13 December ('13/12/18, A Perfect Date to Celebrate', said a banner). All of them shared the values that defined ultra groups around the world. Against modern football. Against commercialisation. Solidarity with your allies. Scorn for your enemies. And, above all, resentment towards the police.

The activism of Freiburg and Hannover's ultras as well as Helen's Supporters Crew had been a success. There had been other campaigns, to try to cut out sexism and homophobia. Corrillo had also been awarded €1,000 by supporter pressure group Fan Supporters Europe for its work in helping refugees, something that would be unthinkable for almost any ultra group anywhere else in the world. But they still felt they were fighting a losing battle. A club like Freiburg would be in serious trouble if 50+1 was abolished. Kind and the big-money advocates that wanted to abolish 50+1 would no doubt be back. The ultras and activists might only have won a stay of execution.

The short walk to the Schwarzwald-stadion showed what could be lost. Manu walked me to the stadium through friendly crowds. Their

fan bar welcomed anyone. Glühwein was sold by the pint for just a few
euros. There had been a long discussion about leaving this place for a
new, expanded stadium near the airport – perhaps the only answer to
Freiburg's survival in a post-50+1 world – but it kept getting wrapped
up in red tape. At the front of the north stand I could almost touch
the ball as Hannover scored the equaliser in front of me. The game
finished 1–1. Kind was not there to see it.

CHEMNITZ, EASTERN GERMANY

THE FLOWERS AT THE MAKESHIFT memorial had begun to brown
and wilt, the candles – long extinguished – had melted down into a
stiff wax puddle. In the centre of the jumble of tributes and obitu-
aries was a plain wooden cross. On one side hung the German flag,
on the other the flag of Cuba. At its base was a picture of Daniel
Hillig, who was murdered on this spot, a minute's walk from the
huge Karl Marx bust in central Chemnitz, a few months earlier.
Hillig had been stabbed by a recently arrived refugee from Syria
who was later convicted of manslaughter.[22] His death sparked a
series of anti-immigrant protests and riots that made international
headlines.[23]

Under communism the city of Chemnitz, in eastern Germany,
was known as Karl-Marx-Stadt, but changed its name once the Berlin
Wall was torn down. Like almost every town and city in Germany
there had been an influx of new arrivals in 2015 after more than a
million refugees, mainly Syrians fleeing war in their home country,
were given leave to remain by Chancellor Angela Merkel. Hailed
around the world as an act of compassion, in Germany's conservative
heartlands, especially in the former communist east which had
struggled economically compared to the richer west due to deindus-
trialisation, it was seen as an act of betrayal. Rather than immigration, eastern Germany had experienced acute *emigration* since 1990.
According to the Institute for Population and Development in Berlin,
1.8 million people left five of Germany's eastern states between 1990

and 2010. Poverty, hopelessness and a largely homogenous population created the perfect conditions for the far right. In the 2017
Bundestag elections, the anti-immigrant AfD candidate narrowly finished second in Chemnitz with a quarter of the vote, almost double
the AfD's national average. The murder of Hillig – a German with
Cuban heritage whose family had experienced their own share of racism in the past – was quickly exploited to help bring those teeming
resentments to the surface.

Shortly after Hillig's death a far-right Chemnitzer FC ultra group
– Kaotic Chemnitz – advertised a protest march on Facebook calling
for fans to meet at the Karl Marx bust for 'Honour, loyalty and passion
for club and home city'. By the second day 6,000 had turned up.
Hundreds later rampaged through the city, giving Nazi salutes and
attacking anyone who looked like they might be a refugee. 'We are
still having a very big, very emotional debate on the refugees movement to Europe, in Germany, which is, I think, mostly racist,' Robert
Claus, the academic who specialises in hooliganism and the far right,
told me. 'Kaotic Chemnitz is not a big group. It seemed like Kaotic
Chemnitz was able to mobilise thousands of people. They are not
more than twenty people but, of course, they are part of a right-wing
network in Chemnitz and that region, where you can, if you look
back on the past twenty years, you will find lots of names of right-
wing organisations which were forbidden by the state which still
exist.' Chemnitz, Claus said, had a long history of nurturing a 'far-
right subculture somewhere between hooliganism and far-right
music and combat sport' that had attracted generations of young
people.

Kaotic Chemnitz had been banned by Chemnitzer FC, the city's
once successful football club which is now bankrupt and languishing
in Germany's fourth tier, since 2012. The group was a thinly veiled
rebrand of HooNaRa, a hooligan group called 'Hooligans, Nazis,
Racists', which had been set up by Thomas Haller, a man with a fearsome reputation in the local far-right and hooligan scene. One of the
most important moments in the evolution of German hooliganism
away from sporadic fights to more organised, trained and arranged

confrontations took place between Frankfurt and hooligans from Chemnitzer FC and Zwickau in 1997.

'Every scene has its own myths and legends,' said Claus. 'This one is the legend of how the eastern German hooligans took over and proved that hooliganism can professionalise.' According to to one of the Frankfurt hooligans who fought that day, they were shocked to see how the Chemnitz and Zwickau fighters 'formed themselves like a Roman squad'. For years Haller's company also organised the security for Chemnitzer FC. 'He [Haller] was there for all his life and was one of the very important economic figures of the far-right scene,' said Claus. Haller gave an interview in 2007 where he admitted to founding HooNaRa. Chemnitzer FC ended their relationship soon after. 'That's the official story,' said Claus. 'In reality, it changed nothing, because Haller security was still working for Chemnitzer FC. But not as Haller security.' Instead they were subcontractors, wearing the shirts of other security companies.

Today the city, the makeshift memorial for Daniel Hillig and the square around the huge Karl Marx head – known locally as the 'Nischel' – are all quiet. A nearby Christmas market had just opened up for the Saturday lunchtime trade. But in a few hours that could all change. Chemnitzer was about to welcome a team that had become one of their fiercest rivals despite coming from Potsdam, 200km away. SV Babelsberg 03 was one of the few teams in the east of Germany to have a prominent left-wing ultras scene. Energie Cottbus, Lokomotive Leipzig and Chemnitzer FC all had a reputation for their far-right ultras. But Babelsberg took a different path. Unlike the other clubs in the former East Germany they kept their stadium's communist-era name: the Karl Liebknecht Stadion, named after the famous German socialist who, along with Rosa Luxemburg, formed the Communist Party of Germany. Both Liebknecht and Luxemburg were executed without trial on the same day in 1919 at the behest of the German government. I had been taken on a tour of the stadium by Barbara, a Babelsberg fan and activist who was responsible for organising Fan. Tastic Females, a project that highlighted the role of women in football's fan culture, including the ultras movement.[24] The stadium was covered in anti-fascist graffiti. There was a creche. Vegan food was served during matches and there were, she told me, regular campaigns to stamp out sexism and homophobia. When the 2015 refugee crisis hit Germany, 'Refugees Go Home' and 'Refugees Not Welcome' banners were common in the east. Babelsberg instead gave free entry to refugees. Perhaps unsurprisingly, games between Babelsberg and pretty much everyone else were classed as the highest risk by the German police. 'It's a horrible away trip, the worst in the league,' Martin Endemann, who works for Football Supporters Europe, told me before I took the train to Chemnitz. 'You have people screaming in your face: "Go home, Berlin Jew".'

Trouble broke out at one game against Energie Cottbus in 2017 that almost put Babelsberg out of business. During the match the Cottbus ultras were seen giving Nazi salutes and heard singing 'Albeit Macht Frei, Babelsberg null drei' – 'Work Sets You Free (the inscription over the metal gates at the entrance to Auschwitz), Babelsberg zero three' – as well as 'Zecken, Zigeuner und Juden', 'Ticks (a common derogatory word for communists), Gypsies and Jews'. The Babelsberg supporters replied with 'Nazi pigs, out!' Fireworks were fired at the home fans and a group of hooded Cottbus fans tried to cross the pitch and get into their end.[25] Incredibly, when the match report was released by the regional football association, it was Babelsberg who were punished, fined €7,000, which they refused to pay on principle. They were threatened with having their licence revoked until it became something of a *cause célèbre* for Bundesliga teams like Dortmund and Cologne. In the end the north-eastern regional football association halved the fine, allowing Babelsberg to spend the other half on anti-racist initiatives, but only if they could provide receipts.[26]

Today's game was considered another high-risk match by the police, and by Babelsberg's Filmstadt Inferno 99 ultras, so named because Babelsberg was home to the German film industry. It was one of the reasons I was standing in front of the Karl Marx head, hours before kick-off, on my own. When I initially contacted Filmstadt Inferno they were extremely wary and wanted to check me out first, and to set out the parameters. Max arranged to meet me at a hipster Moroccan cafe in Berlin. He was young with a thin reddish moustache, large 1980s thin-rimmed glasses and a baseball hat. He solemnly explained how ultras like them were 'shy' of the media. He exhaled loudly when I suggested I wanted to stand in the away end. Eventually we agreed I could, as long as I 'didn't act like a journalist', that I found someone to travel with and, under no circumstances, travelled on the bus from Potsdam to Chemnitz with them. So I took two trains, and three hours later I was in Chemnitz.

The police had flooded the route to the stadium on the outskirts of the city. The first Chemnitzer fan I saw had 'White Power' emblazoned in English on the back of his jacket. The tunnel walls that led underneath the railway track towards the stadium was full of graffiti.

Merkel Must Go.
1312.
White Pride!

I passed three lines of security before I was allowed to wait at the back of the small but tidy Stadion an der Gellertstraße. Nervous-looking fans would arrive in ones and twos, Babelsberg fans from nearby towns and villages hiding their scarves inside their jackets until they were sure they were around allies. Out on the street next to the entrance the police were aggressively strip-searching two Chemnitzer fans who said they were just walking past, although one had a bag with the words 'FCK CPS' on it, which was the likely cause for the police's interest in them. The convoy of coaches from Potsdam finally arrived, in one piece, half an hour before kick-off. According to Tom, an English journalist who travelled incognito with Babelsberg regularly, they feared the bus would be attacked on the way but the police had escorted them from the outskirts of the city. Max cooly nodded in my direction before heading into the game. The tribune was split. There had been a falling-out between some of Babelsberg's groups. The Filmstadt ultras stood at the front whilst the Bulldogs stood at the back, although the space, and the numbers, were so small that they were both essentially stood next to each other pre-tending to ignore the other group. It wasn't entirely clear what slight had led to the split. There was a touch of the Judean People's Front about it all.

There was no pyro, but the ultras did bring a banner that read 'Karl Marx statt Chemnitz', a play on the city's communist name that translates as 'Karl Marx instead of Chemnitz'. It wasn't a happy trip for Babelsberg. By half-time they were down to ten men and ended up losing 2–0 thanks to goals from striker Daniel Frahn. A few months later Chemnitzer FC – and Frahn – would be back in the news. Thomas Haller, the founder of HooNaRa, died after a long battle with cancer. At the next home game, against VSG Altglienicke, Haller's face was shown on the big screen during a minute's silence. The north stand held a banner – 'Rest in Peace, Tommy!' – and a large black flag with a cross. When Chemnitzer's striker Daniel Frahn scored he ran to the bench and held up a T-shirt that read 'Support Your Local Hools'. Frahn later said that was merely fulfilling Haller's dying wish, although he did apologise.[27] There were, wrote journalist Felix Tamsut, similar memorials at Energie Cottbus and in Switzerland at Grasshopper Zurich. When the story that Chemnitzer FC had hon-oured a known neo-Nazi went public, the club's CEO resigned, as did Chemnitzer's fan-liaison officer – who was also a local politician in Chemnitz for the centre-left Social Democratic Party – who had writ-ten a Facebook post praising Haller. The club's stadium announcer was sacked, its main sponsor ended its relationship with the club and the regional football association fined them €12,000.

Germany's ultra scene was perhaps the most political I'd ever encountered. But it was also changing. As the police cracked down harder, the scene had started to become more violent, mixing hooli-ganism and the purer ultra scene that had arrived from Italy in the 1980s. Almost as important as football was the rise of MMA and its international network connecting hooligan firms, ultras and the far right, especially in Eastern Europe. Many of the most active firms, especially Dortmund's 0231 Riot and Northside, Robert Claus pointed out, no longer even go to the football matches. 'The far-right recruitment doesn't need the football that much any more,' he said. 'It's working with combat sports.'

Nothing illustrated this better than the Desperados, set up by Janni in 1999 and run on inclusive, activist principles until he left for South America. Since then, the group moved further to the right. 'It's the most violent of the Dortmund ultra movements,' said Claus. Many of the Northside hooligans had graduated from the Desperados. 'There is no single entity of the German ultra fan in German. I don't think that exists. It's rather about ultra as a cultural code,' said Claus. 'We have ultra groups which are so violent that you cannot really separate them from hooliganism. We have left-wing anti-violence groups, left-wing pro-violence groups, right-wing pro-violence groups and everything in between.' But perhaps that wasn't surprising. The violence had always been there, long before the hooligans were hooligans and the ultras were ultras. The only thing German ultras agreed on, Klaus agreed, was 'their fascination with choreography in the stadiums' and their 'hostility against the police'.

The game passed without any serious incidents. There were no fights, and the Filmstadt ultras avoided having their flag taken, as had happened when Zwickau had visited a few years before. The ultras folded up their *'Karl Marx statt Chemnitz'* banner that they had taped to the wall at the back of the stand and went back to their coaches. It was so cold that a few took pity on me and invited me on the coach home. But the ultras still had the same rules and values, regardless of whether they were in Italy, Serbia or Russia. Twenty minutes into the long coach journey back to Berlin, a delegation of the Filmstadt Inferno approached. Solemnly, they told me that I had broken the rules. Journalists were not allowed. I had been told. The other members were upset, especially if I overheard them speaking. Max, the ultra with the ginger pencil moustache, was looking at his feet.

But I don't speak German. I won't understand what anyone is saying, I said.

'That doesn't matter,' the *capo* replied. 'You were warned.'

I was escorted to the front of the bus and sat in the front seat. The *capo* ordered everyone around me to move to the back of the bus. No one was to sit next to me. Nor was anyone allowed to speak to me. I was placed, effectively, in solitary confinement. It was a two-and-a-half-hour bus ride back to Berlin. The *capo* believed me to be as much an enemy as the neo-Nazis they fought week in week out. I asked the driver to stop the bus at the side of the highway somewhere outside Leipzig, 200km from Berlin, and I walked to the nearest train station instead.

10

Sweden

STOCKHOLM

EVEN BACK HOME AMONGST HIS COUNTRYMEN MIKAEL STOOD OUT.
He was waiting to meet me outside a metro station in the western
suburbs of the city. His long beard was a little longer, his long hair,
tied in a ponytail, poking out under a black baseball cap. Like when
we had first met in Montevideo, he was wearing a West Ham T-shirt,
this time a mocked-up cover of *Never Mind the Bollocks Here's the Sex
Pistols* but in claret and blue. The pink kiss lips tattoo on his neck
glowed, almost neon against the contrasting colours. On the front it
read: 'Never Mind The Tottenham Here's The ICF'. It had been a few
months since we said goodbye in Buenos Aires. Mikael had stayed to
watch a few more Boca matches and to do some shopping. Boca merchandise was hard to find in Sweden. So he filled a suitcase and

brought it back with him. It had been a good ten years since he shuttered his ultras merchandise shop but he couldn't stop collecting and he couldn't stop selling. He knew a bargain when he saw one.

We embraced as if seeing each other after surviving a war and were now safely back in barracks, before getting on a train to the city centre. We were headed for one of the 'last working-class pubs in Stockholm', he told me. Stockholm's centre, the home of his beloved Hammarby, a team still considered the 'people's club' in the city, had become gentrified and had priced people like him out. But there was still one place that served beer for 30 kronor a glass, less than three euros, and didn't judge you for taking an early drink.

In a few days one of the biggest matches in Sweden was taking place, the Stockholm derby between AIK and Hammarby. There were a few Stockholm derbies given the city had three top-division teams. Hammarby shared a new stadium with Djurgårdens, the Tele2 Arena, which for some made that match something special. Djurgårdens, however, considered the match against AIK their *true* Stockholm derby. But AIK–Hammarby was still a big match even if Mikael joked that it wasn't a Stockholm derby at all. AIK's roots were in Solna in the far north of the city. So far north in fact that they were technically from another town altogether. But the opposition wasn't the biggest issue for either team in the run-up to the match. The biggest issue was the police.

Swedish football was often held up as a shining example of how modern football could co-exist with an absolutist ultra culture. Like in Germany, there was a 50+1 ownership model which meant the supporters and their concerns were at the centre of any discussions around the game, whether about ticket prices, transfers or policing. But unlike Germany, Swedish football wasn't that good. UEFA's coefficient ranked Sweden the 19th best league in Europe, behind Wales and Slovakia. But in the stands, Sweden had one of the best fan cultures in the world. There was an active, well-respected and still growing ultras scene. Attendances were big for a country of only ten million people. Hammarby's average attendance was 24,000. Every weekend at dozens of clubs, tens of thousands of ultras would arrange elaborate choreographies or design incredible *tifos. Capos* would stand in specially erected cages to lead the chants with megaphones in hand. Smoke and pyro were ever-present, despite being technically illegal in the stadiums. There were a large number of women involved too. Hammarby claimed that it had the largest proportion of female fans for any men's team in the world: 30 per cent for home games. And the police had a hands-off approach.

It was also, at least for the Swedish league, a pragmatic business choice. As far back as 2010 it was clear that Sweden would never compete financially with the top European leagues. 'You see the big rich leagues get richer from TV rights: the Premier League, Bundesliga, La Liga. But what the hell do you do in a country like Sweden?' said Mats Enquist, the CEO of the Swedish league. 'There aren't any oligarchs and we have the 50+1 rule.' They needed something else. That something else was to concentrate on the fan experience. When Enquist was hired in 2012 he conducted a countrywide survey. It told him what most supporters already knew. They weren't there for the quality of the football, they were there for the atmosphere.

Supporter liaison officers were hired, like in Germany; former ultras who provided the bridge between management and the *curva*. In 2012 the *evenemangspolis* or 'event police' were introduced, a specially trained unit to deal tactfully with the supporters. They would also introduce the so-called 'Supporter Dialogue Police', a pragmatic attempt to bring police and the ultras together for their mutual benefit. 'The police and Bajen Fans have never got along together particularly well. Mutual distrust and bad experiences of previous contact have always made it hard for the parties to talk about various events and incidents in a constructive manner. We have been so far apart,' wrote Maria Lemberg, then the second in charge at Bajen Fans, Hammarby's biggest organised supporter group. She had praised how the police and the supporters had worked together so that there had been less trouble from the *curva*, and that the police had stopped treating everyone at a football match like they were a threat, as they did when they famously pepper-sprayed half of the stand during one Hammarby game in 2012. 'Both supporters and the police are satisfied with the result,' wrote Lemberg. 'The Supporter Dialogue Police have helped in situations where we as supporters need to talk to the police, but where we previously felt that they refused to listen to us.'[1]

And it was, Enquist said, good for business. From 2015 to 2018 the average attendance in the Swedish league doubled. The league's income tripled. There were bigger sponsorship and TV rights deals. 'Violence was down, racism down, drunkenness down,' said Enquist. 'There were so many positives.'

The choreo and the pyro – although illegal – grew and (almost) no one got hurt because of it. Mikael had played a leading role, if not *the* leading role, in this play. He formed Sweden's first ever ultras group, Hammarby Ultras, in 1993. In fact, no one had done more than Mikael to bring the influences of the outside world home. Ever since he'd sat down in front of the TV as a nine-year-old to watch the World Cup final in Buenos Aires in 1978 – with its blue and white ticker-tape hurricane – Mikael had spent his life trying to recreate it. As I'd found out for myself from our time together in Uruguay and Argentina, he'd lived amongst, and forged deep contacts with, Boca Junior's main *barra* La Doce, and with Roma's ultras too. He'd obsessively exchanged photographs of choreographies with like-minded ultras in Sweden and around the world in the 1980s, 90s and into the new millennium before the internet and digital photography made them obsolete. There was a 25,000-picture archive of choreo and *tifos* from around the world filed away at his mother's summer cabin. Every Swedish *curva* had Mikael's fingerprints on it somewhere.

Yet something had changed in recent months. The dialogue stopped. Police raids intensified. The searches as you entered the stadium became more vigorous ('like being sexually assaulted', was how one male ultra described it to me). Arrests had gone up. The dialogue with police ceased to function properly. There had been some problems. There was a small but powerful and active arranged fight scene away from the stadiums. And inside them there had been a few high-profile incidents. The last death in a Swedish football was only in 2014 when a Djurgårdens fan in his mid-forties was killed in a brawl.[2]

In 2016 the Djurgårdens–Hammarby derby was stopped after Djurgårdens ultras started throwing flares on the pitch when they were losing 4–2.[3] There had been a couple of instances of players being assaulted during games, the most famous being Henrik Larsson's son Jordan. Henrik was coach of Helsingborg, and Jordan the team's main striker, but when they were relegated a group of hooded fans took to the pitch and roughed up his son. He quit the next day.[4] In 2018 another Djurgårdens–Hammarby derby saw fighting in the stands.[5]

Since then, though, the trouble had dissipated. But week by week the police and the bureaucracy of the city had weighed heavier and heavier. 'The situation is getting crazy,' Mikael said as he explained what was happening, on the train. He, like many other ultras, thought the situation was linked to a corruption scandal. The man many believed was in charge of this new policing strategy was Björn Eriksson, the president of the Swedish Sports Confederation, and a former police chief and president of Interpol. He had been part of a government commission that had examined football violence in Sweden and made a number of recommendations. The first was the banning of face coverings in the stadiums, which was later introduced by then minister for home affairs Anders Ygeman in 2017. To protest, AIK's ultras wore black niqabs, the Islamic face covering worn by some women (there was an exemption in the law for people who covered their faces in the line of work or for religious reasons).[6] They held up a banner that said: 'AIK's ultras mean well, we're now wearing masks for religious reasons. Freedom for ultras is the goal, thanks Ygeman for the loophole.'

Eriksson had also called for 'police-free' stadiums, due to the cost to the state of policing games. He pushed for more private security in the stadiums instead. But an investigation by the Swedish newspaper *Ekpressen* discovered that Eriksson had been paid millions of kronor as chairman of Sakerhetsbranschen, a lobby group for Sweden's private security industry.[7] 'Basically, he holds the most powerful position in Swedish sports,' Noa Bachner, the journalist who broke the story, told me when I asked him about the scandal. It seemed like a clear conflict of interests. The president of AIK suggested he should probably think about his position. 'When we published our first report on this, it was met with extreme reactions from Swedish football, all the major fan groups, the Swedish football supporters' union and several clubs, most of them calling for him to be removed from his position,' Bachner said. 'He's not seen as the sole reason for the heated conflict, but a key figure.' An investigation was launched into the alleged conflict of interest and Eriksson himself admitted his role at the lobbying organisation, but he denied that it had in any way influenced his decisions. The authorities, at least for now, seemed happy with Eriksson's explanation, who was re-elected to his post amidst the controversy

We met Martin, Fernando and Daniel in Dovas, the bar that sold 30-krona beers. It was tidy and dark; rows of wooden tables filled with groups of students, punks, drunks and pensioners. Martin was wearing thick-rimmed glasses and a black LAFC hat, from one of the newest franchises in America's MLS, which made him look like a semi-pro skater. Fernando was smartly dressed and looked, and spoke, unnervingly like Christoph Waltz's character in *Inglourious Basterds*. Martin had formed Malmo's first ultras group back in the early 1990s with Fernando joining later. Daniel was the youngest and was an active current member of the Hammarby Ultras. It had been a few years since Martin, Fernando and Mikael had been in the same room together. They greeted like old friends, commenting on how much weight each had put on or lost.

Martin founded Malmo FFÖ's first ever ultra group in 1996. Every week Martin would watch *Eurogoals* – a low-budget, quick-fire run-through of all the goals across the main European leagues – on Eurosport, although it wasn't the goals he was actually interested in. 'At the start of the games they showed a bit of the choreography from the ultras,' he explained. 'And I thought that was really cool. And I started to record that little bit on video.' Martin was already plugged into Sweden's underground hardcore and punk scene. He played drums in a short-lived band putting on DIY gigs, making fanzines and T-shirts. He recognised something similar in terrace subculture and began swapping cards and pictures of *tifos* and choreographies with other like-minded supporters, such as Mikael, all across Sweden and then internationally.

'You have glue on the stamps so you could re-use them,' he explained.

'You washed the stamps with soap and used them again,' Mikael added.

By 1993 Martin had joined Malmo's official supporters' club but he wanted more. 'Something extra,' he said. So he showed Fernando his Eurogoals *tifo* montages on VHS and all the photos and cards he'd been exchanging with other supporters. Fernando looked through the trove of pictures Martin had collected and thought it was a great idea to bring some of this to Malmö. So, Martin set up his first group 'Troops of Blue '96' ('after the Sepultura song 'Troops of Doom', Martin told me), and went to the official supporters' club to beg for some money, then collected more in buckets at the stadium so they could buy some supplies from Denmark. By 1996, Martin had made a banner with their name – MFF Tifosi – on it in his parents' basement.

When Martin laid out the paper and card on each seat for the mosaic choreography he'd designed, the other supporters were confused. Ever since 29 November 1969, the day when Swedish national television showed its first ever English football match, Swedish football had followed the English way of supporting their teams. The broadcast had a revolutionary effect, bringing the idea of coordinated chants and singing into every Swedish home. Hammarby, Mikael said, were the first to replicate the English-style terrace chants. The rest, of course, would follow; the violence and the hooliganism. A year after the first live broadcast of an English match, Sweden had its first televised act of hooliganism; IFK Göteborg, who were about to be relegated, were playing Örebro SK. One thousand IFK Göteborg supporters invaded the pitch and the referee halted the game for 45 minutes.[9]

By the early 1980s dedicated fans that stood together and sang were known as *klackarna*. Each club would have its English-influenced *klack*.[10] It took a while for this new, alien, southern European form of ultra culture to take hold. 'We'd hand out the papers, like A2 size, to hold up. People were like: "Why are we holding this up?"' recalled Martin.

'In the beginning, I was not so impressed with Malmö because we were four or five years ahead of them,' said Mikael, rather brutally. 'But then I saw [them] in 1998 and I thought, yeah, Malmö is coming good, coming strong.'

The Swedish ultras scene was now one of the best in Europe, but the police actions of the past year had become a threat. Mikael had seen the same thing happen in Italy and Austria. He'd been expecting this to happen. 'It was the wild west, with supporters fighting on the pitch, and it was difficult for the police to control it when it was new,' said Daniel from the Hammarby Ultras, about how the scene was back when he started in 2005. 'We'd start with five flares. And then it has grown and grown. And it's getting out of control for the police.' For Daniel, Sweden was just catching up with the kind of policing that had swamped the scene almost everywhere else in Europe. It was the same for every youth culture, whether it was graffiti or punk, which 'scare and confuse older people'. The worst part of it all was that Swedish TV, sponsors, everyone who markets the game, loved pyro and the ultra style of support. It was their pictures in the magazines, their videos on the adverts. No one was going to Swedish football because of the quality of the actual football.

'It's shit,' Daniel conceded. Everyone agreed. Martin pointed out that today was the 40th anniversary of Malmö reaching the European Cup final when they were still an amateur team, something that would never, and could never, be replicated in the modern game. 'We will never compete with the top leagues, the top countries,' said Daniel. 'But in the *curva*? That's different.'

Martin and Fernando weren't directly involved in the ultras any more. They lived a long way away from Malmö, which is a good five hours on the train. 'I'm plugged into it but I'm also a DJ, so I plan gigs around games,' he said.

This weekend's derby was taking place at a tense time and Daniel had made some last-minute changes to Hammarby's choreography. There had been some discussions with the AIK ultras, the Black

Army, about their plans for the game. For once they had found themselves on the same side, against the police. The police, he believed,
were trying to separate the club from the ultras, making it financially
and morally impossible to keep up the level of support that the ultras
had enjoyed. Divide and rule. 'We decided there will be a protest for
the first ten minutes. A silent protest between both ultras was agreed,'
Daniel said. 'And then in the tenth minute we will have a little something special.'

Hammarby's training ground is in the heart of the club's home district
of Södermalm. There doesn't seem to be any security as Mikael
breezed into the main office to meet with Henrik Kindlund, the club's
CEO, who had met with the ultras a few times that year. The training
facility had only just been completed. Whilst most owners or board
members try to burnish their terrace credentials, Kindlund had no
need to – he was Hammarby through and through. He'd worked at
the club for years as a volunteer and before that stood on the terraces
watching the team at the old Söderstadion, 'maybe seventy to a hundred' times, before they moved to the Tele2 Arena they shared with
Djurgårdens. 'I was always a part of the culture and grew up in a
neighbourhood where everyone was a Hammarby fan,' he said. 'It was
really green and white.'

Kindlund's position was almost entirely dependent on the support
of the fans. The 50+1 model meant that any policy that went against
what the supporters groups and ultras thought were in their best interest would mean a vote against the board, and he would have to resign.
That affected everything from the club's positioning on ticket prices
(which were planned to go down next season) to the number of standing areas in the stadium. 'The ultras came and said, "We want the
upper short side section as a standing section",' he said. 'And I was
like: "Fucking hell. I have to go to the city and say that."' So the stadium now has three different standing sections, in contrast to shrink-
ing numbers elsewhere. The club found space for the ultras to make
their choreo (although Daniel, the Hammarby ultra, complained they
wouldn't give the ultras a key to the stadium, like they did at Malmö),

let them in the arena days before to arrange it and provided security to 'keep an eye on the other teams' fans. So they don't fuck things up.'

The issue of pyro was a delicate one. 'Because it's illegal,' Kindlund conceded. 'So the formal position of the club is obviously that we don't want it at the arena when it is illegal.' But Kindlund was a pragmatist. The anti-pyro law had been one of the worst enforced laws in Sweden, at least until this year. 'The fans know that we think that you shouldn't use them but that's kind of like me telling my daughter when she rides her bike that she has to wear a helmet out. And sometimes she doesn't. I'm not going to ground her for it.'

There hadn't been a significant increase in violent instances, Kindlund said, that would justify the police cracking down on the ultras. The situation had improved over the past 15 years. The past few games had passed without any recorded incidents at all. The stadium was full, the family section was full. There were still hooligan groups that arranged fights, but that was often far away from the stadiums. There was, of course, always the danger *something* could happen. And that, Kindlund believed, was the problem, when the police wanted to 'control the whole society'.

The system had worked, and then some of the old faces returned. The ROG, Regionala Ordningsgruppen, or the Regional Order Group, a specialised and notorious riot police unit, had been let loose at more and more games. 'That's just a unit of all the police who like to fight,' said Kindlund.

The ROG used to be known as the *tunnelbanepolisen*, or subway police, dealing with disorder on public transport, especially around match days. But they earned a reputation for brutality. Mikael told a story about how his father, who used to work fixing the cars for the secret service, was badly beaten along with his grandfather after a Hammarby game for helping a drunk man on to the metro outside the old stadium. 'My father didn't say he worked for [the] police and he was badly beaten for helping this man into the metro,' Mikael told me. His father passed away a few years ago. 'But my father went to his boss and the police [involved] had to walk in the suburbs for six months,' the equivalent of being demoted to traffic duty. In 2013 the *tunnelbanepolisen* were officially dissolved. Although it was effectively a rebrand. Most of the offices just moved to the newly named ROG.

Everyone knew about ROG. Their mere presence was seen as a provocation. 'The police officers like to fight, they're on their toes,' said Kindlund. 'The fans like to fight. They're on their toes, and our security guards are trained to be non-confrontational and not use their sticks. They, some of them, are also on their toes.' Earlier in the season the ROG were caught beating a group of AIK fans. An investigation by Malena Johansson at the daily newspaper *Dagens Nyheter* found footage, captured on a pair of Snapchat sunglasses (which had a built-in camera), of AIK fans being beaten without provocation. One was threatened with having his finger broken. Johansson spoke to a former member of the unit, anonymously, who quit because of the brutality. 'I'm not one that beats people in the back with [a] baton and threatens to break [people's] fingers and such,' the former ROG officer said. 'I am more professional than that, and therefore I chose to quit.'[11]

Almost everyone I spoke to – fans, ultras, supporters groups, owners, players, even the Swedish league – couldn't understand why this was all happening now. But Enquist, the CEO of the Swedish league, had a theory. 'It boils down to one thing: pyrotechnics,' he said. 'Some of the administrative policemen read the newspapers and thought: "That's enough, we need to show who is in charge." It's a very populistic approach. It creates an inflammatory climate. Instead of the positive developments, there's dark forces in the subculture that feed on this and grow when you get a very clear enemy like the police. We don't know where this is leading to.'

There were the conspiracy theories surrounding Björn Eriksson and his alleged conflict of interests. The second in command of Sweden's entire police force Mats Löfving, was not a big fan of ultras either according to Kindlund. 'He just hates everybody. Everybody who wants to have fun, more or less.' Even a lot of the rank and file police were confused. What they had experienced whilst policing football matches didn't seem to warrant the type of response they had seen. And it was, at least to them, making the job unnecessarily dangerous and feeding into the worst emotions on both sides.

Stefan Holgersson, a Swedish police inspector whose rank had gone up and down depending on how much he criticised his bosses, knew ROG well. As well as policing crowd trouble at football matches and neo-Nazi rallies, he also studied for a PhD and taught part-time at Linköping University. He'd worked inside ROG and had seen how counter-productive aggressive policing was. 'They have people who are really good at handling problematic situations but also have individuals who are not,' he explained when we talked on the phone. What worked, according to Holgersson, was not reacting violently. He admitted that, just like the ultras and the firms, there were those within the police that went out looking for trouble too. 'They like weapons. They like when things happen. They are searching for struggle,' he said. Holgersson's research hadn't exactly made him popular with many in the police. 'These people are strong. If you have a unit of eight calm people, but two offensive people, the calm officer follows the offensive officers. They set the context.'

Holgersson didn't think that Björn Eriksson was the problem, necessarily. Nor any increase in violent fan groups. It was the composition of the upper echelons of the police force. 'The police has moved its focus on to repression,' he said, particularly since the restructuring of the police in 2015, which gave greater influence to those who had experience with anti-terrorism units. They, Holgersson said, 'like the hard stuff.'

For Mikael it was a clear black and white issue. It was purely about control. Ultras, he said, were the biggest subculture in Sweden. And like in England, Italy and even Germany, any subculture, when it became big enough, needed to be controlled by the state. The problem was that, although it broadly worked in larger countries, Sweden was a different case. 'If you get rid of the ultras in Sweden, who're you going to replace them with?' Mikael said. 'Sweden is a small nation, the football is not that great.' In England, he said, they took out the working class and replaced them with the middle class. 'You can do [it] in England and Spain or Germany, but not really in Sweden.'

It wasn't just the ultras protesting against what was happening. The clubs and the players had got involved too. Before the last home game against Norrköping, the team walked out on to the pitch with T-shirts that had a message on the front: '*Supportrar Får Sporten Att Leva!*' 'Supporters Make The Sport Live'. There was a plan to share the same message before Sunday's game against AIK. 'We have a good relationship with the fans,' said Mats Solheim, Hammarby's longest-serving player, who I met as we left – even if they'd had criticism from them.

Why did you decide to wear the T-shirt? I asked.

'We talked to the *tifo* group that came to us and they asked us to take a stand so that they can continue the same atmosphere in the stands. That's us taking a stand for the supporters as well. Because they are important to us.'

Would you be in the stands if you weren't on the pitch? I asked him. He laughed.

'I'd be the one drinking the beer, shouting a lot and having a great time. I don't think I'd be an ultra, but I'd be in the middle of it.'

There was, of course, another game to be played that weekend. A few minutes' walk from Hammarby's training ground, in a bar run by a Syrian Christian refugee, Hugo leaned in and explained what drew him towards the violence. 'I have always been drawn to trouble, and adrenaline and excitement,' he said calmly. 'It's always been that way. I always wanted to be where it happened.'

Hugo was the leader of Hammarby's hooligan firm, the KGB. The fighting didn't interest Mikael. But unlike in Germany, the ultras and the hooligans were clearly demarcated, and had a good relationship. Swedish football was much more apolitical than in Germany or Ukraine and, more importantly, the firms all still went to watch the football. Hugo was in his thirties, prime fighting age, with piercing blue eyes made more intense by the fact that he never seemed to blink. He was calm and softly spoken as he described how he became addicted to football violence. His gateway drug was ice hockey, which had a raucous fan culture with a violent streak. There would be five or six fights against other hockey fans every season, but when Hammarby had a few lean years, and fewer people were turning up, Hugo decided to step it up. 'Then we decided to do organised violence,' he said.

There had been a long tradition of hooliganism in Swedish sport, going back as far as the 1920s.[12] But modern hooliganism emerged in the 1970s, copied from England. 'When I started this, people looked to England. We looked up to the ICF [West Ham's InterCity Firm], the [Chelsea] Headhunters. *That* was the idea of a firm,' Hugo said. But soon the German scene was becoming more influential, with its much stricter organisation, with set numbers of fighters and rules of engagement, and a certain fighting style. At first they called themselves simply Bajen, Hammarby's nickname. The word 'Bajen' came from a sort of joke, Mikael had told me earlier, about how English people would pronounce Hammarby badly. (He tried saying Hammarby in a mock English accent to show me what he meant but I still didn't get it.) There was a rush of people to join the new firm and soon there were 25 dedicated people wanting to be part of the organised fight scene. When the police and the media started to notice they began listing each club's firm: Wiseman of IFK Göteborg (considered the strongest in Sweden), the Firman Boys of AIK and, as far as they were concerned, an unnamed group from Hammarby. 'They wrote that we were "just a gang of mates [*kompisgängt*] that like to fight",' he said. So they took that name, Kompisgängt Bajen, and adapted the Soviet KGB badge – replacing the communist star and the hammer and sickle with the face of St Eric, the patron saint of Stockholm – as their own.

The first big organised fight took place against IFK Göteborg's feared Wiseman firm. It was the first time the KGB had fought when there were no games. 'We met halfway in a town, by the forest, in the square there,' he said, adding that there were about 35 fighters. 'It was [the] middle of the winter with high walls of snow around.' It was, he said, a good fight. Hugo doesn't remember much of it but he remembered the man that he fought. 'He was wearing an Inter Milan hat and he was smiling the whole time.' They lost, of course, and the journey home resembled a war zone medevac. 'There was blood. Noses were off and hands broken. Our leader, he looked like the Elephant Man.' After that, Hugo said, 'I was hooked'.

The early days used to be a little rougher, a little more indisciplined. Fighters would drink. During one of the first away trips for a fight, Hugo recalled, most of the people on the coach were racking up lines of coke. Random mates would be invited along. Some of them swore they were better fighters after a beer or two and would pack a couple of cans into their kit to down before the fight started. But then a new, much more serious, form of fighting emerged – initially from Germany, and perfected in Ukraine, Russia and eastern Europe. Mikael vividly remembered the first time he saw a recording of a forest fight, when a tape turned up for sale at his shop. 'It was in Russia or Ukraine. Nobody had seen that before,' he said. 'I thought: Wow! I was totally shocked. I thought: "What the fuck is this?"'

Unlike the anarchic, booze-fuelled urban fights from the English hooligan era of the 1980s and 90s, the new fighting game was much more serious. Under no circumstances could you use a weapon. The numbers had to be even. When someone was knocked out cold, you had to stop. And, most importantly, the fights took place far away from the football stadiums to avoid the police: forest clearings, railway sidings, farmers' fields.

Firms travelled all over Europe to fight each other, most of the time leaving on good terms. There was a code of honour, respect and sportsmanship. The Ukrainians, Russians and Poles were the undoubted stars of the scene, Hugo said. 'They are small, but they are destroyers,' he told me when I asked about the reputation of Serhii Filimonov and Dynamo Kyiv's Rodychi firm. One Ukrainian fighter told him they fought 90 times a year, not far off twice a week. 'I don't know if we have had so many in Sweden in total!' he laughed. One problem was the greater police control. They had to be innovative to try and avoid detection. There was always the risk that one of their fights could get raided or that a car full of fighters would get stopped along the way. It was perhaps Hugo's greatest skill in the firm: 'thinking outside the box', as he put it. One time, when they were struggling to find a venue, Hugo hired a school in the evening, posing as a lecturer in combat sports. 'We paid them and then we gathered, ninety guys inside the school'. The fight took place, the blood was cleaned up and the school were none the wiser. He admitted he wasn't the best fighter in the group, although he was far from the worst. 'I have the head and the heart because I live for the firm.'

A few weeks earlier the KGB had their greatest success: a victory in a forest fight against Hansa Rostock. A few years ago, when the KGB were still getting organised, Rostock dispatched them in a 30 against 30 fight in under a minute. 'They are considered to be a top firm in Germany,' Hugo said as he looked for the video on his phone. 'We fought them, same conditions three weeks ago and we won in thirty to forty seconds. It felt very good because it showed we have developed a lot the last two years. So the tables turned.'

He found the video and played it for me. It began in a sun-dappled clearing in a lush green forest. Two teams entered on either side, walking slowly together, tight in formation, until they clashed. Hammarby took the advantage, destroying Rostock's formation, before the best fighters peeled away and began picking off their opponents. 'That's me there, in the blue shorts,' Hugo said, as the video showed him knocking a man to the floor. 'Then I push this big fucker here and then I'm out [of shot].' The camera focused on one of the KGB's fighters knocking his opponent to the floor, kicking him over and over in the head as the man on his back tried frantically to avoid each blow.

He's really kicking him in the head. Is that allowed? I asked.

'Yeah,' Hugo said matter-of-factly, 'and then ... BOOM!' The man on the floor went limp as he was finally knocked unconscious. His opponent stopped kicking straight away.

Another Hammarby fighter flew across the screen, taking out his opponent with a flying kick. Hugo had reappeared and was dealing with the final Rostock fighter. 'I'm sitting on him and hammering him,' he said, eyes glued to the screen.

Was he unconscious at this point? I asked.

'No, at this point he's not out,' he said with a pause as the last of Rostock's fighters were mopped up. 'Now. He's out. We actually took his tongue out of his mouth. So he didn't swallow it.'

The new professionalism had its benefits. The fights were orderly, the chances of arrest were lower and the standard had gone up hugely. Hooligans today, Hugo said, were doing 'combat training, MMA, Thai kick boxing'. And the action took place far away from normal society. If they weren't hurting anyone else, the firms reasoned, what was the problem? Still, Hugo preferred fighting in the cities. It felt more real to him, and more free. There were more variables to consider in an urban environment. More angles for attack, more routes to defend. More chances of getting caught. More variables meant more risk. More risk meant more danger. More danger meant more adrenaline. But the police had learned how to control the city. Other firms hadn't adapted to the new world, which meant it was all but impossible to fight. An arranged fight meant that, at the very least, there would be blood.

We were from completely different worlds, Hugo and I. But I felt I understood something of his rationale. I had also been drawn to the danger of the terraces. But rather than find that rush from violence, I found it in undertaking petty acts of vandalism in the hopes of provoking a police chase. As a teenager I must have been arrested a dozen times. Getting caught was almost as big a rush as getting away. Almost. Nothing beat escaping. It was only after I spent one day in Chelmsford prison – a sort of scheme set up to scare potential young offenders into reforming their ways – that I decided that the rush wasn't worth it. Who knows? If I hadn't stopped maybe, like Hugo, I would be trying to recreate that dopamine hit in a forest somewhere in Eastern Europe.

Sweden's scene was small but they were plugged into the new international world of arranged football fights. Facebook, Instagram, YouTube. Sites like GruppaOF (115,000 Instagram followers) and Ultras Tifo (96,000 followers) regularly updated their followers with the number of fighters, the teams, their alliances and the results. Videos of the fights were rarely shared and any pictures had the faces of the fighters blurred out. Encrypted messaging apps, especially Telegram, made communications simpler and hard to monitor for the authorities. Full videos of fights, like the ones Serhii and Hugo had shown me, were difficult to find online. In a world of universal knowledge and surveillance, the subculture of arranged fights could still thrive in something approaching anonymity. 'I don't think that the old school should die because that's what we started this for,' Hugo said. 'And the connection to football must stay and must stay strong.'

That was ultimately the point. Hugo was a Hammarby fan. He loved football and he loved the violence, but he also loved his team. It was becoming more and more common to see firms completely disconnected from the game. In Ukraine, CSKA and Metalist Kharkiv's firms both existed, and thrived, long after their teams had gone out of business. Borussia Dortmund's Northside didn't go to the games. In other countries, Hugo said, organised crime had overtaken the scene. 'I think we have found a way between the new school and the old school,' he said.

Hugo was right. I had been to Poland a few months before, in the city of Kraków. Poland's ultra scene was one of Europe's most vibrant and most violent. Kraków's derby between Cracovia and Wisła was known as the 'Holy War'. In the lower tiers of Polish football, the threat of violence was so high even village teams had specially constructed cages to lock ultras away into. There had been a long-standing truce about using weapons, the so-called Poznań Pact, but that didn't apply during the Holy War. In 2011, the leader of Cracovia's ultras was hacked to death in broad daylight by at least a dozen people using knives and machetes.[13] Several of the accused wore branded T-shirts of Wisła Kraków's main group, the Sharks, in court. Yet it had emerged that some Polish ultra groups had also been involved in the drugs trade, as well as human trafficking. The Sharks even managed to take the club over during a financial crisis and use it as a front for its activities.[14]

The Sharks were led by Paweł Michalski, known as Misiek ('Teddy Bear' in Polish). He became notorious across Europe on 20 October 1998 for throwing a knife at the head of Italian international Dino Baggio when Parma played Wisła Kraków in a UEFA Cup match. Baggio got five stitches, Wisła was banned from European competition for one year and Misiek got six and a half years in prison. But when he came out he organised the Sharks into a group that, according to Szymon Jadczak, an investigative journalist who uncovered the scandal, was a 'Mafia' with connections to the drug trade and a reputation for violence and torturing anyone they believed had talked to the police. They worked out of the White Power gym near the club's stadium, where they would practise for their organised fights. The club, Jadczak told me, became a 'sort of cash machine' for those connected to the leadership of the Sharks. There was also a strong neo-Nazi element. A large group of Sharks were seen giving straight-arm salutes on a visit to the Rome's Stadio Olimpico to watch Lazio play.[15] Fabrizio Piscitelli, leader of Lazio's Irriducibili, had told me that Wisła Kraków's Sharks were one of the few groups ideologically pure enough to deserve a friendship with them. A Lazio shirt hung on the wall of the Sharks' own cafe bar in the grounds next to the club's stadium. A picture of Wisła players giving Nazi salutes before a game in Germany, before the start of the Second World War, had been placed above the till. The Sharks' merchandise shop was full of anti-Semitic stickers and posters against Cracovia (who they disparagingly called 'The Jews'. Cracovia's main ultra group adopted the name and is known as the Jude Gang). Eventually, Poland's Central Bureau of Investigation undertook a series of raids – the largest, according to Jadczak, in the organisation's history – and arrested dozens of hooligans and ultras from Wisła Kraków and Ruch Chorzów. 'This is definitely not the end of the Sharks,' said Szymon. 'They get a lot of money from this.'[16] Misiek eventually cooperated with the police. What was left of the Sharks denounced him with a banner at a home game, calling him a traitor.

Hugo would, of course, be at the AIK–Hammarby derby on Sunday. There was also something special planned with AIK's Firman Boys. It was an impossible scene to get access too. Mikael had warned me that even asking to watch a fight might cause offence. It was highly secretive and off-limits to outsiders. But Hugo readily agreed to let me come along. A fight would be taking place after the game. 'Something different,' he said cryptically. He'd call me closer to the time, on Sunday evening, to let me know where and when we should meet. We exchanged phone numbers and he told me to add him on Telegram. A few hours later I did. Hugo's profile picture showed him, arm in arm with another man, smiling as if they'd just won the lottery, their faces splashed red with what looked like blood.

*

There were perhaps 50,000 people inside the Friends Arena, yet the game between AIK and Hammarby kicked off in silence. As promised, the AIK and Hammarby ultras had worked together to protest on the biggest stage in Swedish football. Mikael was there, as was Daniel. Hugo was in the crowd somewhere too. But there was a diverse crew of ultras and supporters, male and female, young and old, ex-hooligans, skinheads, young children. There was even a large contingent of English supporters who had cut their teeth on the terrace culture at Nottingham Forest, West Ham and Sheffield United. They had found a home here, offering something that was gone from back home: standing, beer (although one of the new regulations meant that only low-strength beer could be served) and a kind of instant camaraderie. 'Football fans should be disorganised,' said Glen, an older Swedish skinhead in a bomber jacket when the match kicked off. He spoke with a slight east London accent, picked up from years of travelling to England to watch West Ham. He still missed the old English terrace way of doing things. 'Facebook and all this, I dislike it,' he said before shouting: 'FUCKING COMMUNISTS EVERYWHERE!'. The crowd around us shushed him quiet.

The ten minutes' silence was unnervingly well observed. It was also incredibly powerful, sucking the importance and the significance out of what was happening on the pitch. The 22 footballers seemed small and irrelevant compared to the weight of self-discipline and control that was bearing down from four sides of the arena. The silence was broken with a flash, like a thunderstorm following an abnormally hot summer's day. Both ends of the stadium lit hundreds of flares, releasing plumes of thick smoke. The referee had to momentarily stop the game. A flurry of banners and choreos were raised. Björn Eriksson, the man that pretty much everyone blamed for the new era of police control, featured prominently. The Hammarby ultras raised their banner: 'Swedish Football Against Swedish Police – National Sport Against An Authority In Crisis'. AIK's Black Army ultras raised theirs: 'Our Songs Against Your Batons'.[17]

And then the two sides of the stadium, the *curva* behind the goals, joined together in a coordinated chant.

'Fuck the police!' Hammarby chanted.

'Football murderers!', AIK replied.

The game was immaterial now, although Mikael wasn't happy. AIK scored a quick-fire two goals in the first half thanks to Sebastian Larsson, the former Sunderland midfielder and current Swedish international, who had recently returned home after playing abroad for 14 years. Hammarby lost two players in quick succession to injuries, including centre back Mats Solheim. But the upset didn't last long. Mikael was here in his natural environment. The place he felt happiest. The place he had helped to build, always striving to replicate that burst of colour, that first burst of love, he'd seen on TV in Buenos Aires in 1978. This scene, the ultras scene, was a young person's game. His girlfriend's oldest son was old enough now to be a leading figure in the Hammarby ultra scene himself. Yet Mikael was ageless. It wasn't necessarily that he looked younger. True, he still had an abundance of hair, a long beard with only a few flecks of grey in it and a rash of tattoos. But he had something greater. Mikael was the godfather of the Swedish ultras scene, not just because he'd started it, or that he had hung on to accrue the benefits of his seniority. This wasn't Argentina or Italy where longevity – survival even – brought with it automatic respect and its own financial rewards. Mikael wasn't going to retire controlling a criminal empire, or be rewarded for his loyalty or for staying alive longer than his rivals. He simply lived and breathed ultra culture. He had dedicated his entire life to it. He didn't have kids. He wasn't married. Everything, every krona he had, every minute he could spare, was dedicated to his team and to the scene. The only thing that could extinguish that passion was the police, the control that was threatening to destroy everything he had helped to build.

The game finished 2–0 and we walked out of the stadium. Mikael was exhausted and was about to head home with his girlfriend and her son. He had decided some time ago that if tensions continued to escalate with the police, he'd stop doing this. 'I'll save my money, go to Boca Juniors two times a year and then I'm fine.' He couldn't bear to see what happened in Rome happen in Stockholm. The thousands of Hammarby fans squeezed back on to the train, towards Medborgarplatsen, the large square that had become central to Hammarby's identity. It was here that more than 30,000 supporters celebrated their first, and so far only, Allsvenskan league title in 2001. At the start of every season, the same number of fans met there and marched the three kilometres together to the stadium for the first home game. After a few hours, the bars and the square emptied of fans and their colours. It was getting late. But then, just as I'd resigned myself to missing the second 'match', Hugo, the leader of the KGB texted me. It was on.

The meeting point was on the edge of a quiet estate, not far from the Medborgarplatsen. It overlooked a steep wooded embankment. It was close to 10pm but Sweden's midsummer nights meant that it was still warm and bright. An old couple walked past with their dog. It was silent, except for the clink of glasses as a waiter cleared a table outside a small pizza restaurant nearby that was closing for the night. It didn't feel like a 120-man brawl would be taking place here any time soon. Perhaps I had missed it. Or, more likely, the KGB had decided at the last minute that I shouldn't ride along. But then a car drove slowly past. Five men with thick necks dressed in black were inside. A second car, 30 seconds later, its occupants also all dressed in black, did exactly the same. I was in the right place.

Hugo was standing in the porch of an apartment block. Another car slowed and stopped. He walked to the kerb and thrust his head into the open window on the passenger side and checked each face to see who they were. Satisfied, he gave directions to where they should meet the others. The nearby pizza bar, it turned out, had always been an old meeting spot for the KGB. But it had recently come under new ownership and the new proprietor threw the KGB out, telling them not to return. The problem was that Hugo liked it, but not because of the pizza. 'You can see far up and down both streets and spot any danger early,' he said. Any attack by a rival firm, if it came, would be easily spotted as they approached thanks to the clear sight lines up and down each side of the long road that passed by. The cliff that fell sharply away in front of us meant they couldn't be attacked from the front. The complex paths and roads of the housing estate behind made it unlikely they would be attacked that way without being spotted well in advance. It also made escape a certainty if the police ever made an appearance. In terms of military strategy, the bar was Hugo's Tower of London. He had plans to return one day, forcing the owner to leave by instigating what he called 'a campaign of low-level terror'. But not today. Today there were more important matters to attend to.

We walked down the hill, over a bridge that crossed a nearby highway and down into Stockholm's deserted meat-packing district where Hugo had left a large van. A group of perhaps 30 men were already there. Hugo instructed them to go ahead to the final meeting point. We had some special guests to pick up. 'I'm in the truck now. I'm on my way to you. Sit tight,' he said down his phone as we drove through traffic. We would be joined by one of Brøndby's top firms, who had travelled from Denmark to be here to fight AIK's Firman Boys. 'We are friends with some of the Brøndby guys,' Hugo explained. 'This was the first derby in three years.'

As he drove we talked about his life, his family, his work in construction. How he had a bad stomach from the stress of work, organising the fights and playing football (he'd made it as far as the third tier of Swedish football as a teenager, he said). He'd found himself in jail for a month after, he said, being misidentified as the aggressor in a bar fight he was trying to mediate. After today, he hoped to take two months off and focus on his family and reading. He was currently enjoying Bernard Cornwell's *Saxon Stories*, a series of historic novels set in ninth-century England following the travails of Uhtred – heir to a Saxon kingdom who was kidnapped as a child and raised as a Dane – who uneasily traversed two worlds that he both recognised and knew he could never be part of.

Hugo was calm, as if he was picking up the congregation for a church service. There was no hint of worry at the forthcoming duel nor any obvious stress about arranging it, even though his phone rang constantly. 'I am very calm but I haven't eaten anything today,' he said. 'It's always the same.' We pulled into the road next to a hotel. 'You guard our space ship,' he said as he got out. He returned with a group of 20 men. They were ready to go, dressed in a mixture of black sportswear and fighting gear, sparring to themselves or jumping up and down. They were perpetually moving in silence.

Their leader, Christian, climbed into the front, sandwiching me in the middle, as the rest of his men were herded into the back of the truck, which had no windows or ventilation. He was jittery but friendly. 'I'm on something else,' he said, laughing, as we headed to the rendez-vous. 'Hammarby is like us. The one difference. We party hard.'

'We do too!' Hugo replied.

'Yeah, but not like us. Cocaine is not a big thing in Hammarby. But it is in Brøndby.'

Brøndby had a feared firm. Christian joined in 2011, when he was 18 years old, and rose to become leader two years later. They had their own MMA gym where a pool of 60 fighters trained three times a week, ensuring that if anyone had to drop out, or had got themselves arrested, or if they were needed at short notice for a street brawl, there was always someone who was up to the job to replace them. It meant they could fight 30 times a year. None of the fighters that were there today were older than 28.

There was no official friendship between Hammarby and Brøndby, only some informal connections, but Christian was after revenge. A fight last year against the Firman Boys had gone wrong. Christian was sure they were wearing shoe coverings that gave them greater grip and could do more damage when they stamped on your head. The rules of honour, respect and sportsmanship had, he believed, been broken. 'I don't mind losing,' he said. 'That's how it is. But I don't like people who act like sportsmen and they are doing things the exact opposite. I don't like snakes.' Behind him, the back of the van was completely silent. No one was talking. I was worried they had suffocated. 'They're just getting in the zone,' Christian reassured me.

Hugo, meanwhile, was receiving bad news. He sighed as he fin-ished the phone call. It looked like the Firman Boys had backed out of the fight. He was embarrassed. The vans were a new thing. Christian hadn't seen that before. 'I like it!' Christian said of the van, rocking slightly in his seat.

But now there was nowhere to go. 'If they don't come we will go to Solna,' Hugo said, referencing the district in northern Stockholm where AIK comes from, 'and we will fucking attack everything.' It was the first time I had seen any hint of anger from Hugo, even if it was just for a split second.

'Why don't we do that first anyway?' Christian offered jovially, as if suggesting a different restaurant to eat in that night. 'Did they say anything about us?'

That, as it turned out, might have been the issue. Hugo's AIK contact had spotted some of the Brøndby lads in the crowd during the game. Someone had posted a picture on social media. He phoned Hugo and asked if a new alliance had been formed. 'They asked me: Are they here? I said sort of.' Recalling the phone call riled Hugo further. 'We will attack them. We will beat them one way or the other.'

'Then I'll sleep very, very well,' said Christian.

'I'm very embarrassed,' Hugo said apologetically. 'I've never ever had this conversation with AIK. Chicken shits. We will go to Solna. And we will see them in the pub. And we will say: "We are here now."'

First, he needed to break the bad news to the expectant crowd. It was almost dark as Hugo parked the van on the edge of a seemingly derelict estate. He opened up the back doors and the Brøndby lads flew out in a blast of hot air. We pushed through a broken wire fence and slid down an earthen embankment until we reached abandoned railway tracks below. The group veered left, following the tracks until we reached a tunnel. There, around 50 more men were waiting, almost invisible in the gloom. They too were silent, shadow-boxing, limbering up, waiting for an opponent that wouldn't arrive. Hugo stood in the middle of the crowd, on one of the rails, and broke the bad news. There was a palpable sense of disappointment. But Hugo had good news too. He knew where AIK's firm would be, he said, and we had transport too. So we would take the fight to them. The men scrambled back up the embankment and filled the waiting cars and vans. The Brøndby hooligans silently clambered back into their windowless, airless sweatbox.

'We'll find them,' Hugo said, reassuring himself as much as anyone else. He fired the engine and the convoy left for Solna.

The convoy headed north and parked in an industrial estate in the heart of Solna. It was silent and tense. I kept expecting a gang of AIK hooligans to jump out before everyone was ready but it never came. Things moved fast. 'Stay at the back,' Hugo said, paternalistically rather than with any anger. He ran to the front. And the mob moved at speed. It was the last time I would see him.

The phalanx moved so quickly I could barely keep up running at full speed. It snaked through a park and then up two sets of concrete stairs. Still no AIK hooligans had turned up. And then came the red flares and the shattered glass. At the first AIK pub the mob had smashed out the front windows and thrown flares and smoke bombs inside. Bodies lay unconscious on the pavement. A woman screamed from a balcony as the street was trashed. I ran past the prostrate men, wondering who they were. Were they Firman Boys? Or just civilians, in the wrong place at the wrong time? One man in a bad way was being cared for by a friend, lifting his head to try and unblock his airways. He looked at me with hate in his eyes. To him I was inseparable from the people that did this.

> The creatures outside looked from pig to man, and from man
> to pig, and from pig to man again; but already it was impossi
> ble to say which was which.

The scene behind me looked like a war zone, with red flames and injured people. I thought of the English hooligan film *I.D.*, and the police officer, John, who went undercover in a violent English hooligan firm only to succumb to its charms. To the people I'd just run past, I was just another face in the mob. My best course of action, I reasoned, was to keep running.

The formation kept its shape and kept moving at speed until it came to a second pub. The front window was smashed out and flares were thrown in. But then the police stormed. Two vans with flashing lights were waiting. I wondered whether this was the fabled ROG. Later I'd find out that there had been another riot in Solna earlier in the evening and a man was in hospital in a coma as a result, which explained why the police were so quickly on the scene. We all turned and fled into the estate next to the parade of shops as the police vans closed in. There was no way I could outrun them, or even keep up with the KGB. I made a split-second decision. I took my hat and jacket off and turned around 180 degrees, walking as calmly as I could back from where I had run. The police fired past me, after the pack.

Trying to walk as normally as I could, I crossed a pedestrian bridge into a park and, once out of view, sprinted into a thicket of trees. Smaller groups were also hiding there. I checked my phone for an escape route, but the Solna train station had been closed by the police because of a 'disturbance'. Soon I was the last person in the park. I had a brainwave. I ordered a cab and waited in the bushes until it arrived. Just as it turned up and parked, a police van mounted the pavement and sped down the cycle path. I span behind the tree until it had passed, then walked to the car. The driver slowly drove past the wreckage. Dozens of flashing blue lights. Smoke was still rising from the smashed-out bar. A police helicopter was in the air. Later, Hugo texted to see if I was OK. He had escaped. All of his crew had got away too, although it had been reported that people were arrested. Two people had been taken to hospital. It made the news the next morning, another example for the media of the violent fan culture that had afflicted Sweden's youth. I wondered whether Björn Eriksson or Mats Löfving had seen it.

The taxi took me back to near my hotel. I waited on the kerb for half an hour to make sure no one had followed me. But there were no flashing lights and no helicopter. It had been vicious and ultra-violent. Victory and supremacy was, of course, the aim. But it wasn't just those things that attracted someone to this life. It was far simpler than any theories of hyper-masculinity. It was the buzz. It was, as Hugo had told me within a minute of us meeting, about the 'adrenaline and excitement'. The trouble that he had always been drawn to. It was throwing yourself into the abyss and somehow scrambling out of it again. The guilt of my proximity would have to be dealt with later. But for a brief few moments, I had felt it too. My heart was beating fast and I felt something approaching elation after my escape. I was fifteen again. I turned on the light in the bathroom and stared at myself in the mirror. I was smiling.

PART FOUR:
THE NEW OLD WORLD

'It's not man's job to think about whether God exists or not, especially when you know that right in front of your eyes one person is stepping on another's neck.'

Eka Kurniawan, *Beauty Is a Wound*

11

Turkey

BEŞIKTAŞ, İSTANBUL

ONCE THE SIGNAL WAS MADE EVERYONE CROUCHED DOWN ON TO THE cobbled stone floor and awaited instruction from the man standing next to the huge eagle statue. Hundreds were doing the same, men and women, old and young, on their knees, the crowd stretching out in concentric circles like ripples spreading through a black and white sea. Before every game, this is where the Çarşı gathered, around the eagle statue that represented them, in the heart of the club's epony-mous district on the European banks of the Bosphorus strait. The Çarşı are the biggest organised supporters group of Beşiktaş. The sta-dium, known nominally as Vodafone Park but still commonly referred to as İnönü, its old name, is a short walk from here. They drank and sang and lit flares – doled out by passing hawkers for 10 lira each

– before making their *entrada*. The Çarşı *capos* at the front urged silence as a drum, beating slowly at first, built to a crescendo. Everybody leapt up and the chant finally deafened the square as the flares were lit and the smoke became so thick I could hear, but not see, people retching next to me.

What are they singing? I asked Bora, a football writer, historian and Beşiktaş fan, who was coming with me to today's match.

I expected a song about the the club, the colours, this labyrinthine district or perhaps even a song about one of the many leftist causes – from environmental issues to animal rights to hailing the author Orhan Pamuk when he won the Nobel prize for literature – that the Çarşı had become famous for. Something smart. Something with meaning.

'The lyrics go: "Suck my dick, Fenerbahçe",' Bora replied sheepishly.

I watched as a well-dressed middle-aged woman, around the same age as my mum, dampened down the crowd, urging them back to their knees, only to ignite them again by screaming that, yes, Fenerbahçe should indeed suck her dick one more time.

'That's it,' said Bora, searching for a drop of deeper meaning. 'Those are the only words.'

It was true, Fenerbahçe was Beşiktaş's biggest rival. Almost all their songs revolved around Fenerbahçe and the various sexual exploits of their rival's fathers and mothers, even when, like today, they weren't playing each other. Beşiktaş and Fenerbahçe, alongside Galatasaray, are known as İstanbul's 'Big Three'. They have dominated Turkish football since all three were founded around the same time over a century ago (although the exact dates and seniority of each respective club was still hotly debated). Since the first recognised championship in 1924, the big three have won 70 of the subsequent 89 titles. The origin story of each moulds the identity of the clubs and their fans to this day, even if the truth is opaque. Galatasaray was founded at an aristocratic elite high school formed in 1481, in the district of Beyoğlu, adjacent to Beşiktaş on the European side of İstanbul. Fenerbahçe came from Kadıköy, a 15-minute ferry ride across the Bosphorus on

the Asian side of the city, with a bourgeois tradition, proud of its connections to Mustafa Kemal Atatürk, the secular founder of modern
Turkey, who they claim was a fan. Recep Tayyip Erdoğan, the country's president whose entire elected career had been defined by
unpicking Atatürk's militant secularism, is also a supporter. Beşiktaş,
meanwhile, saw itself as the outsider, and clung to its working-class
roots even though it was now one of İstanbul's most prestigious neighbourhoods. (A fourth İstanbul team, Kasımpaşa, was rarely mentioned
alongside them.)[1]

'Of the big three, we are the smallest. We're the underdog,' Bora
explained. Beşiktaş also had the oldest and best-known supporters
group. The Çarşı was formed in 1982, essentially, with a leftist, liberal
political identity. You could see their sign spray-painted all over the
neighbourhood: the group's name with the 'a' replaced by the anarchist symbol.

Whilst they became famous for their many political, but witty,
banners and songs at the İnönü, the 2013 Gezi Park protests made
them infamous. What started out as a small protest by a handful of
environmental activists to stop a tiny scrap of public park being turned
into a mall, exploded into the biggest anti-government protests in a
generation.[2] And the Çarşı were at the front battling with the police,
alongside the fans of Galatasaray and Fenerbahçe. Such an alliance
seemed utterly implausible given the long history of violence and hatred
between the three sets of fans. But İstanbul United, as it became
known, showed the power that organised football fan groups can have.[3]
Erdoğan did not forget the role the ultras played in Gezi. The protests
were, eventually, crushed, and a new era of government control – over
society and especially over Turkey's ultras – began. Political chants
and political choreography were immediately banned. But the Çarşı
endured. Another tactic would have to be used to challenge the big
three on and off the pitch. And, in 2014, it looked like Erdoğan and his
ruling Justice and Development Party, the AKP, had found it.

Today's match was against İstanbul Başakşehir, a new İstanbul
team that had found itself both at the top of the league with a handful
of games to go, and in the good graces of the country's president. The

two appeared to be connected. The team came from the outer suburb of Başakşehir, a reliably pro-AKP voting district, and was built from İstanbul's almost forgotten municipality team. In four years they had established themselves as one of Turkey's best. Arda Turan had signed a €3m-a-year contract on loan from Barcelona. Robinho had signed in the winter transfer window. They played at the brand new Fatih Terim Stadium, named after Turkey's greatest living coach, who was currently in charge of Galatasaray. But where did this money come from? It wasn't from the fans. Even though Başakşehir had their own, newly formed supporters group – 1453, named after the year Constantinople fell to the Ottomans – they were lucky to have a few thousand supporters at any given home game. But Erdoğan had often boasted that Başakşehir was his team. Although there was no proof of direct government funding, the team's lavish sponsors were all connected to the AKP. The club's president was related to Erdoğan by marriage. And now they were top of the table and on course to win their first ever title. The big three was about to become the big four.[4]

This weekend there was a hitch. A few weeks earlier İstanbul held its mayoral elections. İstanbul is vast, a sprawling city of 15 million people, Turkey's economic powerhouse. It had always been seen as vital to Erdoğan's political project – a mixture of neo-liberal capitalism, Islamism and authoritarianism. Indeed, Erdoğan launched his own political career by becoming mayor in 1994. But his preferred AKP candidate, the former prime minister Binali Yıldırım, had narrowly lost to the opposition CHP candidate Ekrem İmamoğlu a few days before. Erdoğan wasn't accepting the loss of his power base well, and had suggested there had been irregularities. Turkey's election board was looking into whether the vote should be re-run, incensing the opposition who viewed it as another step on Erdoğan's journey towards despotism. A decision was expected imminently at perhaps the worst time. Four İstanbul teams were due to play in the city the same weekend.

'Forget Beşiktaş v. Başakşehir. Fenerbahçe v. Galatasaray is on,' Bora said. The Intercontinental Derby was the biggest game in Turkey, if not one of the biggest in the world. Tens of thousands of ultras and organised football fans would be on the streets. 'The government wouldn't want the fans to react to a political decision during derby weekends,' Bora added. 'There would be mayhem.'

The Çarşı moved as one towards the stadium, past the lines of trucks with water cannons, thousands of riot police with shields, helmets, truncheons and tear-gas canisters. There had been a rumour that İmamoğlu would turn up today, a symbolic gesture of defiance during a symbolic fixture: a team that represented İstanbul's liberal, secular culture against a team that represented the patronage network that had entrenched Erdoğan's power. Beşiktaş versus Erdoğan FC. The crowd began to chant 'Cheers, Tayyip!' whilst clinking beer bottles, a tongue-in-cheek reference to the time the government massively increased the tax on alcohol. Thousands of flares were lit as the crowd began to chant pro-İmamoğlu slogans and headed for their seats.

Turkey's first self-declared ultra group, Galatasaray's UltrAslan, was formed in 2001. Its own rich and storied indigenous fan culture existed long before that, of course. But the new millennium brought with it new influences. Technology and globalisation had allowed cultural exchange to occur on a scale, and at a speed, that had never been seen before. In 1950 it took five months for the sound of Brazil's *torcida*, the sound of Jayme de Carvalho's Charanga, to travel back by boat to Croatia with the Yugoslavia national team, percolate by word of mouth, and then emerge in some rough form far from Brazil's Platonic ideal at Hajduk Split's Stadion Stari plac stadium. In the 1980s it took weeks for Mikael to process the pictures he took on his camera of his early *tifos* and then exchange them by post with like-minded obsessives in Sweden and elsewhere. In the 1990s, the snippets of choreography and chants on programmes like *Eurogoals* would be heard by those who were paying close attention to the 30 seconds at the start and end of the broadcast once every seven days. As the internet became as ubiquitous as football, that exchange of ideas became instantaneous. It wasn't just speed, the world got smaller too. Over the next ten years the combination of the Italian terraces,

English hooliganism, Argentinian *barras bravas* and Brazilian *torcida* now mashed into an exportable concept of the 'ultras' spread to every part of Europe, to Asia, North America and North Africa.

North Africa and the Magreb had been particularly enthusiastic about adopting the aesthetics of this ultra culture 2.0. Whenever there was a club centenary or a trophy to celebrate, the ultras from Morocco, Algeria and Tunisia put on a pyro show – known as a *craquage* – that would rival anywhere in the world. When Tunisia's Espérance celebrated its centenary in 2019 they did so with a *craquage* that wasn't just restricted to the stadium. Three days before the actual event, the ultras arranged for a football-pitch-sized *craquage* that spelt out Espérance in Arabic. When it came to game day the government restricted the number of fans headed to the game to 5,000. The ultras boycotted it, and 20 times that number headed to the training complex instead. Flares were lit in every city and town in Tunisia. It was perhaps the first country-wide *craquage*.[5]

But the ultras were adopting more than just the aesthetics of the movement. The ultras' organisational structure, tightly knit groups difficult for outsiders to penetrate, in a public space that was impossible to control by the authorities proved to have a much more political effect. The best example was in Egypt. In 2007 I went to the Cairo derby between Al Ahly and Zamalek. It was the biggest game in African football but it was also the debut derby for Al Ahly's first ultra group, which would later come to be known as the Ahlawy. There I had met Assad, the group's founder and *capo*. He had been heavily influenced by the *curva* in Italy, English football and the ultras in Serbia. At that game they unveiled their first *tifo*, aimed at Zamalek, commemorating their biggest ever victory, a 6–1 mauling back in 2002.

'The two biggest political parties in Egypt are Ahly and Zamalek,' Assad explained. At the time Egypt had been under decades of autocratic rule by Hosni Mubarak. There was little political space to do anything and the ultras then were staunchly apolitical. The stadium was a release from what was going on in Egyptian society rather than an extension of it. It was too dangerous to do otherwise. Ahly's enemy was Zamalek, and vice versa. But the Ahlawy, and Zamalek's equivalent the Ultras White Knights, would go on to carve a political space for themselves in Egypt's football stadiums.

Over the next few years their numbers would grow from a few hundred to tens of thousands. What couldn't be expressed on the street or through the ballot box could be said in the freedom of the *curva*. Increasingly political chants could be heard, especially against police brutality. The Ahlawy were on the front line of Mubarak's increasingly hostile police state every week simply because they spent a lot of time in their company. The journey to matches, the shakedown outside the stadiums, the aggressive policing inside them all left their mark Every match had a thousand reminders of the absence of freedom. Over time the chants became more anti-authoritarian and anti-police. 'ACAB' made an appearance on a few banners. Their leaders would be arrested – although not Assad – and their members roughed up regularly before, during and after games. But far from subduing dissent, the authorities were fanning its flames. When Egypt finally revolted in 2011, hundreds of thousands of people filled Tahrir Square demanding that Mubarak step down. When the police attacked, there was only one group that had any front-line experience.

Like in Ukraine three years later, Egypt's ultras knew how to confront the police. Each group announced that they were staying neutral, but individual members could attend. Once there it was clear who knew what to do and who didn't, as ultras from all of Egypt's clubs found themselves at the centre of the fight. 'The whole concept of any independent organisation didn't exist, not unions, not political parties,' Assad told me when we met again in Cairo shortly after Mubarak was forced from power. 'At the time it was just sport. But to them it was the youth, in big numbers. They feared us. Of course, I don't want to say we were solely responsible for bringing down Mubarak. But our role was to make people dream, letting them know if a cop hits you, you can hit them back. During the revolution, there was the Muslim Brotherhood, the activists and the ultras. That's it.'

The Ahlawy were an absurdly diverse group. There were men and women, secularists and devout Muslims, obscenely rich and dirt poor.

In the months after the revolution it was striking how much influence the ultras had on the other activists and protesters. The pyro and the flags were the most immediate example. But they had also adopted the sound of the stadiums, especially the chants, which became anthems heard at every protest.

> *They say violence is in our blood*
> *How dare we fight for our rights*
> *Stupid regime*
> *Hear what we say*
> *Freedom!*
> *Freedom!*
> *Freedom!*

Over the next few years I travelled back regularly to Cairo and saw how the revolution fell apart. At first the ultras were branded as simple hooligans, but as their role in the revolution became clearer, they were then hailed as heroes. But within the security state, they were despised and targeted for revenge. On 1 February 2012, 72 Al Ahly fans, many of them Ahlawy, were killed in a stadium crush after a game against Al Masry in Port Said. Someone had turned the lights off shortly before the Al Masry fans ran across the the pitch to attack the opposite stand. But a mixture of violence, mendacity, bad luck and ineptitude led to unfathomable bloodshed. The single gate out of the stand had been locked.

'We are victims for our values, our ideology and what we stand for,' Assad had told me, after we had travelled to Alexandria to visit the grave of one of the ultras who died that day. 'We are one of the purest entities in the country and they are trying to destroy us. Seventy-four people [the 72 that died in Port Said plus two members who died during the revolution] is not enough. If you want to terminate our ideas then you have to finish us all. We'll die for it if that is what it takes.'

The Ahlawy campaigned remorselessly for answers. They effectively prevented the football league from re-starting until the courts had delivered justice. Which they did. An Egyptian court later found that the city's security authorities had colluded with Al Masry's ultras to launch the attack. On social media and in the graffiti on Cairo's streets you would see the same code: 'JFT74', 'Justice For The 74'. The phrase was taken from Liverpool fans who for years campaigned for justice for the 96 that died at Hillsborough in the face of an indifferent state. Port Said was Al Ahly's Hillsborough, but in reverse. There was only a short window for any kind of justice. Soon after, Egypt's first democratically elected president Mohamed Morsi was ousted in a coup, replaced by the former director of military intelligence Abdel Fattah el Sisi. A month later his forces moved in on two pro-Morsi protest camps. It's estimated that as many as 1,200 civilians were killed at the Rabaa massacre. [Morsi would later die in prison.] The crackdown had begun. Almost exactly three years after Port Said, 22 members of Zamalek's Ultras White Knights were killed in a crush outside a stadium caused by the police firing tear gas into an enclosed space. Supporters have largely been banned from club matches ever since.[6]

Egypt's ultras would eventually be outlawed. In May 2015 Cairo's Court of Urgent Matters passed a law banning them after a private prosecution brought by Mortada Mansour, the chairman of Zamalek and a staunch ally of Hosni Mubarak. Mansour had long hated the ultras, calling them terrorists and thugs. The ultras responded by throwing a bag of urine over him. Hundreds would end up in Egypt's jails in the years that followed. The repression became too much and the Ahlawy released a video in 2018 of them burning their main banner, the internationally recognised sign that an ultras group was disbanding. The Ahlawy's Facebook account was deleted. Ultras White Knights followed a few days later. Assad and the group's other leaders – at least those who weren't in jail – melted back into their ordinary lives, unable to speak of the time they were considered heroes of the nation.

There are very few civil organisations who would survive a toe-to-toe fight with the state. The ultras in Egypt were no different. But they were a unique phenomenon: at first non-political, but avowedly anti-authoritarian actors who were in the right place at the right time to make just the right amount of difference. There was no manifesto.

They were simply a loose confederation of friends who shared two loves: football and the desire for a free space. Yet even as they were outlawed and disbanded, their banners burned and the graffiti painted over, one thing endured that couldn't be erased. The songs and chants. The lexicon of the terraces seeped into everyday use. Even now, supporters were being arrested in Egypt for singing revolution-era songs or chanting for the release of those arrested for being ultras.

Unlike Egypt and Tunisia, Algeria didn't have its Arab Spring. But at the start of 2019 mass protests broke out when the country's ailing president, Abdelaziz Bouteflika, announced his intention to stand for a fifth term. Bouteflika was in his eighties and in bad health, wheelchair-bound after a recent stroke. He had already been in power for 20 years and had twice altered the constitution to get around presidential term limits. Fearful of large groups of organised men roaming the streets, the government suspended the football league. But for years Algerian ultras had been chanting highly political songs about poverty, government corruption, mass youth unemployment and disenchantment. They all seemed to reference drug use and how the government turned a blind eye to it to pacify the population. El Bahdja, the ultras group of USM Alger, were, according to Maher Mezahi, an Algerian journalist who documents North African ultra culture, the masters of songs that could 'last six or seven minutes, and everyone knows the words'. The most famous chant was 'La Casa del Mouradia', named after Bouteflika's presidential palace and effectively a poem that tells the story of the president's 20 years in charge.

It's dawn and I can't sleep,
I'm sitting here, slowly getting high,
What is the cause and who can I blame?
We're sick of this life we live.

The first [term] they tricked us with reconciliation,
The second it became clear that this is La Casa del Mouradia,
In the third the country suffered because of personal interest,
In the fourth the puppet [Bouteflika] died and nothing changed.[7]

Bouteflika stepped down without violence and bloodshed but 'La Casa del Mouradia' remains the sound of the protests.

In Morocco, the government found it equally as difficult to eradicate something as ephemeral as a song. Raja Casablanca's first ultras group, the Green Boys, was formed in 2005, although they quickly split in 2006 with a group forming the Ultras Eagles. There were now three distinct groups within Raja; Green Boys, Ultras Eagles and Derb Sultan. Often there were clashes between the three. In 2016 two people were killed at the Mohammed V Stadium when members of the Green Boys and Ultras Eagles clashed.[8] The government banned the ultras and jailed Raja's head *capo*, Zakaria 'Skwadra' Belkadi.[9] He was released two years later and the ultras were allowed to return. Morocco also escaped its Arab Spring but that didn't mean there wasn't an undercurrent of alienation and unhappiness with the government and the police over the same issues that had afflicted the youth in Egypt, Algeria and Tunisia: corruption, unemployment and, especially, abuse by the police.

Like in Algeria, a song from the *curva*, this time from the Mohammed V Stadium, had also become an anthem for doomed youth: 'F'bladi Dalmouni'; 'They've Oppressed Me in My Country':

They've oppressed me in my country
Who can I complain to?
To God, the most high
Only He knows

In this country we're living under a dark cloud
Asking for peace
Give us victory, God

They offer us drugs from Ketama [a famous hash producing area of Morocco]
And abandoned us like orphans
We'll get our due on judgment day

Many talents you have destroyed
With highs [from drugs], *you've crushed them*
How else do you want to see it?

Other clubs had also written popular anti-government anthems, but 'F'bladi Dalmouni', written by Gruppo Aquile, was by far the most popular, and the catchiest. I went to Casablanca for the derby between Raja and Wydad in the hope of meeting the leaders of the Green Boys and the Ultras Eagles. It had been difficult making contact. They feared being arrested and thought they were being monitored. Being seen talking to a foreign journalist would almost certainly bring more unwanted heat on to them. After weeks of back and forth we had agreed to meet in Casablanca when I got there. As my taxi headed from the train station to the centre, through the city's shabby French colonial streets, the driver turned on the radio. Even though it was midday, midweek, it was the unmistakable sound of Arabic football commentary.

Who's playing? I asked my driver.

'Raja,' he replied.

We headed straight there, but not to the vast Mohammed V Stadium, which was under renovation. It was one of the reasons why the derby was being played a three-hour train ride away in Marrakesh. We arrived instead at the Stade Père Jégo, the home of Racing Athletic club, the same club where the famed Inter coach Helenio Herrera – who had played his part in growing Italy's ultra movement – spent two seasons as a player in the early 1930s. The stadium's stone-coloured wall had the club's name written in faded green paint in both French and Arabic. A few dozen supporters were sat on top of the high wall, watching the game, a full ten-metre drop behind them.

The Père Jégo was completely full for Raja against Ittihad Tanger. It was cool and overcast and three sides of the stadium had no cover, but the largest, along one side of the pitch, was overflowing; an almost unbroken mass of green. Fights seemed to be breaking out within small groups that spilled out on to the wide concourse in front. It was chaos. Within a minute a man both wider and taller than me grabbed my arms and dragged me away. 'This place is not for you, go!' He was pointing at my camera. He pushed me away and went back to sorting out a melee that had broken out.

On the other side of the stadium I could see the stand in its full glory; a swaying mass of green shirts with green smoke bellowing from the fireworks that had just been let off. There were several Palestinian flags and a banner calling for a free Palestine; another said 'Until Death'. But then I heard what I had come for. The entire stadium started singing 'F'bladi Dalmouni', a beautiful and haunting melody.

> *You killed the passion*
> *You started the provocation*
> *Fear is your invention*
> *And you applied that to us*
> *You want to rule with it*
>
> *Because of flares you forced us to play behind closed doors*
> *And you banned the tifos*
> *You're warring with the ultras*

A short man in expensive-looking clothes sidled up to me and asked who I was. He introduced himself as Nabil, the head of police, and asked for my ID. He took a look at it and started quizzing me as to why I was there and who I had spoken to, something that would happen frequently in Morocco. When I told him I was there to see the fans, he took a moment to take it in before his face cracked into a wide smile. 'Of course, I can help you! We have a good relationship with the ultras!' he said. The other ultras had noticed the policeman talking to me. I wanted to get away as quickly as I could. 'They are pillars of our society,' he said. He took my number, and gave me his, and told me to call him, day or night, if I wanted to talk to any ultras. He was good friends with them, he said. He would sort everything out.

At that moment I knew that I would never hear from my contact from the Green Boys again. And I didn't.

BEŞIKTAŞ, İSTANBUL

CEM YAKIŞAN'S BAR COULD BE found a few minutes' walk from the eagle statue in the centre of Beşiktaş, deep in its maze of cafes and kebab shops. Inside the walls were covered in pictures of counter-cultural icons: Kurt Cobain, Che Guevara, The Clash and Hrant Dink, a Turkish-Armenian journalist who was murdered by an ultra-nationalist in 1997. A black and white flag had been hung on the crisscross of wires that tangled between buildings outside. Above all else, Cem's first love was Beşiktaş, both the club and the neighbour-hood. The two are impossible to untangle. He turned on an outside heater to fight off the damp, cold İstanbul winter's day. Almost every-one who walked past, it seemed, stopped to say hello. A few asked for money, and he always obliged. This was his neighbourhood. He was born and grew up here, and never left.

'The first thing we learned from living here was sharing,' he said. His mother, he recalled, would send him out to buy bread but insist he bought three loaves instead of two, so it could be shared with oth-ers on his walk home. 'That is how we grew up and that is reflected in our terrace culture.'

Cem was the founder of the Çarşı. Or, at least, one of the found-ers left alive. In 1982, alongside 17 other young, radical Beşiktaş fans, they set up a supporters group in the darkest days of dictatorship fol-lowing the 1980 military coup. They named it after the market, or bazaar, at the heart of the neighbourhood. The leading figure back then was Optik Baskan (a *nom de guerre* for Mehmet Isiklar that came from the fact he used to wear very strong glasses) a master's student and history teacher who moulded the early leftist ideals of the group. It was his idea to make the 'A' of Çarşı an anarchist symbol. He died of a heart attack in 1997, shortly after coming out of prison for drug offences. He was 38. At his funeral the Çarşı chanted in honour of 'the last hooligan'. Almost all the rest have left or been killed. In 2011 Alen Markaryan, one of the Çarşı's terrace leaders, was shot by another member during a dispute. He made a full recovery but didn't return.[10]

Cem was one of the last left standing, offering a memory of the turbulent early years of the group. He was not a young man any more. He had grey, receding hair but sharp blue eyes behind thin-rimmed glasses. His principles have remained unchanged. 'We don't care if you are Kurdish, Armenian, Greek, German, a woman, man, factory owner or shoeshine boy,' he said when I asked him to define Çarşı's values. 'As long as we are in those stands together, we are together.'

As a group Çarşı were difficult to pin down. Depending on which members you speak to, they are either an ultras group or a hooligan firm; they are either deeply political or so broad as to make them virtually apolitical; they are either a driven group of social activists that raise money for earthquake victims and animal shelters, or simply an excuse to escape the grind of daily life for 90 minutes. One famous Çarşı banner proclaimed, '*Çarşı, her seye karsı!*': 'Çarşı is against everything!' There was even one banner that declared that '*Çarşı is against itself*'. There's no membership. They don't sell merchandise. They were, Cem said, a feeling. A state of being that brought people together in the hope of something better. And there was a long list of actions that Cem was proud of in recent years. The drive to donate blood in 2011 after the Van earthquake in the far east of the country (the Çarşı stripped down to their underwear and threw their scarves and clothes on to the pitch as donations during one game). There was the Greenpeace protest when activists climbed the main covered stand at the İnönü and hung on ropes for 90 minutes, 10m in the air, with a banner that said: 'Nuclear Free Turkey. Çarşı.'

But before all that came the bloodshed. The 1980s were a dark time on Turkey's terraces, a period of such violence that they have become known as 'The Terrace Wars'. At that time, each team's supporters groups were loose confederations of fans, whose leader was known as the 'Amigo'. The Çarşı was the most organised. In fact, it was the only group with a distinctive name.

The epicentre of 'The War' was one terrace in particular. The İnönü, although Beşiktaş home, also hosted Fenerbahçe and Galatasaray for long periods. When the two played, the stadium was split down the middle: 50 per cent of the tickets were allocated to both home and away fans, which was asking for trouble. But the hard-core all wanted to stand in the same place: the *Kapalı*, or covered, stand. About 6,000 could stand here, Cem, explained. The roof wasn't just for shelter: it also amplified the chants. It was prime terrace real estate and three groups of supporters wanted it. So, every time two of the teams played, the two sets of fans literally fought each other for the right to stand in the middle. Eventually, groups of supporters were sleeping there overnight, waiting for their opponents to arrive. When the police got wise to that, they would simply arrive at 5am instead.

Cem had fond memories of those days. He enjoyed the fighting. And he was good at it, even if it left him with 'seven or eight stab wounds. And a bullet wound in my leg.' The violence got worse, with groups arranging to meet up and fight. The fighting spilled over from match day until it became an everyday occurrence, like a low-level urban guerilla war across the city. But with no rules and weapons frequently used – a long, thin doner kebab knife was a favourite weapon of choice, and guns weren't uncommon – the situation was getting out of control. 'You have to understand that it wasn't just on game day that we were fighting. It was every single day,' he said. 'Those were the bad days.'

Something had to be done. 'I received a phone call from my most violent rivals,' Cem said. So, in 1996, the leaders of the supporters's group at Galatasaray, a man called Sebahattin Şirin, and Fenerbahçe, led by Pepe Metin, contacted Cem to arrange a meeting at Abasagga Park, close to his bar in Beşiktaş.

'It was actually a serious scene,' Cem recalled of that day. They agreed to meet at dusk. Cem brought 40 Çarşı with him, the leaders of Galatasaray and Fenerbahçe the same. But soon he realised that, around the edge of the park, partially obscured by the darkness, were hundreds more. At first Cem thought that it was a trap and that this, finally, would be the moment he was killed. But when the streetlights came on, he realised that they were Beşiktaş fans who had followed him to the park for protection. They were his people. He grabbed the two other leaders and walked to a nearby coffee shop, leaving their followers to pace around outside like expectant fathers, waiting for news to arrive. A truce was discussed. Hands were shaken. What became known in Turkish football as 'The Peace' was agreed. And mostly it has held ever since.

That's not to say there hasn't been violence in Turkish football since. There was the infamous murder of two Leeds United fans before a UEFA Cup semi-final game in 2000.[11] Referees and players have been attacked on the pitch. In 2015 the Fenerbahçe team bus, with Dirk Kuyt and Emre Belözoğlu inside, was shot at after a game.[12] Several fans have been killed in individual incidents too. A Fenerbahçe fan was stabbed to death only a few weeks before the Gezi Park protests. And it is violence that has been given as a pretext by the government every time a new law restricting football fans is discussed and then invariably implemented. But the mass, organised violence between the supporters was largely a thing of the past.

Whilst the Çarşı's mix of social consciousness and extreme loyalty made them the biggest and most recognised supporters group, there was no real hierarchy. 'An understanding of strict hierarchy is unthinkable for us,' Cem said. 'What happens is that we decide together. What you have to know is that, in this group, dissent is not something that you learn or try to achieve. It is in our nature.' Everything from what songs to sing to what banners to make to what food they should eat on away trips are all put to the vote: one member of the Çarşı, one vote. It was how the group became involved in the Gezi Park protests. For Cem, Gezi began weeks before. The Çarşı had tried to march on Taksim Square for the May Day protests but had been denied by the police. And then there was the last days of the İnönü Stadium. It was being ripped down and rebuilt, part of Erdoğan's football stadium rebuilding zeal. The last game of the season against Gençlerbirliği was packed. As many as 100,000 people were there according to Cem. 'It was an emotional day and, stupidly, a police officer fires a gun in the air and it's mayhem after that.' Beşiktaş won that game but the headlines in the Turkish press were about riots, tear gas and gunshots.[13]

Two weeks later, the police were indiscriminately tear-gassing peaceful protesters and burning down their tents on Gezi Park. 'On the first day, 24 May, I was there with fifty people,' said Bağış Erten, a Eurosport journalist who was at Gezi from the beginning. 'The next day it became two hundred. The next day more than a thousand. And by 31 May, that night, more than a million people were ready for the tear gas.' The increased violence saw Erdoğan dismissing the protestors out of hand, declaring they were 'çapulcu' ('looters') and 'godless'. 'I will not seek permission from hoodlums to implement my plans for Taksim [Gezi Park],' he told a large crowd at a rally. The heavy-handed tactics were winning. No one had any experience fighting the police. Cem watched the violence on TV and decided it was time to go and help. It was put to a vote. Everyone agreed. 'We started our first march with five hundred people from this neighbourhood. By the time we reached it [Gezi] there was almost ten thousand people.'

The moment that the Çarşı arrived in Gezi was captured in the documentary *İstanbul United*. 'I'll never forget that scene [with] fans wearing jerseys the moment the Çarşı came in,' said Bora. 'You have come literally to save us. People were crying. It was incredible.' A confederation of supporters from the big three had come together and marched, although the Çarşı were by far the biggest and most visible presence. They brought banners and songs.

Come and shoot,
Come and shoot us with tear gas,
Take off your helmet,
Put away your baton,
And we will see who is the boss.

They also turned one of Erdoğan's slogans against him.

The çapulcu [looters] are coming.

More importantly – like in Tahrir Square in Egypt and Maidan in Ukraine – Turkey's ultras had experience of what to do when the police attacked. How to deal with tear gas and rubber bullets. How to use vinegar to counteract the effects. When to run and when to stand your ground. 'At Gezi we did what we trained for,' said Cem. 'We knew how to deal with police pressure. We knew how to deal with tear gas. We knew how to deal with a water cannon or night-sticks.' The ultras could only ever provide a limited protection, though. By 15 June the government had crushed the uprising. Eight protesters had been killed and 8,000 injured. Eleven had been blinded. The Gezi Park redevelopment was stopped, but that wasn't the end of the matter.

When the 2013/14 season began, the government and the football federation banned political chants and banners. 'We are adding bad political and ideological slogans to the list of illegal demonstrations in football stands, or behaviour not complying with sporting ethics,' said Turkey's interior minister Muammer Güler. 'It is clear that political and ideological slogans do not comply with sport's spirit ... That includes profanity or non-sporting behaviour.'[14] But still you could hear the chants on the terraces from the 34th minute (34 is the vehicle registration code for İstanbul): 'Everywhere is Taksim, everywhere is resistance'. The ultras would be controlled even more tightly from now on. There was already the hated 6222 law, brought in in 2011, that gave the police sweeping surveillance powers. It laid the bedrock for the introduction of an equally despised e-ticket system, the Passolig card, alongside cameras that could take pictures of individual faces in the crowd. The system was doubly controversial because the card forced you to sign up for an account with Aktif Bank, where Erdoğan's son-in-law was the CEO of the bank's holding company. There was a countrywide boycott of stadiums when the scheme was introduced. The average attendance in Turkey's Süper Lig halved, from 14,000 to 7,000.

Cem Yakışan, meanwhile, had bigger problems to deal with. After Gezi he and 34 other members of the Çarşı were arrested. He was charged with running a criminal organisation and with attempting to topple the government. Either charge, if found guilty, would lead to life in prison.[15] 'I was the prime suspect,' said Cem. 'I said, yes, OK, but I founded the group in 1982. We've been around for more than thirty years. Aren't you a little late to charge me with this legal shit?' The coup charge threw him somewhat. His lawyers had gamed every eventuality that might come up in the court room, but not that. 'I looked at the judge and said: "If I was strong enough to topple the government I would have made Beşiktaş champions."' It was an unarguable riposte. He won the case.

BAŞAKŞEHIR, İSTANBUL

COMPARED TO THE FRENETIC BUSTLE of central İstanbul, Başakşehir was quiet, almost deserted. It took a long time to get here from the Bosphorus: a bus, three trains and a taxi. It felt like a different city. In İstanbul every inch of space had been accounted for. But Başakşehir had wide empty streets. Whole neighbourhoods had popped up overnight; lines of identikit, sandy-coloured high-rise flats with families playing with children in parks at the front. Construction sites were everywhere, even around the Fatih Terim Stadium. A large plot of land outside the stadium was being excavated, surrounded by a long fence of spiked metal panels. Attached to each one were tarpaulin-like banners, alternatively orange and blue, the crest and then the owl, the colours and the symbols of the stadium's tenant, and league leaders, Başakşehir. A group of five women walked past, all dressed in full black burqas with a veil. Rolling, scrubby hills rose in the near distance. Aside from the burqas, it reminded me of Israeli settlements I had seen spring up in the West Bank; a place built in a hurry for the true believers, the young families who would put down roots and forever stake their claim here.

The football club was unmistakably at the centre of Başakşehir. In the club shop nearby a scale model showed how the area would look when it was finished. A family-friendly maze of parks and apartment blocks, anchored by the stadium. I counted 14 football pitches and stadiums planned for an area no bigger than a couple of blocks. There were few places that could encapsulate, could mirror, Erdoğan's 20 years in power better than Başakşehir: frenzied real-estate construction, the primacy of football and a deepening Islamic religiosity.

Erdoğan launched his political career by becoming İstanbul's mayor in 1994. His personal vision was to meld a moderate form of Islam with the benefits of modern capitalism and democracy. At least, that was the rhetoric. He tapped into a well of resentment from those who had been marginalised over the years due to the primacy of Atatürk's secularism. In 1997 the Islamist prime minister Necmettin Erbakan was, effectively, forced to stand down by the military for mixing religion with matters of the state. He was banned from office, as was his Welfare Party. Erdoğan was a member and, a year later, he was jailed for reading out what was claimed to be a banned religious poem in public. He served four months of a ten-month sentence. In 2001, sensing an appetite for non-secular politics, he helped form the Justice and Development Party (AKP). They won the 2002 general election by a landslide and, although there were several attempts to have the party banned over the next few years (and Erdoğan himself was initially banned from taking office due to his stint in jail) Erdoğan was able to entrench himself – first as prime minister and then as president – to oversee something of an economic boom in Turkey fuelled by credit and construction.

But his personal story was dominated by football. 'Reis', or 'The Big Man', came from a poor, devout family from Kasımpaşa. He sold *simit* – stale, sesame-seed bread – on the streets but excelled in religious studies and sport. He was obsessed with football and his legend has been burnished thanks to tales by sycophantic biographers of him single-handedly leading his young team to victory. He has, in various public pronouncements, declared that he was an artful midfielder, a striker and a goalkeeper. The biggest claim was that Fenerbahçe wanted to sign him. There is very little evidence of any of this happening but it hasn't stopped Erdoğan invoking football to show his virility and 'man of the people' credentials. Erdoğan wove football and his Islamic credentials together as early as 1994, just before he was elected İstanbul's mayor. When a biopic of Erdoğan was released in 2019 it had a young version of him scoring an overhead winner, coming on as a substitute when the score was 9–9. 'Soner Yalcın, a journalist who has written a 400-page take down of Erdoğan, makes no effort to conceal his contempt,' wrote John McManus in *Welcome to Hell?*. 'He believes that the entire Fenerbahçe story is fabricated. Yalçın also claims Erdoğan spent his first two years at Camıaltıspor as assistant to the kit man.'[16]

Whatever the truth of Erdoğan's playing career, there was no doubt he had made the game a developmental priority when he came to power. According to Patrick Keddie's political history of Turkish football, *The Passion*, Erdoğan's AKP built its hegemony through the construction sector, setting up a network of patronage that enriched allies, building a new elite to counter the old secular powers in the country. In 2013, at the time of Gezi, the government had $100 billion worth of construction projects in the pipeline. İstanbul, and the rest of the country, was changing quickly. Thirty new football stadiums were built across 27 cities. Galatasaray and Beşiktaş got new stadiums, although only Beşiktaş was allowed to stay in the same location. Galatasaray fans saw their Ali Sami Yen Stadium destroyed, sold to developers for a new mall, and the team moved miles away to what was then the Türk Telekom Arena. (As Keddie points out, Erdoğan later banned the word 'arena' being used, forcing stadiums to change their names. 'I am against "arenas". You know what they do in arenas, don't you? People were dismembered there [by animals],' Erdoğan said in a 2017 speech. 'I have given the instruction to the minister and we will remove the name "arena" from stadiums.')[17]The relocation contributed to one of the most embarrassing moments of Erdoğan's political career. When the Türk Telekom Stadium (née Arena) was opened in 2011, with a match against Ajax, Galatasaray's fans booed Erdoğan. Completely unprepared for public displays of dissent, he angrily left at half-time. To avoid a repeat when Beşiktaş' new stadium was opened, only VIPs were invited. But Başakşehir was home turf. When the Fatih Terim Stadium was opened in 2014, Erdoğan played in an exhibition match wearing number 12 on the back of his shirt, shortly after becoming Turkey's 12th president. He scored a hat-trick too: the first a decent finish from the outside of the right boot, the second a superb chip over the goalkeeper. The third saw the opposition basically stop and let him score. There was enough there to show he had *some* ability on the pitch, even if the jury was still out on whether that was enough to have pricked the interest of Fenerbahçe when he was a young man. The club retired the number '12' jersey afterwards, not for the fans like at Hajduk Split, Lazio, Red Star Belgrade and Hammarby (or, closer to home, Beşiktaş and Fenerbahçe), but in honour of Erdoğan.[18]

Still, Gezi Park proved there was one area of football Erdoğan could not fully control. The big three, and in particular their fans. So in 2012 a group of directors connected to the AKP bought the old municipality team of Başakşehir and transformed it. The team's colours were now the same as the AKP flag. The chairman, Göksel Gümüşdağ, was an AKP official, married to the niece of Erdoğan's wife Ermin. The club's key sponsors were all connected to Erdoğan's patronage network. The company that built the stadium, Kalyon Group Holding, was the company charged with redeveloping Gezi and had been a frequent recipient of government contracts including one of Erdoğan's prized projects, the newly opened İstanbul airport. Medipol, the club's biggest sponsor, was run by Dr Fahrettin Koca, the Erdoğan family's personal physician. He was also appointed Minister of Health in 2018. Erdoğan has himself, on occasion, boasted about being the founder of 'his' team. 'They insist that there is no official government support,' says Bağış Erten, the Eurosport journalist. 'I'm not convinced. The sponsors were quick to be convinced. If you want to do business with the municipality, with government, it's a good idea to be seen positively by the government.'

By 2014 the club was in the top tier, with a new stadium and money to burn, finishing fourth, fourth, second, third, and second in the following five seasons. At today's game against Beşiktaş, the squad would include Arda Turan, Emmanuel Adebayor, Demba Ba, Gaël Clichy, Gökhan İnler and Robinho. Also in the squad was goalkeeper Volkan Babacan, who was chipped by Erdoğan at the opening of the stadium. The big three in İstanbul was truly now the big four. The problem was that hardly anyone showed up for the games. Attendances bumped along at around 2,000. This had not gone unnoticed. When

Erdoğan dropped into the district's AKP office he chided them for the empty seats.[19]

Outside the stadium, by a terrace of cafes, a handful of buses were parked up. Police leaned lazily on their riot shields, bereft of their usual militarised equipment. If there was to be any trouble today, clearly the police didn't think it would be here. 'We are an İstanbul club and İstanbul was conquered by the Ottoman empire in 1453. That's why we chose the name,' said Cafer, a large man with a greying beard waiting for the rest of his people to arrive. He was the *capo*, or *amigo*, of 1453, the supporters group of Başakşehir. He was wearing an orange hoodie with the year in big letters on the front, surrounded by dozens of young ultras. There would be, he said, around 500 to 1,000 of them travelling to Beşiktaş for the game today. He laughed when I asked whether the club and its supporters were pro-Erdoğan, believing it was jealousy that was driving the critics. Or fear. The big three's monopoly was, he believed, about to be shattered, with the new neighbourhood creating a community culture which would bring fans to the club. Of course, that meant the club's supporters rejecting their previous allegiances, something akin to heresy for most people from İstanbul. Cafer wouldn't say what his club was when he was growing up. 'We are a new club, yes. But in Europe we have seen new clubs breaking taboos and winning titles. And that is what we will do as well.'

In the cafe next door Burak Bilgili was taking phone calls and arranging the transport for Başakşehir's away support. 'Eighty per cent of our fan base are students,' said Burak, a young man with a red beard and a prematurely receding hairline. 'This is a record.' Burak was one of the founders of 1453, charged with building a fan culture to match the success of the team on the pitch. Moving to the new stadium had helped, he said, to build more of a neighbourhood spirit. 'The neighbourhood resembles the fan group,' he said. 'First, the area is very young too. Second, we are gentle people. Fair people. Respectable people. We don't believe there should be swearing or violence in the stands. We never swear and we never commit violence. What we want from this fan group and our stands, families should be able to come, watch our game, and have no problem whatsoever.'

There was little to find wrong with what he said. Who wants to condone violence? Who doesn't want families at football? But the language was very similar to Erdoğan's and his allies. No swearing. Families. Respect. Manners. Piety juxtaposed against the behaviour of the *çapulcu* and the 'godless'. Burak wanted to move 1453 away from the ultras model at other clubs. There was one ultras-esque group but overall they wanted to be a moderate group. 'Officially speaking we are a fans association ... unlike the European ultras.'

He was cut off by a loud series of bangs from outside. A few hundred members of the 1453 had arrived outside the cafe and were lighting flares and letting off smoke bombs for a local TV crew. The police were unmoved. 'They are not condoning violence!' Burak added quickly.

The biggest problem was always how to persuade residents to switch teams. So Burak went from door to door to campaign for the club. 'We went to houses. We talked to people about how important it is to support a neighbourhood team. In the end they were convinced.' The AKP had done much the same in the aftermath of losing İstanbul's mayoral election: turning up at doors asking who they had voted for and why. Burak seemed a kind soul, but I wondered how much his campaign gave the appearance of persuasion and how much felt like coercion to break a habit of a lifetime. He denied that this was Erdoğan's or the AKP's team. 'There are three, four hundred fans outside. Go out, ask them, you will see as many different political ideologies. What is happening [is] we are playing good football and deserving what we are winning.' Burak sincerely believed a title for Başakşehir would be good for Turkish football, that the big three 'could learn something' from the success of a team run properly.

What will it be like here if you win the title? I asked.

'This will be an insane zone,' he said. 'But maybe we'll celebrate our title all across İstanbul. And we can all celebrate the title together.' On a TV above him, there's no mention of today's game, just wall-to-wall coverage of tomorrow's clash between Fenerbahçe and Galatasaray. Burak was nothing if not optimistic.

Outside the young ultras of the 1453 were getting ready to leave for the biggest match of the season. Win and they would go nine points clear. Başakşehir's first title would be all but assured. The plan would have been a success. A group crowded around me.

'We will win 8–0! People will be very confused!' shouted one.

'*Allez, allez, allez, allez*, ultras, ultras!' shouted another.

'Beşiktaş!' shouted a third.

Aren't you supposed to be a Başakşehir fan? I asked the supporter who shouted for Beşiktaş.

He showed me his arm. It was full of black and white Beşiktaş tattoos. Suddenly they were all showing me their tattoos. 'I'm UltrAslan!' shouted another, holding orange prayer beads. He pulled down his shirt to reveal the red UltrAslan symbol, the sign of Galatasaray's ultra group, marked on his chest. The group start chanting, mixing all the teams in together.

'I'm a Fenerbahçe fan but I live here. It's impossible to get to Kadıköy, so why not support Başakşehir?' said Yusuf, a young fan going to the game. He said he was a member of Genç Fenerbahçeliler, GFB, or Young Fenerbahçe supporters, the club's main ultra group.

Was the game against Beşiktaş the biggest game this weekend? I asked.

'Nah, I still support Fener,' he replied. 'I'm going to the derby tomorrow.'

Burak had quite a job on his hands. The 1453 started to get ready to leave for the long drive to Beşiktaş, whilst we went back to the Bosphorus, taking a taxi, three trains and a bus.

'At least we got this game,' a bored policeman said to his colleague as we walked past. 'I'd hate to be at Fener–Gala tomorrow.'

BEŞIKTAŞ, İSTANBUL

As kick-off approached, the Çarşı streamed down past the Dolmabahçe Palace, the home of the last of the Ottoman Sultans, before turning right near the clock tower and the mosque. Some of the İnönü's almost art-deco facade had been kept, incongruous underneath the bright-red splash of the 'Vodafone Park Stadium' sign. 'We don't care about Başakşehir. We don't care about the other teams,' said Emre, a Çarşı member, as he was about to go in. 'They will never have this feeling. Ten years from now they will be nowhere.' Bora, however, would not be joining me. 'I've boycotted the games ever since they introduced the Passolig card,' he explained. It was a story I would hear frequently, of bans and boycotts.

Inside, the 1453 were here in the corner, filling up only half of their space. There was no pyro or smoke bombs. Çarşı's banners were lined up at the bottom of the north stand, barely visible from anywhere else in the stadium. A large coloured banner of Beşiktaş's symbolic eagle with the words 'Always Towards Victory' was hoisted along the east stand. Behind the goal was another that said: 'This Is Beşiktaş: Everybody Stand Up'. Çarşı banners weren't banned, Bora told me before I entered the stadium. Not officially anyway. 'But there is a loophole for the police,' he said. 'If they believe the message on the banner is of a political nature they have the right to not allow it in the stadium.' Earlier this season one member of the Çarşı was stopped before the Fenerbahçe game with a banner that said *Hasta la Victoria, Siempre*', a famous quote of Che Guevara that means 'Until victory, always!' The police confiscated it.

The noise was still deafening as the game began but Başakşehir dominated the early stages and were only kept out by a couple of great saves from Loris Karius, who was rebuilding his career at Beşiktaş after his humiliation in the 2018 Champions League final with Liverpool. Robinho, though, eventually found a way through. The title looked to be all but headed to the suburbs until Beşiktaş equalised when the veteran Canadian midfielder Atiba Hutchinson scored an acrobatic close-range volley before half-time. During the break the Çarşı behind the goal started to stir, slowly at first, before a chant engulfed the whole stadium.

'Give him the mandate! Give him the mandate!'

Whilst the AKP were busy trying to find any pretext to have İstanbul's mayoral election annulled, İstanbul's mayor-elect Ekrem

İmamoğlu had, indeed, shown up at the Beşiktaş game. In an interview on Fox TV during his campaign İmamoğlu had said that he had no interest in funding and supporting a football team – a thinly veiled reference to Erdoğan and Başakşehir – as the city already had three big clubs. 'My job is not to create and support a sports club,' he said. There was no doubt who supported him in the stadium now. The Beşiktaş crowd responded with a chant demanding that his election be officially verified, something that had not yet happened thanks to very public pressure from Erdoğan. He got up out of his seat as the chants got louder and louder until someone at the club realised what was happening. Given that political chants were now banned, the stadium's speaker system cranked, unexpectedly, into life, blasting ear-splitting Turkish rock music in the hope of smothering the pro-İmamoğlu chants.

In the second half Beşiktaş attacked and took the lead with a superb goal from Burak Yilmaz. Başakşehir responded, even sending their goalkeeper up for a corner in the final minutes, but it was to no avail. The closest they got to an equaliser was when a Beşiktaş defender chested the ball down and accidentally nutmegged Karius before the ball dribbled inches wide. The stadium erupted at the full-time whistle. Beşiktaş was back in the title race, Başakşehir had been thwarted and İmamoğlu had been feted. The significance of the match, and the chanting, was lost on no one.

BEYOĞLU, İSTANBUL

SELIM HAD ARRANGED TO MEET me on the edge of Taksim Square. It was night-time, that day's rainfall had only recently finished, and the square was a buzz of activity: hawkers, tourists, lovers and beggars all crisscrossing each others' paths. Behind me stretched Gezi Park, looking scrappy and neglected. Selim arrived by bumping up on to the pavement with his moped, throwing me a helmet and telling me to get on the back. He drove west, deeper in to Beyoğlu, past the Galatasaray Lisesi, the 500-year-old elite school that gave birth to

Galatasaray football club, before turning north into a maze of single-lane streets. We stopped, finally, at a tea shop. In the back room framed posters of great Turkish football teams from the past, in brilliant Technicolor, were hung on the walls: the 1969/70 title-winning Fenerbahçe team, dressed in yellow and black. The claret and blue of Trabzonspor. The red and green of Diyarbakirspor, the now-defunct team from Diyarbakir, Turkey's largest Kurdish city. And, on the left, the gold and red of Galatasaray, Selim's team.

'How can they pay Arda Turan three million euros a season? How can they pay Adebayor's wages?' asked Selim, shaking his head. It was a question that every fan had about Başakşehir, but Selim was more focused on the weekend's other business. Galatasaray was playing Fenerbahçe, across the water, in Kadıköy. It was the biggest game of the season. It was always the biggest game of every season. Beşiktaş's victory against Başakşehir opened the door for Galatasaray to catch up and perhaps win a title that seemed impossible at the turn of the year. The two were due to play at the end of the season too. If they were within striking distance, Selim reasoned, the title would be decided then. 'It will be a symbolic victory definitely,' said Selim. 'We really don't want Başakşehir to be champions.'

Selim had been a member of Galatasaray's ultra group, UltrAslan, since it was founded in 2001. The name is a portmanteau, combining 'Ultras' with *aslan*, the Turkish word for lion. Their founding was a pivotal moment in Turkish fan culture. Before 2001, during the era of 'The Terrace Wars' and the subsequent peace, the terraces were run by the *amigos*. 'It was a different time,' Selim said of the violence back then. 'They used to attack with knives, guns, axes. Imagine, at that time the influence of the 1980 military coup was felt to one's bones.' Selim felt that the violence wasn't an unexplainable, uncontrollable phenomenon. It was by design. 'The government gave way to this violence,' he believed. 'You guys play around here, so you don't interfere with political things. They let fans kill each other. They let this violence grow.'

By 2000 the reputation of Turkish football fans, internationally, was in the gutter. 'The Peace' may well have stopped mass violence in

Turkey, but individual murders still took place every season and then there was the international outrage that followed the murder of two Leeds United fans. On the pitch Galatasaray was building a different legacy. They won the UEFA Cup, becoming the first Turkish club to win a European honour. And European football meant European away days. The fans were heavily influenced by what they saw, especially from Italy's ultras. 'We saw Milan fans, the Fossa dei Leoni. Madrid Ultras Sur. Going to England, seeing their fans. Lazio, Roma,' explained Selim. They wanted to be as unified, with a proper name.

There were two central figures leading UltrAslan: Alpaslan Dikmen and Sebahattin Şirin, who was one of three *amigos* who made 'The Peace' with the Çarşı and Fenerbahçe fans in 1996. Dikmen, a big man with a clean shaved head, took charge of the day-to-day organisation. The group began to introduce pyro and choreography, Selim's specialisation.

UltrAslan is made up of 300 separate groups, sometimes divided by geography or ethnicity or, like Selim's, for students. The chants, adapted from Italy and Argentina, were simple enough for the Turkish terraces. The choreography though, with its complex organisation, was far harder to implement. It was, Selim said, a case of trial and error. 'We failed a lot of times!' he laughed. But there were successes too: a *Godfather* choreography against Bayer Leverkusen; a Fred Flintstone choreography against Fenerbahçe, decrying the fact they hadn't won the Turkish Cup for 30 years. Within a year every Turkish team had its own ultras and were producing their own material, often satirical, sometimes political, but always telling the stories of the issues that were important to them at that time: 'We'd have a brainstorm two weeks before a match and in the end we come up with an idea,' Selim said when I asked about the process of making the *tifo*. 'We never took one lira from the club. It was all funded by us. We had an architect who drew things on the computer. The templates were printed out in large scale in Beşiktaş and then we would buy the cloth, go to the tailor for it to be cut. And then we organised some place huge to paint it.' There was only one time, Selim recalled, when the absolute secrecy of the choreo was broken, when one member sent a picture to a friend, who sent it a friend, and so on. He was never invited back. 'It is like a huge treason,' said Selim.

Unlike the Çarşı, UltrAslan had a strict hierarchy. It trademarked its name and sold merchandise that outsold the official club shirts. It was so successful that, when Galatasaray was on the verge of bankruptcy in 2002, UltrAslan transferred the copyright to the club for three years, raising millions of euros. It saved the club. Also unlike the Çarşı, UltrAslan's politics couldn't be easily pinned down. The club had a national fan base, covering every ethnicity and class. Even Abdullah Öcalan, the jailed leader of the Kurdish PKK terrorist movement, was a Galatasaray fan.[20]

'Fan culture in Turkey is ridiculously heterogeneous so they don't usually have a common social or political identity,' said Cem Dizdar, a journalist who co-hosts *Sports Headlines*, a popular football chat show on TV. 'They don't share anything else apart from the team colours. Instead you have some factions that have the same social beliefs.'

Dikmen, Selim says, managed to connect UltrAslan's young liberal, Westernised factions with its more conservative elements. 'What made him special was he was a bridge from the more educated Western ultras and the more working-class poor people. We had this division. We still do.' Up until then UltrAslan was, Selim believed, largely apolitical. That changed in 2008 when Dikmen died in a car accident. He was 42. Sebahattin Şirin took control, and he had a different outlook. He was a devout Muslim and prayed five times a day. 'Nowadays it is safe to say that UltrAslan are on the right wing. It is a mixture of nationalism and also Islam.' The conservative faction was in power. But the enemies remained the same. Fenerbahçe and Beşiktaş, of course, but also the authorities. 'The police was and has always been the enemy,' said Selim.

It was the anti-police ethos – 1312 – that meant when Gezi Park erupted, Galatasaray fans headed to Taksim Square too. Although it wasn't quite, at least for Selim, the 'İstanbul United' moment that many have spoken about. The people involved were fans – Selim was there, but not in club colours – but the leaders of UltrAslan and Fenerbahçe's GFB didn't officially sanction it, like they did when a

march was arranged in 2016 to protest the attempted coup against
Erdoğan that was – Erdoğan believed – organised by his old ally, now
exiled, Fethullah Gülen. Or when the fans of the big three came
together to protest the introduction of the Passolig card, or during
protests before a constitutional referendum that would transform
Turkey into an executive presidency. Or even when they mourned
together after 48 people, 36 of them police officers, were killed in a
2016 bombing by Kurdish militants outside Beşiktaş's stadium.[21]

'It's a romanticised version, they didn't come together to be honest,' said Selim of the Gezi protests. 'Although I don't like them very
much, it's fair to say that the Besiktas fans gave the biggest contribu-
tion to the Gezi Park protests.' Yet Gezi would fundamentally change
the relationship between the ultras and the authorities. 'The government saw there was a threat in the football stadium,' Selim believed.
'They thought: "We have to do something about this or we will face
some open protests." And, as you might have noticed, our government
is not fond of any criticism.' The 6222 law was properly implemented,
surveillance stepped up and supporters were tracked, nominally to
prevent violence even though, according to Selim 'the violence wasn't
that bad anyway'.

There was another reason for the crackdown: political protest.
'People were shouting in the stadium, "Erdoğan, resign". The police
can catch you very easily. They can lock you up. You can be labelled a
terrorist. It's that easy to have something happen to you.'

There had, at least, been one positive recent development.
Away fans were allowed into the stadiums once again having been
banned for six years. A convoy of buses would be leaving the Türk
Telekom Stadium and cross the Bosphorus to Fenerbahçe's stadium. It would be under a heavy police presence. Everyone would
be searched for pyro, the bridge would be closed and they would be
escorted by the police all the way. At least UltrAslan would be in
the stadium. But not Selim. He had become a victim of football's
new security regime.

'It's a tragic story,' he said, shaking his head as he explained the
absurdity of his experience. A few months earlier he had travelled to

an away game in İzmir, against Göztepe. Galatasaray won the game after Göztepe missed a penalty and several chances, incensing the home crowd. 'So we started making fun of them and they noticed us, so they are making gestures that they will kill us and we're laughing.' After the game, as he was leaving, Selim made a hand gesture, where you poke your thumb between your second and third finger: a milder Turkish version of doing the 'wanker' sign, or giving the finger. Four weeks later Selim received a court order in the post, instructing him to go to his nearest police station. The policeman told him he'd been banned and had to go there to sign a register every kick-off time, and 45 minutes later, to make sure he wasn't sneaking into the stadium. He had no idea for what until the policeman showed him a high-definition picture and a video of him making the thumb sign. His friend also got banned. 'He was caught with a power bank in the stadium. Charging his phone. I've been waiting for this match for one year. Even my mum laughed about it.'

The security crackdown, the increased control, was killing Turkey's terrace culture. Selim decried what was happening to it. It used to be, he said, 'much more chaotic in a positive, natural way. It kind of resembled a jungle with its own rules. But you survived if you followed certain codes.' The choreo still continued and, Selim admitted, had improved from his day, even if he wasn't on board with some of the more nationalistic messaging. Although even seemingly apolitical banners could still get you in trouble. A recent 3D choreo of Rocky with the words 'Stand up; they look big because you are kneeling,' made international headlines. Sylvester Stallone tweeted his admiration of it. The Turkish government was less impressed. In its post-coup zeal to weed out suspected 'Gülenists', allies of the Erdoğan nemesis Fethullah Gülen, the authorities launched an investigation into the choreo, forcing UltrAslan's leader Sebahattin Şirin to make a statement to the police. The wording, they believed, was similar to the words in a poem 'Stand up, Sakarya', which Gülen had read in a recent sermon. The club said it was a 'pathetic attempt' to discredit them. 'We will use all our legal rights against any institution, person or social media account that tries to put the name of Galatasaray alongside that of the leader of the heinous terrorist organisation,' they said in a statement.[22]

For Selim, he would have to leave the country and travel to Greece and watch PAOK to find the fan culture he fell in love with. 'I have never felt safer than with the Gate 4 in Toumba,' he said. 'There is no state control whatsoever. But you feel safe because you are part of that community. I feel safer in that jungle than this one.' So, at 5pm on Sunday afternoon, Selim wouldn't be coming with me to the derby as I'd hoped. He would instead be arriving at his local police station to sign his name.

Do you think I'll be allowed to take a bus to the game with UltrAslan? I asked doubtfully.

Selim made a phone call. 'Be at the stadium, tomorrow. One o'clock.'

SARIYER AND KADIKÖY, İSTANBUL

IN AN UNDERPASS NEXT TO the Türk Telekom Stadium, two lines of coaches stretched over the horizon, as far as the eye could see. At least 2,000 members of UltrAslan were here, singing songs and letting off firecrackers as 1pm approached. The Türk Telecom Stadium seemed to be as far from Galatsaray's roots as Başakşehir was from the Bosphorus; a soulless industrial area next to a motorway. 'There's 2,600 here, in fact,' said Güven, a friend of Selim, correcting me on the numbers. A few of them had made a banner for the occasion: 'No Ban For Selim'. 'He is sick he can't be here,' said Güven. 'It's probably the most important game of the year.'

The chaotic mass of gold and red squeezed past three lines of security, frisked by each to make sure no pyro got through, before the police urged the ultras on to each coach one at a time. Once it was jammed full, they forcibly shut the doors as if overpacking a holiday suitcase. Each coach jolted forward into a convoy on to the motorway in single file, led by police officers holding machine guns. Inside the noise was ear-shattering as the ultras sang and swayed. As soon as we hit the road, the ultras forced the doors open, as they did on every other bus. They hung on to the door and swung out on to the motor-way as police motorcycles sped past, chanting louder and louder until we crossed the the Fatih Sultan Mehmet Bridge, named after Mehmed the Conquer who sacked Constantinople in 1453. Usually the road would be jammed, and the journey would take hours. But not today. The police had blocked every side road. The long, snaking convoy arrived 20 minutes later with smoke bombs and the flares that had been smuggled past the police and detonated outside the doors. One by one the ultras spilled out of the coaches and marched along the cleared highway towards the stadium, stopping only to abuse the groups of Fenerbahçe fans who had gathered on the bridges above.

On the other side of the stadium, in Yoğurtçu Park, tens of thousands of Fenerbahçe fans had gathered around the statue of Alex de Souza, the Brazilian striker who became captain of Fenerbahçe. The fans funded the statue a few months before he returned to Brazil. Thousands upon thousands of flares were being lit, the smoke completely obscuring parts of the crowd, all soundtracked by a Turkish band. If the game was important for Galatasaray's title chances, this was all that was left of Fenerbahçe's season. At one point they had been flirting with relegation – an unthinkable prospect. The GFB, Fenerbahçe's ultras group, was nowhere to be seen. 'Our fan bases don't come from the same class or historical or political background,' Cem Dizdar told me before the game. 'They are fragile, so when the team does bad ... take Fenerbahçe this year. The GFB has disap-peared. They are just a mass of forty thousand people going to the game.'

For the 'mass of 40,000' there was still some pride that could be salvaged today. Galatasaray hadn't won here in two decades. 'It's so important for us,' said one Fenerbahçe fan, his five-year-old son on his shoulders. His son was holding an angry, fizzing flare at arm's length to avoid the fire spitting in his face. 'We'll fight Galatasaray.' But nobody wanted to talk about football. Everyone I approached, even with the most anodyne question about the title race, wanted to talk about politics. A crowd would jostle around me every time I spoke to someone.

'My leader is Mustafa Kemal Atatürk. My team is Fenerbahçe,' answered one man when I asked about Başakşehir.

'No Tayyip Erdoğan! Fuck you, Galatasaray,' was the reply when I asked another what the score would be today.

'I love Ekrem İmamoğlu!' said another when I asked what the atmosphere would be like outside, after the game, if Galatasaray broke their curse. Someone even tried to convert me to Islam when I asked about their latest signing, Nigeria international Victor Moses.

Once inside, the atmosphere in the Ülker Stadium turned dark. A four-stand choreo of blue and yellow had been arranged with a long banner across the middle of the east stand that read: 'Fenerbahçe Are The Kings Of This Realm'. But, after a disastrous season, this was not a happy place. A whirling, poisonous atmosphere followed every Fenerbahçe mistake, made worse when the referee used VAR to reduce Fenerbahçe to ten men. Ekrem İmamoğlu turned up at this game too, but got a more mixed reaction. Some Galatasaray supporters welcomed him, some were against, mirroring how Salim had described the factions within UltrAslan. Some Fenerbahçe ultras started chanting that İmamoğlu was a Gülenist, using a convoluted logic that he had been an enthusiastic backer of the club being punished for a match-fixing scandal in 2011. The case was a huge embarrassment for the club, but any punishment had been bogged down in various court cases. In post-coup Turkey, even a match-fixing scandal had transformed into a nefarious plot to bring down Erdoğan's club by Fethullah Gülen. Just as the crowd was getting confident in holding Galatasaray at bay – chanting, 'Galatasaray, you couldn't beat us if we were dead' – Galatasaray took the lead through Henry Onyekuru. Fenerbahçe's fans started fighting each other in the stands. But, even though they were down to ten men, Fenerbahçe equalised thanks to Elif Elmas, preserving their 20-year run against Galatasaray.

'I've never experienced a derby like this before in my life, to be honest,' Victor Moses told me as he left the ground. The Fenerbahçe fans dispersed quickly after the game, grateful for the unexpected draw.

After the game, I took the ferry from Kadıköy back to Beşiktaş. A few Fenerbahçe and Galatasaray fans were scattered on the seats, dozing on the short journey back, shattered from their exertions. The title was in the balance, as was the election. Turkish fan culture had shown how powerful it could be, politically, inside and outside the stadiums. Gezi Park was one moment, but Erdoğan recognised the potential for trouble from the stands and had forcibly gentrified the game, looking at England as a blueprint. But the squeezing out of the traditional, organised and difficult-to-control ultras wasn't a bug. It was a feature. More was to come too. A new raft of even stricter regulations, connected to the hated 6222 law, were planned to be brought in soon.

Most people outside Turkey saw Gezi as a failure, but not the ultras and activists who were there. 'What people learned there, what they were reminded of, was the solidarity of sharing things,' said Cem Yakışan of the Çarşı. As long as there are two people who understand what it stands for and say, "I am a member of Çarşı," the spirit will live.' Others believed it was Gezi which had brought a more unified civil spirit to İstanbul, one which was able to be harnessed to give İmamoğlu a narrow win in the election. 'If Erdoğan was in his situation I would have chanted his name too,' Cem told me. 'İmamoğlu has been treated unfairly. He won the election. Give the election to the man. What we cannot stand is unfairness and injustice. We don't care who the subject of that injustice is.'

A few weeks later President Erdoğan got his way. Ekrem İmamoğlu's narrow victory in the İstanbul mayoral election, by just 15,000 votes, was annulled.[23] The AKP had petitioned the Supreme Election Council, claiming that there had been 'irregularities' in the vote and, besides, 15,000 votes in a city of 15 million was too small a margin to fairly declare a definitive result.

'It is illegal to win against the AK party,' tweeted Onursal Adıgüzel, the deputy chairman of the CHP, İmamoğlu's opposition party.[24] A new vote would have to be held. But, in the meantime, there was

another unforeseen problem. If İmamoğlu had been barred from fulfilling his mandate, who would run İstanbul until the second vote
could be held a month later? Recep Tayyip Erdoğan knew just the
man for the job: Göksel Gümüşdağ, the president of Başakşehir.[25]

12

United States

LOS ANGELES

AFTER A DOZEN PEOPLE ALL DRESSED IN BLACK HAD PLACED THE different-coloured pieces of paper on to the corresponding seat numbers, everyone stood back and watched to see if their big plan would work.

'OK, OK, and now the national anthem,' shouted Pat Aviles through a megaphone before clearing his throat and singing the last line from 'The Star-Spangled Banner'.

'... and the home, of the, braaaaaave.'

He chopped his arm down to make the signal as he finished the last note, and the black banner slowly jerked upwards. Behind, in the north stand of the Banc of California Stadium, home to Los Angeles FC, two members of the club's *tifo* committee pulled hard on ropes connected to pulleys fastened to the roof. The thin, black, vertical banner, with the words 'We Will', eventually revealed itself as it unfolded on its way, ten metres up, to the top left of the stand. Pat, the club's permanently cheerful supporter liaison officer, was moderately happy with the results.

It was the night before LAFC was due to play the Montreal Impact. LAFC was one of Major League Soccer's newest franchises, although they hadn't taken long to grow accustomed to the league. With the former US and Egypt national team coach Bob Bradley in charge they had reached the play-offs in their first year. This was their sophomore season and they had made mincemeat of their division, scoring goals for fun. The *LA Times* had dubbed them the 'Manchester City of US soccer'. Mexican international Carlos Vela had outshone everyone in the league, even Zlatan Ibrahimović, the star of LAFC's cross-city rivals the LA Galaxy. Their stadium was a small but beautifully crafted piece of architecture in downtown LA. It was a soccer-specific stadium with safe standing in the north stand, home to the 3252, the umbrella independent supporters' organisation that brought together LAFC's nine ultra groups. 'Black Army, District 9 Ultras, Los Lucky's, Cuervos, Expo Originals, The Tigers, The Krew, Armada, Empire Boys,' Pat proudly reeled off when I asked whether he could remember them all.

The name, Pat explained, came from the crowd capacity of the north stand where the nine groups, and their various sub-groups, all stood during home games. They were all represented here after spending weeks organising, painting and then sewing this week's *tifo,* which had been voted for by the 3252's *tifo* committee, a group of L.A. artists and soccer fans who were in charge of what ended up being displayed in the stand. It was the first time they'd ever used a pulley system, and no one was really that sure how it would all turn out.

'What is an ultra? An ultra is someone who has passion, love for this game, who doesn't come to just cheer a little bit, drink a little bit. We're here for 90 plus giving it in the stands, home and away,' said Mauricio Fazio, a leader of the District 9 Ultras and a vice-president of the 3252. Maurico was a big guy with an Amish-style beard who wore a black T-shirt with 'Los Angeles Against ICE' on it, a reference to US Immigration and Customs Enforcement. ICE was the hated force that implemented President Trump's crackdown on illegal immigrants, which had spread wider into LA's Latinx community. 'It's a statement for our people, and football is about the people,' he replied when I asked him about it. 'As ultras it's our duty to voice the opinions of the people because it's the common man's sport.'

The group was named after the location of their stadium, in LA city council's District 9. Their emblem was a skull in a top hat with the Latin phrase *'Noi Soli Sine Metu'*: 'Us Alone Without Fear'. Their rules were laid out on their website. There was zero tolerance for racism, bullying and hate speech. Violence was forbidden (although 'self-defence is anyone's right') and under no circumstances would stealing any opponents' flags or banners be accepted. 'WE ARE NOT A GANG thus we do not condone any sort of gang-like behaviour,' they wrote.

'That's why this feels like home,' said Mauricio. 'Because we all live in different regions here in the city. Different ethnicities, different cultures, different backgrounds of football, but we all come together here come match time.'

LA is a vast and diverse city. Mauricio had Mexican roots and his early soccer memories came from south of the border. 'My parents and my uncles, they come from the *barras bravas* in Mexico, they taught me the supporter culture,' he said. When he was a kid he would go with his father and uncles to the Estadio Azteca, and couldn't work out why they weren't wearing team colours nor why they were picked out for particularly intimate searches by the police. 'It was because they were ultras, and they showed me how to be an ultra from being a kid. I always waited for my own club and it finally happened here. And it took until now, to the ripe old age of fifty-one, to find a home.'

It was common for Mexican-Americans to grow up with soccer, but without an MLS team to pour themselves into. They thought that had changed with the creation of Chivas USA, which focused its attention on the city's Latinx population. But its focus was too narrow and it went out of business after ten years. 'Chivas USA is how I learned to love this league, you know?' said José Salcedo, another leader of the District 9 Ultras. 'Chivas USA gave me the opportunity to help build a culture in the United States.' LA, he said, had always been a soccer city, even before MLS arrived. As a multi-ethnic, heavily Latin-influenced city, soccer had deep, multi-generational roots. As we spoke Pat gave the order and a second banner was raised, to the right of the north stand. This time it unfolded much more smoothly as it was winched up, revealing its message in black and gold, the club's colours: 'Rock You'.

Chivas USA folded on Monday, 27 October 2014. On the following Thursday LAFC was officially born, attracting ex-Chivas fans and others who never felt LA Galaxy represented them.[1] Part of the reason was location. The club was far from downtown. So far, in fact, that LAFC fans dismissively refer to the Galaxy as 'Carson', the city within LA County where the club is based. Still, the new LAFC embraced its diversity. Tomorrow's game was a case in point. It had been dubbed 'Pride Night'. The *tifo*, the pyro, the flags and the pre-game rituals were in honour of Los Angeles' LGBT community. Ten thousand rainbow-coloured captain's armbands (sponsored by Dollar Shave Club) would be given out before the match. One would be worn by club captain Carlos Vela on the pitch. The last home game had been 'Women's Night'. The *tifo* that evening was in honour of America's greatest player, and LAFC co-owner, Mia Hamm. The three *capo* cages at the front of the north stand were led by women and there were other flags dedicated to inspirational women: the Pakistani activist Malala, the US Supreme Court Justice Ruth Bader Ginsburg and Congresswoman Alexandria Ocasio-Cortez. I wondered how such a move would be welcomed in Kyiv, Kraków or Rome.

With the two vertical black banners in place, the main *tifo* on white satin-finished cloth was unfolded on the pitch. The figure at the centre was roughly cut from the canvas and dragged on to an even bigger black mesh. The *tifo* committee each took an edge, punched a small hole in the canvas and secured it in place before it was hauled to the stand and attached to the pulley system. Mauricio, José and the rest of the 3252 held their breath. If the cloth ripped it was game over for tomorrow. Pat picked up his megaphone, gave his cue, and sang the last line of the national anthem. Everyone waited nervously as the *tifo* slowly cranked up for the first time. It unfurled perfectly. Pat and the ultras took a step back to admire their work. 'How fucking cool does that shit look,' Pat said proudly. 'Fake it until you fucking make it!'

There has long been a fundamental tension between the supporter culture in American sports and how football is structured in the rest of world. Whether it was American football, baseball, ice hockey or basketball, US sports made vast amounts of money, largely by being cartels. There was no such thing as promotion or relegation. All that mattered was whether your franchise continued to make money, and didn't prevent the others from making money too. Membership of this club was determined by the other franchises rather than merit. Franchises could frequently be moved between cities when the ownership felt they could get a better deal elsewhere, leaving the people who had supported them – sometimes for decades – bereft. Very few franchises gave any truck to the supporters or their views. To them fans were merely passive consumers of a product. Supporters were essential to the business, as long as they handed over their money and didn't expect to have any say in return, much like buying a Netflix subscription or a cinema ticket.

But the anger and sense of betrayal that followed when a team was moved from one city to another was proof that the fans wanted and expected more. When the Arsenal owner Stan Kroenke successfully agitated to move the St Louis Rams NFL franchise back to Los Angeles in 2016 – a team which had itself moved from LA 20 years before – it provoked a furious reception in a city that had poured its heart and soul, and money, into their team.[2] I'd seen first-hand how the move alienated a whole city, not just against Kroenke, but against the NFL. Court cases were still ongoing in St Louis to try and claw back some of the money that the city and its citizens had poured into Kroenke's pockets in the form of stadium tax breaks and season passes to unsuccessfully keep the Rams in the city. Kroenke's new LA

Rams now played one hundred metres from here, across Exposition Park, at the LA Memorial Coliseum, until their new multibillion-dollar stadium – which was shaping up to be the most expensive sports stadium ever built – was finished.

When America's MLS was founded in 1996, in the afterglow of the country's hugely successfully 1994 World Cup, it was set up along the lines of other US sports, with a closed league of franchises that nonetheless had aggressively expanded from 10 teams in its inaugural season to 24 in 2019. Another four will be added in the next two years, including the David Beckham-owned Inter Miami. It has been wildly successful. As soccer has grown in popularity, crowds have boomed, from total attendances of 2.8 million in 1996 to almost 8.5 million in 2018.[3] But football around the world had a different relationship between the clubs' ownership and their supporters. Clubs were viewed as the property of the community, and owners merely temporary custodians. That relationship had manifested itself in a wide range of different outcomes. The system of membership owners in Spain with its *socios,* the 50+1 model in Germany and Sweden that made big-money takeovers impossible and made clubs hugely reliant on the wishes of their supporters. The ultras in Italy, *barras bravas* and *torcida* in South America, all had power and influence over their clubs, for good and ill. The question was, how do you build a supporter culture in a US soccer franchise from scratch, mixing commerce and passion whilst avoiding being inauthentic, the single worst crime for most supporters around the world?

American ultra culture was seen as an oxymoron over the Atlantic, fuelled by cringe-worthy viral videos like the 2015 clash between supporters of New York Red Bull and New York City FC when mockney-inflected chants of 'Who are ya?!' could be heard ringing out.[4] Or the time when Derek 'Diablo' Alvarez of the Miami Casuals (a hooligan group nominally attached to Miami FC, a team bumping around in the lower leagues of American soccer) recorded a video calling out Millwall's hooligans. Alvarez – a self-declared ex-communist anti-fa skinhead – was derided for the video but he has persisted. He produced another video in 2018, this time calling out Liverpool fans and declaring himself as 'the most talked-about football hooligan and casual in the world!' He announced plans to try and introduce, as he called it, 'forest fighting' – the *okolofutbola* that Serhii in Ukraine and Hugo in Sweden were involved in – to America. 'Everyone I've shown videos of forest fighting has said: "This is awesome. Is anybody making money off this? You could be the [UFC President] Dana White of this thing" … To me, it's the evolution of hooliganism. I want to turn it into a sport. I could see firms doing it wearing their teams' colours. Is society going to like putting a load of hooligans on TV? Well, what's the difference between this and MMA?'[5] Was it possible to start something that matched European and South American terrace culture without, well, appearing as plastic as Alvarez?

LAFC was financially backed by a host of celebrities. Mia Hamm, Will Ferrell and Magic Johnson were part of the 31-person ownership group that included billionaire titans of the tech industry. And Vincent Tan.[6] From the start, according to Pat Aviles, the ownership tried to bridge the gap between the front office and the supporters. Pat was hired, in his words, to 'go to the bars where people got up at four o'clock in the morning' to watch European soccer. He would do the same at Griffith Park, a famous pick-up soccer spot in LA, and try to persuade the players he found to join the new project. Like almost everyone I'd spoken to, he had generations of soccer heritage. His Chilean grandfather was a crazy Colo-Colo fan. Pat was born in LA, and always loved soccer, especially the international game. When he was a child he tried to get behind the Galaxy but when he got older something about them left him cold. Instead he discovered a love for club football through a VHS of Manchester United's treble-winning season when he was ten years old.

Like the EPL barflies he converted, he hadn't found a true home until LAFC came knocking. The first problem to solve was how to bring together such a diverse group of fans. So, when the supporter groups began to form, the club took the *capos* to Germany to learn from who they saw as the best example to follow when it came to supporter engagement: Borussia Dortmund, The Unity and its vast *Südtribüne*, the Yellow Wall. When they got there they didn't get the

reception they had expected. For one, they were told by Dortmund's
management they couldn't visit the Yellow Wall on match day because
their safety could not be guaranteed. 'Somehow The Unity found out
that this was happening ahead of time, and they were upset at their
front office,' Pat recalled. 'They said: "What are you doing messing
around with people from LA, this is Dortmund, care about Dortmund.
What you doing wasting your time?"'

Still, they learned enough from the trip to base the 3252 on The
Unity. For Pat, LAFC was the Dortmund to LA Galaxy's Bayern
Munich; one was a plucky underdog whose strength came in unity
versus the elite royalty, the big-money champions. 'In America, we
always say, we don't want to be like the Yankees,' said Pat. 'We want
to be like the Chicago Cubs. Their fans go a hundred years without
winning the World Series. But they still show up every single game.'
The difficulty was how to bring the essence of the ultras, and the
independence of spirit encapsulated in them, to LAFC in a way that
Dortmund had succeeded in doing. Although even the German ultra
scene was seen as a little too organised and progressive for some
European purists. For them, any accommodation with the owners,
with the system, was betrayal. The US system, even somewhere as
outward-looking as LAFC, was Disneyland compared to even
Germany. Only the English Premier League, which had a similar
knack for commercialism whilst managing to treat the fans even
worse than most American franchises, came close in comparison.

The fact that MLS was playing catch-up – first against other US
sports then against other leagues in world soccer – meant that a space
for a more independent supporters movement (with a particularly progressive outlook) had been carved out from the start. St Pauli,
Hamburg's famously left-wing club, had been hugely influential. Yet
the league's rules had become stricter about what was and wasn't
acceptable as the product and the money grew. Several US ultra
groups had fallen out with their management for not toeing the line
and had been ostracised, Toronto FC's Inebriatti, New York Red Bulls'
Garden State Ultras and Chicago Fire's Sector Latino amongst them.[7]
The league had even taken the decision to ban all anti-fa flags and

symbols in a bid to remain apolitical. By following England, with its heavy restrictions on the nature of messages and banners at matches, and Italy, with its ban on pyro, MLS had been successful in recreating a European stadium atmosphere, just not in the way it perhaps intended to. The outcry by MLS ultras saw the ban reversed, for the 2019 season at least.[8]

LAFC's management had at least agreed to some suggestions that the 3252 made, something anathema to the English Premier League. Safe standing was only brought in after the 3252 demanded it when consulted by the stadium's architects. A supporters' bar, at the top of the north stand, with discounted beer, was also added at the supporters' insistence. But the front office kept a tight leash on the aspects of ultra culture that were held as sacrosanct. All *tifo* had to be club approved, by Pat. There was a specific 'sticker wall' at the top of the north stand to try and keep them all in the same place: stickers of Andy Capp in black and white, holding a beer, with the words 'Los Angeles Faithful' around him; others that read 'Don't Be A Dick', 'Love Beer, Hate Racism', the ICF's British Rail sign and the word 'Beermug', 'ACAB 2016' and '*Chinga Tu Madre* Trump' ('Fuck Your Mother, Trump'). There had also been a zero-tolerance approach to chanting, especially the use of *puto*, roughly translating in Spanish as 'faggot', a commonly used and controversial curse in Mexican football for decades that had seeped into the US game too.

What about the flares? I asked Pat. He explained that only controlled pyro, done by pyrotechnic companies, was allowed.

Usually they would just have black smoke but for Pride Night different colours would be used to try and replicate a rainbow if LAFC scored. Which, given their record so far this season, was highly likely. But the most unusual element of the 3252 was the role of women. Everywhere I had been around the world, women had mostly been pushed to the periphery of terrace culture, but not in US soccer and especially not at LAFC. 'Women are leading the charge in the *capo* stands, and that's not just that night [women's night],' Pat explained.

*

The next day hundreds had turned up for LAFC's pre-match tailgate party in Christmas Tree Lane Park. All nine of the 3252 groups were represented, each with their own merch stalls and sound systems creating a mix of heavy metal, West Coast hip-hop and Latin pop music. Every stall had a rainbow flag as the ultras chugged beer and Micheladas, a kind of Mexican Bloody Mary that uses cold beer instead of vodka. 'It actually involves a lot of work,' said Celi about her role as an LAFC *capo* as she handed me a Michelada. She was a member of the District 9 Ultras and had worn rainbow-coloured eye shadow for the occasion.' You actually have to be up in the *capo* stand directing the chants, you have to make sure everybody in your section is loud.'

Celi never thought she would ever be the kind of person that would lead the chants for a few thousand people at a soccer game. She was from downtown LA and loved soccer, but had never found a club team she felt she could root for. When she came to the first season at LAFC, just a few blocks down the road from her home, she knew she had found what she was looking for. There were a few groups back then but she felt at home with the District 9 Ultras, which Celi said instantly 'felt like a family'. One day, she accidentally found herself in the cage. 'I was lucky,' she said. 'Last season at women's night I got the opportunity to be up in the *capo* stand. And I guess from there, people in my group saw that I had the potential.' She had been up there ever since. There were no nerves, even though, as she described, 'you have all eyes on you'. She already knew the chants and the routine. She had already learned all the songs, which had been adapted from chants heard from Europe or, more frequently, South America. There were former *barras bravas* from River Plate and Boca Juniors who had made LA their home and were now part of the 3252. A bank of drummers, men and women, were installed, a mix of Argentinian, Brazilian and Mexican beats. They would practise in the week before the game at their various meet-ups, adopting what worked, and discarding what didn't.

'The love and the passion that you have for the sport and the love and the passion that you have for the team, once you're up there, it's something totally unbelievable,' she said of the adrenaline she felt. 'It's really not something that you can explain. You just feel it.'

It was hard work, but she didn't feel tired until she had finished. She was there two hours before a game, and an hour after. There were now hundreds of women like Celi who had thrown themselves into the culture and had proved they were every bit as capable of leading a chant, or designing a *tifo* or organising the groups' merch as anyone else. Soon enough, as the sun drained away, Christmas Tree Lane Park emptied as the 3252 headed for the north stand. Celi left too, to take her place at the front.

The north stand was rocking, a broiling sea of black and gold, as kick-off approached. A large banner at the top of the stand, written in Spanish, declared that the 3252 were from the 'Barrio Angelino'. A bank of drums in the centre formed the heartbeat of the stand as the *capos* in the three cages conducted the chants. Celi was there, to the left, sweeping her arms back and forth as the crowd turned to 'do the Poznań, jumping up and down in the style of the Polish team who gave the phenomenon its name. When they were all facing the right way they chanted, helped by the lyrics flashing up on the big screen opposite.

> *Dale, dale, dale, Black and Gold!*
> *Jump for LA Football Club, ole! ole!*

Around us scarves were held up with a mix of messages in Spanish and English.

> *'El Hinchada Popular'*
> *'Casuals'*
> *'Shoulder to Shoulder'*

'We are at the front line of football fan culture, right on the edge,' said Sal, a *capo* from Los Lucky's who, a few moments earlier, was up in the cage with a megaphone. And, in a way, he was right. The globalisation of fan culture had found its natural home in Los Angeles, a place Sal called 'a city of the future'. It had the aesthetics of the ultras and a desire to be an anarchic outsider against the system, even if it was still a hyper-corporate environment where every element of the experience was tightly controlled. It had some of the organisational stricture of the *barras bravas*, who were heavily involved in the club's affairs and who, in turn, courted and co-opted the *barracapos* for their own ends. Except it wasn't for political or criminal power; it was to keep the business thriving whilst giving just enough atmosphere to keep the fans engaged, and enough material for TV. It used the language of the hooligans, of the casuals, but it was inclusive, non-violent and progressive. Maybe this was the future of a subculture that, around the world, was being slowly controlled and constricted. Maybe the word 'ultra' would exist just as that; a name, a label.

Los Lucky's was one of the nine groups that made up the 3252. Its name came from the Lucky Baldwins pub in Pasadena where like-minded souls would find themselves at 4am to watch English football. When LAFC arrived they formed their own group, enjoying much more freedom than supporters in the country whose football they idolised. 'The EPL has pretty much banned fan culture,' Sal said. He'd been a little disappointed by what he found when he visited London and watched a Chelsea game a few years ago. The efforts to wipe hooliganism from the game had made English football safer. But there wasn't anything like this in England, where you could stand, drink a beer as you watched a game and had some kind of two-way dialogue with your club. A few ultra-type groups had been set up, most notably at Crystal Palace and Celtic in Scotland, but they were few and far between. When Manchester City banned flags being hung from the second tier of the Etihad Stadium, after the introduction of a wraparound digital screen, the club had a bright idea. They decided to have electronic flags instead, something almost as inauthentic as Derek Alvarez's hooligan call-out videos. Compared to the EPL today, LAFC was miles ahead when it came to the supporter experience.

Los Lucky's was a relatively new name. It had to be changed as they were originally called Lucky Boys, but the influx of women into the group made that name a little outdated. The person who had driven that change was a woman named Breezy. 'People will laugh at her on the Instagram page,' said Sal, 'but she grew up in the projects, hearing gunshots every night.'

I found Breezy at the front of the stand. She couldn't have been much more than five foot tall, and slightly built. Like Celi, she'd never thought she'd find her way into a *capo* cage, but once up there – at a rare game in LA where in rained – she never wanted to leave. She was soaked wet and covered in beer. She'd lost count of the number of goals LAFC scored that day. But she was hooked. 'Being up there as a *capo*, representing the women out there, knowing football isn't just for men, it's for women too. We can love football. We can love drinking beer, too. That's what we like to say about the women here.'

Like Pat, Breezy had been a Manchester United fan since she was a kid but it was no substitute for the real thing. 'When you grow up, you're like, what am I? What am I supposed to do in my life? What am I supposed to be?' she said. 'I know I've always wanted to be a voice for the women and a voice for this football culture.' She described her passion almost like she had no control over it. As if it was an infection. Like typhus. 'I didn't know this was in me. But everyone else saw it in me.' She was a totally different person in the cage, she warned me.

As the players came out, so did the flags, one for each of the 3252's nine groups, alongside nine rainbow flags. The national anthem cranked up and the stadium sang a full-throttle version. Pat was at the front waiting for the cue.

'... and the home of the brave.'

He pumped his arm down and the pulleys cranked into life. The two black banners smoothly glided up to the top of the stand. 'We Will' on the left. 'Rock You' on the right. In the middle a huge *tifo* of Freddie Mercury doing a star jump in tight white trousers and yellow jacket unfolded as the rest of the 3252 held up coloured cards to form a rainbow mosaic. The crowd (including Will Ferrell and Matthew McConaughey, who would later come down on to the field to meet the 3252) stamped their feet and sang 'We Will Rock You'. It had, after all, gone to plan.

LAFC destroyed Montreal Impact, winning 4–2. Breezy took to the cage and did indeed seem like a different person. She had climbed up on to the second rail, her back to the game, urging the 3252 to sing louder. She seemed 12 feet tall. When the fourth goal went in, scored by Tristan Blackmon in front of the north stand, the league-approved pyro kicked in, belching a thick, multicoloured fog that consumed Breezy and her cage. It was the fire, but without the fury.

13

Indonesia

SOMEWHERE ON THE AH 152 HIGHWAY OUTSIDE BANDUNG, INDONESIA

WHEN YOU BELIEVE YOU ARE ABOUT TO DIE – TRULY BELIEVE THAT THE end is upon you – your body changes. After the adrenaline of survival, and your options close, it becomes warm and soft, as if it is preparing to absorb impact. There is a light-headedness, like anaesthetic. You can no longer feel the beat of your heart which, moments early, was thumping so hard you suspected you might cough it up. It's now fluttering above you at an exponential frequency.

I had felt this fear only a few times before. Once in Lebanon, another time in Egypt. This time, though, I wasn't in a civil war. At least not in the traditional sense. I was standing on the side of an Indonesian highway with a hundred fans of Persija, the biggest club from Indonesia's teeming capital, Jakarta. We were on our way to the south-eastern coast of its main island Java to watch Persija play in a preseason tournament. This might sound unimportant to most fans. It wasn't a derby or a championship-defining league game or even a cup final. But that didn't seem to matter in Indonesian football. Persija's supporters group, Jakmania, and its network of ultras, were taking 12,000 people to the game against PSS Sleman in the 2019 President's Cup. *12,000.* Our coach was just one of dozens moving in convoy, at night, to avoid being attacked by the ultras of Persija's biggest rival, Persib Bandung, from the city of Bandung 150km southeast of the capital.

I'd been told that Indonesia had one of the most extreme fan cultures in the world, an ecosystem of ultra groups that take their names from Italian *curve* and English terraces. As European, and especially Italian, fan culture spread around the world it was also adopted in Asia. Japan had a thriving ultras scene, as did Malaysia. Like the huge fan bases that followed big European teams, it had often been derided as plastic, a cheap copy of European culture with none of the roots or integrity. Indonesia didn't seem to fit that description. It had one of the most violent fan scenes in the world. Since the 1990s, 74 people had been killed there in football-related violence.[1] And the deadliest rivalry of all was between Persija and Persib Bandung.

'Wait here, DO NOT MOVE FROM HERE!' Bimo shouted at me. Bimo was the leader of the Rain City Bois, a Persija ultras subgroup from Bogor, where he was from. Bogor was a short train ride south of Jakarta, a colonial city where the Dutch kept their summer retreats during their near three centuries of empire. We had boarded our coach and sung songs, often adapted from English terrace chants. And then, inexplicably, our coach stopped here, just outside Bandung. An unfathomable bureaucratic mix-up meant we all had to get off, at the side of a busy six-lane highway with traffic whizzing past at 100kmph, and wait for a new bus to come. The driver had breezily reassured Bimo that a replacement would arrive soon before he sped off and left us in the dark. Thirty minutes later there was still no sign of our replacement bus.

Bimo was getting agitated, chain-smoking and pacing past me. 'This is dangerous,' he said. 'If Persib find we are here, they will come for us.' And they did.

Bimo noticed them first, clustered on a nearby bridge crossing the highway, waving what looked like clubs as they screamed down at us. The mass disappeared off the bridge and cascaded down the embankment and through the trees, until they too were gathered at the edge of the highway. A group of about 20 Persija ultras ran to confront them. 'Stay here,' Bimo urged me again. He grabbed a friend and instructed him not to leave my side at all costs. He ran into the distance too.

I had been warned this might happen. The night before, as we watched Liverpool play Bayern Munich in the Champions League at 3am, I was told that it was likely our coach would be attacked by rival firms as we passed Bandung. It had become a regular hazard for all away trips. I had also been warned that if we ever got into trouble that I should not, under any circumstances, fall over. 'If you fall, you're dead,' Fadhil, one of the Rain City Bois, told me. 'They don't stop until you are dead.' There is a phrase you often see on the back of football shirts in Indonesia, especially Jakarta: '*Sampai mati*', 'until death'. The last death was six months before. A 23-year-old Persija fan, Haringga Sirla, was killed by Persib fans at a game in Bandung.[2] Away fans are banned when the two play now, but Sirla had gone incognito. When Persib's ultra group, the Vikings, grabbed him they demanded to see his ID. When they saw he was from Jakarta the mob beat him to death. 'He was stabbed, his head was fractured, his neck broken, his nose broken. How can I not think about that every single day?' his grieving mother told Australia's ABC news.[3] A horrific video of the incident was shared on GruppaOF's Instagram account, where violent fight videos were commonly posted. But this video was too much, even for their audience. Almost every comment demanded they delete it. If you wanted to survive Indonesia's terrace culture you had to keep moving.

A few seconds later Bimo and the rest of the Persija ultras were running back. The Persib fans weren't holding clubs but machetes.

Machetes.

We all ran together, women and men, away from the mob of machete-wielding maniacs. And then we stopped. Another group cascaded down the embankment in front of us. We were trapped, front and back.

Was all this worth it? I asked myself.

As my body softened and my heart raced, I thought about my family, my young daughter, being told the news that her father had been tragically killed. Not in an accident or peacefully in bed, after an illness. But hacked to death on the side of an Indonesian motorway by a mob of marauding ultras.

It didn't feel like it was worth it.

We looked left and right as the two mobs, only just visible in the darkness thanks to the headlights of passing cars, closed in.

What do we do? I finally asked Bimo.

He thought for a second.

Without looking left or right, Bimo ran across the highway. Everyone followed.

JAKARTA

BIMO HAD AGREED TO MEET me at a coffee shop in central Jakarta after he had finished work at the warehouse. Before he sat down he made a quick scan of the clientele just to make sure. You could, he told me, never be too sure who you might bump into. Bimo lived for Persija and its ultra culture. He was young, in his early twenties. He had taught himself English by watching football and videos on YouTube. *Green Street Hooligans* had been a major influence. He spoke with a slight English inflection with the odd word thrown in from English casual culture: other supporters were 'lads', leaders were 'top boys'. The fashion was 'clobber'. So enamoured was Bimo of English casual culture that he had started up his own micro-fashion label, FC Tribun Kultur, fashioning retro bags and accessories from old football shirts, stylish copies of casual staples, like bucket hats and

Fred Perry-esque polo shirts as well as second-hand tops and Adidas trainers. Even though he was from Bogor, he had been a Persija fan since his father took him to watch his first game of football – or *sepak bola* in Indonesian – at the vast Gelora Bung Karno Stadium, where they now play their home games. He started going on his own when he was 11 years old. As he got older and more involved in the scene he joined one of the dozens of ultra sub-groups that now existed, each with their own flag to fly at the Gelor Bung Karno, or during away days.

We'd been messaging for weeks and agreed to meet for two reasons: so that I could pay the equivalent of £20 for the return bus fair to travel with the Persija fans on their away day against PSS Sleman, and also to check me out. Persija's ultras, like virtually every ultras group in the world, were deeply distrustful of outsiders and journalists, blaming them as much as the police for spreading a negative reputation of them around the world. They were hard to meet, 'just like the Grobari and Delije' in Serbia, he told me. 'If they find out you're a journalist, everything is cancelled.' He was trying to arrange a meeting with the leader of one of Persija's most notorious firms who were holding a screening in the city tomorrow afternoon. Persija was playing in the AFC Cup (Asia's equivalent of the Europa League). I scrubbed all my social media accounts of the word 'journalist' just in case, and hoped for the best.

The club's fan culture was vast and complex. In 1997 the main supporters group was formed. Jakmania brought together the disparate groups and firms into a recognisable whole. They wore orange shirts and introduced organised chanting and choreo displays. Below that were dozens of sub-groups taking their names from Italian and English terrace culture. There was the Curva Nord Persija, which sat in the north stand of the stadium and included groups like the Orange Street Boys (who used a picture of Alex from *A Clockwork Orange* on its banner), Sector 5 Ultras and the Tiger Bois. In the Curva Sud Persija there was the Sudbois and Garis Keras – which literally translates as 'the hardliners' – who were known for being at the front when fights broke out with their opposite numbers, the Vikings of Persib

Bandung. Jakmania Bogor sat in the south tribune as well, where Bimo's Rain City Bois were a sub-group. Bogor was known for its excessive rainfall, hence the name.

'You have to meet Bung Ferry,' Bimo says. Bung Ferry was a legendary figure in Jakarta. He set up Jakmania and was treated almost like a rock star by younger ultras. But he was respected too. Bimo recalled how, when a riot broke out during a home game, Jakarta's governor was unable to stop the fighting. So they called on Bung Ferry, and the fighting stopped. 'He's like Arkan, of Delije,' he had told me. 'But he has no army or political concern.'

After half an hour Bimo seemed reassured. He contacted Curva Nord Persija and let them know. Later that evening he texted me with good news. Curva Nord Persija's *capotifosi* had agreed to meet me. 'But change your profile picture,' Bimo wrote. 'You look like a journalist.'

The next day the *capotifosi* of Persija's Curva Nord sent me a location pin to where I needed to go, a bar just south of central Jakarta, to watch his team's next match. There was no chance of making this away trip. Persija was playing Shan United from Myanmar in the AFC Cup, a trip of over 4,000km. So the ultras met at an industrial hipster pub. Their black flag was flying over the door: an orange and green tiger circled with the words 'Curva Nord Persija'. Inside, Rio greeted me, cooly at first. He had given the all-clear for me to be there but was still a little wary. There were around 50 in the room, including Abdul, the previous *capotifosi* who had, nonetheless, stuck around with the group. 'I handed over the leadership of the Curva Nord to Rio in 2017,' he said. He needed an operation on his kidney and couldn't really carry on with the same intensity. Abdul still couldn't stay away. He was wearing a grey Curva Nord sweatshirt and orange Persija baseball cap. 'I became a member of Jakmania in 2001 because I supported Persija when I was a kid.' He was in his thirties now, and had started to go to the stadium alone, without his father, in 1998. In 2004, he was part of a small group that formed Curva Nord, looking for a new way to support their team. The Curva Nord had gained some international fame for its choreo on social media. Before one

2018 AFC Cup match, they raised a 3D banner of an anthropomor-
phised tiger, flexing his bulging biceps. The rest of the north curve
fanned pieces of red, yellow and orange card, which gave the illusion
of flames raging around it. The Curva Nord, Abdul said, had very
strict rules to follow. They posted them on their Twitter, Facebook
and Instagram accounts: no individual ultra group banners until after
the show, do not tear the paper card, listen to all the instructions from
the crew, and under no circumstances take a selfie.

The game didn't start well for Persija. They quickly went 1–0
down. It was mid-afternoon, midweek, but the bar was still full. 'Have
you tried Intisari?' Rio asked me. I hadn't heard of it before. It was, I
was told, what fuelled the Indonesian fan scene, at least for Persija. I
gave Rio some rupiah and he came back with three big bottles of it.
Intisari was a thick, black wine, somewhere between Jägermeister and
Buckfast. Soon we were knocking back large glasses of it. Any tension
evaporated. 'To be a leader you have to be a charismatic figure,' said
Ryo, who now had his arm around my neck. 'That's why we believed
in him,' he said, pointing to Abdul. Soon enough everyone was on
their feet. Persija scored twice in ten minutes, and then added a third.
Everyone was chanting and swigging from the bottles of Intisari. Rio
was now topless, arms outstretched, belting out a version of 'Allez,
Allez, Allez', occasionally beating his chest.

Abdul didn't drink, but he couldn't stay away from the group he
had helped to found. When I asked about the violence, he laughed.
'No, when Persija play Persib Bandung there is no away support so we
never fight. The *capos* never fight face to face.' In fact, no one really
had a straight answer as to why Persija and Persib Bandung hated
each other so much. It seemed arbitrary and spontaneous. There were
none of the organised meet-ups of the Eastern European ultra scene.
One ultra told me very confidently that it was due to a perceived slight
when their bus was attacked in Bandung without warning 18 years
ago. Another said that a bureaucratic mix-up meant three coaches of
Persija fans once turned up for a game when they were expecting one,
which angered Bandung's Vikings for some reason. Another suggested
an ethnic element. Jakarta is a mix of people representing Indonesia's

vast geography and diversity. Bandung is the capital of West Java, home to the Sundanese, the biggest ethnic group in the province. Jakarta is effectively an island on the edge of their territory. Whatever the reason, whatever the slight, it had led to escalating tit-for-tat violence. For Abdul it was simpler than all that. 'I was born in Jakarta and I should support Jakarta's football team. In Bandung, Bandung fans support their local team. It's geography. Only geography,' he said.

I could feel the Intisari changing my perception. Rio was still on the chair at the final whistle, singing not to Persija, but an ode to Intisari, in English. We all joined in. I remembered a story I'd read, years ago, about how Buckfast, a sickly, caffeine-enriched fortified wine similar to this, had fuelled a violent crime wave in Scotland.[4] Buckfast was made at Buckfast Abbey in the south-west of England by well-meaning monks who sold their brew to pay for the abbey's upkeep. The problem was that 10 per cent of their total sales was in Coatbridge, a town of just 40,000 people in Scotland. Strathclyde Police mentioned Buckfast in 6,500 crime reports in two years between 2010 and 2012. Maybe Intisari was the reason for the intense violence at the Persija–Persib derby. It was as good an explanation as any other.

'We learned from other groups, we have connections in Germany and Italy,' Rio told me when he sat down and put his shirt on. An Eintracht Frankfurt ultra came and stayed for four days, four years ago, and gave some advice on how to build the scene. Some would soon be coming from Marseille's Commandos Ultras 84, France's longest serving group. Online the YouTube videos of Dynamo Dresden impressed Rio the most, but it was difficult making connections and friendships with European groups. 'The problem is there's so much racism like in England,' he said. I'd almost forgotten amongst the shower of Intisari that Indonesia was an overwhelmingly Islamic country, the most populous on earth.

Just before the rain stopped I got a message from Jakmania. Bung Ferry was ready to receive me. Rio knew the way and threw me a helmet and I jumped on the back of his motorbike before slaloming north through Jakarta's clogged streets, the light from skyscrapers smearing past on either side.

Jakmania's office was in a terrace of shops and fast-food stalls, wedged between the main highway heading south out of central Jakarta and the small but tidy Soemantri Brodjonegoro Stadium. A university campus was adjacent and the courtyard in front full of life. A monsoon had just passed through and a regiment of young women were practising Muay Thai outside during the gap in the rain. Jakmania's office was at the very end, lights on, with a sign above the door: 'The Jakmania Persija Fans Club'. The J had been replaced by the drawing of a left hand, forefinger and thumb stretched out, the symbol that every Jakmania member gave to show their allegiance. Underneath was the date of the group's founding: 19 December 1997.

Inside, Bung Ferry – middle-aged, grey at the temples and wearing 1950s-style glasses – was sitting cross-legged on the floor, a TV behind him flickering with an old Indonesian football match in black-and-white. A dozen or so Jakmania district leaders sat in rapt silence listening to his talk. There was a lot to organise. More than 10,000 Jakmania would be headed to the other side of Java in a few days' time for the match against PSS Sleman. Tickets and bus seats had to be allocated throughout the 70 different districts that Jakmania operated in the capital. And there was, of course, the perennial issue of safety; how to get everyone there and back in one piece. The opposition wasn't the problem. Jakmania had a good relationship with PSS Sleman's group Brigata Curva Sud, even if there was a good chance they wouldn't be at the game.

The BCS had announced it was boycotting the game because of the club's poor management. They had released a manifesto with eight demands that had to be met before they would consider returning, ranging from 'build a training ground' to 'stop releasing mixed messages'.

The danger came from the highway. The most violent part of Indonesian football these days was the coach journey to away games. Away fans were only barred when Persija played Persib Bandung, but simply passing Bandung, or an area known to have a large Persib fan base, was dangerous. And Persib Bandung were not in the best of moods presently. A few days before their Montenegrin coach Miljan

Radović had been attacked in the dugout during a game after Persib had gone 3–1 down against Persebaya Surabaya. Bimo had sent me the video. He had to be escorted off the pitch by three soldiers but was attacked again before reaching the tunnel.[5] He was gone before the start of the season.

Although Jakmania was founded officially in 1997, its genesis was the 1986 World Cup finals in Mexico. 'There were no supporters like now. They only just watched the game and that's it. There was no specific culture in the 1970s and 80s,' said Bung Ferry after we greeted one another and sat down outside. Next to him were two of Jakmania's lawyers, who usually dealt with members when they were arrested. But today they worked as translators. Until that World Cup people would go to football matches, watch and leave. But the colour and the noise of Mexico 86 made Bung Ferry realise that there was no reason the same thing couldn't happen in Indonesia. 'In the 1980s, I come to the stadium and Persija has no support. I wanted to make a supporters group for Persija to attract people. And I made some chants and songs.'

Bung Ferry started singing, the first of many songs he would sing to me over the next 90 minutes. This one was to the tune of Boney M's 'Rivers of Babylon':

> *Come on Tiger,*
> *Never surrender,*
> *Persija*
> *Persija come on*

His greatest hit, though, was a hymn that he wrote for Jakmania, which I'd already heard being sung a dozen times.

> *We are one soul*
> *We have one aim*
> *We have one love*
>
> *Persija*

For our victory
For our glory
For our unity
Persija

This was new to Jakarta and it took a few weeks for the singing to catch on. To help, Bung Ferry would handwrite the lyrics to songs, photocopy several hundred leaflets and hand them out at the entrance. He felt that the songs were the way to create a unified identity amongst the fans. 'I wanted to establish with Jakartans our own culture, our own songs, not to identify with anybody else like ultras in Italy or hooligans in England.'

That was a difficult job, given Indonesia's size. The country was made up of 17,000 islands. More than 1,300 local languages were spoken by 800 different ethnic groups. A huge movement of people from the countryside to the city had seen Jakarta's population more than double since 1970. It also created an even mix of ethnic groups: Javanese, Betawi (from Jakarta) and Sundanese, as well as large ethnic Chinese and Malay populations. It was because of this mix that Bung Ferry believed that Jakarta needed something like Persija, and Jakmania, to find a common identity. Most people still clung to their identities, and their football teams, from their 'home' region. Bung Ferry wanted to make Jakarta, and by extension, Persija home, a kind of city-state nationalism not dissimilar to Italy's archipelago of regional identities. But there was little space for such free expression. From the 1960s Indonesia was ruled by President Suharto, a corrupt, anti-communist autocrat who seized power with the help of the military in 1966 as part of his 'New Order' movement. With the tacit consent of his allies in the West, turning a blind eye to abuses as long as Indonesia's leftists were kept in check, he crushed all internal dissent and oversaw a foreign policy that led to as many as a quarter of million deaths when his army invaded East Timor.[6]

Suharto was brought down by the 1997 Asian financial crisis, which devalued the currency by 80 per cent and led to mass inter-ethnic rioting. But Indonesia emerged a much freer place, fuelled

largely by the student-led *Reformasi* movement. 'Censorship and ideological conformism had been the dominant mood of the 30-year New
Order era,' wrote Dr Andy Fuller, one of the few academics who had
studied Indonesian football culture. 'Its decline saw an often-euphoric
embracing of youth subcultures, often mashed together in curious
ways.'[7]

Football subculture was one that flourished, mishmashing the
exploding punk rock scene with Italian ultra culture – newly arrived
on Indonesian TV in the 1990s – and English hooligan films like *The
Firm*, *The Football Factory* and later *Green Street Hooligans*. The
Tawuran, (semi-organised street battles) had long existed in Indonesia.
The game had arrived with the Dutch and was by far the most popular sport in the country. It gave the game's supporters a look, a sound
and a hierarchy. And Jakmania gave an identity to a disparate group of
the young and the poor. The military police took little notice in the
beginning, but within two years Jakmania had 15,000 members –
then the police started to take note.

Bung Ferry began collecting money and arranging trips, although
there probably wasn't anywhere in the world as difficult to traverse for
an away day as Indonesia. In one memorable game, Bung Ferry and
500 members of the Jakmania took a two-day ferry to Makassar. They
received a hostile reaction and slept under their banners for two days,
lost the game, and then took the two-day ferry back.

The early days of Jakmania were captured in *The Jak*, a documentary by Yusuf Andibachtiar, a film-maker who has documented
Indonesian football culture, seeing it as a mirror to understand the
country's disenfranchised. He followed Bung Ferry and explored
Jakmania's rise in Indonesia's post-New Order era. In the film Bung
Ferry is thinner, less grey but much more militant. He describes how
he had initially been part of 'The Commandos', a supporters group
for Pelita Jaya, before changing his allegiance with seven other members. The Commandos never forgave him for that. He spoke about
the violence that followed Jakmania. How it was a natural state of
things in Indonesia when people offend each other, whilst blaming
the police and the authorities for inflaming the situation. 'The police

in Indonesia doesn't maintain security,' he told me. 'If one of us are rioting, they punch us, fight with us. In their mind they have to punch. In those conditions it makes us angry and makes the stadium like a bowl of soup when it boils. That's the police.' The media, he added, were just as much to blame for automatically blaming Jakmania.

The Jak ends with two scenes. In the first, a match is about to take place at Persija's old Lebak Bulus Stadium in the heart of the city. The capacity was only 12,500, perhaps a third of what was needed to accommodate the Jakmania, and the stands were packed. Supporters were standing in deep crowds right up to the sidelines and on the pitch. Bung Ferry can be seen on the pitch, in his number 12 shirt, directing and negotiating with the police, who had no idea what to do. The film ends in 2005, with the final championship play-off between Persipura Jayapura and Persija. Persija lost in extra time and a vicious riot followed, with the Jakmania setting fire to some parts of the stadium. The last scenes are of bloody, unconscious fans being taken to hospital. One member of Jakmania died. Bung Ferry decided to quit after that. 'It needed fresh ideas,' he said. 'In fan culture regeneration is the most important thing. So in 2005 I decided to leave and plan my succession.'

Yusuf would return to football when he made his first feature film. Romeo & Juliet was a reimagining of Shakespeare's famous play but set in Jakarta with the Montagues as Persija fans, the Capulets supporting Persib Bandung. The opening scene sees a coach full of celebrating Persib Bandung fans travelling home from a victory. They sing:

Viking or Bonek [the ultras group of Persebaya] are the same
As long as we're not the Jak
Because they're the bitches.

Moments later they are attacked on the highway by 'The Jak'. Through brutal, window-shattering violence and the haze of tear gas, Romeo (Rangga) and Juliet (Desi) lock eyes and fall in love. Desi, it turns out, is the young sister of Persib Bandung's head capotifosi, a Tybalt-esque hothead.

For Bung Ferry, the violence was inherent. Football clubs were treated as deities – 'like a demi-god', Bung Ferry explained – so any slight or offence led quickly to violence. 'We take it fairly seriously. Most Indonesians are struggling. So football is an expression of freedom from their tough life. So if someone mocks our football club they take it fairly seriously and when we have a clash we have to make them die.'

The arrival of European influences in the 1990s didn't encourage violence. It had always been there, waiting for an outlet. There was, though, one major difference between Europe and Indonesia. 'When you fight like the Europeans if your opponent is beaten up, you are finished. It is over,' he said. 'But it is different in Indonesia. If your opponent is beaten up, we still punch him out until they die.' I thought of what one of the Rain City Bois had told me. *Don't fall over.*

The last few years had seen the worst of the violence. It got so bad that Bung Ferry came out of retirement. Persija was bankrupt and the league was a mess. Corruption, match-fixing and non-payment of players' wages were rife. FIFA stepped in several times. On one memorable occasion they called for the election of the president of the Indonesian football federation, PSSI, to be re-run. The winner was in prison serving a sentence for corruption. Eventually a breakaway league was formed to try to clean up the game, but this saw FIFA suspend Indonesia, who then had a long period in the wilderness.[8] At that time, Bimo told me, 'Jakarta was like a war zone.' There was a cycle of violence. One side would attack the other out of a perceived injustice, and the other side would reply in kind. In May 2016 a young Persija fan, Muhammad Fahreza, was killed during a game. His brother claimed that he had been beaten by the police. At the next game Jakmania rioted against them. One fight, Bimo told me, saw ten policemen injured and the stadium was set on fire. One of the officers was left in a coma and lost his left eye. Thirty Jakmania were arrested. The slogan 'All Cops Are Bastards' was found in one of Fahreza's notebooks at home after his death.[9]

Bung Ferry felt he had no choice but to return and bring back some order. There hadn't been any major trouble since. 'People wearing shirts with ACAB and 1312, that is a European thing and I don't like those things,' he said. 'If we don't like the police, we share our opinion with our voice. Not with the shirt. We have to share our opinion with our voice. If we have to fight, we have to fight. If you hate the police, if you have your problem, face it alone, not with Jakmania.' Bung Ferry's power was clear. 'Bung' means 'big brother' or 'comrade' and is only bestowed on those who command huge loyalty and respect (Indonesia's first post-independence president Sukarno is widely known as Bung Karno). Even Rio, one of the top boys of the Curva Sud, was deferential when he spoke. 'No one dared to arrest me, even the police, military, government,' Bung Ferry said. 'They were afraid. Because if they arrested me Jakmania would defend me. All of Jakmania.'

Bung Ferry wouldn't be taking the bus east. He had to fly to Sleman tomorrow, where he would be meeting with the local police chiefs and PSS Sleman's ultra groups to arrange the security. But he would be at the game. 'It always rains at dawn and dusk in Sleman,' he told me. 'Bring an umbrella.'

BOGOR, INDONESIA

IT WAS A BOILING-HOT DAY and the Pakansari Stadium looked empty, but it didn't sound empty. The AFC Cup game between PSM Makassar and Toyota Laos had just kicked off. The stadium was built for the 2018 Asian Games but was in the middle of nowhere, a good 45 minutes in a taxi from Bogor. That was the easiest part of the journey. Around 500 ultras from PSM Makassar were here, from the island of Sulawesi, around 1,800km away. PSM's stadium wasn't deemed up to scratch by the AFC so the game was hosted here instead. The journey wasn't quite as hard as in Bung Ferry's day, when he had to take a six-day round trip over land and sea. But still, filling one sector behind the goal was an achievement. The metal fence at the front was covered with banners and flags, with a line of drummers keeping the songs in rhythm. On top of the metal fence, holding a megaphone, was PSM's *capo*, a man approaching 50 who was wearing a white Islamic prayer cap and had tattoos covering both arms. He prayed every time PSM scored, which was a lot given that they had gone 4–1 up with half an hour still to play, before scrambling down and organising another song. 'In Indonesia we have tradition with religion,' says Imam, the leader of PSM's ultra group, PSM Fans. 'We have strong roots, we always pray with the goals.'

I was due to meet up with the Rain City Bois that night before heading east with Jakmania's convoy. But Bimo had told me another big match was taking place and I should see it. Imam's group numbered about 500 in total and the terrace was a mishmash of influences: English, Italian, Sulawesi, Indonesian, Islamic. One flag read: 'Away Days, With PSM Makassar', in English. Underneath was the old British Railways logo that had been appropriated by West Ham United's infamous InterCity Firm (so called because they would use British Rail's InterCity service to travel to away games). Underneath that was the phrase 'You'll Never Fight Alone'. One ultra wore a T-shirt: 'No One Likes Us We Don't Care', a chant made famous by Millwall. In the middle was the PSM's ultras symbol, crossed hammers. Imam had a Stone Island jumper over his shoulders, despite the heat. 'In Indonesia it's about the ultras and the hooligans,' he explained. PSM were scoring goals for fun now. It was 7–2. 'There were some books but the biggest influence was by film. *The Firm*, *Away Days*, *Football Factory* … *İstanbul United* from Turkey. I love the way the ultras supported their club.'

The biggest influence of all was *Green Street Hooligans*. 'Green Street Hooligans 1, 2 and 3,' Imam stressed. It had been one of the few constants of my travels over the past ten years. Of all of my country's vast cultural output – the Beatles, Shakespeare, Dickens, *Only Fools and Horses* – according to almost every group of ultras I had met anywhere in the world the single most popular piece of art was *Green Street Hooligans*. Elijah Wood played the improbable role of a recently expelled Harvard student sent to London to stay with family so he can have a long, hard think about his future. He falls in with a bunch of West Ham fans, of which Charlie Hunnam plays a top boy from the infamous Green Street Hooligans (clearly based on the ICF), who go out fighting other clubs' firms, especially their hated rivals Millwall. And so begins the unlikely journey from golden-hearted Hobbit to rabid American soccer thug. It is memorable for one thing in particular: Charlie Hunnam's absolutely appalling attempt at an East London accident.

And yet it has also served as a kind of blueprint for young football fans around the world who idolised the nihilistic terrace culture in 1980s England. The first time I realised the power of the film was in Israel, shortly after its release. I was meeting with the members of La Familia, the hardcore ultras of Beitar Jerusalem, a club famous for its anti-Arab views. An Arab had never played for the club, and La Familia had violently protested whenever it was suggested an Arab might do so. They were suspicious of foreigners and journalists, and spoke very little English. But when they heard I was English they broke out in song: 'I'm West Ham 'Til I Die' in a mockney accent. It wasn't just the songs, but the fashion too. Burberry caps. Stone Island jumpers. C.P. Company jackets with goggles. The film was widely mocked in England, and *Green Street Hooligans* 2 and 3 make the first one look like Werner Herzog in comparison. But young fans, usually teenagers, saw *Green Street Hooligans* as a 'how to ...' manual. The same thing happened when I met the ultras of Borac Banja Luka in Bosnia or Steaua Bucharest in Romania or Drita in Kosovo. *Green Street Hooligans* fetishised the violence of a bygone age, one that doesn't really exist in England any more thanks to the gentrification and criminalisation of football fandom in the Premier League era. But the film's influence remains, even though it was meant as a warning about how even the most unlikely people can be drawn to violence. It had become a self-fulfilling prophecy: a film that warns of the proximity of violence in young men, inspiring casuals culture on almost every continent on the planet.

Imam, though, wasn't into the violence. It was, he said, all about the clothes and the chanting.

The game ended 7–3. PSM's *capo* was on the drums banging a slow rhythm as the players stood in front of the fence and the ultras responded with an Icelandic thunderclap. They chanted the word 'Ewako', a south Sulawesi word that, according to Imam, means 'to be brave' in Buginese. As the players clapped back they broke out in song, again in their local language:

> We are always here
> We are always there too
> Don't be afraid, we'll always be there
> Go my PSM

> Reclaim the glory
> We miss that time
> History speaks about us
> And I'm sure you can do it

Everything had been thrown into the melting pot: Italy, England, Iceland, Indonesia, Sulawesi and Islam. It wasn't a poor facsimile of European culture. It was the latest iteration of influence, cross-pollinated across borders and assimilated with that which had been here for decades already.

That night I met with Bimo and his Rain City Bois in Bogor. Saif, a cherub-faced regular, Bagus, wearing a beanie hat and a green hoodie with the symbols of all the world's major religions on the front and the slogan 'Religion Is Not Crime; Allah Taught Us To Be A Good Person'. Fadhil who had hair like Dave Grohl, and Andri, who looked too young to be here. We drank Intisari on the streets of Bogor, bought from a street stand that sold it in plastic bags. You drank it by chewing off a corner and gulping down the arch of thick black liquid that shot out. A large, noisy group of Persib Bandung fans had taken over the city's central square, letting off flares and blue smoke bombs. It was the club's 86th birthday. We left them to it. Liverpool were playing Bayern Munich in the Champions League. English and Italian football was followed almost as religiously as the domestic league. Bimo sent me a video from 2017, of a riot that broke out in a mall following a Manchester United–Liverpool game. But there would be no trouble tonight.

The next day, hungover, we met at a KFC. Bimo had gathered his drums and flags as we waited for our coach, as night fell, on the edge of the city. He held it up for me, just before what we thought was our coach arrived to take us on the long night trip east: it was black, a British Railways sign in the middle surrounded by a Fred Perry-style laurel wreath. Around it were the words: 'Rain City Bois, Persija Jakarta, We Will Follow You Over The Land And Sea.'

SOMEWHERE ON A HIGHWAY OUTSIDE BANDUNG, INDONESIA

As THE HUNDRED OR SO members of the Jakmania sprinted across the six-lane highway, the passing traffic screeched and honked their horns. We managed to reach the middle intersection just as metal crunched and glass shattered behind us. A mini-van was sliding towards us sideways, inches from toppling over, its front caved in. At first I'd thought one of us had been hit, and that we would almost certainly be dealing with a dead body. There would have been no chance of survival. But everyone was accounted for, bunched up on the island in between the two directions of traffic. The van had swerved to avoid us and hit another passing car. The two now blocked the entire three lanes of traffic headed east. The drivers and passengers got out unharmed, even if their vehicles were now wrecks. The accident may well have saved our lives. The highway patrol quickly turned up to see what was going on. The two groups of Persib Bandung ultras waited, in the shadows, as if held back by the flashing yellow lights, for the authorities to leave before they could resume their attack. But the highway was a mess. The Jakmania ran back across the highway and huddled together waiting for the replacement coach to turn up. One lane was reopened. We waited, knowing that if the car with the flashing lights left, we would be attacked from two sides. What felt like hours passed until, finally, our coach careered around the roadblock, screeched to a halt as the doors hissed open. The driver had a wide smile and gave us a thumbs-up, oblivious to what had just happened. We swamped the coach. Inside Bimo and the Rain City

Bois screamed at people to close the curtains. We weren't out of trouble yet. The coach still had to pass under a bridge 50m away. It would be Persib's last stand. The doors were closed and we sat in the dark, in silence, away from the windows, sweating and bracing for impact. As the coach approached the rocks rained down on top of the metal roof in a staccato machine-gun of bangs. They stopped for a heartbeat as we passed underneath, and then resumed again on the other side. And then it stopped. The bus erupted in joy as everyone hugged each other and began chanting Persija's hymn, written by Bung Ferry 20 years before.

We are one soul
We have one aim
We have one love

Persija

For our victory
For our glory
For our unity

Persija

We were, Bimo told me, almost safe. There was only a 50/50 chance of being attacked again. But in four hours' time, once we'd passed the city of Banjar on the border of West and Central Java, we should be clear. Bagus sat next to me and handed me a bottle of Intisari. I drank deeply.

It turned out that we had been the lucky ones. Another coach, the one that inexplicably dropped us off at the side of the highway, was attacked by rock-throwing Persib fans, some of its windows smashed out. A second coach was also attacked by rocks and, in the escape, it flipped over and slid down an embankment. Eight Jakmania were taken to hospital. At the next few rest stops we divided those left uninjured amongst the rest of the convoy, filling our coach until it was standing room only. A disco ball was turned on as everyone sung Indonesian pop songs blasted through the coach's crackly speaker system, drinking Intisari, the air thick with sweet clove-scented tobacco smoke. Next to me Bagus was dropping in and out of consciousness, alternatively falling asleep on my shoulder and retching into a plastic bag. Bimo was singing constantly, mainly English terrace chants:

> *Persib Bandung!*
> *Is full of shit!*
> *Oh, Persib Bandung is full of shit!*

And (to the tune of 'Achy Breaky Heart' by Billy Ray Cyrus):

> *Don't take me home*
> *Please don't take me home*
> *I just don't wanna go to work*
> *I wanna stay here and drink all the beer*
> *Please don't, please don't, take me home.*

There was also an ode to Intisari. The coach was rocking until, gradually, the Intisari ran out. It got quieter and slurrier. By dawn virtually everyone was asleep. We stopped at a local town to buy noodles and, as it was Friday, so that half the bus could go and pray at the local mosque. By the time our coach entered Slemen we had been on the road for 23 hours. It pulled into a field that had been turned into a coach park. There were hundreds of coaches from all around Java. Hawkers were selling scarves and pin badges: Away Days, Ultras Persija, The Jak Mania, Forza Persija, Against Modern Football. Badges of Sergio Tacchini, C.P. Company, Ellesse, English flags with the British Rail logo, the Union Jack with 'Jakartans' running across the middle. Exhausted casualties lay on any patch of ground they could find. It felt more like the dying hours of a 72-hour music festival; one last headline act before the long march home.

*

What do you see when you watch a game of football? Do you see a game of numbers and tactics? Do you see an entertainment product? Or do you see something else? That something else was the essence of writing *1312*. Every ultra, *barra brava*, *torcedores*, hooligan or casual I spoke to had the same origins story. The same recollection. They looked at the pitch, but were drawn to the danger and the noise of the crowds behind the goals. They didn't just want to watch football. They wanted to feel it too. I had felt that when I first started going to football on my own. At 13 I would take the train to the Boleyn Ground and pay £5 to stand on the North Bank amongst the hooligans of West Ham United. I couldn't see a thing when the game was played. But I could *feel* the game, and the crowd, around me. That sense of being part of something bigger, a sound that you could lose yourself into and the excitement that something dangerous could happen at any moment. I can still feel some of that today. Or at the very least, recall the outline of its memory. That's why the Italian word *tifosi* had such resonance. It spoke of something you had no choice over. Once infected, you were never really cured.

When I started out I wanted to know what the ultras were and to tell the stories of the people who had dedicated their lives to football supporter culture. Even after visiting 25 countries and speaking to hundreds of people, I was still no closer to a single definition. If anything, the journey had made it harder. Every single person from foot soldiers to *capos* had a different idea of what an ultra was. There was the Italian definition, of course. To go beyond, to dedicate oneself to a club and a group seven days a week. But it was easier to define what it was against: the mistrust in any type of authority. The despair at the commercialisation of the modern world. The others who weren't them, unless a very specific alliance had been made. Spending time with ultras sometimes felt like it was them – us – against the rest of the world. The closest definition I'd heard was in Split. *Dišpet*. Anti-everything, a kind of noble morality that you followed to the end, even if that sometimes led to your own destruction.

But even that didn't tell the whole story. There was a moral compass, even if you didn't agree in which direction the needle was pointing. Fallen enemies were honoured and money raised for their families. Help was given for refugees. Campaigns had been launched *against* refugees. There had been coordinated campaigns of racist abuse. Food banks for the poor. Funds to repair dilapidated churches and mosques. Help for the victims of floods, fires or earthquakes, even if it was a hated rival who had suffered. Others had agitated for political change. For justice. Against corruption. *For* racial purity. Anti-racist campaign had been launched. Many became foot soldiers for the far-right, who found a deep pool on the terraces to recruit from, whether it was in Italy, Eastern Europe or Germany. It was a movement of extremes, without compromise. Centrist ultras were as rare as snow leopards.

This, of course, led to a whole web of contradictions. Ultras claimed to despise politics yet almost everything they did was political. Even being apolitical was a political decision. They hated the media and journalists who painted them as thugs, but would also freely admit that violence was an integral part of the scene. Many basked in, and indeed built their reputations on, the media coverage that followed. It was about the single focus of supporting a team. Yet the movement attracted a surprising number of leaders who had no interest in football. They were outsiders, yet at times had been co-opted by government forces, mafias or political movements when it was expedient. The truth was that there was no all-encompassing definition. Being an ultra was a feeling, an anti-authority urge that found a home in football and could be channelled into myriad of different places. Its appeal was in part due to its adaptability. It could become a focus and a vehicle for revolutionary change against dictatorships. Or be adapted into a money making mafia exercise. Or into an organised, illegal fight club. Or into a huge art collective.

When I started, I wanted to document one of the biggest youth subcultures in the world. And that's true. There are millions of ultras, if not tens of millions. But ultras, in the classic Italian sense, are going the same way as English hooligans: killed by police control, stadium bans and – the biggest culprit to the older generation of *capotifosi* – social media. Today's ultra culture was an amorphous thing, mashing together different aspects of hooligans, *barras bravas* and *torcida*, all wrapped up in the aesthetics and rules forged in 1970s Italy. But if you wanted to find the true spirit of the modern ultra movement in the second decade of the twentieth century, Italy might not be the place to look. You would have more luck searching for it in Germany, Indonesia, Sweden, Morocco, maybe even in LA.

It was one of the reasons why Mikael – back in Sweden – had made some big plans. He had finally decided to do something with the thousands upon thousands of *tifo* photos that had been sorted and stored at his mother's summer house outside Stockholm. It was perhaps one of the great untapped archives of the ultra movement. Nearly 40 years of painstakingly collected and collated memories. Not just photos, but scarves and shirts and stickers and programmes and literature. At some point the scene that Mikael had dedicated his life to had become a bygone age, so he had decided that he wanted to write the definitive ultras encyclopedia. Someone had to write the names down before they disappeared and were forgotten forever. And there was no one better than Mikael. I suggested 'Ultrapedia' as a title but he wasn't that keen on it. He was also working with a producer on a film about the history of *tifo*. But day to day was all about Hammarby. He was, as ever, travelling to every game home and away. There was a big run of matches coming up and there was an outside chance they could win the title.

Meanwhile, the police had continued their crackdown on the ultras, and the ultras had responded in an increasingly creative fashion. In August 2019 the Swedish police decided to reduce the number of tickets available to AIK's Black Army ultras in the north stand for a Europa League qualifier against Sheriff Tiraspol from 4,000 to 2,750. Their justification was persistent standing in the walkways, which the ultras saw as little more than a pretext to shut them down. So they emptied the entire stand and covered it in blue and white police crime-scene tape, ensuring that the crackdown got wide international coverage. A few weeks later, Celtic's away support got a taste of the new regime too. According to the *Scottish Herald*, "'around 20" police officers stormed in among the Hoops [Celtic] contingent and there were allegedly weapons used during the melee'.[10] Mikael had decided to just carry on as normal and to hell with the consequences. 'We don't care about the police,' Mikael said. 'All the matches we'll be preparing big *tifos* and a lot of pyro, so we'll go for it, you know?' Which is what Hammarby did. The championship came down to the final game of the season between three teams: Malmö, Djurgårdens and Hammarby. Djurgårdens went 2–0 down in their game and Hammarby were winning. For a brief few moments they were top of the league. But Djurgårdens came back and their hated rivals won the championship. Mikael was distraught. Not least because his other team had also lost. The much anticipated Boca Juniors-River Plate Copa Libertadores semi-final – the match feared by Argentina's president Mauricio Macri – went ahead without incident. But Boca, even with Carlos Tevez and the newly arrived Daniele De Rossi, were no match for River Plate. There was some good news for Rafa di Zeo, though. Macri was voted out of office. A new government aligned with Cristina Fernández de Kirchner was being formed. Perhaps Rafa, as he predicted, would be returning to the Bombonera now that the political winds had changed.

Meanwhile, Hugo's KGB was going from strength to strength. I would occasionally see posts on social media detailing their fights. A month later the KGB enjoyed a victory against much-vaunted German opposition: a 13-vs-13-man brawl against Chemie Leipzig. 'Hard fight. 2 Min. KGB win,' was how it was reported in GruppaOF's Insta account. There was also a rematch with AIK's Firman boys. Hugo had told me that AIK's firm had claimed they were being followed by the police, which was why they didn't turn up last time. There were 170 fighters for the rearranged match. Hammarby won. 'We crushed them,' said Hugo.

Serhii Filimonov had a bit more time to dedicate himself to *okolo-futbola*. After the Ukrainian presidential elections were won by Volodymyr Zelenksy, the former actor who had got famous by playing a fake Ukrainian president on Netflix, the country's parliamentary elections were brought forward. As a rising star in the National Corps, Filimonov thought he would be on the party's electoral list. But, in the weeks before, the main far-right and ultra-nationalist political parties had decided to form an electoral pact. It was unlikely that individually they would gain the 5 per cent of the votes needed to win seats in the Rada. So they pooled their resources and redrew their electoral lists. Rodion Kudryashov, the former leader of the Dnipro ultras, was on there, near the top. But Filimonov wasn't. When the elections took place the new far-right bloc barely got 3 per cent.[11]

Shortly afterwards Filimonov quit the party, not because he wasn't on the list, but due to the reality of Ukraine's political system and the ability for those close to it to enrich themselves. Over the previous months it was revealed that several figures connected to Azov had become very rich, very quickly. Like Sergei Korotkikh, a Russian-Belarusian who was once a leading figure in Russia's largest (and now outlawed) neo-Nazi group, the National Socialist Society[12], before moving to Ukraine to become head of intelligence for Azov. He was personally handed a Ukrainian passport by the former president Petro Poroshenko for his efforts in the war against Russia.[13] When Korotkikh filed his tax return – he had a role with the police, and a legal require-ment for all civil servants is to publicly disclose your assets – he had managed to accrue a million dollars, one and a half Kyiv apartments and a private plane in less than a year, and all on an official salary of $237 a month.[14,15] Filimonov was clearly doing well for himself since returning to civilian life, but not that well. He left, remaining on good terms with the National Corps' leader Andriy Biletsky but decided to return to his own direct-action firm, Honor. He'd also helped to set up a 'Street Protest Academy', a class that – he said – taught non-violent protest techniques. The poster had a picture of a Molotov cocktail on it. 'I decided that I have my own way,' he told me. A few months later Filimonov and Maliar were back in the news again after they were both pictured at street protests in Hong Kong.[16] Their links with the far-right were highlighted. They were called 'protest tourists'. The Russian and Chinese media, looking to discredit the Hong Kong pro-testers, found what they were looking for in Honor. Filimonov said that they were simply on holiday and weren't giving any instruction to the protesters. 'Of course they are interested in discrediting us,' Filimonov replied when I messaged him shortly after the story broke. 'It's so that Hong Kong will not support Ukraine in return.' Once he was home Filimonov said he would be going back to his roots, focusing on *okolofutbola* and 'preparing for next year's fights.' I was sure this wouldn't be the last protest I'd see Filimonov and Maliar attend.

In Turkey İstanbul's mayoral election was re-run after it was cancelled on dubious grounds at the behest of President Erdoğan. It was, as it turned out, a huge tactical error. The residents of İstanbul were furious at what they perceived to be an electoral trick mostly pulled in banana republics. There were many problems with Turkish democracy, but the votes themselves had been relatively clean. It was the base of Erdoğan and the AKP's legitimacy. Winning fair elections, but then using that power to bend and break the rules away from the ballot box as it saw fit. So, when the vote was re-run (with Başakşehir's president running the city until the right candidate won) İstanbul gave Erdoğan an even bloodier nose. Ekrem İmamoğlu increased his winning margin from a wafer-thin 13,700 votes to over 806,000 votes. It was a record victory in any İstanbul election, both by percentage and by numbers.[17] Erdoğan couldn't count on any better news from his pet football project. After losing to Beşiktaş – the game where the crowd chanted for İmamoğlu – Başakşehir collapsed. They lost their crunch game against Galatasaray 2–1, despite going ahead.[18] Galatasaray won the title and hundreds of thousands of fans filled Thaksim after the game with flares and smoke bombs. Not that Selim was allowed to watch the game. The police had upheld his ludicrous ban and he would not be able to return to the stadium until March 2020.

But the government was not to be thwarted for long. Shortly after the end of the season a new crackdown on all supporters was announced. Big fines were introduced for swearing. Prison sentences for anyone starting a discriminatory chant. Any pyro would mean jail, even if it was let off far from the stadium on a boat or on a bus. 'The bill introduces prison terms of up to three years to anyone "disrupting the course and security of the competition",' reported the pro-government paper the *Daily Sabah*. The purpose of the bill, they wrote, was to 'cleanse sports of "violence, insults and swear words" and "to create an atmosphere of sportsmanlike conduct for players and fans".'

Başakşehir may have lost the title, but the game was being remoulded in both their and Erdoğan's image.[19]

One man whose image was certainly on the up was Ivan Savvidis, the gun-toting owner of PAOK. On the one hand he was still banned from Greek football stadiums for walking on to the pitch with a gun when he disagreed with a referee's decision against rivals AEK of Athens. His alleged involvement in trying to swing the name-change referendum in neighbouring Macedonia – where he was accused of funnelling money to nationalist Macedonian ultras – hadn't gone to plan either. Even though the opposition boycotted the referendum so that the vote would not reach the 50 per cent needed to validate it, prime minister Zoran Zaev pushed ahead anyway. When I started this book, the country was called the former Yugoslav Republic of Macedonia. When I finished it, it was the Republic of North Macedonia. FIFA changed the name of the national team shortly afterwards as well. It's now listed under 'N', rather than 'F' like before. But Savvidis was still a hero in Thessaloniki. After nearly four decades, PAOK finally won the title in 2019. Toumba was transformed into its Ring of Fire. The harbour was lined with hundreds of thousands of people as Savvidis was greeted like a returning hero. 'Let those in Athens think with a clear head: what they did to us made us stronger by the day,' he told the crowd.[20] Even though Savvidis wasn't allowed to enter Toumba until his ban ended in March 2021, it appeared that he was going nowhere. But that hadn't stopped the controversy. In December 2019 a Greek investigation by the ONE TV station alleged that Savvidis was, through a complex network of companies, the man that ultimately controlled another top tier Greek league club, Xanthi FC.[21] If true it would be a huge scandal that would likely relegate both clubs and see Savvidis banned from football for life. PAOK furiously denied the accusation. 'The ridiculous antics and fairytales coming out of Olympiacos and those behind the club continue,' PAOK said in an official statement.[22] ONE TV station is owned by Evangelos Marinakis, the owner of Olympiacos. As with everything in Greek football, the truth was always mired in conspiracy.

In Rio, Cláudio was working hard to reform Raça and bring them back to the stadium. He had invited all the disparate groups to the Stuck Cow to talk it out. His plans to bring a form of parliamentary democracy and social conscience to the *torcida* were still on track. Some were worried that they would lose huge numbers of people if they kicked out the most violent members. 'I said: "Fuck! I started with eight people. Me, my brother and six more."' But, as ever with politics, uncomfortable compromises had to be made. A meeting was set up with Rio's governor Wilson Witzel. Witzel was a former judge and ally of Jair Bolsonaro, who was elected on a law-and-order platform that promised a trigger-happy shoot-to-kill policy, 'a slaughter' of Rio's drug gangs.[23] One tactic the police were now using was firing at crowds of suspected criminals from a helicopter. There had been mass protests in Rio against Witzel after a police officer shot an eight-year-old girl in the back after firing wildly at two men escaping on a motorbikes. She died that night in hospital.[24]

Witzel was also the man who could lift the ban on Raça. Aware that there were hundreds of thousands of potential votes in it, Witzel met with three leaders of Raça and was pictured with a Flamengo shirt. Cláudio refused to go. Witzel, Cláudio said, was a 'Nazi, fascist'. He didn't blame Raça for meeting with him. 'I said: "My brother, I don't like it, but I won't criticise you either." I know if it wasn't done Raça would never come back to the stadiums.' And Raça, Cláudio believed, was needed now more than ever. 'Not even in 1964 did we have such a fascist country,' said Cláudio. 'We will have to fight this, fight this from below.'

In Serbia President Aleksandar Vučić finally had enough of the goading from the terraces. His finance minister Siniša Mali gave a press conference to release figures that proved Red Star and Partizan Belgrade were being given roughly the same amount of money and that accusations of favouritism were unfounded.[25] If anything, they claimed, Partizan's football team received *more* state funding than Red Star since 2014. 'The reason we are coming out with the numbers is not to have the clubs argue, but for the citizens know how much we are trying to make it balanced and that they function in the best way.

That they represent our country well. As is evident, the money is evenly distributed,' said Mali.[26] Meanwhile Partizan's terrace war continued. Ljubomir Marković, one of the Alcatraz leaders jailed for the killing of the French fan Brice Taton, was shot twice in the head on a Belgrade street.[27] 'His death shows that there is a shift in power,' said Bojana Pavlović.

Ismail Morina, meanwhile, had been enjoying his anonymity. He had been working hard and studying for his EU truck licence. There hadn't been any more problems with the Serbian authorities. There had, however, been a few copycat incidents. At a Europa League match between F91 Dudelange and Azerbaijani team Qarabag in Luxembourg, a drone was flown over the pitch carrying an Armenian flag.[28] Although based in the Azeri capital of Baku, Qarabag were originally from Agdam, a now abandoned city in the region of Nagorno-Karabakh which Armenia and Azerbaijan frequently go to war over. The pilot had learned from Morina's mistake during the Serbia–Albania game, never flying it too close to the players, who tried and failed to bring it down. They were so desperate they started firing footballs at it. They all missed. There was also nearly a revenge drone incident too. The day before the Czech Republic played Kosovo in a 2020 European Championship qualification match, a group of Czech fans were stopped and searched outside the Fadil Vokrri Stadium in Pristina. They discovered flares, a knife, a drone and a flag with the words 'Kosovo is Serbia'.[29] The phrase had found solidarity amongst ultra-nationalist Eastern European ultras to show kinship with their Slavic brothers. Kosovo came from behind to win 2–1.

Still, Ismail couldn't stay away for long. When I contacted him he had just got back from France after an unsuccessful mission. France played Albania in Paris and Ismail had made a white banner, 20m long, to display at the game. It read, in black letters: 'Hands off From Kosovo', with the 'v' in Kosovo replaced by a pink heart. He sent me a picture of it laid out on the floor. It was four times longer than his work van. The message was intended for the French. Ismail had got steadily angrier about the impasse in Kosovo, especially in the north where there was a large Serbian population. It also had, Ismail said, rich mining and water reserves, which he thought the French were after. But the French never saw the banner. Security stopped Ismail and his friends from unfolding it and they were aggressively ejected from the match. 'It's like I am a terrorist,' he messaged me. I had a feeling that Ismail Morina's story might have more chapters to write.

Whilst Ismail was planning his next provocation outside Milan, the 2019/20 Italian football season began without one of its most infamous leaders. On 4 August, Fabrizio Piscitelli, Diabolik, the leader of Lazio's Irriducibili who I had sat down with in his headquarters next to a portrait of Mussolini, was sitting on a bench in Rome's Parco degli Acquedotti. It was only a short walk from his home. Just before 7pm, in broad daylight, a man dressed as a jogger approached Diabolik and shot him in the back of the head, behind his left ear, with a 7.65 calibre pistol. He died instantly. He was 53 years old. In the days that followed, the place where he was executed became a shrine of flowers and messages from across Italy and the world. A banner appeared on a walkway next to the Colosseum, a favourite place for the Irriducibili to send out public messages, that read: 'Diabalo Lives'. Far-right ultra groups travelled to Rome to pay their respects.

No one was arrested as speculation about the motives behind his death were discussed in the Italian media and on social networks. Straight away it was clear that this wasn't connected to the actions of the Irriducibili. The death was too violent, too professional. The weapon, the manner it was done, the fact that the killer was well disguised and had easily escaped, all suggested it was a professional hit. Diabolik had certainly made plenty of enemies and there were any number of lines of enquiries. His involvement in drug trafficking seemed to be a good place to start. The Albanian mafia was suggested as one potential culprit. He had been named in the Mafia Capitale corruption case, another line of enquiry. Anything from business dealings in arms to human trafficking to gold were suggested. Even his connections to far-right politics. But still no one was arrested.

The most pressing problem, though, was the funeral. The authorities viewed it as a potential flashpoint for the far-right and other ultra groups from around Europe. So they banned a public funeral and pencilled in the service for 6am a week later. Piscitelli's family was incensed, took legal action and refused to collect the body from the morgue, forcing the city into the farcical situation of renegotiating the terms of the burial. As the days ticked by, the start of the Serie A season approached, as did the first Rome derby of the season between Lazio and Roma. At all costs, the funeral had to take place before then. And it did. In the end, a compromise was agreed. One hundred people could attend the funeral. It didn't keep the ultras away. The route to the church was lined by hundreds of people, letting off blue smoke bombs and flares, wearing T-shirts in honour of him. One read: 'Jackals can feast on the corpse of a lion, but he remains a lion and they remain jackals'. When the hearse moved slowly past, the coffin could be seen inside, sleek black with the famous cartoon eyes of the comic character Diabolik painted on the front. Dozens gave Roman salutes. The funeral passed without violence.[30]

The new season started with Inter Milan's Boys SAN arranging a mosaic choreography of Diabolik's eyes across the *curva nord*. Boys SAN and the Irriducibili had a long and deep friendship based on their shared far-right world view. Underneath the choreography a banner read: '*Fabrizio Con Noi*'; 'Fabrizio Is With Us'.[31] Despite the worry, the Rome derby passed without incident too. Lazio, famed for their choreography, displayed a huge image of Diabolik's face that covered the *curva nord*. The ultras were silent for the first half, to protest that the club had failed to pass on its condolences. Or even mention officially that Diabolik had been murdered. The Irriducibili had banned players from celebrating in front of the *curva nord* too. When Luis Alberto scored the equaliser for Lazio in what turned out to be a diplomatic 1–1 draw, he complied.

Diabolik's murder had shown how the ultras had diminished in Italian football. At the height of their powers at the start of the millennium, they virtually ran Lazio, making huge sums from merchandising. They could breeze in and out of the training complex. They could force transfers if they fell out with a player or prevent one from leaving if they so chose. Today, the club wanted nothing to do with Diabolik and didn't fear the consequences of ignoring his demise. Lazio's president Claudio Lotito, Diabolik's long-time nemesis, announced that Lazio was cracking down on the racist chants. 'We're tired of our image being dragged through the mud,' he said. 'After fifteen years, I am tired of still having to deal with these situations.'[32] Which was not to say Italian ultras were fading into the night. A recent police crackdown against Juventus ultras uncovered a complex plot to extort money and tickets from the club by threatening to make racist chants, knowing that big fines would follow.[33] Another raid on a Juve ultras group uncovered a cache of assault weapons, a trove of Nazi memorabilia and a surface-to-air missile. 'Connections were found between these neo-fascist and neo-Nazi groups and ultras groups, in particular, Juventus and the Drughi Giovinezza section,' said police chief Carlo Ambra.[34]

But, during the first Rome derby of the season, on the other side of the Stadio Olimpico, the fraternity that ultras felt in death was clear. Roma's ultras had done something Lazio's management had refused to do. They commemorated the death of Fabrizio Piscitelli with two simple banners.

'Rest in Peace, Fabrizio.'
'Fly High! Ciao Diablo.'

*

The Maguwoharjo Stadium looks like a mini San Siro. Each corner has wide spiral walkways to enter the stadium. We pushed through the crowd until we were the crowd. Thousands surged forward as we corkscrewed upwards, flare smoke making it impossible to breathe. As we neared the top, the chanting gave way to angry screaming. The police had only opened one small door for the mass to squeeze through. A lone security guard impotently shouted at us to move back as hundreds joined the back every minute. But we couldn't. We were caught in a pressure point. The crowd was slowly imploding, crushing our ribs and pushing the air from our lungs. Fathers lifted their children up and screamed for the security to save them. Eventually the police officer gave up and smashed open a second door, relieving the pressure as we swarmed through the gates. Bimo hadn't even broken sweat. It was always like this, he said.

We found our place ten minutes before kick-off. It was getting dark and the Maguwoharjo Stadium was already full. PSS Sleman's Brigata Curva Sud had cancelled their boycott. They flew thousands of flags in the south *curva*, periodically letting off flares. The Jakmania filled the entire east stand. They had brought 16,000 people with them, in the end. Each ultra sub-group covered the front fence with their flag, an important ritual of belonging. Bimo tied his black Rain City Bois flag to one of the last spaces he could find. Atop the fence, half a dozen *capotifosi* had climbed up with megaphones to lead the chants. Rio was there, further down, urging his followers to sing louder. Bung Ferry was there too, stopping every few steps for selfies and autographs. As the game kicked off each of the *capotifosi* shouted through their megaphones, urging the crowd to sing the hymn written by Bung Ferry louder.

We are one soul
We are one aim
We are one love

Persija

For our victory
For our glory
For our unity

Persija

The Jakmania sang its haunting melody, at a higher pitch than you would hear at a European or South American stadium. Yellowish, acrid smoke enveloped us, mixing with sweet clove tobacco smoke and the hot, humid air. The football was incidental, the great dirty secret at the heart of football's obsessive fan culture. The chanting was only broken by euphoria when Persija scored twice. Persija won 2–0 and were through to the knockout stages. But none of that really mattered. Like in every country's fan culture, what mattered were the ties that bind. The friendship and the unity. Indonesia hadn't blindly aped Italy's fan culture, no more so than English fans had aped the Italian ultras. Or Russian fans had aped ultra-style choreo and flares. Indonesian fan culture had been influenced by Europe but each group had grafted that influence on top of an already deep and devout culture. Far from being an embarrassing facsimile of European culture, as many European ultras derided the Asian scene, Indonesian fan culture bore a striking resemblance to England in the 1980s. This was a working-class space. Bimo worked in a warehouse. The rest of the Rain City Bois sold Persija merchandise on the streets. The Jakmania I had just travelled with for almost 24 hours were waiters, barmen, delivery drivers. It was full of youth and anger and belonging. It was one of the few places Jakartans could afford to gather and express their discontent. Jakmania had become what Bung Ferry had always hoped it would; a home for the homeless.

The singing didn't stop at the final whistle. The crowd moved back down the spiral staircases and out towards the front of the stadium. Bimo and his Rain City Bois stood by the entrance and bought some cigarettes, stealing themselves for the long coach ride home. This, Bimo told me, was one of the last times his crew would be all together. It might even be *the* last. 'Next week I start a new job, in the east of the country,' Bimo said. He would have to make do with watching home games on TV. Away days like this would be all but impossible. Bung Ferry would also announce his retirement later in the year, wanting to promote young talent, new blood. And so it continued, the cycle of renewal and regeneration.

The damp, hot air suddenly gave way to the monsoon, arriving just on time. Bung Ferry was right. In Sleman, it always rained at dusk.

Endnotes

INTRODUCTION

1 *Encyclopedia of the Ottoman Empire* (Infobase) by Gabor Agoston and Bruce Alan Masters P.252
2 Hajduk Split's website has a great section outlining the club's wartime history, in English https://hajduk.hr/eng/history/1941–1950
3 'Meet Yugoslavia's ballerina Beara, once the best keeper in the world', by Jonathan Wilson, *The Guardian*, 5 August 2008, https://www.theguardian.com/football/2008/aug/05/europeanfootball
4 Beara, and a host of other surviving members, were interviewed in the 2012 Croatian documentary *1950: Hajduk and Torcida*. He died in 2014.
5 Ibid.
6 *The Politics of Football in Yugoslavia: Sport, Nationalism and the State* (I.B. Tauris) by Richard Mills, Chapter 4. Mills' book is one of, if not the best book about football in the region. It's a trove of information on how football and politics often collided in Yugoslavia.
7 Ibid.
8 Ibid.
9 Ibid.
10 'Dinamo's glory made into a political football', by Chris Stephen, *The Observer*, 24 October 1999, https://www.theguardian.com/world/1999/oct/24/theobserver1

11 'Dinamo Zagreb football supremo convicted of fraud', by Anja Vladisavljevic, Balkan Insight, 6 June 2018, https://balkaninsight. com/2018/06/06/croatian-football-supremo-sentenced-for-money-embezzelment-06–06-2018/

12 'Why did Croatia fans disrupt their Euro 2016 match against Czech Republic', by Aleksandar Holgar, *The Guardian*, 18 June 2016, https:// www.theguardian.com/football/2016/jun/18/why-croatia-fans-disrupt-euro-2016-match-czech-republic

13 'Euro 2016: Croatia apologizes over Nazi swastika on its home pitch', by Paul Gittings, CNN International, 13 June 2015, https://edition.cnn.com/2015/06/13/football/nazi-swastika-croatia-football/index.html

14 'Zdravko Mamić Objavio Otvoreno Pismo Torcidi Pred Cijelom Hrvatskom', *Sportske Novosti*, 21 June 2017, https://sportske.jutarnji. hr/nogomet/nogomet-mix/zdravko-mamic-objavio-otvoreno-pismo-torcidi-pred-cijelom-hrvatskom-sjecate-li-se-sanadera-vidosevica-rozica-svaguse-pokrovca-fiorentinija/6286661/

15 The show was called 'Toward a Concrete Utopia: Architecture in Yugoslavia 1948-1980' https://www.moma.org/calendar/exhibitions/3931

16 'Operation Storm: Croatia's Triumph, Serbia's Grief', Sven Milekić, Marija Ristić and Ivana Nikolić, Balkan Insight, 3 August 2015, https://balkaninsight.com/2015/08/03/operation-storm-croatia-s-triumph-serbia-s-grief-07–31-2015/

PART ONE: LOS PRIMEROS HINCHAS

URUGUAY

1 Much of the history that is known about Prudencio Miguel Reyes has been collected and can be found in a booklet, *El Primer Hincha*, produced by Nacional's Comision De Historia Y Estadistica.

2 Ibid.

3 'Pargarles a barras bravas: el arma de doble filo que vuelve a apuntar contra Nacional', *El Observador*, 30 April 2019, https://www.elobservador.com.uy/nota/pagarle-a-barras-bravas-el-arma-de-doble-filo-que-vuelve-a-apuntar-contra-nacional-201942921267

4 'Uruguay's 'Barras Bravas' have become cartels: Soccer official', by David Gagne, Insight Crime, 24 April 2017. https://www.

insightcrime.org/news/brief/uruguay-barras-bravas-have-become-cartels-soccer-official/. For a deeper dive into the links between organised crime and football in South America, Insight Crime has a comprehensive database in English.

5   'Slayer of Beltan [sic] Prisoner After Duel. Victim's Body Lies in State – Uruguayan Politics in Ferment', the *New York Times*, 2 April 1920.

6   'Abdón porte & Nacional: An eternal declaration of love', In Bed With Maradona, http://inbedwithmaradona.com/journal/2017/4/29/abdon-porte-nacional-an-eternal-declaration-of-love

ARGENTINA

1   'Who is the 12th Man Tonight' by Pål Ødegård, Josimar, 9 December 2018. http://josimarfootball.com/who-is-the-12th-man-tonight/

2   Gustavo Grabia is the most prolific writer on the *barras* in Argentina. His book *La Doce: La verdadera historia de la barra brava de Boca* (Sudamericana) was hugely controversial.

3   'Lista de víctimas', Salvemos al Futbol, http://salvemosalfutbol.org/lista-de-victimas-de-incidentes-de-violencia-en-el-futbol/

4   *The Palgrave International Handbook of Football and Politics* (Palgrave Macmillan) by Pablo Alabarces, José Garriga Zucal, Verónica Moreira, Gabriela Garton and María Nemesia Hijós.

5   *Football Against the Enemy* (Orion) by Simon Kuper.

6   'Argentine president: I'd rather not have a Boca-River Copa Libertadores final' by Agencia EFE, 24 October 2018, https://www.efe.com/efe/english/sports/argentine-president-i-d-rather-not-have-a-boca-river-copa-libertadores-final/50000266-3791327

7   'Argentina: Buenos Aries mayor Macri on political plans and current situation' released by Wikileaks, written on 5 February 2010, https://wikileaks.org/plusd/cables/10BUENOSAIRES81_a.html

8   By far the best take on the whole super-*Superclasico* debacle was Copa90's feature length Derby Days documentary, *The Biggest Game of All Time*, presented by Eli Mengem. https://www.youtube.com/watch?v=rIG13KfUSkI9 'Argentina losing hooliganism battle – Vélez chief' by Rex Gowar, Reuters, 20 April 2015, https://www.reuters.com/article/soccer-argentina-hooliganism/interview-soccer-argentina-losing-hooliganism-battle-velez-chief-idUKL4N0XH4TA20150420

9   'Argentina losing hooliganism battle – Vélez chief' by Rex Gowar, Reuters, 20 April 2015, https://www.reuters.com/article/soccer-argentina-hooliganism/interview-soccer-argentina-losing-hooliganism-battle-velez-chief-idUKL4N0XH4TA20150420

10 Ibid.

11 'After second test, Maradona is out of World Cup' by Sam Howe Verhovek, *The New York Times*, 1 July 1994. https://www.nytimes.com/1994/07/01/sports/world-cup-94-after-second-test-maradona-is-out-of-world-cup.html

12 'Canigga to play for Benfica' by *Associated Press*, 17 August 1994, https://www.nytimes.com/1994/08/17/sports/sports-people-soccer-caniggia-to-play-for-benfica.html?searchResultPosition=2

13 'Snapshot of a nation: How Argentina's new president deals with the occupied factories will be hugely significant' by Naomi Klein, *The Guardian*, 28 April 2003, https://www.theguardian.com/world/2003/apr/28/usa.globalisation

14 'Violence, Power, Soccer and Drugs: Argentina's Barras Bravas' by Miriam Wells, Insight Crime, 5 June 2014, https://www.insightcrime.org/news/analysis/violence-power-soccer-and-drugs-argentinas-barras-bravas/

15 'El día que Di Zeo les "enseñó" cómo ser barrabravas a los Ultra Sur del Real Madrid' by Gustavo Grabia, Infobae, 4 December 2018, https://www.infobae.com/deportes-2/2018/12/04/el-dia-que-di-zeo-les-enseno-como-ser-barras-brava-a-los-ultra-sur-del-real-madrid/

16 Ibid.

17 *Angels With Dirty Faces: The Footballing History of Argentina* (Orion) by Jonathan Wilson.

18 '128 members of Boca Junior's barra brava banned from attending matches' by *Buenos Aires Times*, 4 April 2019, https://www.batimes.com.ar/news/sports/128-members-of-boca-juniors-barra-brava-banned-from-attending-matches.phtml

BRAZIL

1   'The Stuck Cow' is the closest translation. Another was 'Cow stuck in the mud'. There's also a Brazilian dish of the same name: beef ribs in a thick sauce; a cow stuck in mud.

2   'Soccer's Deadliest Fans: The Troubled World of Brazil's "'Organiza-
     das'" by James Young, *Rolling Stone*, 28 May 2014, https://www.roll-
     ingstone.com/culture/culture-news/soccers-deadliest-fans-the-trou-
     bled-world-of-brazils-organizadas-92741/

3   One caveat with these murder rates. The 2018 figure was astronomically
     high, but it marked a drop of 13 per cent from 2017. 'Brazil's murder
     rate finally fell – and a lot' by Robert Muggah, *Foreign Policy*, 22 April
     2019, https://foreignpolicy.com/2019/04/22/brazils-murder-rate-final-
     ly-fell-and-by-a-lot/

4   'Jair Bolsonaro: Brazil's firebrand leader dubbed the Trump of the
     Tropics' by BBC News, 31 December 2018, https://www.bbc.co.uk/
     news/world-latin-america-45746013

5   'The slave trade in the U.S. and Brazil: Comparisons and Connec-
     tions' by Professor Leonardo Marques, Yale University Press Blog, 21
     November 2016, http://blog.yalebooks.com/2016/11/21/slave-trade-u-
     s-brazil-comparisons-connections/

6   The best book about Jayme de Carvalho was actually written in 2007
     by Cláudio Cruz, alongside Wilson Aquino. *Acima de Tudo Rubro-
     Negro: O Album de Jayme de Carvalho* tells his life story alongside a
     trove of pictures and documents from the era.

7   Ibid.

8   Ibid.

9   There is a brilliant description of Jayme, and how carnival entered
     Brazil's stadiums, in Alex Bellos's seminal *Futebol: The Brazilian Way
     of Life* (Bloomsbury).

10   *Football and the Boundaries of History: Critical Studies in Soccer* (Pal-
     grave MacMillan), Chapter 15, 'The Competitive Party: The Forma-
     tion and Crisis of Organized Fan Groups in Brazil, 1950–1980' by
     Bernardo Buarque de Hollanda.

11   *Futebol Nation: A Footballing History of Brazil* (Penguin) by David
     Goldblatt.

12   Whilst British Pathé has a few videos of the Queen's visit to Brazil
     in 1968, footage of her in the Maracanã was only released by their
     Brazilian counterparts. 'Rainha Elizabeth II No Maracanã – 1968' on
     YouTube, https://www.youtube.com/watch?v=stQDN3RBXzQ

13   'Brazil: 18 months on, authorities must not let Marielle Franco
     killing remain unsolved' by Amnesty International, 12 Septem-

ber 2019, https://www.amnesty.org/en/latest/news/2019/09/brazil-authorities-must-solve-marielle-franco-killing/

PART TWO: NO FACE, NO NAME

ITALY

1   *Football Fascism and Fandom: The UltraS of Italian Football* (Blooms-bury) by Alberto Testa and Gary Armstrong.

2   A good, concise explanation of Italy's ultras can be found in *The Ital-ian ultras: From local divisions to national co-operation* by Dr. Mark Doidge (University of Brighton).

3   'Roma fan "lashed out" at Irishman Sean Cox before Liverpool match' by Eleanor Barlow, *The Irish Times*, 11 October 2018. https://www.irishtimes.com/news/crime-and-law/roma-fan-lashed-out-at-irishman-sean-cox-before-liverpool-match-1.3660168

4   'Liverpool vs Roma: Lawyer representing Italian men charged over violence says both clubs should be punished' by Luke Brown, *The Independent*, 27 April 2018. https://www.independent.co.uk/sport/football/european/liverpool-news-vs-roma-anfield-attack-champions-league-sean-cox-condition-merseyside-police-a8324251.html

5   Aside from his legal career, Contucci also runs a hugely popular AS Roma website that charts the history of the club's ultras http://www.asromaultras.org/

6   A good introduction to the politics of the time is *The Archipelago: Italy Since 1945* (Bloomsbury) by John Foot. In fact, his excellent book on Italian football *Calcio: A History of Italian Football* (HarperCollins) is also well wroth reading.

7   *The Archipelago: Italy Since 1945* (Bloomsbury) by John Foot

8   'La Roma: Soccer and Identity in Rome' by Francesco Ricatti, Annali d'Italianistica Vol. 28, Capital City: Rome 1870–2010 (2010)

9   'Football Violence in Italy' by Antonio Roversi, *International Review for the Sociology of Sport*, 1 December 1991.

10 'Our History', Inter Official Site, https://www.inter.it/en/inter_club/inter-club-history

11 'The Ultras, Racism and Football Culture in Italy' by Carlo Podaliri and Carlo Balestri, in *Fanatics! Power, Identity and Fandom in Foot-ball* (Routledge) ed. Adam Brown.

12 'The Bloody Battle of Genoa' by Nick Davies, *The Guardian*, 17 July 2008, https://www.theguardian.com/world/2008/jul/17/italy.g8

13 'Rumour of police killing triggered Rome match riot' by Peter Popham, *The Independent*, 23 March 2004, https://www.independent.co.uk/news/world/europe/rumour-of-police-killing-triggered-rome-match-riot-5355197.html

14 'Organised crimes' by Vanda Wilcox, *When Saturday Comes*, April 2007, https://www.wsc.co.uk/the-archive/103-Politics/194-organised-crimes

15 'Italian anti-terror law enacted' by BBC News, 30 July 2005, http://news.bbc.co.uk/1/hi/world/europe/4731711.stm

16 'Italy fans rampage after killing' by BBC News, 12 November 2007, http://news.bbc.co.uk/1/hi/world/europe/7090017.stm

17 'Ciao Capitano: The life and tragic death of Roma legend Ago di Bartolomei' by Paul Grech, The Gentleman Ultra blog, 28 November 2016.

18 '16 yrs for De Santis over Esposito' by ANSA English, 25 September 2018, http://www.ansa.it/english/news/general_news/2018/09/25/16-yrs-for-de-santis-over-esposito_3ab5dbf9-1772−4538-8d5f-8224a74b6630.html

19 'Inter fined for "existential" harm to Napoli fan' by Reuters, 5 August 2008, https://uk.reuters.com/article/soccer-inter-existential/soccer-inter-fined-for-existential-harm-to-napoli-fan-idUKL531838020080805

20 'Inter ultra nabbed for fan death' by ANSA English, 31 December 2019 http://www.ansa.it/english/news/2018/12/31/soccer-inter-ultra-leader-nabbed-for-fan-death_36ad00b4-1673-43e5-b416-94fc0edb-02cb.html

21 'The accidental terrorist' by Anne Hanley, *The Independent*, 6 May 1997, https://www.independent.co.uk/news/the-accidental-terror-ist-1259973.html

22 *Hooligans* was was a three-part BBC documentary series. The 'Foreign Fields' episode looked at ultras, *barras bravas* and hooligans around the world. It aired in 2002 but remains a peerless examination of global football fan culture around that time, http://news.bbc.co.uk/2/hi/programmes/hooligans/1960433.stm

23 'Seven held after "mafia attempt" to buy Italian football club Lazio' by Associated Press, 23 July 2008, https://www.theguardian.com/world/2008/jul/23/italy.internationalcrime

24 'Fallita scalata alla Lazio, la procura: "Otto anni agli Irriducibili"' by Lavinia Di Gianvito, *Corriere Della Sera*, 1 October 2013, https://roma.corriere.it/notizie/cronaca/13_ottobre_1/scalata-lazio-chieste-condanne-2223404322730.shtml

25 '"Diabolik": "Bomba sede Irriducibili movente politico, siamo pronti"' by Silvia Mancinelli, AdnKronos, 6 May 2019, https://www.adnkronos.com/fatti/cronaca/2019/05/06/diabolik-bomba-sede-irriducibili-movente-politico-siamo-pronti_EOqukOqMFhn08AiNjPkz5K.html

26 Ibid.

SERBIA

1 Mihajlović's original interview was in *France Football* but Barry Glendenning's feature in *The Irish Times*, from 3 September 2018, gives a good account in English; https://www.irishtimes.com/sport/soccer/out-of-the-shadow-of-the-iron-curtain-red-star-belgrade-are-back-1.3617227

2 By far the best retelling of this story, in English, is 'Hajduk Split v Crvena Zvezda (abandoned)' by Charles Ducksbury in *The Blizzard*, 1 December, 2015, https://www.theblizzard.co.uk/article/hajduk-split-v-crvena-zvezda-abandoned

3 'What Punk Rock Meant to Communist Yugoslavia' by Miljenko Jergović, *The New York Times*, 18 September 2017, https://www.nytimes.com/2017/09/18/opinion/punk-rock-communist-yugoslavia.html

4 'Yugoslavia: 1918-2003' by Tim Judah, BBC History, 17 February 2011, http://www.bbc.co.uk/history/worldwars/wwone/yugoslavia_01.shtml

5 *Yugoslavia: Death of a Nation* (Penguin) by Laura Silber and Allan Little

6 *Yugoslavia: A Concise History* (Palgrave) by Leslie Benson.

7 'Zulu Warriors' for Vice Srbija, https://video.vice.com/rs/video/zulu-warriors/5acf2ffaf1cdb30e574f05b8

8 You can still track down old copies of *Ćao Tifo* in Serbian second hand markets. It's a remarkable read. Not only can you see pictures, taken of and by ultras across Yugoslavia, people would send in artwork too. Pictures would be printed from *curve* all across the world. But the most remarkable section was 'Pišem, Pišeš". I write, you

write. Ultras from across the country would write back and forth to each other in the letters' page about issues of the day. You can browse one issue, number 6, online: https://issuu.com/lokozine/docs/cao_tifo_6__1990_/82

9   *The Serbs: History, Myth and the Destruction of Yugoslavia* (Yale University Press) by Tim Judah.

10 Ibid.

11 Ibid.

12 Ibid.

13 Ibid.

14 There is a large body of academic work that plays down the game's role in the starting of the war. But '1990 Football Riot Becomes National Myth in Croatia' by Sven Milekic, 13 May 2016, for Balkan Insight gives a good summary in English, https://balkaninsight.com/2016/05/13/1990-football-riot-remains-croatia-s-national-myth-05–12-2016/

15 'UN appeal court convicts Serb radical Seselj of war crimes' by BBC News, 11 April 2018, https://www.bbc.co.uk/news/world-europe-43729348

16 The full interview is a very interesting read. Vučić isn't exactly the kind of person you would think to be an ultra, but almost everyone I've interviewed about this agrees that Vučić was likely there. 'Slučaj "Maksimir" – dvadeset godina posle' by Zoran Majdin, *Vreme*, 20 May 2010, https://www.vreme.com/cms/view.php?id=931952

17 As translated in Richard Mill's excellent book, *The Politics of Football in Yugoslavia: Sport, Nationalism and the State'* (I.B. Tauris).

18 There's a wealth of material out there on the crimes of Arkan and his Tigers. Very few people have been convicted. 'Arkan's Paramilitaries: The Tigers Who Escaped Justice' by Balkan Insight, 8 December 2014, is a good place to start. It includes the dark photos of Ron Haviv, who escorted the Tigers as they swept into Bijeljna in eastern Bosnia. His photos, including one of a Tiger kicking a recently executed middle-aged woman in the head, helped to cement Arkan's bloodthirsty reputation in the West. http://www.balkaninsight.com/2014/12/08/arkan-s-paramilitaries-tigers-who-escaped-justice

19 The opening chapter of Franklin Foer's *How Soccer Explains the World* (Harper Perennial) has some interesting details about Arkan

from this period. He also interviews his widow, the singer Ceca, who became the club's president after Arkan's death.

20 *The Butcher's Trail: How the Search for Balkan War Criminals Became the World's Most Successful Manhunt* (Other Press) by Julian Borger.

21 Ibid.

22 The full ICTY indictment can be found on their website and is grim reading;   http://www.icty.org/x/cases/zeljko_raznjatovic/ind/en/ark-ii970930e.pdf

23 'The Three M's: Milosevic, Mugabe, And Maduro' by Steve H. Hanke, African Liberty, 15 May 2019, https://www.african liberty.org/2019/05/15/3-ms-milosevic-r-mugabe-and-maduro/

24 *The Butcher's Trail* (Other Press) by Julian Borger

25 *The Fall of Milosevic: The October 5th Revolution* (Palgrave Macmillan) by Dragan Bujošević and Ivan Radovanović

26 Ibid.

27 '(Im)potent State? Part Two' an Insajder investigation for b92, 10 December 2009, https://www.b92.net/eng/insajder/index. php?yyyy=2009&mm=12&dd=10&nav_id=74525

28 'Serbian President's Brother Met With Infamous Criminal' by Stevan Dojčinović and Bojana Pavlović, OCCRP, 15 April 2019. https://www. occrp.org/en/investigations/serbian-presidents-brother-met-with-infa-mous-criminal

29 'BIRN: Serbian president's brother linked to alleged criminal' by N1, 17 April 2019, http://rs.n1info.com/English/NEWS/a476931/BIRN-Serbian-president-s-brother-linked-to-alleged-criminal.html

30 'BIRN: Stop Targeting Slobodan Georgiev' by Balkan Investigative Reporting Network, 18 April 2019, https://birn.eu.com/news-and-events/birn-stop-targeting-slobodan-georgiev/

31 'KRIK: Probe into Kosovo Serb politician murder includes two more people' by N1, 19 April 2019, http://rs.n1info.com/English/NEWS/a477704/Kosovo-prosecutor-extends-probe-to-two-more-Serbs.html

32 'Nikolić: Hteli su da nas likvidiraju' by M. R. Petrović, Politika, 30 July 2008, http://www.politika.rs/sr/clanak/50381/Nikolic-Hteli-su-da-nas-likvidiraju

33 'Football hooligan extradited to Serbia' by b92, 22 February 2012,https://www.b92.net/eng/news/crimes.php?yyyy=2012&mm=02&dd=22&nav_id=78901

34 'Serbian soccer fans: hooligans or gangsters?' released by Wikileaks, dated 29 October 2009, https://wikileaks.org/plusd/cables/09BELGRADE1266_a.html

35 'Serbia football fans jailed for 2009 Brice Taton murder' by BBC News, 25 January 2011, https://www.bbc.co.uk/news/world-europe-12279960

36 'Vučić: Pušten uhapšeni koji nikoga nije ni pipnuo' by *Politika*, 19 May 2016, http://www.politika.rs/sr/clanak/355372/Vucic-Pusten-uhapseni-koji-nikoga-nije-ni-pipnuo

37 'Authorities accused of "controlling" right-wing hooligans' by b92, 12 February 2016, https://www.b92.net/eng/news/politics.php?yyyy=2016&mm=02&dd=12&nav_id=97023

38 'Serbia's Deadly Mix: Football, Politics and Crime' by Devin Windelspecht, OCCRP, 27 January 2017, https://www.occrp.org/en/blog/6016-serbia-s-deadly-mix-football-politics-and-crime

39 'Foul Play: Serbia's Football Hooligans Get Down to Business' by Ivana Jeremić, Balkan Insight https://balkaninsight.com/2019/07/22/foul-play-serbias-football-hooligans-get-down-to-business/

40 'Splićani u Beogradskom Kaosu. Izjave i fotografije otkrivaju: Hrvati ratovali s Grobarima' by Index HR, 14 December 2017, https://www.index.hr/sport/clanak/detalji-kaosa-u-beogradu-izjave-i-fotografije-otkrivaju-splicani-pomagali-frakciji-grobara-u-napadu/1013648.aspx

GREECE AND MACEDONIA

1 'Greek league suspended after PAOK club president invades pitch with a gun' by Sandy Thin, CNN International, 12 March 2018, https://edition.cnn.com/2018/03/12/sport/paok-aek-team-owner-gun-pitch-invasion-spt/index.html

2 'AEK ends Greek season with first league title in 24 years', Associated Press, 5 May 2018, https://eu.usatoday.com/story/sports/soccer/2018/05/05/aek-ends-greek-season-with-first-league-title-in-24-years/34601979/

3 'Greece wrestles with fan violence' by Niki Kitsantonis, *The New York Times*, 19 April 2007, https://www.nytimes.com/2007/04/19/sports/19iht-GREEKS.1.5350626.html

4 'Greek youths riot after police shoot boy' by Lee Glendinning, *The Guardian*, 7 December 2008, https://www.theguardian.com/world/2008/dec/07/greece

5 'AEK Athens get suspended ban over crowd trouble', BBC Sport, 22 February 2019, https://www.bbc.co.uk/sport/football/47334506

6 'Greek club owners and players prosecuted for match-fixing' by Andy Brown, the Sports Integrity Initiative, 1 March 2018 https://www.sportsintegrityinitiative.com/greek-club-owners-players-prosecuted-match-fixing/

7 'Statement by Ivan Savvidis' by Ivan Savvidis, PAOK FC, 27 April 2017, https://www.paokfc.gr/en/news/20160427-dilosi-ivan-savvidi/

8 'Evangelos Marinakis: Nottingham Forest owner rejects drugs link', BBC Sport, 24 March 2018, https://www.bbc.com/sport/football/43527262

9 'Greece's neo-fascists are on the rise … and now they're going into schools: How Golden Dawn is nurturing the next generation' by Nathalie Savaricas, *The Independent*, 2 February 2013, https://www.independent.co.uk/news/world/europe/greece-s-neo-fascists-are-on-the-rise-and-now-they-re-going-into-schools-how-golden-dawn-is-8477997.html

10 'Are Greek Policemen Really Voting in Droves for Greece's Neo-Nazi Party?' by Max Fisher, *The Atlantic*, 22 June 2012, https://www.theatlantic.com/international/archive/2012/06/are-greek-policemen-really-voting-in-droves-for-greeces-neo-nazi-party/258767/

11 'Olympiakos vs. PAOK abandoned after Oscar Garcia hit by object from crowd' by PA Sport, 26 February 2018, https://www.espn.co.uk/football/olympiakos/story/3398484/olympiakos-vs-paok-abandoned-after-oscar-garcia-hit-in-face-by-object-from-crowd

12 'FIFA warns of "Grexit" if action is not taken to purge Greek soccer,' Ekathimerini, 14 March 2018, http://www.ekathimerini.com/226727/article/ekathimerini/sports/fifa-warns-of-grexit-if-action-not-taken-to-purge-greek-soccer

13 'Ivan Savvidis' by PAOK FC, https://www.paokfc.gr/en/the-club/the-shareholder/

14 Ibid.

15 'The New Greek Oligarchy' by Alexander Clapp, The American Interest, 5 January 2018, https://www.the-american-interest.com/2018/01/05/new-greek-oligarchy/

16 'Savvidis sells Donskoy Tabak and Greek subsidiary to Japan Tobacco' by Ekathimerini, 16 March 2018, http://www.ekathimerini.

com/226804/article/ekathimerini/business/savvidis-sells-donskoy-tabak-and-greek-subsidiary-to-japan-tobacco

17 'Let them eat Alexander the Great statues' by Valerie Hopkins, Foreign Policy, 19 June 2016, https://foreignpolicy.com/2016/06/19/let-them-eat-alexander-the-great-statues-skopje-2014-macedonia-colorful-revolution/

18 I had reported on the wire-tapping scandal in Macedonia before. You can find more background on that issue in 'Bombs of Skopje', POLITICO Magazine, 24 May 2015, https://www.politico.com/magazine/story/2015/05/bombs-over-skopje-118218_Page2.html

19 'Thousands clash with police in Athens over Macedonia name deal' by Philip Andrew Churm, Euronews, 20 January 2019, https://www.euronews.com/2019/01/20/thousands-clash-with-police-in-athens-over-macedonia-name-deal

20 'Greece to expel two Russian officials amid Macedonia dispute' by Kerin Hope, Financial Times, 11 July 2018, https://www.ft.com/content/68e75e3a-8511-11e8-96dd-fa565ec55929

21 'Russian Businessman Behind Unrest in Macedonia' by Saska Cvetkovska, OCCRP, 16 July 2018, https://www.occrp.org/en/investigations/8329-russian-businessman-behind-unrest-in-macedonia

22 'Macedonia Suspects A Greek-Russian Billionaire Paid For Violent Protests To Prevent It From Joining NATO' by J. Lester Feder, Buzzfeed News, 16 July 2018, https://www.buzzfeednews.com/article/lesterfeder/macedonia-russia-nato

23 'In Pictures: Macedonia "Name" Protest Turns Violent' by Siniša Jakov Marušić, Balkan Insight,18 June 2018, https://balkaninsight.com/2018/06/18/in-pictures-macedonia-name-protest-turns-violent-06–18-2018/

24 You can read Tarčulovski's ICTY Indictment here: http://www.icty.org/x/cases/boskoski_tarculovski/ind/en/bos-ii050309e.pdf

25 'Macedonia Made Huge Payments to War Crimes Convict' by Siniša Jakov Marušić, Balkan Insight, 19 October 2017, https://balkaninsight.com/2017/10/19/macedonia-paid-hefty-sum-to-war-crimes-convict-10–19-2017/

26 'Macedonia Puts Mob Invaders of Parliament on Trial' by Siniša Jakov Marušić, Balkan Insight, 22 August 2018, https://balkaninsight.

com/2018/08/22/trial-starts-in-macedonia-parliament-rampage-case-08–22-2018/

27 'Balkans' political football keeps hooligans close to heart of power' by Aleksandar Manasiev, *The Guardian*, 29 November 2012, https://www.theguardian.com/football/2012/nov/29/balkans-political-football-hooligans-power

28 The role of ultras in anti-LGBT attacks in the region at the start of the decade is summed up in 'LGBT Violence in the Balkans' by Valerie Hopkins, Open Democracy, 23 May 2013, https://www.opendemocracy.net/en/5050/lgbt-violence-in-balkans/

ALBANIA AND KOSOVO

1 'Serbia v Albania: surreal provocation and violence show lessons not learned' by Nick Ames and Saša Ibrulj, *The Guardian*, 15 October 2014, https://www.theguardian.com/football/2014/oct/15/serbia-albania-provocation-violence-lessons-not-learned

2 'There was a familiar face in Serbia v Albania riot – but why was he there?' by Vladimir Novaković, *The Guardian*, 16 October 2014, https://www.theguardian.com/football/blog/2014/oct/16/serbia-albania-riot-ivan-bogdanov

3 'Disciplinary decision on Serbia-Albania match', UEFA.com, 24 October 2014, https://www.uefa.com/insideuefa/disciplinary/news/newsid=2172207.html

4 *The Serbs: History, Myth and The Destruction of Yugoslavia* (Yale University Press) by Tim Judah.

5 'On a Garage Floor in Kosovo, A Gruesome Serbian Harvest' by Chris Hedges, *The New York Times*, 10 March 1998, https://www.nytimes.com/1998/03/10/world/on-a-garage-floor-in-kosovo-a-gruesome-serbian-harvest.html

6 'Masked ringleader of crowd trouble during Italy-Serbia clash identified by tattoos', *The Daily Telegraph*, 13 October 2010 https://www.telegraph.co.uk/sport/football/teams/serbia/8061619/Masked-ringleader-of-crowd-trouble-during-Italy-Serbia-clash-identified-by-tattoos.html

7 'Autochthonous', Top Channel, 14 July 2015, https://www.youtube.com/watch?v=2_ii1w5hBLo

8 'Tifozat Kuq e Zi/ Slovenia – Shqiperi/ Ballist Morina', YouTube, 10 September 2013, https://www.youtube.com/watch?v=MJNKyn14wvM

9 'Macedonia blames Kosovans for deadly Kumanovo clashes', by BBC News, 10 May 2015, https://www.bbc.com/news/world-europe-32680904

10 'Guns, Drones and Burning Flags: The Real Story of Serbia v Albania', Copa90, 17 October 2015, https://www.youtube.com/watch?v=WuUUGIn8QuE

11 'Ending an Albania-Serbia Game and Inciting a Riot, With a Joystick' by James Montague, *The New York Times*, 7 October 2015, https://www.nytimes.com/2015/10/08/sports/soccer/as-albania-faces-serbia-meeting-the-drone-pilot-who-ended-their-last-match.html

12 *Modern Albania: From Dictatorship to Democracy in Europe* (New York University Press) by Fred C. Abrahams

13 'Albania's Big Dream Comes True – With a Little Help From PM,' by James Masters, CNN International, 13 October 2015, https://edition.cnn.com/2015/10/13/sport/albania-football-european-championships-france-2016/index.html

14 'Albania trying to prevent extradition of Morina from Croatia', B92, 7 September 2017, https://www.b92.net/eng/news/region.php?yyyy=2017&mm=09&dd=07&nav_id=102259

15 'Legija poručio Morini: Robijaši će te je*ati čim stigneš', Telegraf, 31 August 2017 https://www.telegraf.rs/vesti/hronika/2891932-legija-porucio-morini-robijasi-ce-te-jeati-cim-stignes

16 'Albanian fan wanted for sparking soccer match violence freed', by Llazar Semini, Associated Press, 10 July 2018, https://apnews.com/0553b27c81494e199be844dc2357e9ca/Albanian-fan-wanted-for-sparking-soccer-match-violence-freed

PART THREE: AGAINST MODERN FOOTBALL

UKRAINE

1 'Kateryna Handziuk: Ukraine activist, 33, died from acid attack' by Madeline Roache, Al Jazeera, 5 November 2018, https://www.euronews.com/2019/06/06/kateryna-handziuk-five-men-jailed-over-acid-attack-on-ukraine-anti-corruption-activist

2 'Skin growths saved poisoned Ukrainian president' by Andy Coghlan, *New Scientist*, 7 August 2009, https://www.newscientist.com/article/dn17570-skin-growths-saved-poisoned-ukrainian-president/

3   This is a deep and complicated subject. Tymoshenko is no angel but her arrest in the run-up to Euro 2012, which Ukraine was co-hosting with Poland, became a scandal; https://edition.cnn.com/2012/05/08/sport/football/football-euro-2012-ukraine-tymoshenko/index.html

4   'From Glasgow to Marseille: the story of Russian football hooliganism' by Avram Liebenau, Pushkin House, 1 April 2019, https://www.push-kinhouse.org/blog/2019/4/1/from-glasgow-to-marseille-the-story-of-russian-football-hooliganism

5   'Soccer Wars Heating Up: When It Comes to Violence, Soviet Fans Can Hold Their Own With Rest of World' by United Press International, *Los Angeles Times,* 14 November 1987, https://www.latimes.com/archives/la-xpm-1987–11-14-sp-5299-story.html

6   Ibid.

7   A good article I came across was this *Guardian* Long Read by Simon Parkin called 'The Rise of Russia's neo-Nazi Football Hooligans'. Whilst the headline is a little sensationalist, Parkin speaks to Denis Nikitin, who had become one of the most important figures in the far-right football scene in Europe; https://www.theguardian.com/news/2018/apr/24/russia-neo-nazi-football-hooligans-world-cup

8   Ibid.

9   'Ultras: The Brave Hearts' by Dima Kolchinsky, https://www.youtube.com/watch?v=7IA5GrQKAzc&t=137s

10 'How Canada's embassy in Ukraine was used as pawn in 2014 uprising' by Murray Brewster, the Canadian Press, 12 July 2015, https://www.macleans.ca/news/world/how-canadas-embassy-in-ukraine-was-used-as-pawn-in-2014-uprising/

11 'Ukraine crisis: the neo-Nazi brigade fighting pro-Russian separatists' by Tom Parfitt, *Daily Telegraph,* 11 August 2014, https://www.telegraph.co.uk/news/worldnews/Europe/ukraine/11025137/Ukraine-crisis-the-neo-Nazi-brigade-fighting-pro-Russian-separatists.html

12 Some of the best reporting around Ukraine's far-right, especially Azov, has been done by Canadian journalist Michael Colborne. 'Inside the Extremist Group That Dreams of Ruling Ukraine' by Michael Colborne, *Haaretz,* 23 February 2019, https://www.haaretz.com/world-news/europe/.premium-inside-the-extremist-group-that-dreams-of-ruling-ukraine-1.6936835

13 I first recounted this story in my previous book *The Billionaires Club: The Unstoppable Rise of Football's Super-Rich Owners* (Bloomsbury)

14 'Metinvest Announces Financial Results For 2018', Metinvest Holding, https://metinvestholding.com/Content/CmsFile/en/finreleases__Metinvest_Financial%20release_IFRS%20FY2018%20results.pdf

15 'Ultras: The Brave Hearts' by Dima Kolchinsky, https://www.youtube.com/watch?v=7IA5GrQKAzc&t=137s

16 Ibid.

17 'The Battle of Ilovaisk' by Oksana Grytsenko, *Kyiv Post*, 5 April 2018, https://www.kyivpost.com/ilovaisk-intro?cn-reloaded=1

18 'Sol Campbell warns fans to stay away from Euro 2012' by BBC News, Panorama Euro 2012: Stadiums of Hate, 28 May 2012, https://www.bbc.co.uk/news/uk-18192375

19 'Who Are Ukraine's "Ultras"?' by Daisy Sindelar, Radio Free Europe, 27 January 2014, https://www.rferl.org/a/ukraine-protests-sports-fans-euromaidan/25244357.html

20 FARE regularly updates a document that shows examples of far-right and other discriminatory symbols, words, banners and phrases displayed at football matches in Europe and around the world. Ultras are constantly looking for the identity of anyone who might represent FARE at their matches, who they view as spies; https://farenet.org/get-involved/report-discrimination/global-guide-discriminatory-practices-football/

21 'Ukraine's National Militia: "We're not neo-Nazis, we just want to make our country better"' by Marc Bennetts, *The Guardian*, 13 March 2018, https://www.theguardian.com/world/2018/mar/13/ukraine-far-right-national-militia-takes-law-into-own-hands-neo-nazi-links

22 'Ukrainian Far-Right Fighters, White Supremacists Trained by Major European Security Firm' by Oleksiy Kuzmenko, Bellingcat, 30 August 2018, https://www.bellingcat.com/news/uk-and-europe/2018/08/30/ukrainian-far-right-fighters-white-supremacists-trained-major-european-security-firm/

23 'Interior Ministry denies connection with National Corps Party' by UNIAN, 11 March 2019, https://www.unian.info/politics/10475469-interior-ministry-denies-connection-with-national-corps-party.html

24 'With Axes and Hammers, Far-Right Vigilantes Destroy Another Romany camp in Kyiv' by Christopher Miller, Radio Free Europe,

8 June 2018, https://www.rferl.org/a/ukraine-far-right-vigilantes-destroy-another-romany-camp-in-kyiv/29280336.html

25 'Joint Letter to Ukraine's Minister of Interior Affairs and Prosecutor General Concerning Radical Groups', Human Rights Watch, 14 June 2018, https://www.hrw.org/news/2018/06/14/joint-letter-ukraines-minister-interior-affairs-and-prosecutor-general-concerning

26 'Ukraine's National Militia: "We're not neo-Nazis, we just want to make our country better"' by Marc Bennetts, The Guardian, 13 March 2018, https://www.theguardian.com/world/2018/mar/13/ukraine-far-right-national-militia-takes-law-into-own-hands-neo-nazi-links

27 'Dynamo Kiev defy Ukrainian FA and refuse to play in Mariupol over safety fears' by Mark Baber, Inside World Football, 23 August 2017, http://www.insideworldfootball.com/2017/08/23/dynamo-kiev-defy-ukrainian-fa-refuse-play-mariupol-safety-fears/

28 Ibid.

29 'Mariupol against Dynamo and the shadow of Mariupolgate' by Vadim Furmanov, Futbolgrad, 30 March, 2018, http://www.futbolgrad.com/mariupol-dynamo-mariupolgate/

30 'Despair in Luhansk as residents count the dead' by Shaun Walker, The Guardian, 11 September 2014, https://www.theguardian.com/world/2014/sep/11/despair-luhansk-residents-count-dead

31 'Football in Crimea: The club split in two by Russia's invasion' by Shaun Walker, The Guardian, 11 June 2018, https://www.theguardian.com/world/2018/jun/11/crimea-football-russia-annexation-divided-tavria-simferopol

GERMANY

1 'Borussia Dortmund considering share flotation', BBC World Service, 5 October 2000, http://news.bbc.co.uk/1/hi/world/europe/956894.stm

2 Dortmund very nearly went out of business in 2002 according to Thomas Tress, the CFO at the time. 'Back from the brink: Borussia Dortmund's remarkable recovery' by Eoin Connolly, SportsPro, 20 May 2013, http://www.sportspromedia.com/analysis/back_from_the_brink_borussia_dortmunds_remarkable_recovery

3 By far the best account of Borussia Dortmund's fan culture is given in Building the Yellow Wall: The Incredible Rise and Cult Appeal of Borussia Dortmund (Weidenfeld & Nicolson) by Uli Hesse.

4   Ibid.

5   'Borussia Dortmund – Malaga C.F. CHOREO Champions
     League', YouTube, 11 April 2013, https://www.youtube.com/
     watch?v=HCNm5EPTFDo

6   Of all the people writing about German football and fan culture,
     the most incisive and illuminating is Matt Ford. 'Fear on the Yellow
     Wall: Borussia Dortmund ultras threatened by right-wing hooligans'
     by Matt Ford, Deutsche Welle, 19 November, 2018, https://www.
     dw.com/en/fear-on-the-yellow-wall-borussia-dortmund-ultras-threat-
     ened-by-right-wing-hooligans/a-46364501

7   Ibid.

8   Ibid.

9   One of the best resources on fascist and anti-fascist banners in Ger-
     man football is the Twitter account of Deutsche Welle journalist Felix
     Tamsut, @ftamsut, 16 September 2018, https://twitter.com/ftamsut/
     status/1041343412086235141?lang=en

10   Ibid.

11   Felix Tamsut, @ftamsut, 18 November 2018, https://twitter.com/
     ftamsut/status/1064122038892277760

12   Ibid.

13   'Konspiratives Rechtsrock-Konzert bei Hannover geplant', *Die Zeit*, 16
     May 2011, https://blog.zeit.de/stoerungsmelder/2011/05/16/konspira-
     tives-rechtsrock-konzert-bei-hannover-geplant_6296

14   '"They destroyed my husband's life": When German hooligans ram-
     paged in France', Matt Ford, Deutsche Welle, 21 June 2018, https://
     www.dw.com/en/they-destroyed-my-husbands-life-when-german-
     hooligans-rampaged-in-france/a-44331562

15   'Werder-Fans provozieren Polizeieinsatz gegen Rechtsradikale',
     Der Spiegel, 9 November 2008, https://www.spiegel.de/sport/
     fussball/in-bochum-werder-fans-provozieren-polizeieinsatz-
     gegen-rechtsradikale-a-589325.html

16   'Anti-Islamist Riots in Germany: Hooligans Against Salafists',
     VICE News, 17 December 2014, https://www.youtube.com/
     watch?v=NRZiTreKcCk

17   'Dynamo Dresden fined £54,000 over severed bull's head thrown by
     fans', *The Guardian*, 8 November 2016, https://www.theguardian.
     com/football/2016/nov/08/dynamo-dresden-fined-fans-severed-bulls-
     head-pitch-red-bull-leipzig

18 'Dortmund's south stand to be closed for Wolfsburg match', Deutsche Welle, 13 February 2017, https://www.dw.com/en/dortmunds-south-stand-to-be-closed-for-wolfsburg-match/a-37528838

19 'When chants become crimes: Borussia Dortmund fans fined for defamatory songs' by Matt Ford, Deutsche Welle, 3 June 2019, https://www.dw.com/en/when-chants-become-crimes-borussia-dortmund-fans-fined-for-defamatory-songs/a-49010074

20 'Bundesliga clubs vote to retain 50+1 rule and VAR' by Matt Ford, Deutsche Welle, 22 March 2018, https://www.dw.com/en/bundesliga-clubs-vote-to-retain-501-rule-and-var/a-43089324

21 'Why Jadon Sancho was pelted with black tennis balls during Borussia Dortmund's match at Nurnberg', *Irish Mirror*, 18 February 2019, https://www.irishmirror.ie/sport/soccer/soccer-news/jadon-sancho-pelted-black-tennis-14017726

22 'Syrian Is Convicted in Stabbing Death That Set Off Riots in Germany,' by Melissa Eddy, *The New York Times*, 22 August 2019, https://www.nytimes.com/2019/08/22/world/europe/chemitz-stabbing-germany-riots.html

23 'German right-wing extremists planned "hunt" of migrants: reports' by Cristina Burack, Deutsche Welle, 26 August 2019, https://www.dw.com/en/german-right-wing-extremists-planned-hunt-of-migrants-reports/a-50176487

24 The stories of women in football fan culture are criminaly undertold. But there's loads of great stories to be found on the Frantastic Females website: https://www.fan-tastic-females.org/index.php/de/

25 'Babelsberg to stay in German leagues after compromise deal on Nazi controversy' by Matt Pearson, Deutsche Welle, 7 March 2018, https://www.dw.com/en/babelsberg-to-stay-in-german-leagues-after-compromise-deal-on-nazi-controversy/a-42871536

26 Ibid.

27 'Why was a Neo-Nazi hooligan mourned at a football game in Germany?' by Felix Tamsut, Deutsche Welle, 14 March 2019, https://www.dw.com/en/why-was-a-neo-nazi-hooligan-mourned-at-a-football-game-in-germany/a-47856332

SWEDEN

1 '"Rebuilding Confidence" – The Introduction Of Supporter Dialogue Police In Stockholm' by Maria Lemberg, *Conflict And Cooperation – Dialogue-based work in Swedish football: challenges and working methods* (Enable Sweden)

2 'Swedish game called off after fan killed', Associated Press, 30 March 2014, https://apnews.com/53b8180b88ff4c13a36422aa57eeb995

3 'Planstormning avbröt derbyt: "Skam"' by Jonathan Kvarnström, SVT Sport, 17 October 2016, https://www.svt.se/sport/fotboll/orligheter-i-dif-klacken-avbrot-derbyt

4 'Henrik Larsson steps in as son Jordan is attacked by masked hooligans after Helsingborgs suffer relegation' by Spencer Morgan, *Daily Mail*, 20 November 2016, https://www.dailymail.co.uk/sport/sportsnews/article-3954834/Henrik-Larsson-steps-son-Jordan-attacked-masked-hooligans-Helsingborgs-suffer-relegation.html

5 'Shocking scenes as fans fight in the stands during fiery Swedish derby between Hammarby and Djurgårdens' by Liam Prenderville, *The Daily Mirror*, 20 April 2018, https://www.mirror.co.uk/sport/football/news/shocking-scenes-fans-fight-stands-12454937

6 'Swedish soccer hooligans wear Muslim niqabs to get around newly imposed mask ban' by Marissa Payne, *Washington Post*, 4 April 2017, https://www.washingtonpost.com/news/early-lead/wp/2017/04/04/swedish-soccer-hooligans-wear-muslim-niqabs-to-get-around-newly-imposed-mask-ban/

7 'Fem punkter som avslöjar RF-basen Björn Eriksson' by Frida Sundkvist and Noa Bachner, *Expressen*, 3 June 2019, https://www.expressen.se/sport/fotboll/allsvenskan/fem-punkter-som-avslojar-rf-basen-bjorn-eriksson/

8 'TV the key to Sweden's long love affair with English football' by Phillip O'Connor, Reuters, 6 June 2018, https://uk.reuters.com/article/us-soccer-worldcup-swe-eng-television/tv-the-key-to-swedens-long-love-affair-with-english-football-idUKKBN1JW10T

9 'Sweden' by Aage Radmann and Torbjörn Andersson, *The Palgrave International Handbook of Football and Politics* (Palgrave Macmillian)

10 Ibid.

11 'Polisen lämnade kritiserade gruppen: "De vill ha situationer där man kan använda våld"' by Malena Johansson, *Dagens Nyheter*, 27 July 2019 https://www.dn.se/sport/fotboll/polisen-lamnade-kritiserade-gruppen-de-vill-ha-situationer-dar-man-kan-anvanda-vald/

12 'Sweden' by Aage Radmann and Torbjörn Andersson, *The Palgrave International Handbook of Football and Politics* (Palgrave Macmillian)

13 'Krakow Police Hold Five for Machete Killing' by Thomas Crestodina, *The Krakow Post*, 19 January 2011, http://www.krakowpost.com/2496/2011/01

14 '"The Hooligans were the club"' by James Montague, *The New York Times*, 17 February 2019, https://www.nytimes.com/2019/02/17/sports/wisla-krakow-hooligans-kuba.html

15 'Wisła Krakow football hooligans give Nazi salutes at Roma Lazio derby match" by Anthony Casey, *The Krakow Post*, 27 May 2015, http://www.krakowpost.com/9475/2015/05/wisla-krakow-football-hooligans-give-nazi-salutes-at-roma-lazio-derby-match

16 Szymon Jadczak went on to write a book about the goings on at the club called *Wisła w ogniu* (Wydawnictwo Otwarte) or 'Wisła on fire" https://www.tvn24.pl/magazyn-tvn24/jak-wisla-zaplacila-fortune-pielegniarce-czyli-wielki-szwindel-w-polskiej-pilce,234,4043

17 'Protestaktionerna under Stockholmsderbyt" by Frida Fagerlund, *Aftonbladet*, 2 June 2019, https://www.aftonbladet.se/sportbladet/fotboll/a/70jdVK/protestaktionerna-under-stockholmsderbyt

PART FOUR: THE NEW OLD WORLD

TURKEY

1 There are two fantastic books in English on the history and politics of Turkish football. *The Passion: Football and the Story of Modern Turkey* (I.B. Tauris) by Patrick Keddie and *Welcome to Hell? In Search of the Real Turkish Football* (W&N) by John McManus.

2 'The Legacy of the Gezi Protests in Turkey' by Özge Zihnioğlu, Carnegie Europe https://carnegieeurope.eu/2019/10/24/legacy-of-gezi-protests-in-turkey-pub-80142

3 'Istanbul United: protests bring rival fans together, for now' by Darren Butler, Reuters, 4 June 2013, https://www.reuters.com/article/us-turkey-protests-soccer/istanbul-united-protests-bring-rival-fans-together-for-now-idUSBRE9530ZE20130604

4 'Political football: 'pro-government' club shakes up Turkish league' by Laura Pitel, *Financial Times*, 29 March 2018, https://www.ft.com/content/d18a2dc4-2dfe-11e8-a34a-7e7563b0b0f4

5 'Born in a Cafe, Raised to be African Champions: 100 Years of Esperance de Tunis' by Maher Mezahi, Copa90, 14 February 2019, https://www.youtube.com/watch?v=wRF4sYhzmoI

6 I go into more detail about Egypt's ultras in my first book, *When Friday Comes: Football, War and Revolution* (deCoubertin).

7 'How Algerian Football Fans Helped Topple a Dictator' by Maher Mezahi, Copa90, 15 May 2019, https://www.youtube.com/watch?v=lj-unztOgzQ

8 'Two dead and 49 injured after violent clashes during Raja Casablanca match', Associated Press, 20 March 2016, https://www.theguardian.com/football/2016/mar/20/two-dead-49-injured-violent-clashes-raja-casablanca

9 'Hooliganisme. Ultras Raja: le tribunal condamne Skwadra, alias Belkadi, à 6 mois de prison ferme' by Hassan Benadad, 360 Sport, 23 April 2016, http://sport.le360.ma/botola-pro-1/hooliganisme-ultras-raja-le-tribunal-condamne-skwadra-alias-belkadi-6-mois-de-prison-ferme-8640

10 'The View from the Stands' by Elif Batuman, *The New Yorker*, 27 February 2011. https://www.newyorker.com/magazine/2011/03/07/the-view-from-the-stands

11 *Welcome to Hell? In Search of the Real Turkish Football* (W&N) by John McManus gives a thorough account of the events surrounding the murder of the two Leeds United supporters.

12 'Fenerbahce want league suspended after bus shooting', BBC Sport, 5 April 2015, https://www.bbc.co.uk/sport/football/32189667

13 'Police, Beşiktaş fans clash before last game at historic Istanbul stadium' by Hürriyet Daily News, 11 May 2013, http://www.hurriyetdailynews.com/police-besiktas-fans-clash-before-last-game-at-historic-istanbul-stadium-46690

14 'Turkish government to ban political slogans in football games' by Hürriyet Daily News, 31 July 2013, http://www.hurriyetdaily-

news.com/turkish-government-to-ban-political-slogans-in-football-games–51773

15 'Turkish football fans face life in prison for "coup attempt" during Gezi protests', Hürriyet Daily News, 8 September 2014, http://www.hurriyetdailynews.com/turkish-football-fans-face-life-in-prison-for-coup-attempt-during-gezi-protests-71428

16 *Welcome to Hell? In Search of the Real Turkish Football* (W&N) by John McManus

17 *The Passion: Football and the Story of Modern Turkey* (I.B. Tauris) by Patrick Keddie

18 Ibid.

19 'Erdoğan "AK gençliği" Başakşehir tribününe çağırdı: Şampiyonluğa oynuyorsunuz', Diken, 14 April 2018, http://www.diken.com.tr/erdogan-ak-gencligi-basaksehir-tribunune-cagirdi-sampiyonluga-oynuyorsunuz/

20 'Ocalan plea over Galatasaray match', BBC News, 17 May 2000, http://news.bbc.co.uk/1/hi/world/europe/752329.stm

21 'Istanbul Besiktas Turkey: Stadium blasts kill 38 people', BBC News, 11 December 2016, https://www.bbc.co.uk/news/world-europe-38276794

22 'Gülen probe launched into Galatasaray's 'Rocky' poster', Hürriyet Daily News, 24 October 2017, http://www.hurriyetdailynews.com/gulen-probe-launched-into-galatasarays-rocky-poster-121323

23 'Turkish authorities cancel Istanbul mayoral election' by Zia Weise, POLITICO, 6 May 2019, https://www.politico.eu/article/turkish-authorities-cancel-istanbul-mayoral-election/

24 'Outcry as Turkey orders rerun of Istanbul mayoral election', Reuters, 6 May 2019, https://www.theguardian.com/world/2019/may/06/turkey-orders-rerun-of-istanbul-election-in-blow-to-opposition

25 'Election chiefs order re-run of Istanbul poll Erdogan lost' by Hannah Lucinda Smith, *The Times*, 7 May 2019, https://www.thetimes.co.uk/article/election-chiefs-order-re-run-of-istanbul-poll-erdogan-lost-fwrkqd2h9

UNITED STATES

1 'How LAFC rose from the ashes of Chivas USA and aims to be the team of Los Angeles' by Kevin Baxter, *Los Angeles Times*, 27 April

2018, https://www.latimes.com/sports/soccer/la-sp-lafc-creation-20180427-htmlstory.html

2 Back in 2016 I travelled to St Louis for Super Bowl 50, just as the Rams were being moved to LA. Anger at Kroenke, and the NFL, was widespread. There's a chapter dedicated to it in my book *The Billionaires Club: The Unstoppable Rise of Football's Super-Rich Owners* (Bloomsbury).

3 '2018 MLS Attendance', Soccer Stadium Digest, 28 October 2018, https://soccerstadiumdigest.com/2018-mls-attendance/

4 'New Jersey Red Bulls and New York City fans clash ahead of derby', *The Guardian*, 10 August 2015, https://www.theguardian.com/football/video/2015/aug/10/new-jersey-red-bulls-new-york-city-fans-clash-ahead-of-derby-video

5 'I Want to Import British Football Hooliganism into the US' by Nick Chester, VICE, 23 January 2019, https://www.vice.com/en_uk/article/8xy9bb/i-want-to-import-british-football-hooliganism-into-the-us

6 LAFC lists all its owners on their website: https://www.lafc.com/club/ownership

7 'MLS Ultras: plastic wannabes or sign of a thriving league?' by Graham Ruthven, *The Guardian*, 25 September 2018, https://www.theguardian.com/football/2018/sep/25/mls-ultras-fans-supporters-groups

8 'MLS Lifts Ban on Signs Featuring the Iron Front', *New York Times*, 24 September 2019, https://www.nytimes.com/2019/09/24/sports/soccer/mls-iron-front.html

INDONESIA

1 'Indonesia's hooligan football culture has killed 74 fans', ABC News, 11 February 2019, https://www.abc.net.au/news/2019–02-12/indonesia-football-culture-has-killed-74-fans/10794186

2 I wouldn't recommend watching the mobile-phone footage of his death, which was widely shared on social media in Indonesia: https://www.scmp.com/sport/football/article/2165681/indonesian-football-fan-beaten-death-rival-supporters-persib-bandung

3 Ibid.

4 'Buckfast crimewave revealed' by Stuart Macdonald, *Daily Record*, 4 May 2013, https://www.dailyrecord.co.uk/news/scottish-news/buckfast-crimewave-revealed-police-figures-1868308

5   'Persib fan attacks manager Miljan Radovic following loss to Perse-
     baya Surabaya,' Fox Sports Asia, 8 March 2019, https://www.foxsport-
     sasia.com/football/asian-football/1054996/persib-fan-attacks-manag-
     er-miljan-radovic-following-loss-to-persebaya-surabaya/
6   For a more in-depth look at this bloody period of Indonesia's history,
     watch the Oscar-nominated documentary *The Act of Killing*, https://
     www.newyorker.com/news/news-desk/the-propaganda-precursor-to-
     the-act-of-killing
7   *The Palgrave International Handbook of Football and Politics* (Pal-
     grave), 'Indonesia' chapter by Dr Andy Fuller.
8   'Thanks to FIFA and National Politics, Indonesian Soccer is a Giant
     Mess' by Rowan Kane, VICE, 10 March 2016, https://www.vice.com/
     en_au/article/yp8g35/thanks-to-fifa-and-national-politics-indonesian-
     soccer-is-a-giant-mess
9   'Jakarta's hooligan problem: violence and deaths surround "Jakmania"
     football fans' by Larissa Huda, *The Guardian*, 21 November 2016,
     https://www.theguardian.com/cities/2016/nov/21/jakarta-hooligan-
     violence-jakmania-persija-football-fans
10   'Celtic fans "brawl with police" in AIK stadium at half-time in
     Europa League qualifier', *The Herald*, 29 August 2019, https://
     www.heraldscotland.com/sport/17869364.celtic-fans-brawl-
     police-aik-stadium-half-time-europa-league-qualifier/
11   'The Far Right Just Got Humiliated in Ukraine's Election – but
     Don't Write It Off Just Yet' by Michael Colborne, *Haaretz*, 22 July
     2019,   https://www.haaretz.com/world-news/europe/.premium-the-
     far-right-just-got-humiliated-in-ukraine-s-election-but-don-t-write-it-
     off-1.7563138
12   'The Skinhead Terrorists' by Charles Clover, *Financial Times*, 3 De-
     cember 2010, https://www.ft.com/content/21553438-fcda-11df-ae2d-
     00144feab49a
13   'Friday Night Fights With Ukraine's Far Right' by Michael Colborne,
     New Republic, 9 July 2019, https://newrepublic.com/article/154434/
     friday-night-fights-ukraines-far-right
14   'Бывший гражданин Беларуси из "Азова" купил квартиры в Киеве
     и самолет, а также заработал $1 миллион', Nasha Niva, 19 January
     2017, https://nn.by/?c=ar&i=183990&lang=ru

15 Publicly available documents like this have been uncovered and digitised by Kancelarska Sotnia (The White Collar Hundred), part of Bihus.Info, a Ukrainian anti-corruption NGO: https://declarations.com.ua/en/declaration/nacp_15a4f059-f27b-4b89-9ad9-d3546de6a309

16 'Far-right Ukrainian activists say they were 'only in Hong Kong for protest tourism' as concerns grow they could help authorities delegitimise movement' by Alvin Lum, *South China Morning Post,* 4 December 2019, https://www.scmp.com/news/hong-kong/politics/article/3040625/far-right-ukrainian-activists-say-they-were-only-hong-kong

17 'Turkey's opposition wins rerun of Istanbul mayoral vote' by Tessa Fox, Al Jazeera English, 24 June 2019, https://www.aljazeera.com/news/2019/06/erdogan-candidate-concedes-defeat-istanbul-vote-190623162700306.html

18 'Galatasaray win 22nd Turkish title after beating closest rival' by Ece Toksabay, Reuters, 19 May 2019, https://uk.reuters.com/article/uk-soccer-turkey-championship/galatasaray-win-22nd-turkish-title-after-beating-closest-rival-idUKKCN1SP0PJ

19 'Lawmakers draft bill against fan violence in Turkey', Daily Sabah, 26 June 2019, https://www.dailysabah.com/football/2019/06/26/lawmakers-draft-bill-against-fan-violence-in-turkey

20 'Backed by Russian billionaire, Greek city celebrates title' by Costas Kantouris, Associated Press, 22 April 2019, https://apnews.com/c611b4cfc2be49868a866f434cd635c0

21 'PAOK's gun-slinging owner Savvidis in new shoot-out over report he also owns Xanthi' by Paul Nicholson, Inside World Football, 4 December 2019, http://www.insideworldfootball.com/2019/12/04/paoks-gun-slinging-owner-savvidis-new-shoot-report-also-owns-xanthi/

22 'A media statement from PAOK FC', PAOK FC, 3 December 2019, https://www.paokfc.gr/en/news/20191203-anakoinosi-pae-paok/

23 'Wilson Witzel diz que vai 'abater' criminoso que 'coloque em risco' a sociedade e promete criar 500 mil consultas médicas', Globo, 18 September, 2018, https://g1.globo.com/rj/rio-de-janeiro/noticia/2018/09/18/wilson-witzel-vai-abater-criminosos-que-coloquem-em-risco-a-sociedade-e-promete-criar-500-mil-consultas-medicas.ghtml

24 'Brazilians blame Rio governor's shoot-to-kill policy for death of girl' by Dom Phillips, *The Guardian*, 22 September 2019, https://www. theguardian.com/world/2019/sep/22/brazilians-blame-rio-governors- shoot-to-kill-policy-for-death-of-agatha-felix-girl-8

25 'Serbian Finance Minister: Red Star, Partizan supported equally', N1, 22 October 2019, http://rs.n1info.com/English/NEWS/a537055/Serbi- an-Finance-Minister-Red-Star-Partizan-supported-equally.html

26 'Minister reveals which club received more money from the state – Red Star or Partizan!', *Telegraf*, 22 October 2019, https://www.tele- graf.rs/english/3114637-minister-reveals-which-club-received-more- money-from-the-state-red-star-or-partizan

27 'Hici u Beogradu: Ubijen Kića Alkatraz, vođa navijača Partizana?', Mondo.rs, 1 November 2019, https://mondo.rs/Info/Crna-hronika/ a1245050/Pucnjava-u-Beogradu-ubijen-Kica-Alkatraz.html

28 'Qarabag–Dudelange game suspended after drone flies onto field with Armenian flag', AS, 3 October 2019, https://en.as.com/en/2019/10/03/ football/1570133127_128697.html

29 'Drone seized as soccer fans held in Kosovo before Euro game', AP, 7 September 2019, https://www.apnews.com/23bb678c99914545a83f2 e7eb65d2488

30 'Roman salutes for Lazio ultra coffin', ANSA, 11 August 2019, http:// www.ansa.it/english/news/general_news/2019/08/21/roman-salutes- for-lazio-ultra-coffin_29658ddb-46de-4923-80ce-7fbb7dfe1f7c.html

31 'Diabolik, la scenografia della Curva Nord dell'Inter per Fabrizio Piscitelli', Solo La Lazio, 26 August 2019, https://www.sololalazio. it/2019/08/26/diabolik-curva-nord-inter-scenografia/

32 'Lotito: "Zero tolerance on racism"', Football Italia, 10 October 2019, https://www.football-italia.net/145112/lotito-zero-tolerance- racism

33 'Juventus "ultras" arrested over allegations they blackmailed officials for tickets', BBC Sport, 16 September 2019, https://www.bbc.co.uk/ sport/football/49712955

34 'Italian police seize rocket launcher and neo-Nazi material in raid on Juventus 'ultra' fans', *The Jewish Chronicle*, 15 July 2019, https://www.thejc.com/news/world/italian-police-seize-rocket- launcher-and-neo-nazi-material-in-raid-on-juventus-ultra-fans- 1.486490

Acknowledgements

Belgrade, January 2020

There were literally hundreds of people who helped in making this book happen, and no one did more than Martino Simcik Arese (Twitter: @Martino_Tifo), who opened so many doors for me that I doubted whether I, rather than he, should have written this book. Neither would this book have happened without the guidance of Mikael from Stockholm, one of the most knowledgable people about the scene I have ever met. I wouldn't have even got to this point if it wasn't for Andrew Goodfellow at Ebury giving me the opportunity to write this book (and keep the title). And especially my editor Robyn Drury who was patient and engaged throughout and now can't unsee the 'ACAB' stickers around her neighbourhood. And, as ever, my agent Rebecca Winfield without whom I'd probably still be selling double glazing in Essex. There's nothing wrong with selling double glazing in Essex but I wasn't very good at it so would probably have gone hungry most months.

I'd like to thank all those who took the time to read what I had written and given me important advice. Especially Juraj Vrdoljak (@JurajVrdoljak), Rainier Jaarsma (@Rjaarsma) who gave me some important pointers about covering North Macedonia, Matt Ford (@matt_4d) in Germany, Cas Mudde (@CasMudde) and especially James Corbett (@james_corbett). Charles Ducksbury (@cducksbury) also gave some essential and invaulable insights. Some chapters found their roots in commissions. Without them the various reporting trips that made this book possible would have been impossible: Andrew Das at the *New York Times*, Sean Fay, Alex Chick and Will Tidey at the Bleacher Report, Richard Padula at the BBC World Service, Lawrence Tallis and especially Neil Stacey at Copa90, everyone at *Delayed Gratification*, Jonathan Wilson at *The Blizzard* and Andrew Gray at Politico. Some elements of the story about Egypt's revolutionary ultras came from my first book, *When Friday Comes: Football, War and Revolution in the Middle East*, and are used with kind permission from James Corbett at deCoubertin.

In Uruguay Martin da Cruz, a founding member of the Uruguayan Football Historians and Researchers Association, was particularly helpful. As was Jonathan Wilson for putting us in touch. In Argentina Carola was an exceptional guide on the ground whilst Verónica-Pía López provided brilliant, forensic translations. As always, thank you to Seamus Mirodan for pointing me in the right direction. In Brazil Rafael de Moura Machado introduced me to Cláudio Cruz, which would later lead to us all travelling from Rio to Qatar to watch Flamengo in the Club World Cup final against Liverpool. But that is a different story entirely.

Serbia is a country I am lucky to have called home for the past few years. Jack Davies (@jackoozell), Ralph & Jelena van der Zijden and Jovan Terzic (@joca_t) have provided much needed encouragement when I needed it. As did Tim Julian, during a rare trip back to London. I'd also like to thank Vladimir Ninković (Serbia's number one cricket evangelist) and Stevan Dojčinovič (@StevanOCCRP) for sharing their knowledge. Aleks Eror (@slandr) was a great help and the kafana crew have been an invaluable well of support too. I wrote most of 1312 in an isolated house in Vršac, thanks to Maja Ivanov. Sorry about the stove. I also want to thank Ada and Aart Mudde in the Netherlands. I wrote my last book *The Billionaires Club* in their weekend house in 't Heitje, Hengelo, but forgot to thank them last time. Apologies!

In Greece I'd like to thank Thomas Farines (@thomasfarines) for his help when I was in Thessaloniki and in Macedonia both Ilcho Cvetanoski (@IlchoCvetanoski) and Cvetin Chilimanov (@Cvetin). In Albania – well, Belgrade – I'd like to thank Idro Seferi (@idroseferi), without whom I'd never have found Ismail Morina. In Ukraine Dima

Kolchinsky wasn't just a superb film maker and translator. He also deserves a bravery medal for driving us from Kyiv to Mariupol (and back) in the dead of winter along a pitch black, pot-hole strewn highway. I'd have never found him without the help of Jake Hanrahan (@Jake_Hanrahan), who's the brains behind a great podcast on irregular warfare called Popular Front (popularfront.co). Sasha Feinberg provided peerless Ukrainian translations too. Michael Colborne (@ColborneMichael) and Oleksiy Kuzmenko (@kooleksiy) gave me some great insights too.

In Kosovo I'd like to thank Jack Robinson (@SunflowerShells), Xhemajl Rexha (@xhemajl_rexha), Xili Ismaili and Elizabeth Gowing (@ElizabethGowing). Thanks for the Nietzsche quote!

In Germany, I want to thank Barbara Paech for showing me around Babelsberg at Christmas and telling me about Fan.Tastic Females. Traditional football fan culture is dominated by men and can veer into toxic masculinity. But Fan. Tastic Females (www.fan-tastic-females.org/index.php/en/) showed me a different side of terrace culture. I wouldn't have been able to write about Dortmund's ultra scene if it wasn't for the help of Uli Hesse. Martin Endemann (@EndemannMartin) from Football Supporters Europe (@fanseurope) was a great help in me trying to understand German fan activism and thanks also to Tom Gennoy (@TG94__) for enlivening a bitterly cold match. Sorry for getting you banned from the bus.

Mikael made everything happen in Sweden but I also wanted to thank Dennis Mårtensson (@Dmarten82) who co-hosts a podcast (intebarafotboll.podbean.com) and spoke to me at length about the issues of policing football in the country. In Turkey Tan Morgül (@tanmorgul) was a huge help. Without him I wouldn't have found Bora Isyar (@boraisyar), the editor of Turkey's version of The Blizzard (@TurkiyeBlizzard) who was essential for me to navigate the city's complex rivalries. I'd thank Patrick Keddie (@PatrickKeddie) too but the night dissolved into amnesia. Angelos Giakoumidis and George Lentzas were a great help when I met them at the Intercontinental Derby, and continued to give me advice about the Greek supporter scene, as did George Georgakopoulos in Athens.

In the United States a big thank you – as ever – to Bob and Lindsay Bradley, who opened all the doors for me at LAFC. In Morocco Youssef

Moutmaïne (@YMoutmaine) from Le Matin was a great guide when we went to the Casablanca Derby in Marrakesh. Maher Mezahi (@MezahiMaher) was a fountain of knowledge when it came to anti-regime terrace chants in north Africa, and helped me out with the translations for many of them. Whilst journalists rarely get access, academics have been deeply involved in documenting football fan culture for decades. There is a wealth of fantastic research out there, often hidden behind paywalls. If you haven't come across their work then track down anything by Dario Brentin (@DarioBrentin), Dr. Martha Newson (@martha_newson), Loïc Tregoures (@Ltregoures) and Dr. Andrew Hodges (@dr_andyhodges) in particular. That's a tiny proportion of what's out there. There's loads more to find. And a big thank you to David Goldblatt (@Davidsgoldblatt) who is always an inspiration, but also managed to find some great academic literature I'd otherwise have missed.

Having a child – and a partner who is a much better and more accomplished journalist – has meant that I've been utterly dependent on Kristina Militar and Mina Kuršumlija in Belgrade to look after my young daughter on several reporting trips. And especially Margriet and Reza Nazar. Maria and John Montague, as well as Laura Montague, Rob Reddy and Berrin have also been invaluable over the past two years.

I've quoted various authors and used several epigraphs. The quote from *The Naked Civil Servant* by Quentin Crisp is reprinted by permission of HarperCollins Publishers Ltd and Richard Gollner. The quote from *Beauty is a Wound* by Eka Kurniawan, translated by Annie Tucker, is reprinted by kind permission of Pushkin Press. And the quote from *Soccer in Sun and Shadow* by Eduardo Galeano is reprinted by permission of Abner Stein. I've also sought permission from authors I have quoted more extensively, especially *Golazo!: A History of Latin American Football* by Andreas Campomar and published by Quercus, *The Politics of Football in Yugoslavia: Sport, Nationalism and the State* by Richard Hill and published by I.B. Taurus, and *Building the Yellow Wall* by Uli Hesse and published by Weidenfeld & Nicolson. I found their work profound and inspiring.

Finally, I apologise to Mitra and Mila. Both of their lives were made harder by my prolonged absences and the pressure that it brought. I won't make the same mistake again.